GOU-DERE SORA NAGIHARA 3

SUU MINAZUKI

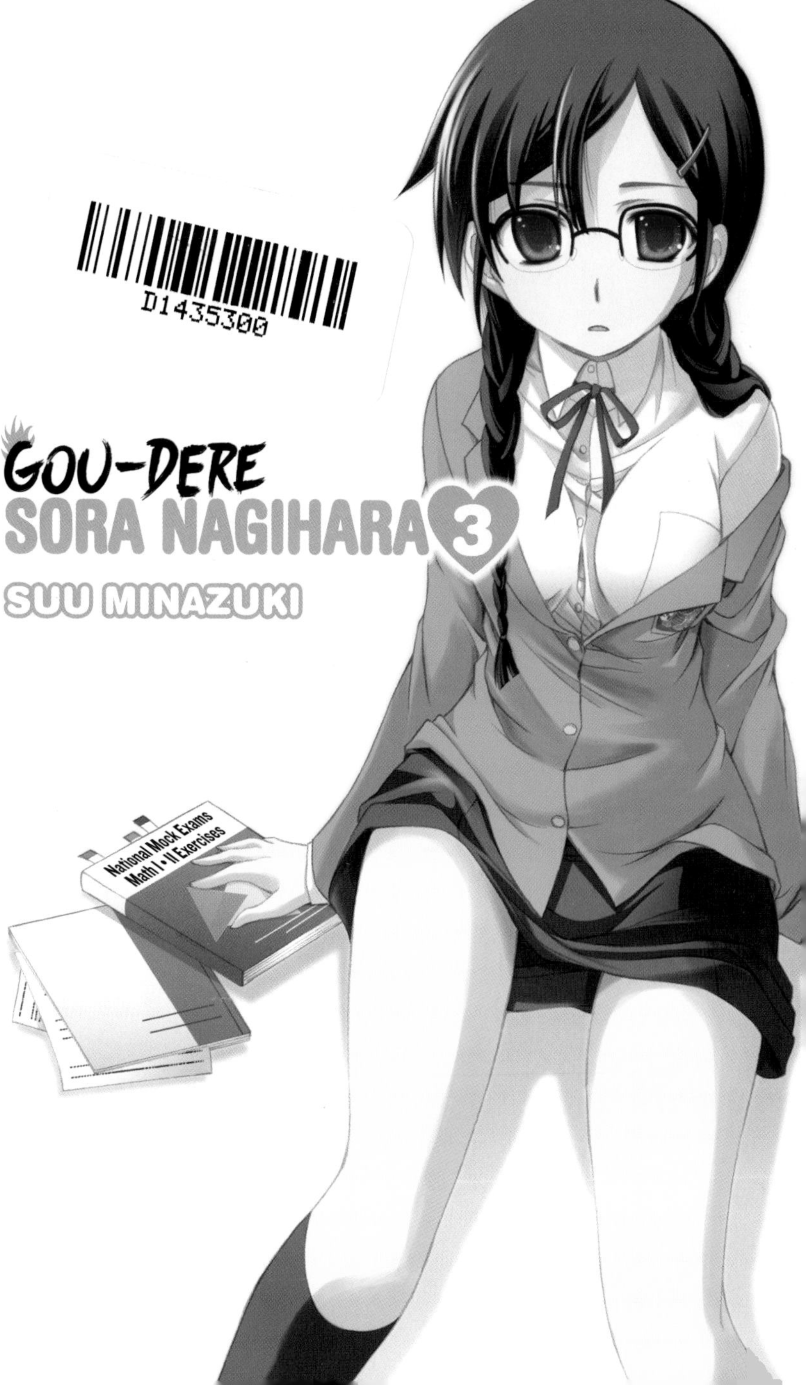
National Mock Exams
Math I • II Exercises

CONTENTS

SORA NAGIHARA

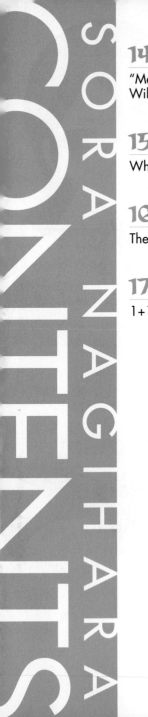

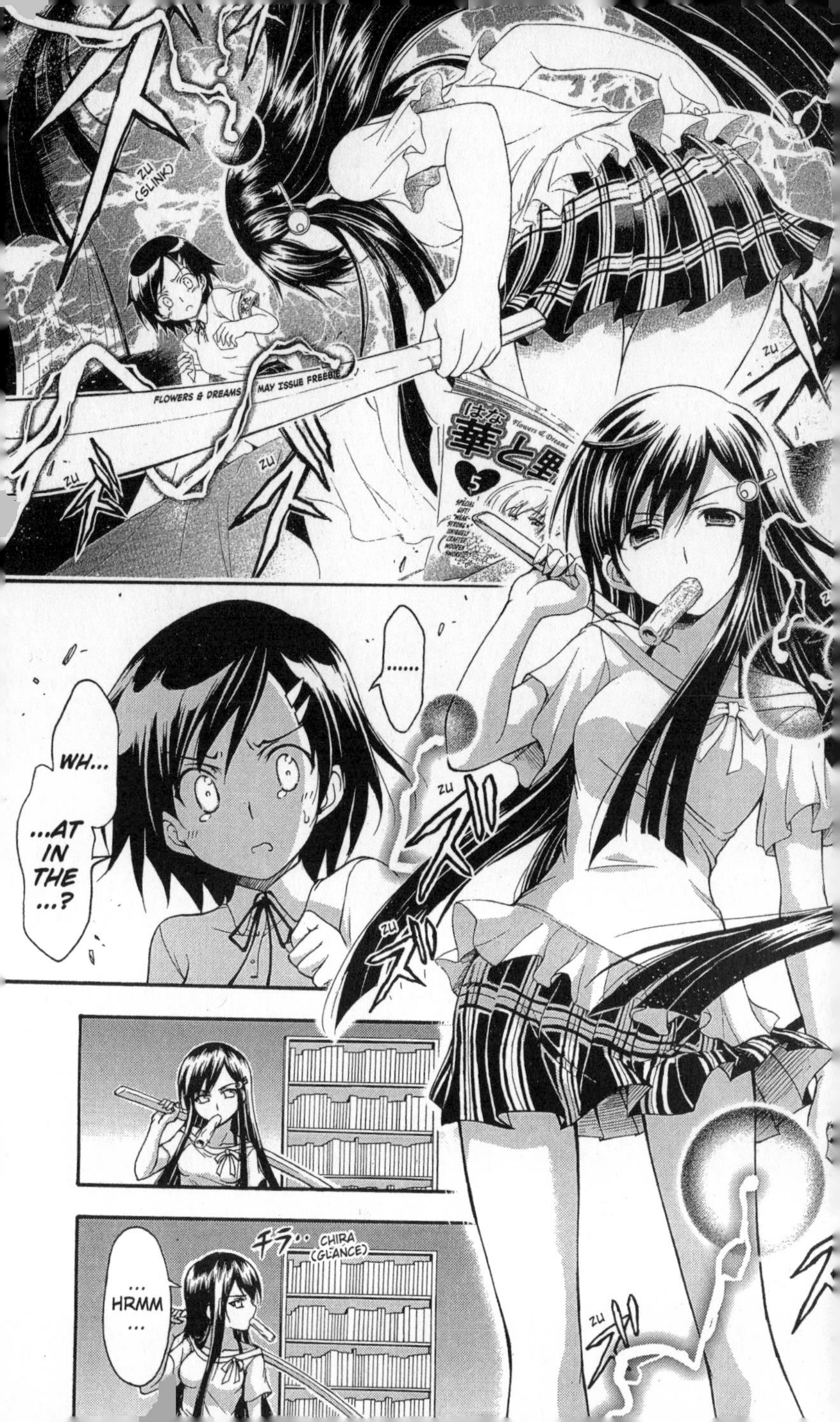
ZU
はな 華と里 Flowers & Dreams 5
SPECIAL GIFT! "WEAK-STRONG★" UNIQUELY CRAFTED WOODEN
ZU (SLINK)
FLOWERS & DREAMS MAY ISSUE FREEBIE
ZU
ZU
......
WH... ...AT IN THE ...?
ZU
ZU
ZU
チラ CHIRA (GLANCE)
... HRMM ...

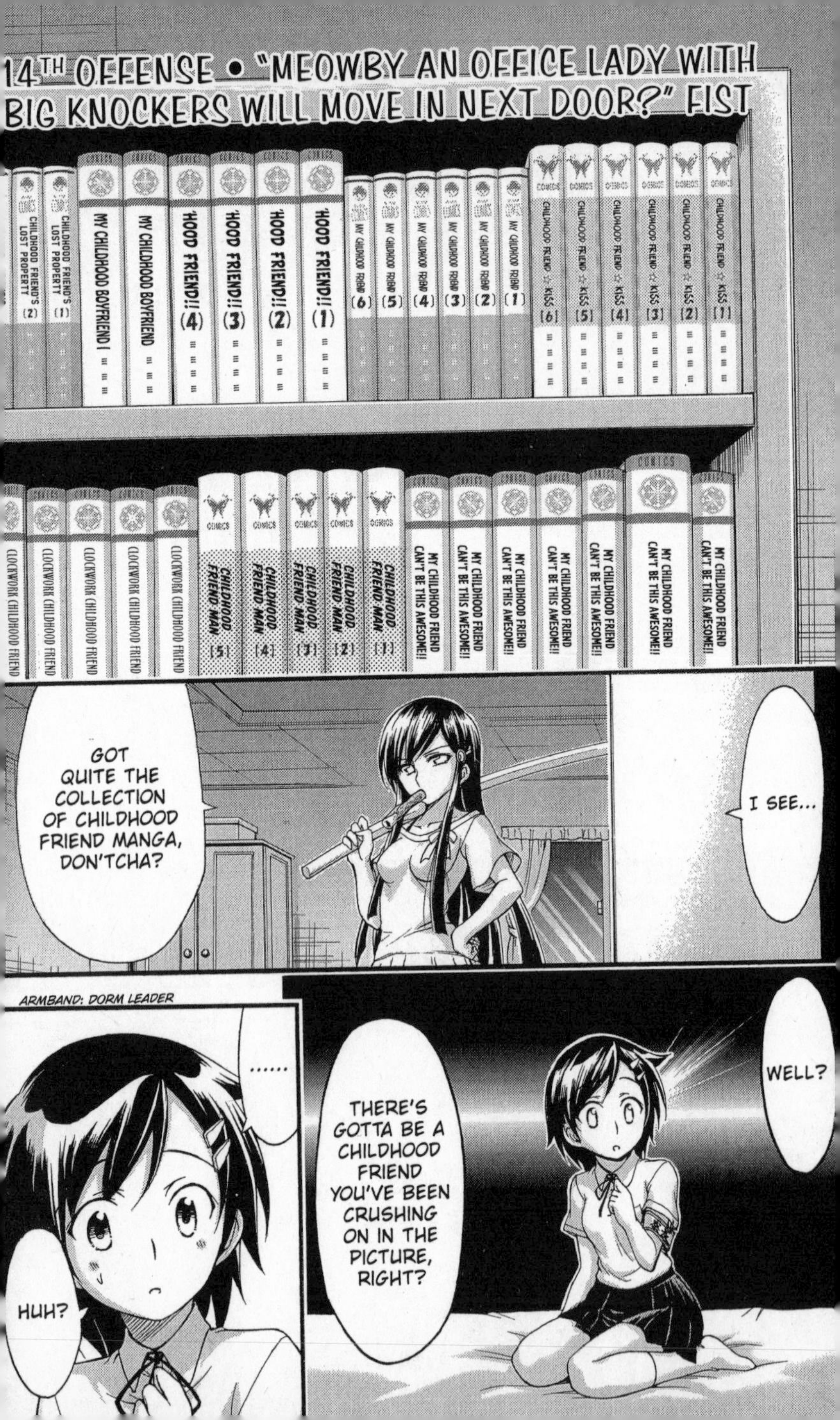
14TH OFFENSE • "MEOWBY AN OFFICE LADY WITH BIG KNOCKERS WILL MOVE IN NEXT DOOR?" FIST
CHILDHOOD FRIEND ☆ KISS [1]
CHILDHOOD FRIEND ☆ KISS [2]
CHILDHOOD FRIEND ☆ KISS [3]
CHILDHOOD FRIEND ☆ KISS [4]
CHILDHOOD FRIEND ☆ KISS [5]
CHILDHOOD FRIEND ☆ KISS [6]
MY CHILDHOOD FRIEND (1)
MY CHILDHOOD FRIEND (2)
MY CHILDHOOD FRIEND (3)
MY CHILDHOOD FRIEND (4)
MY CHILDHOOD FRIEND (5)
MY CHILDHOOD FRIEND (6)
'HOOD FRIEND!! (1)
'HOOD FRIEND!! (2)
'HOOD FRIEND!! (3)
'HOOD FRIEND!! (4)
MY CHILDHOOD BOYFRIEND
MY CHILDHOOD BOYFRIEND
CHILDHOOD FRIEND'S LOST PROPERTY (1)
CHILDHOOD FRIEND'S LOST PROPERTY (2)
MY CHILDHOOD FRIEND CAN'T BE THIS AWESOME!!
MY CHILDHOOD FRIEND CAN'T BE THIS AWESOME!!
MY CHILDHOOD FRIEND CAN'T BE THIS AWESOME!!
MY CHILDHOOD FRIEND CAN'T BE THIS AWESOME!!
MY CHILDHOOD FRIEND CAN'T BE THIS AWESOME!!
MY CHILDHOOD FRIEND CAN'T BE THIS AWESOME!!
MY CHILDHOOD FRIEND CAN'T BE THIS AWESOME!!
CHILDHOOD FRIEND MAN [1]
CHILDHOOD FRIEND MAN [2]
CHILDHOOD FRIEND MAN [3]
CHILDHOOD FRIEND MAN [4]
CHILDHOOD FRIEND MAN [5]
CLOCKWORK CHILDHOOD FRIEND
CLOCKWORK CHILDHOOD FRIEND
CLOCKWORK CHILDHOOD FRIEND
CLOCKWORK CHILDHOOD FRIEND
CLOCKWORK CHILDHOOD FRIEND
I SEE...
GOT QUITE THE COLLECTION OF CHILDHOOD FRIEND MANGA, DON'TCHA?
WELL?
THERE'S GOTTA BE A CHILDHOOD FRIEND YOU'VE BEEN CRUSHING ON IN THE PICTURE, RIGHT?
ARMBAND: DORM LEADER
......
HUH?

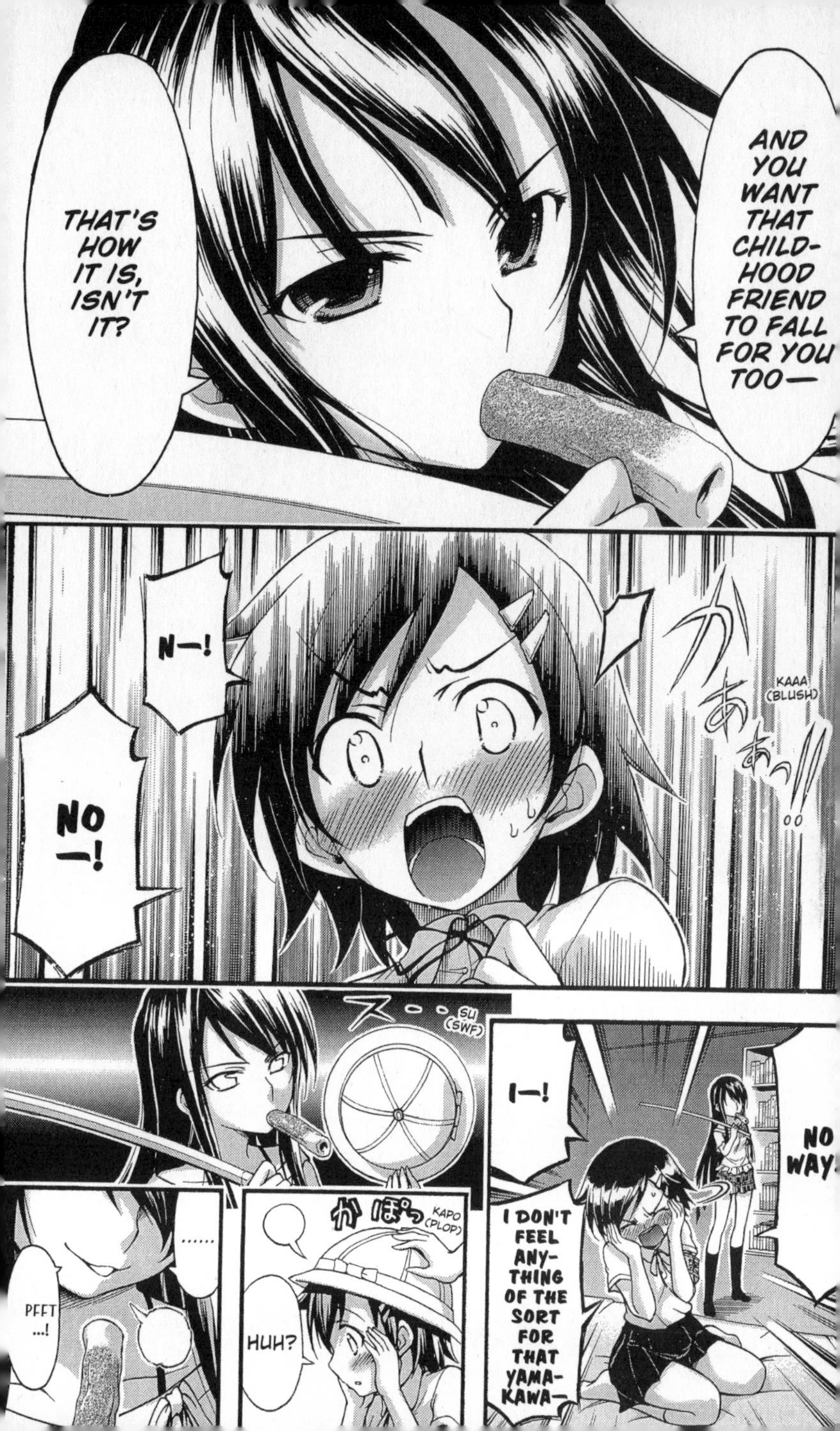
AND YOU WANT THAT CHILDHOOD FRIEND TO FALL FOR YOU TOO—
THAT'S HOW IT IS, ISN'T IT?
かあぁっ!!
KAAA (BLUSH)
N—!
NO—!
I—!
NO WAY.
I DON'T FEEL ANYTHING OF THE SORT FOR THAT YAMAKAWA—
ス…
SU (SWF)
かぽっ
KAPO (PLOP)
HUH?
......
PFFT...!

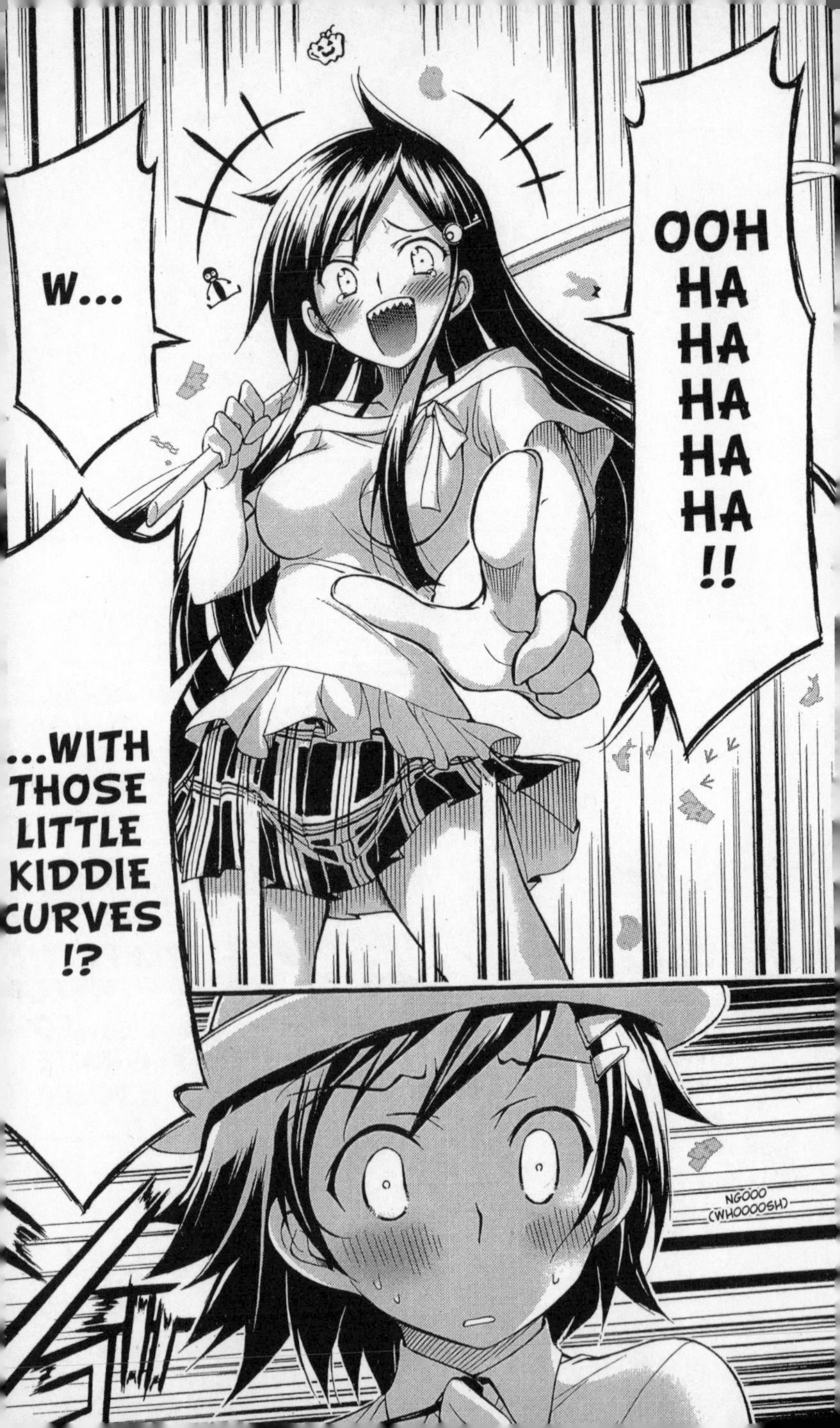
OOH HA HA HA HA HA HA!!
W...
...WITH THOSE LITTLE KIDDIE CURVES!?
NGOOO (WHOOOOSH)

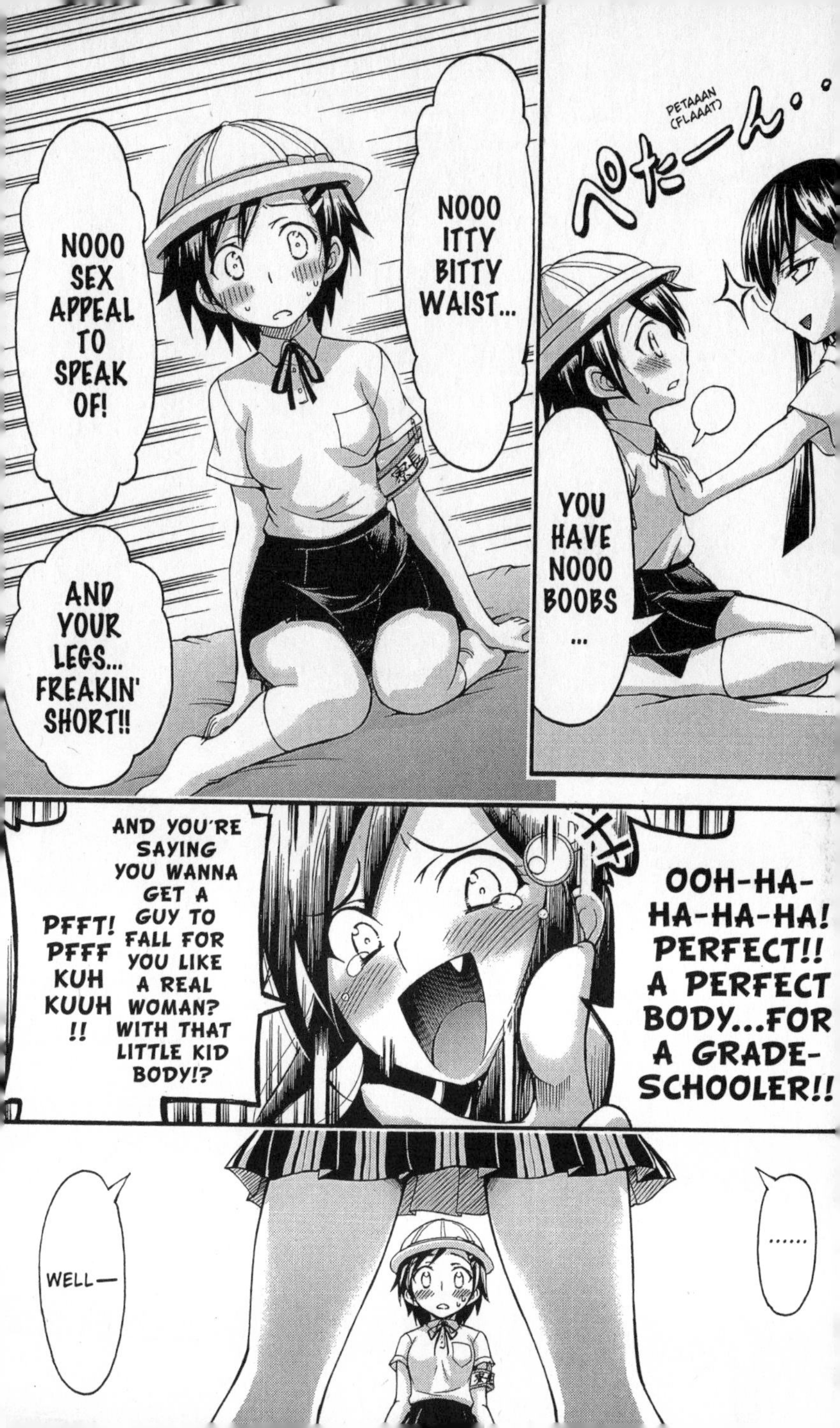
ぺたーん。。
PETAAAN (FLAAAT)
YOU HAVE NOOO BOOBS ...
NOOO ITTY BITTY WAIST...
NOOO SEX APPEAL TO SPEAK OF!
AND YOUR LEGS... FREAKIN' SHORT!!
OOH-HA-HA-HA-HA! PERFECT!! A PERFECT BODY...FOR A GRADE-SCHOOLER!!
AND YOU'RE SAYING YOU WANNA GET A GUY TO FALL FOR YOU LIKE A REAL WOMAN? WITH THAT LITTLE KID BODY!?
PFFT! PFFF KUH KUUH !!
......
WELL—

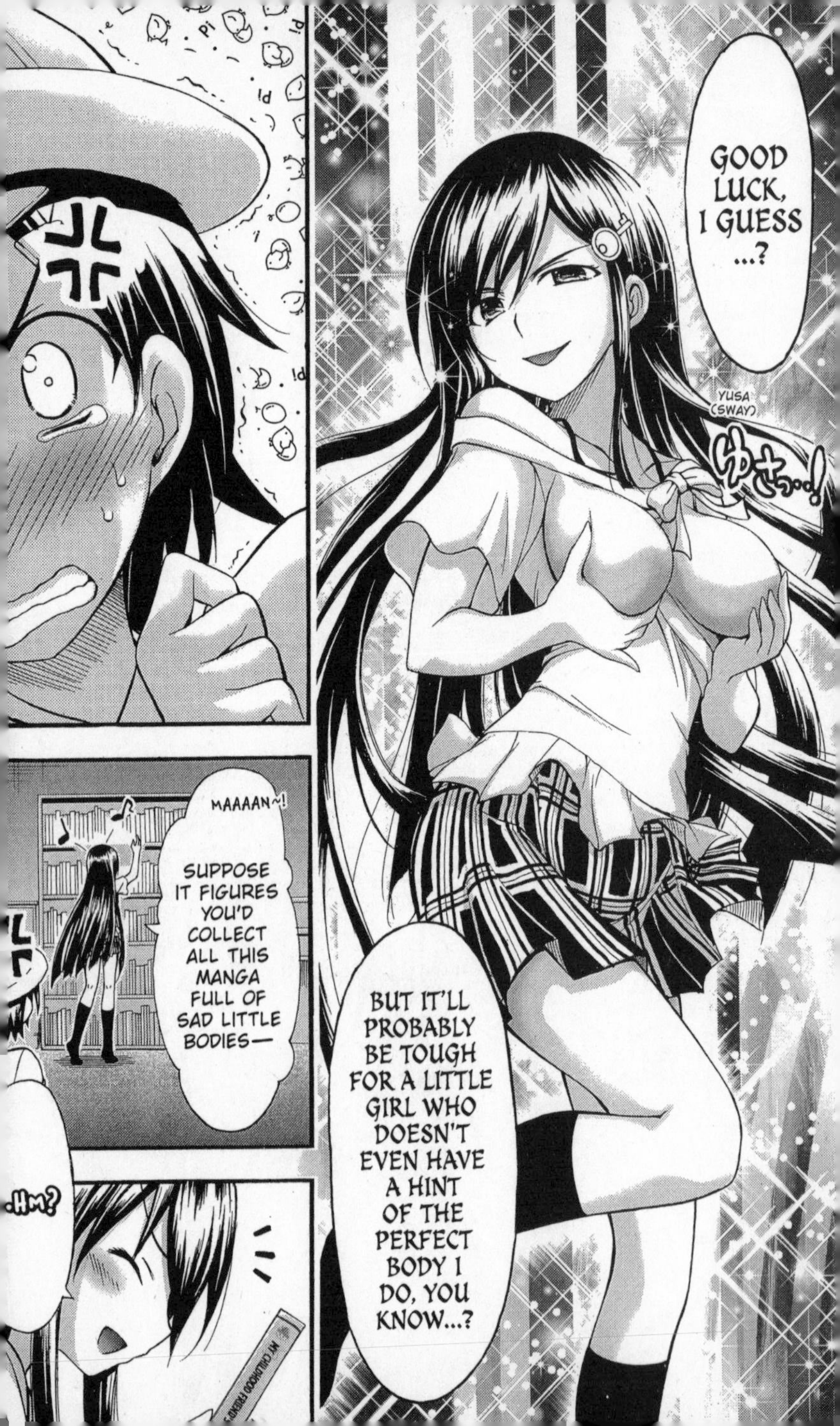
GOOD LUCK, I GUESS ...?
YUSA (SWAY)
BUT IT'LL PROBABLY BE TOUGH FOR A LITTLE GIRL WHO DOESN'T EVEN HAVE A HINT OF THE PERFECT BODY I DO, YOU KNOW...?
Pi
Pi!
MAAAAN~!
SUPPOSE IT FIGURES YOU'D COLLECT ALL THIS MANGA FULL OF SAD LITTLE BODIES—
...Hm?

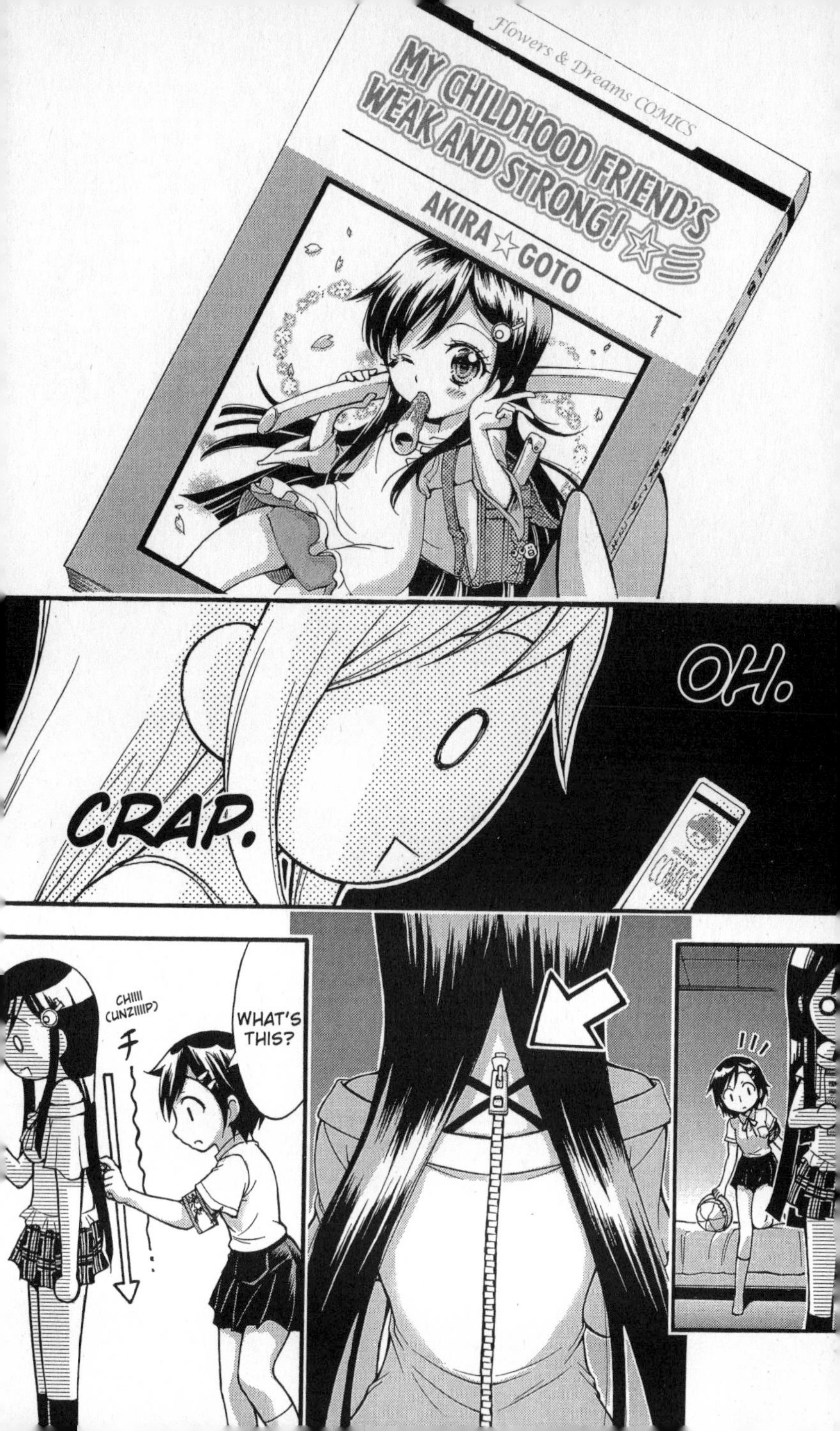
Flowers & Dreams COMICS
MY CHILDHOOD FRIEND'S WEAK AND STRONG! ☆彡
AKIRA☆GOTO
1
OH.
CRAP.
COMICS
WHAT'S THIS?
CHIIII (UNZIIIIP)
チ

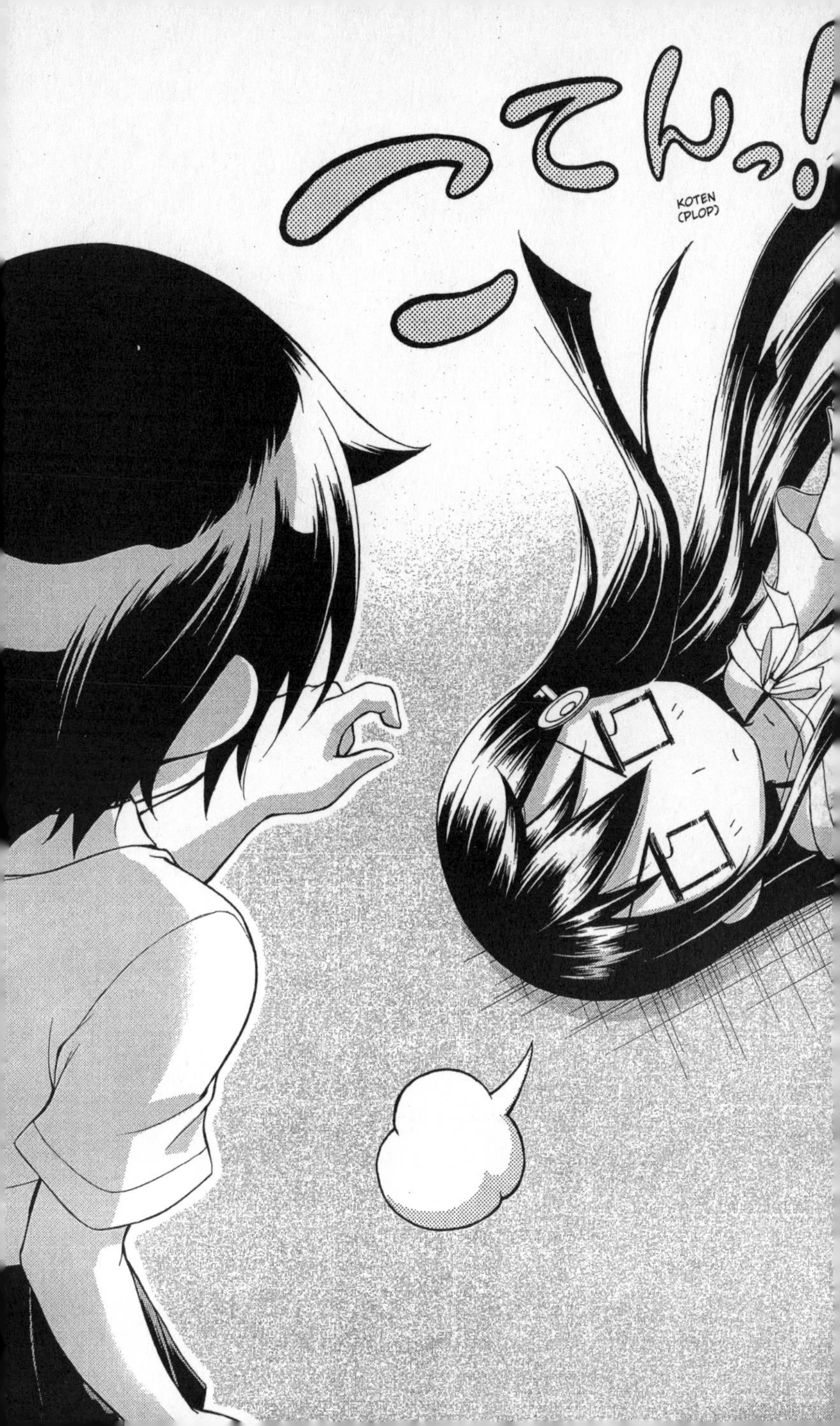
こてんっ!
KOTEN
(PLOP)

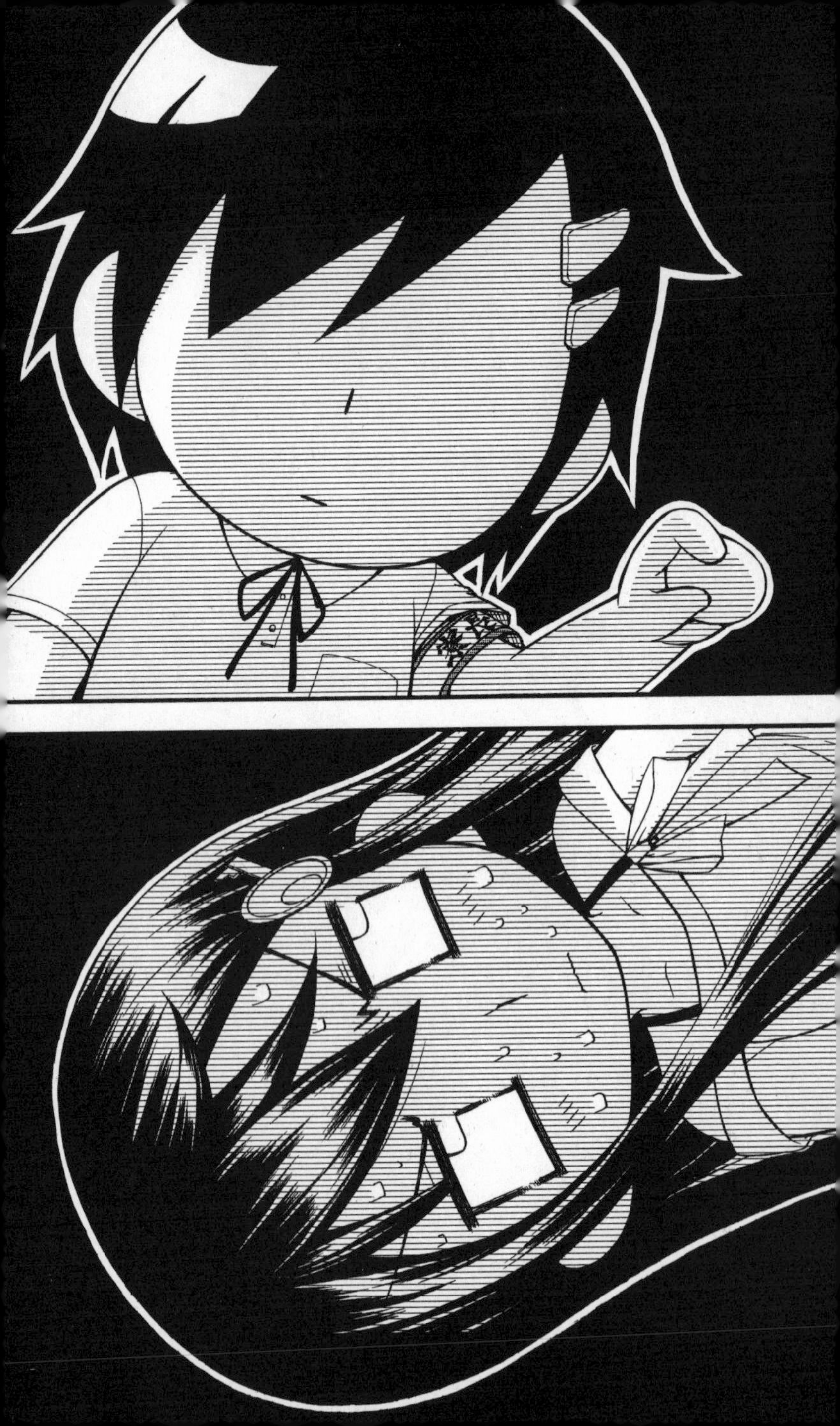

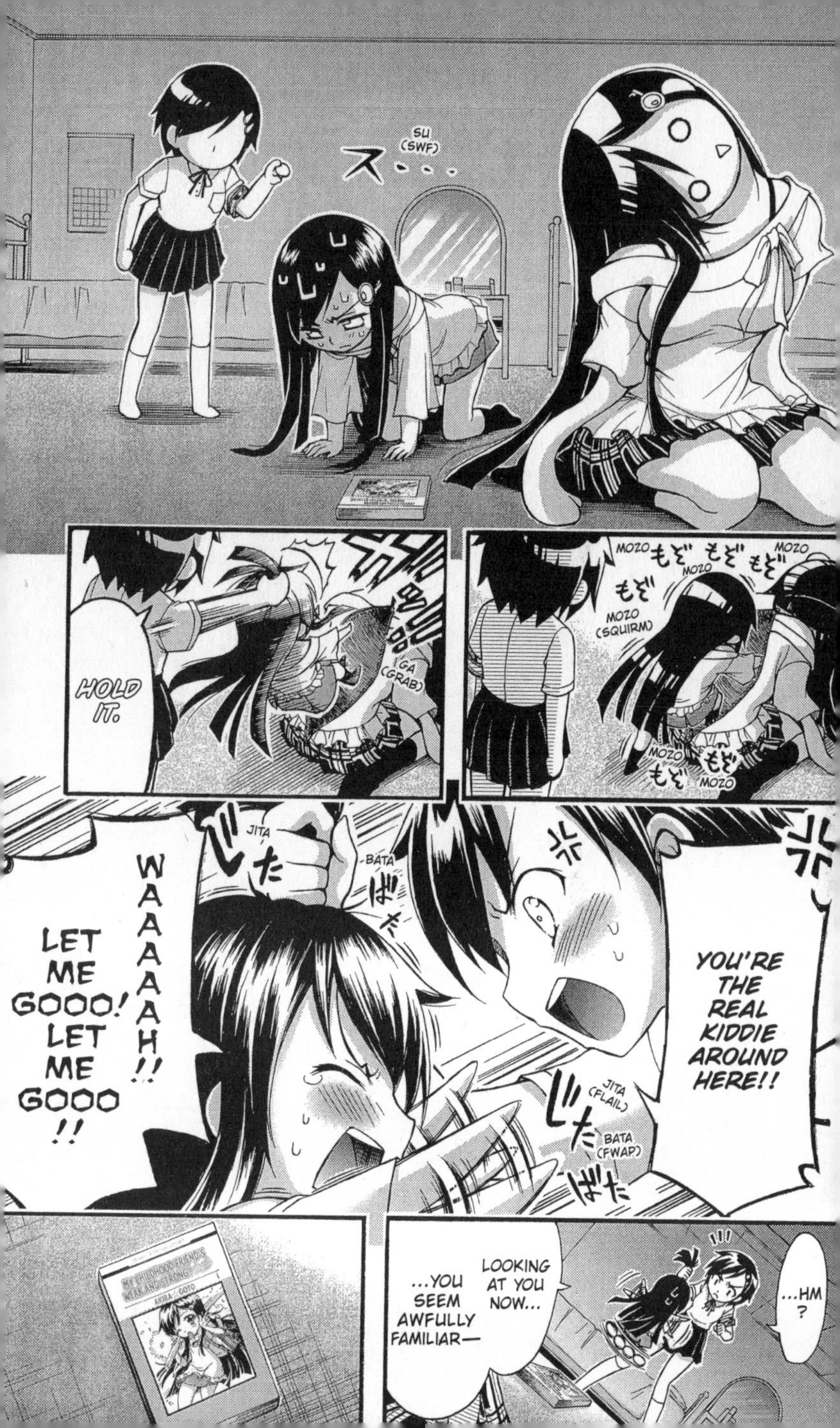

SU (SWF)
ス…
MOZO もぞ
MOZO もぞ
MOZO もぞ
MOZO (SQUIRM) もぞ
MOZO もぞ
MOZO もぞ
GA (GRAB)
HOLD IT.
YOU'RE THE REAL KIDDIE AROUND HERE!!
JITA (FLAIL) じた
BATA (FWAP) ばた
JITA じた
BATA ばた
WAAAAAAH!!
LET ME GOOO! LET ME GOOO!!
...HM?
LOOKING AT YOU NOW...
...YOU SEEM AWFULLY FAMILIAR—
MY CHILDHOOD FRIEND'S WEAK AND STRONG
AKIRA GOTO

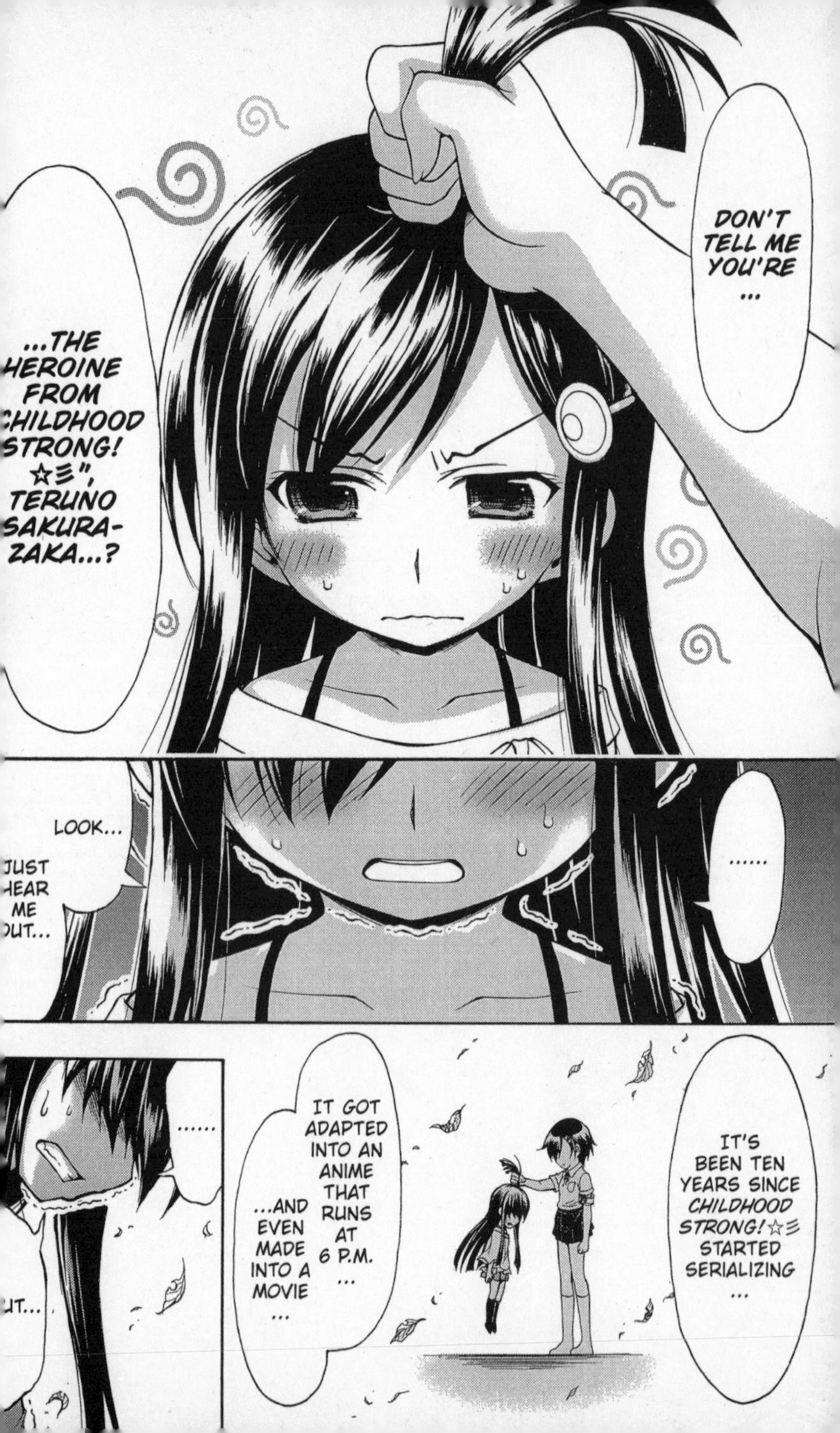
DON'T TELL ME YOU'RE ...
...THE HEROINE FROM CHILDHOOD STRONG! ☆彡", TERUNO SAKURA-ZAKA...?
......
LOOK... JUST HEAR ME OUT...
IT'S BEEN TEN YEARS SINCE *CHILDHOOD STRONG!☆彡* STARTED SERIALIZING ...
IT GOT ADAPTED INTO AN ANIME THAT RUNS AT 6 P.M. ...
...AND EVEN MADE INTO A MOVIE ...
......
UT...

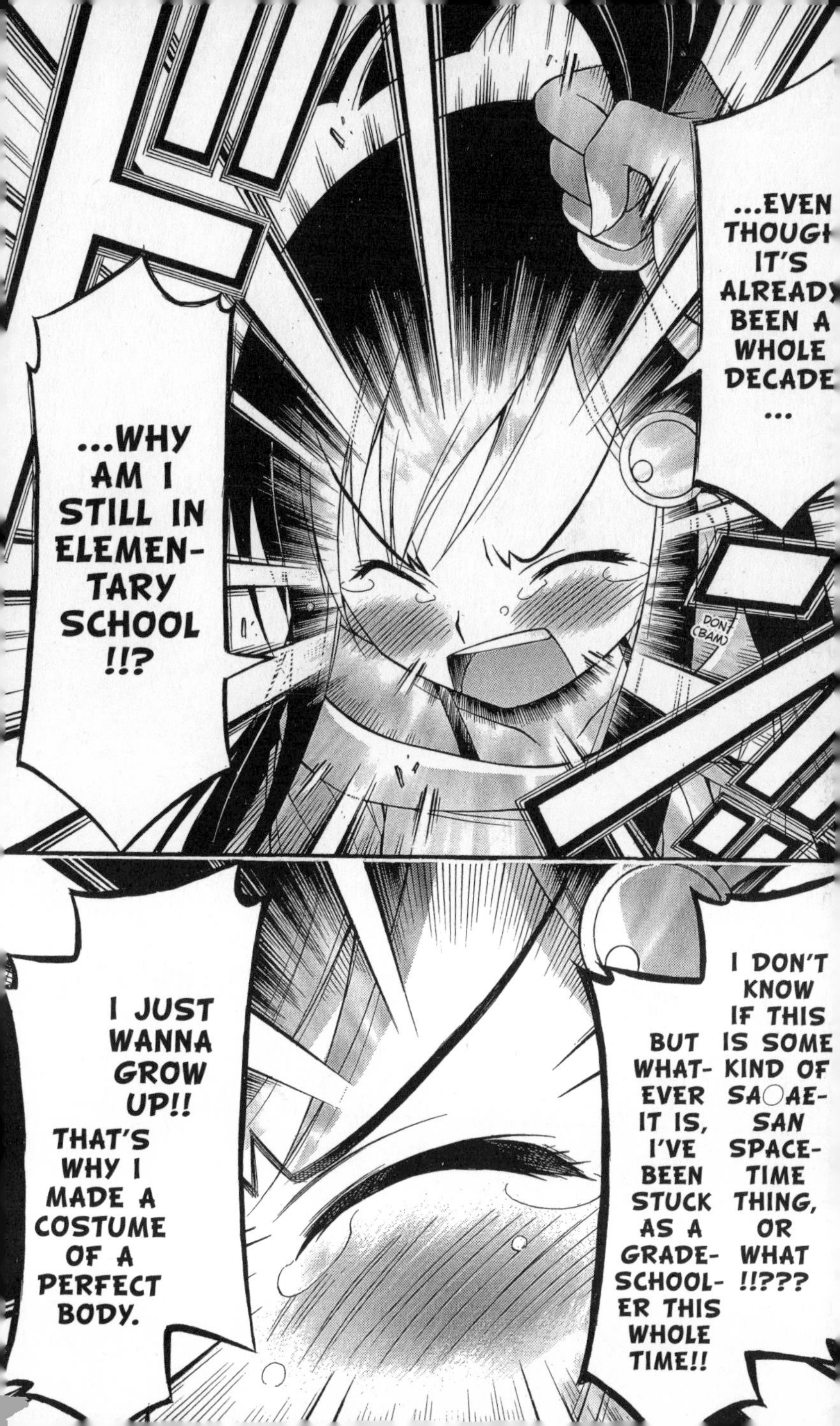
...EVEN THOUGH IT'S ALREADY BEEN A WHOLE DECADE...
DON (BAM)
...WHY AM I STILL IN ELEMENTARY SCHOOL!!?
I DON'T KNOW IF THIS IS SOME KIND OF SA○AE-SAN SPACE-TIME THING, OR WHAT!!???
BUT WHATEVER IT IS, I'VE BEEN STUCK AS A GRADE-SCHOOLER THIS WHOLE TIME!!
I JUST WANNA GROW UP!!
THAT'S WHY I MADE A COSTUME OF A PERFECT BODY.

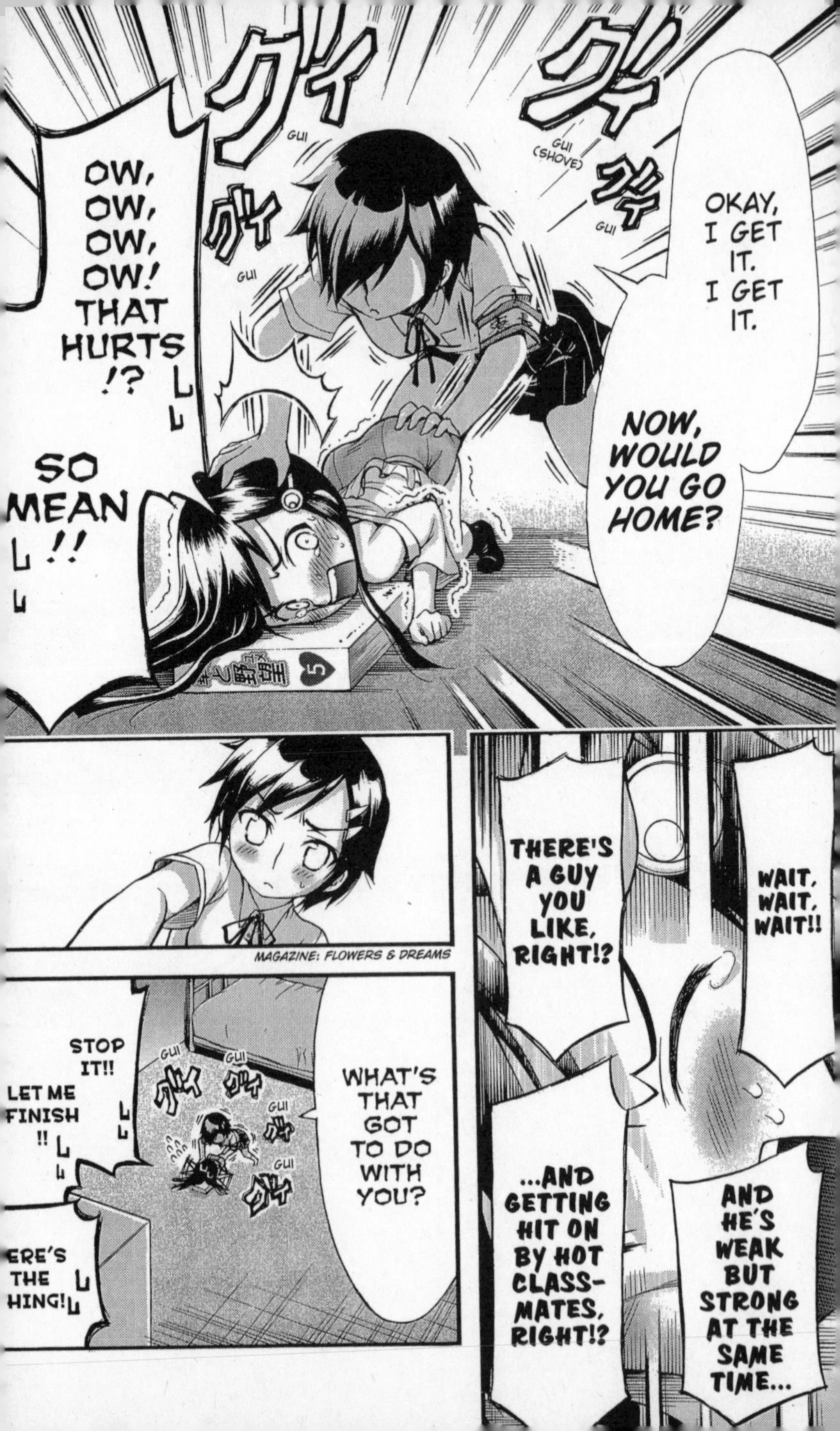
OKAY, I GET IT. I GET IT.
GUI (SHOVE)
GUI
GUI
GUI
NOW, WOULD YOU GO HOME?
OW, OW, OW, OW! THAT HURTS!?
SO MEAN!!
WAIT, WAIT, WAIT!!
THERE'S A GUY YOU LIKE, RIGHT!?
AND HE'S WEAK BUT STRONG AT THE SAME TIME...
...AND GETTING HIT ON BY HOT CLASSMATES, RIGHT!?
MAGAZINE: FLOWERS & DREAMS
WHAT'S THAT GOT TO DO WITH YOU?
GUI
GUI
GUI
GUI
STOP IT!!
LET ME FINISH!!
ERE'S THE HING!

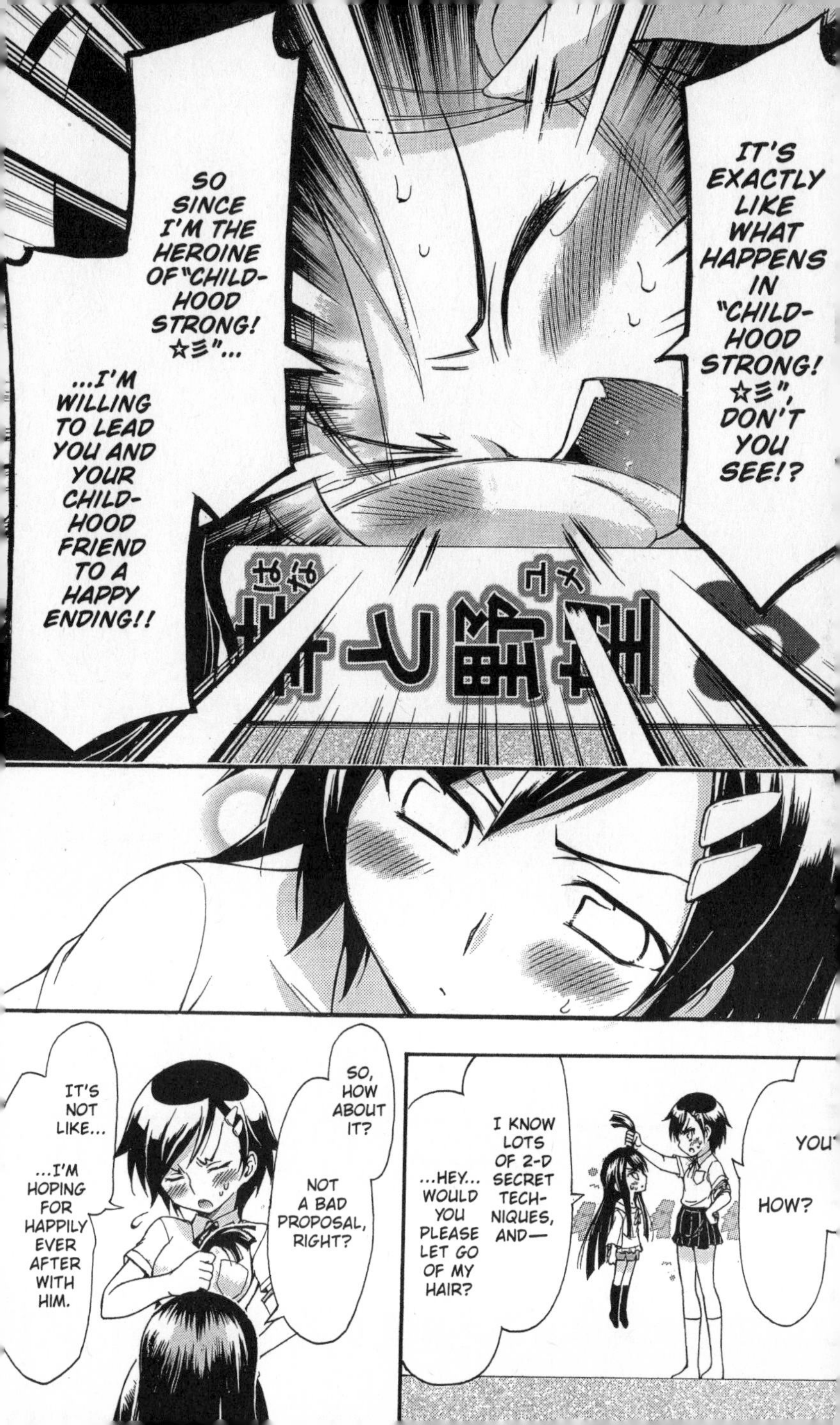
IT'S EXACTLY LIKE WHAT HAPPENS IN "CHILDHOOD STRONG! ☆彡", DON'T YOU SEE!?
SO SINCE I'M THE HEROINE OF "CHILDHOOD STRONG! ☆彡"...
...I'M WILLING TO LEAD YOU AND YOUR CHILDHOOD FRIEND TO A HAPPY ENDING!!
YOU'
HOW?
I KNOW LOTS OF 2-D SECRET TECHNIQUES, AND—
...HEY... WOULD YOU PLEASE LET GO OF MY HAIR?
SO, HOW ABOUT IT?
NOT A BAD PROPOSAL, RIGHT?
IT'S NOT LIKE...
...I'M HOPING FOR HAPPILY EVER AFTER WITH HIM.

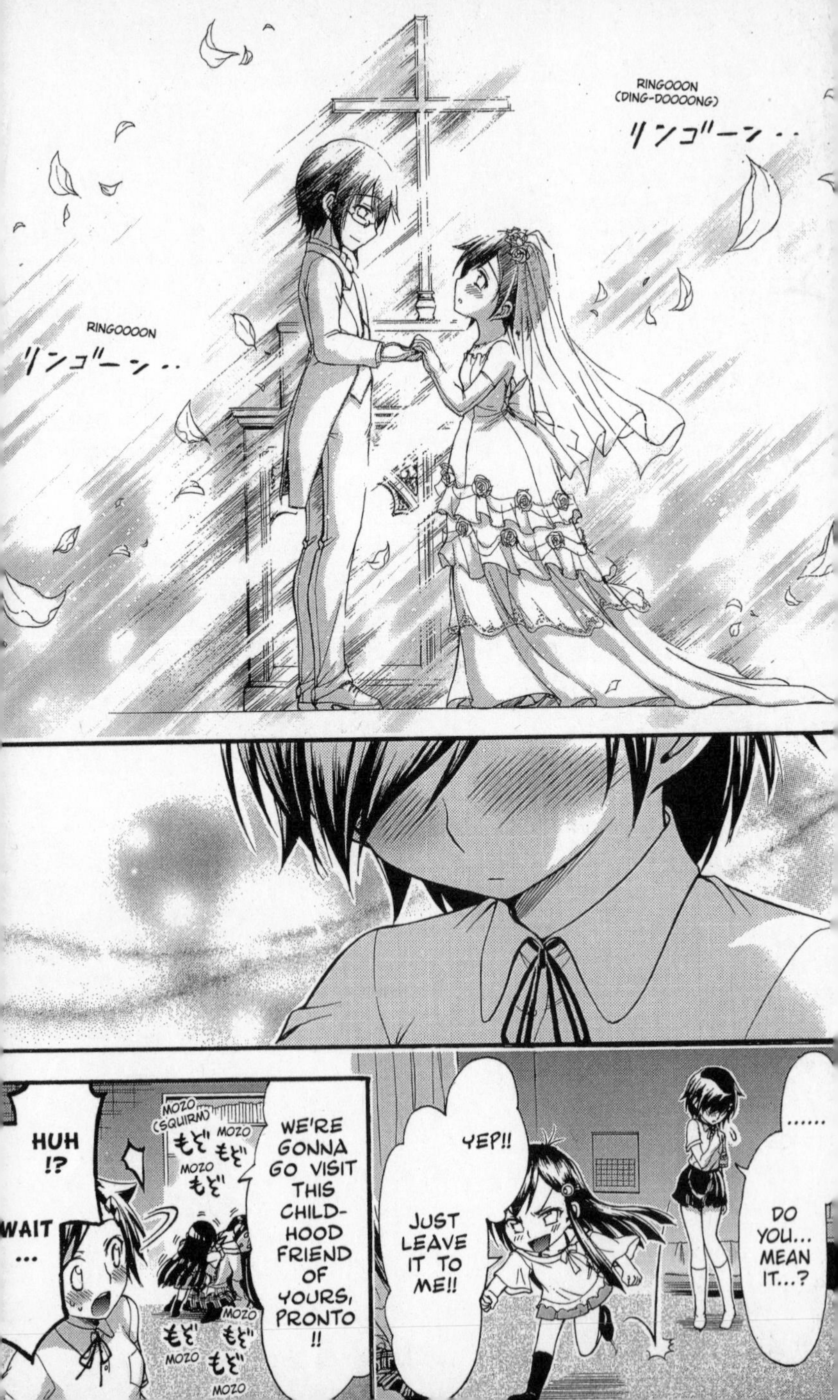
RINGOOON (DING-DOOOONG)
リンゴーン‥
RINGOOOON
リンゴーン‥
......
DO YOU... MEAN IT...?
YEP!!
JUST LEAVE IT TO ME!!
WE'RE GONNA GO VISIT THIS CHILD-HOOD FRIEND OF YOURS, PRONTO!!
MOZO (SQUIRM) もぞ MOZO もぞ MOZO もぞ
MOZO もぞ もぞ MOZO もぞ MOZO
HUH !?
WAIT ...

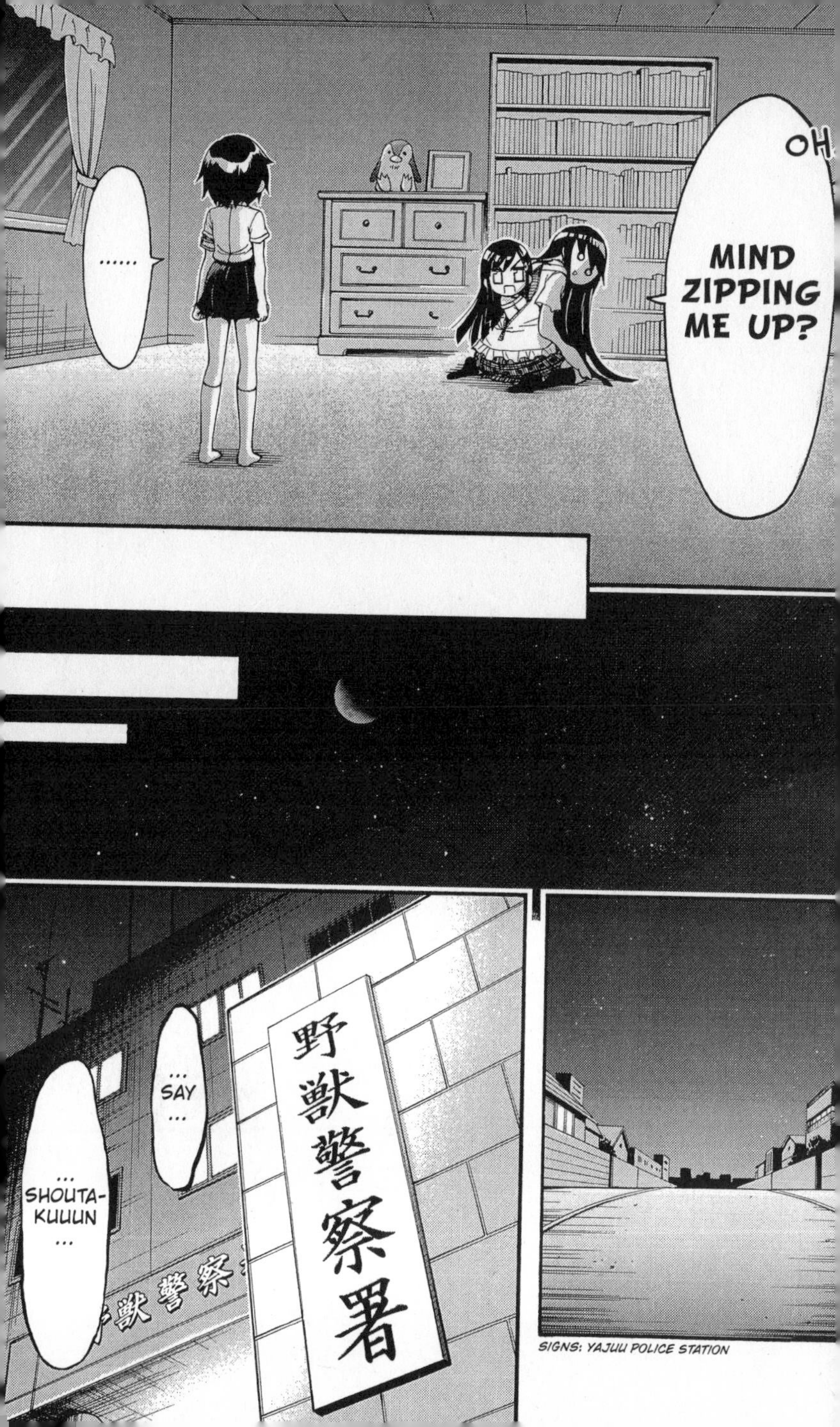
OH
MIND ZIPPING ME UP?
......
野獣警察署
...SAY...
...SHOUTA-KUUUN...

SIGNS: YAJUU POLICE STATION

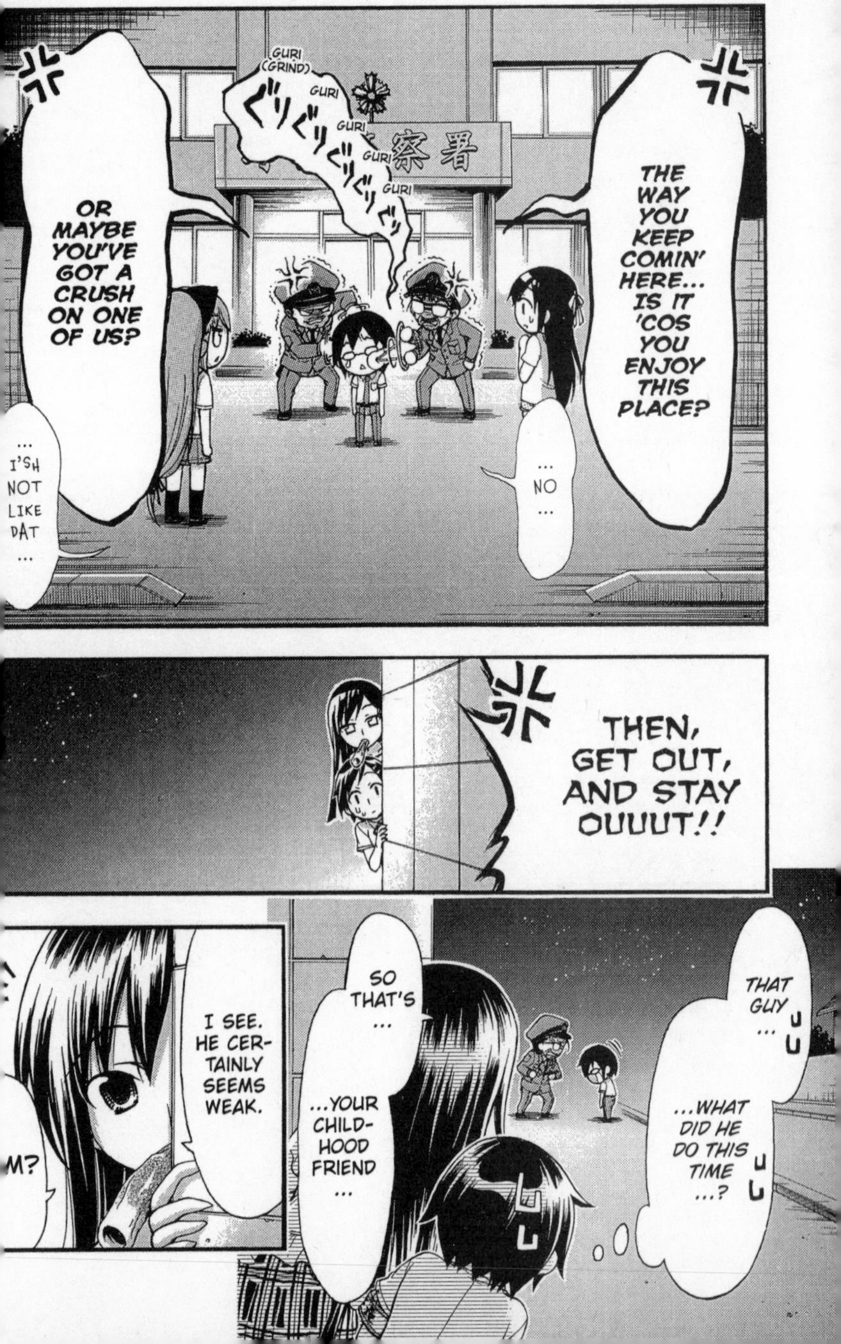
THE WAY YOU KEEP COMIN' HERE... IS IT 'COS YOU ENJOY THIS PLACE?
... NO ...
察署
ぐりぐりぐりぐりぐり
GURI (GRIND) GURI GURI GURI GURI
OR MAYBE YOU'VE GOT A CRUSH ON ONE OF US?
... I'SH NOT LIKE DAT ...
THEN, GET OUT, AND STAY OUUUT!!
THAT GUY ...
...WHAT DID HE DO THIS TIME ...?
SO THAT'S ...
...YOUR CHILD-HOOD FRIEND ...
I SEE. HE CER-TAINLY SEEMS WEAK.
M?

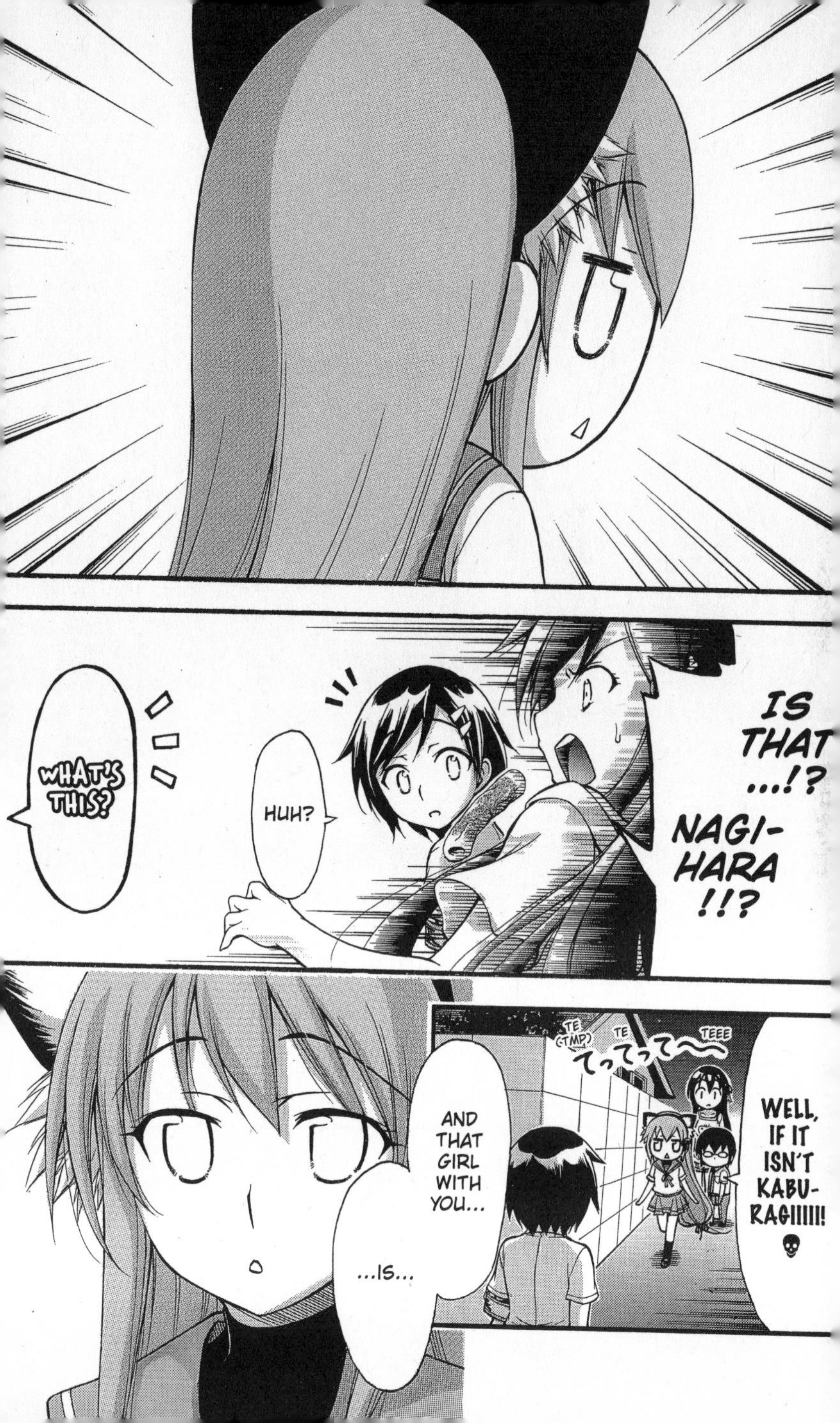
IS THAT ...!? NAGI-HARA!!?
HUH?
WHAT'S THIS?
TE (TMP) TE TEEE
てってって～～
WELL, IF IT ISN'T KABU-RAGIIIIII!
AND THAT GIRL WITH YOU...
...IS...

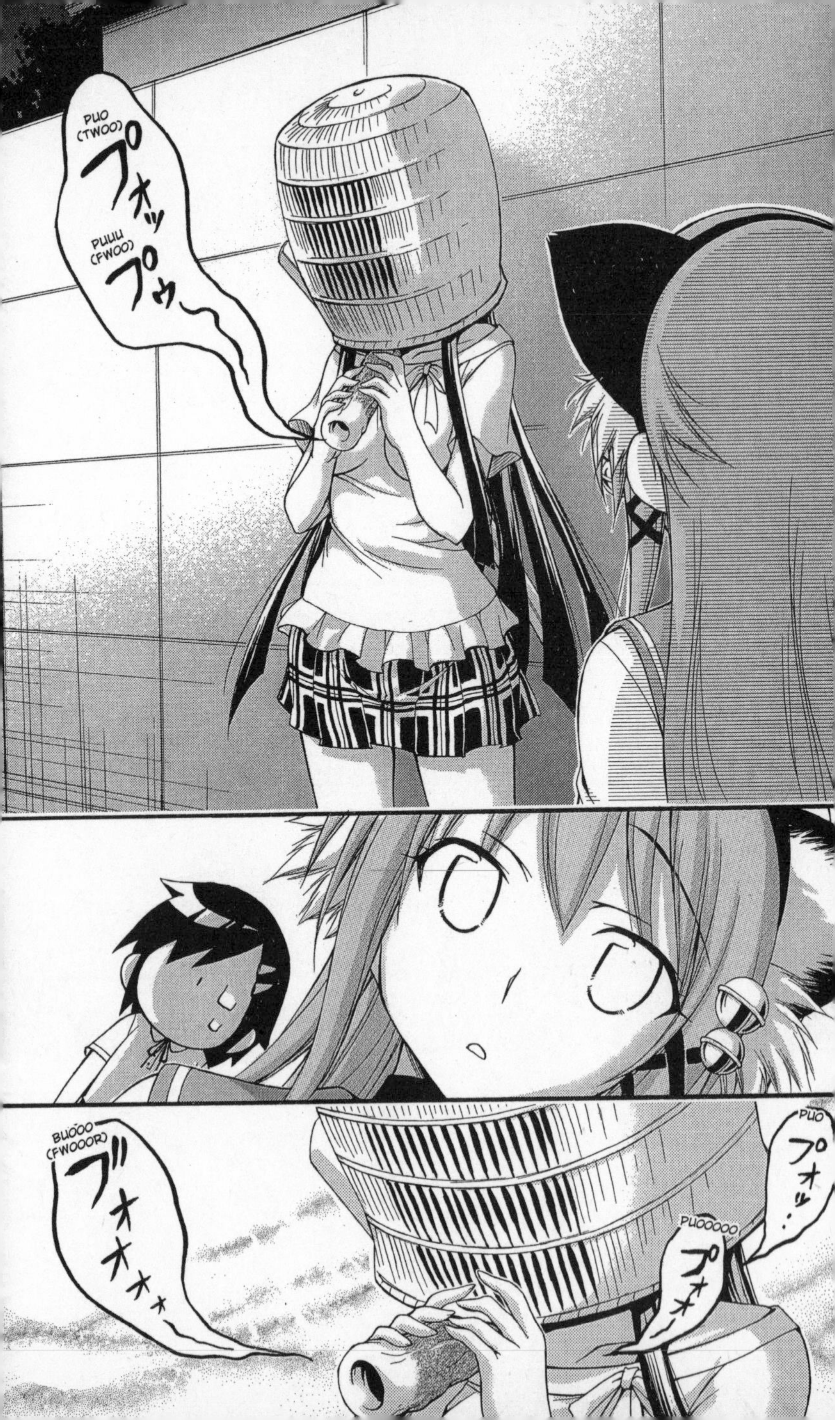
PUO (TWOO)
プオッ
PUUU (FWOO)
プウ～
PUO
プオッ‥
PUOOOOO
プオオ
BUOOO (FWOOOR)
ブオオオオ～

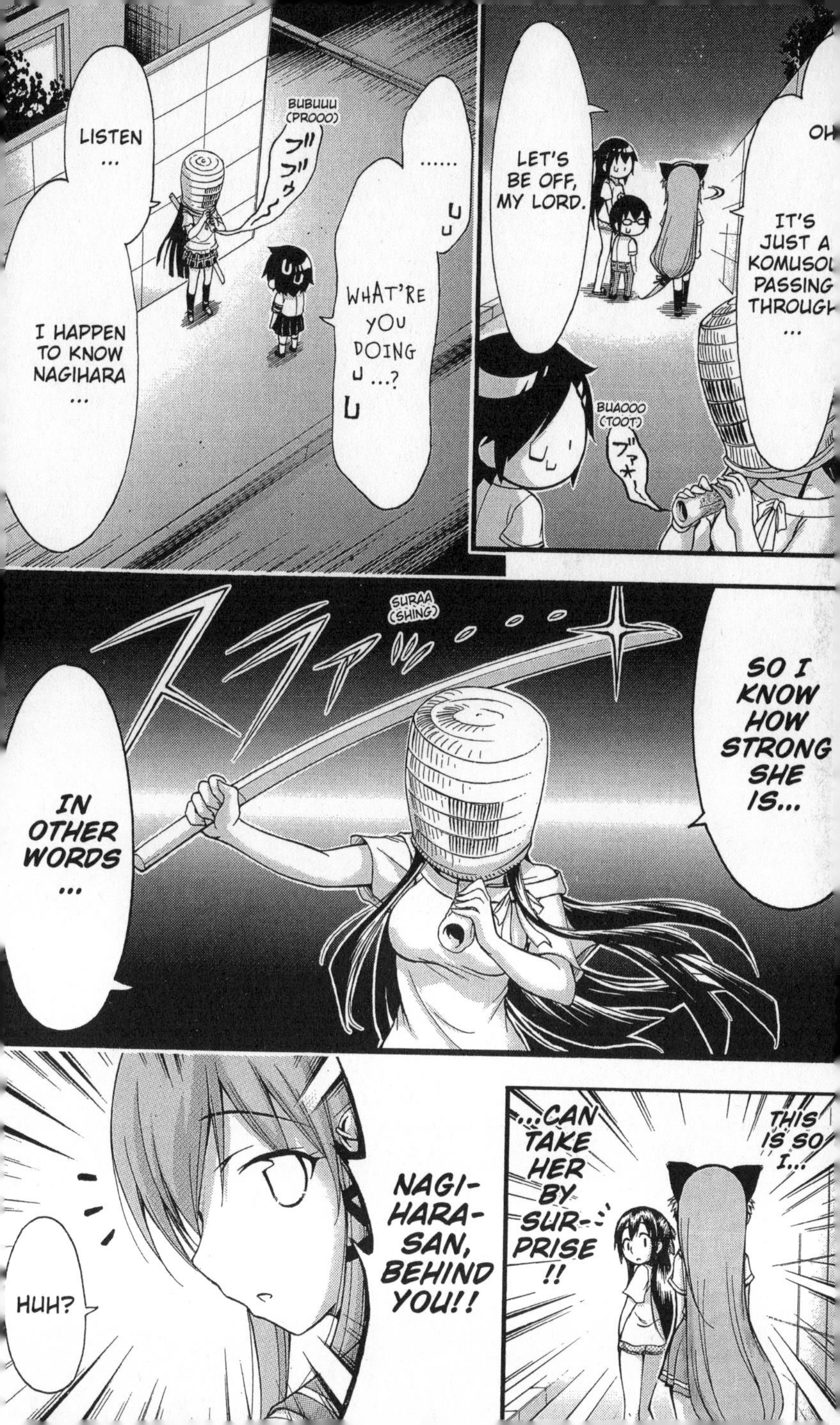
OH
IT'S JUST A KOMUSOU PASSING THROUGH...
LET'S BE OFF, MY LORD.
BUAOOO (TOOT)
ブァ〜
......
WHAT'RE YOU DOING...?
BUBUUU (PROOO)
ブブゥ〜
LISTEN...
I HAPPEN TO KNOW NAGIHARA...
SO I KNOW HOW STRONG SHE IS...
SURAA (SHING)
スラァッ
IN OTHER WORDS...
THIS IS SO I...
...CAN TAKE HER BY SURPRISE!!
NAGIHARA-SAN, BEHIND YOU!!
HUH?

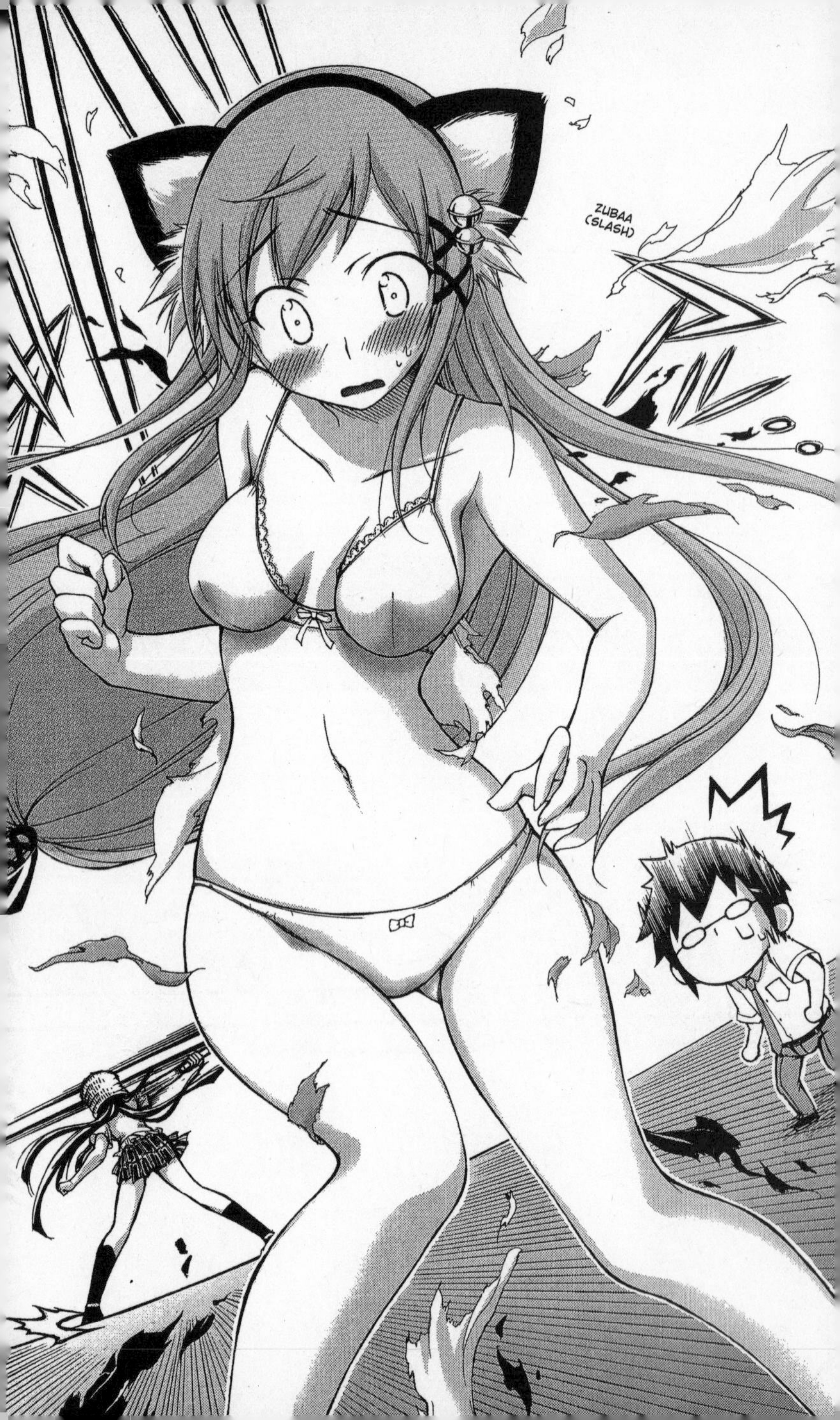
ZUBAA
(SLASH)

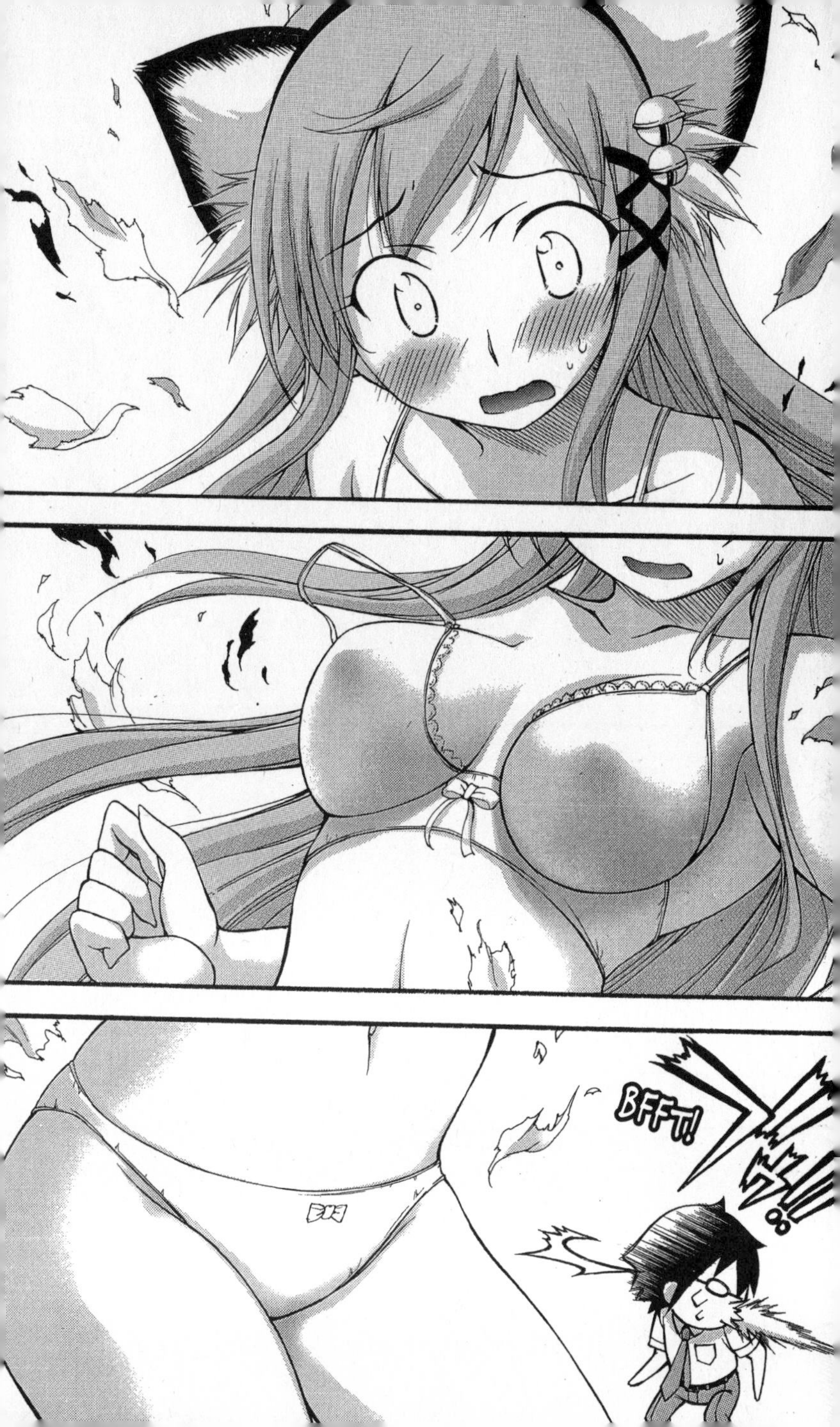
BFFT!

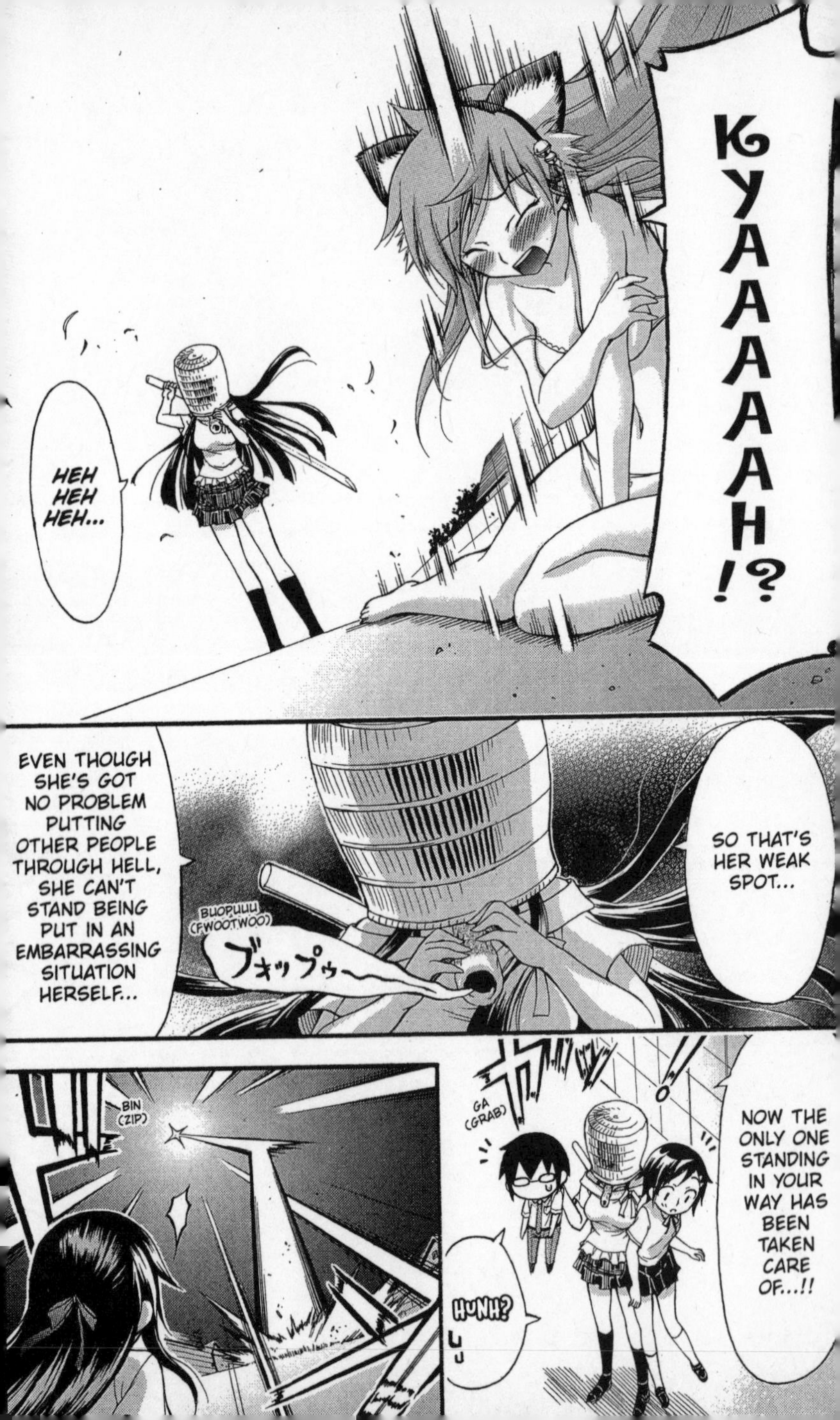
KYAAAAAH!?
HEH HEH HEH...
SO THAT'S HER WEAK SPOT...
EVEN THOUGH SHE'S GOT NO PROBLEM PUTTING OTHER PEOPLE THROUGH HELL, SHE CAN'T STAND BEING PUT IN AN EMBARRASSING SITUATION HERSELF...
BUOPUUU (FWOOTWOO)
ブオップゥ~
NOW THE ONLY ONE STANDING IN YOUR WAY HAS BEEN TAKEN CARE OF...!!
GA (GRAB)
HUNH?
BIN (ZIP)

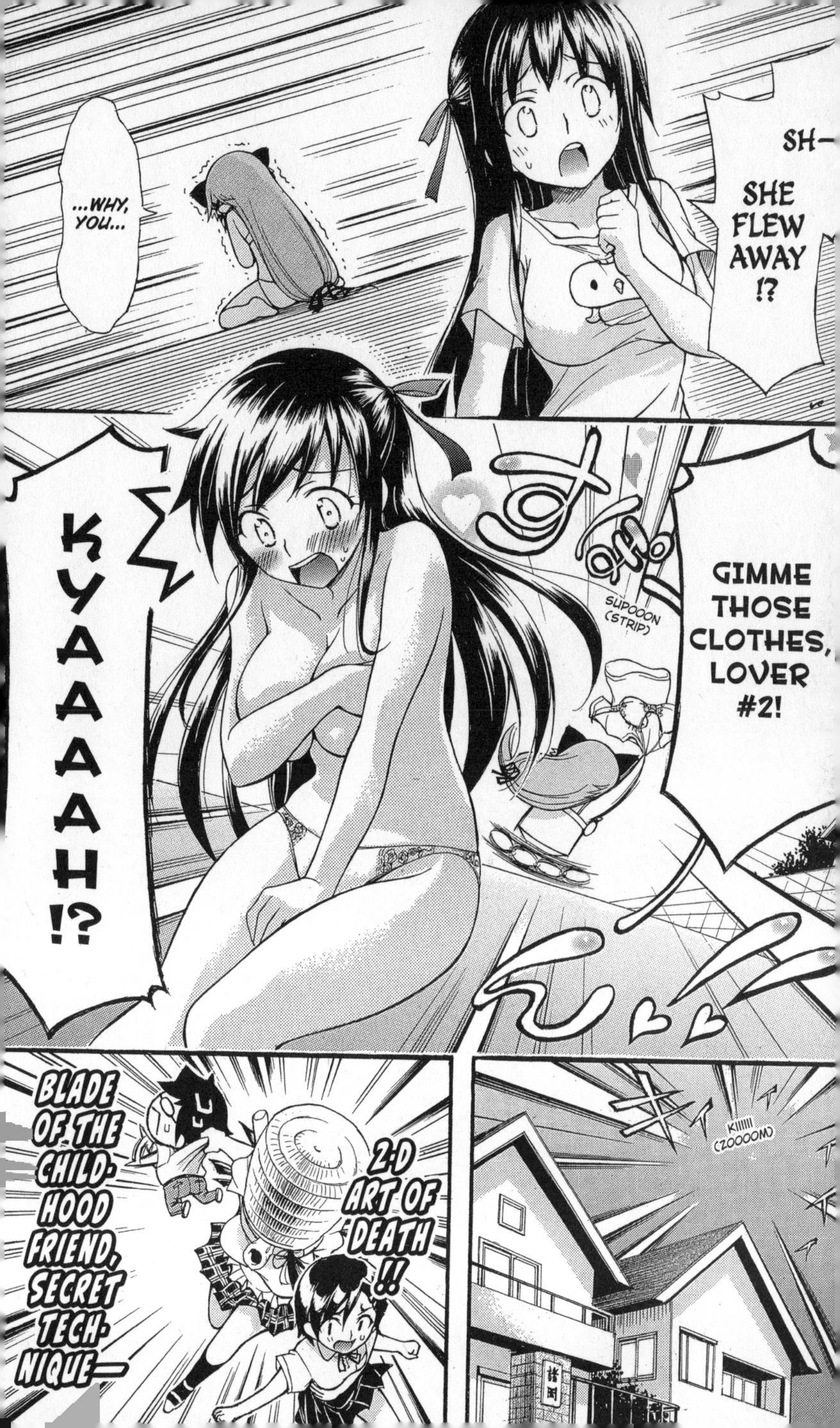
SH—
SHE FLEW AWAY !?
...WHY, YOU...
GIMME THOSE CLOTHES, LOVER #2!
SUPOOON (STRIP)
KYAAAAAH !?
KIIIIII (ZOOOOM)
BLADE OF THE CHILD-HOOD FRIEND, SECRET TECH-NIQUE—
2-D ART OF DEATH !!

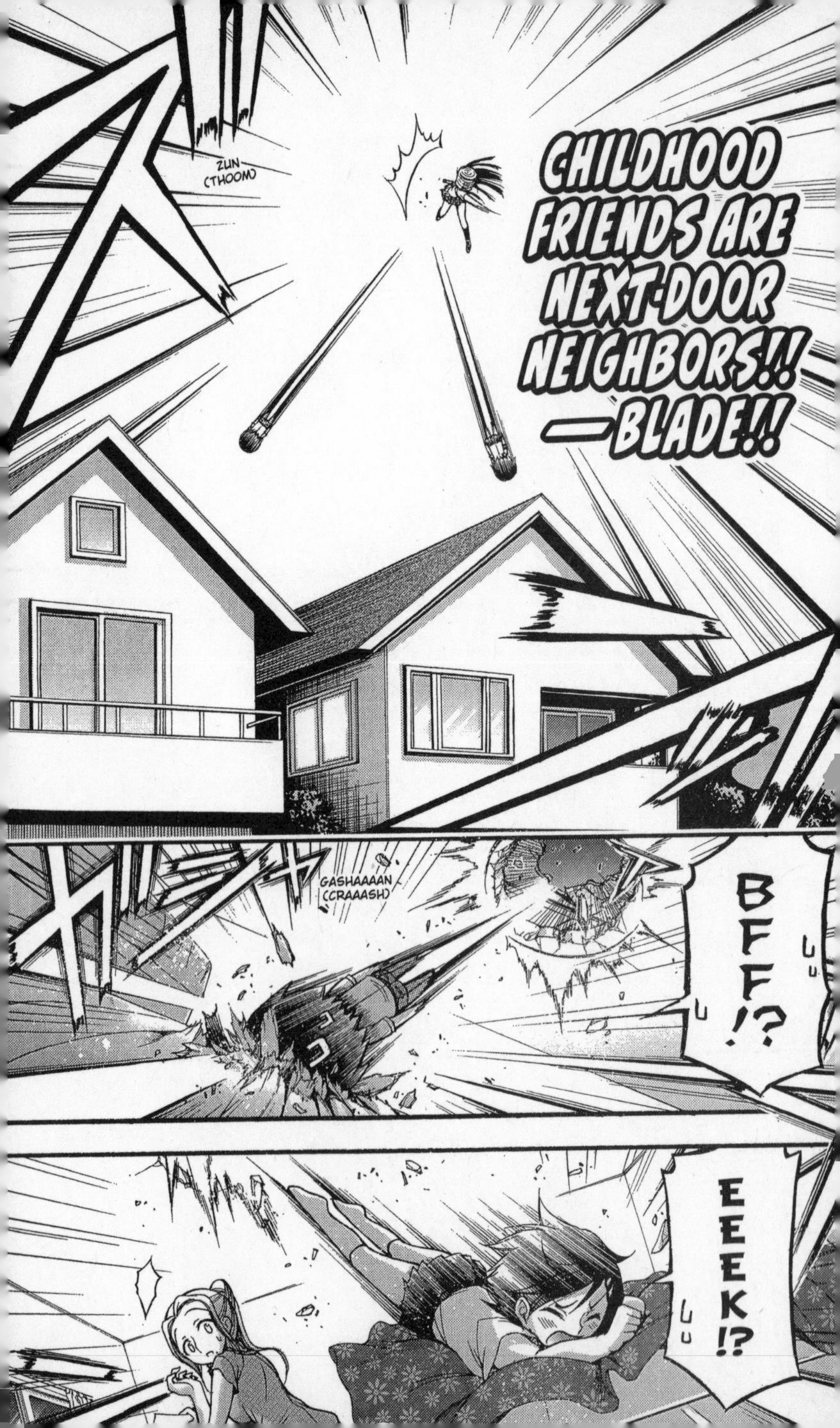
CHILDHOOD FRIENDS ARE NEXT-DOOR NEIGHBORS!! —BLADE!!
ZUN (THOOM)
BFF!?
GASHAAAAN (CRAAASH)
EEEEK!?

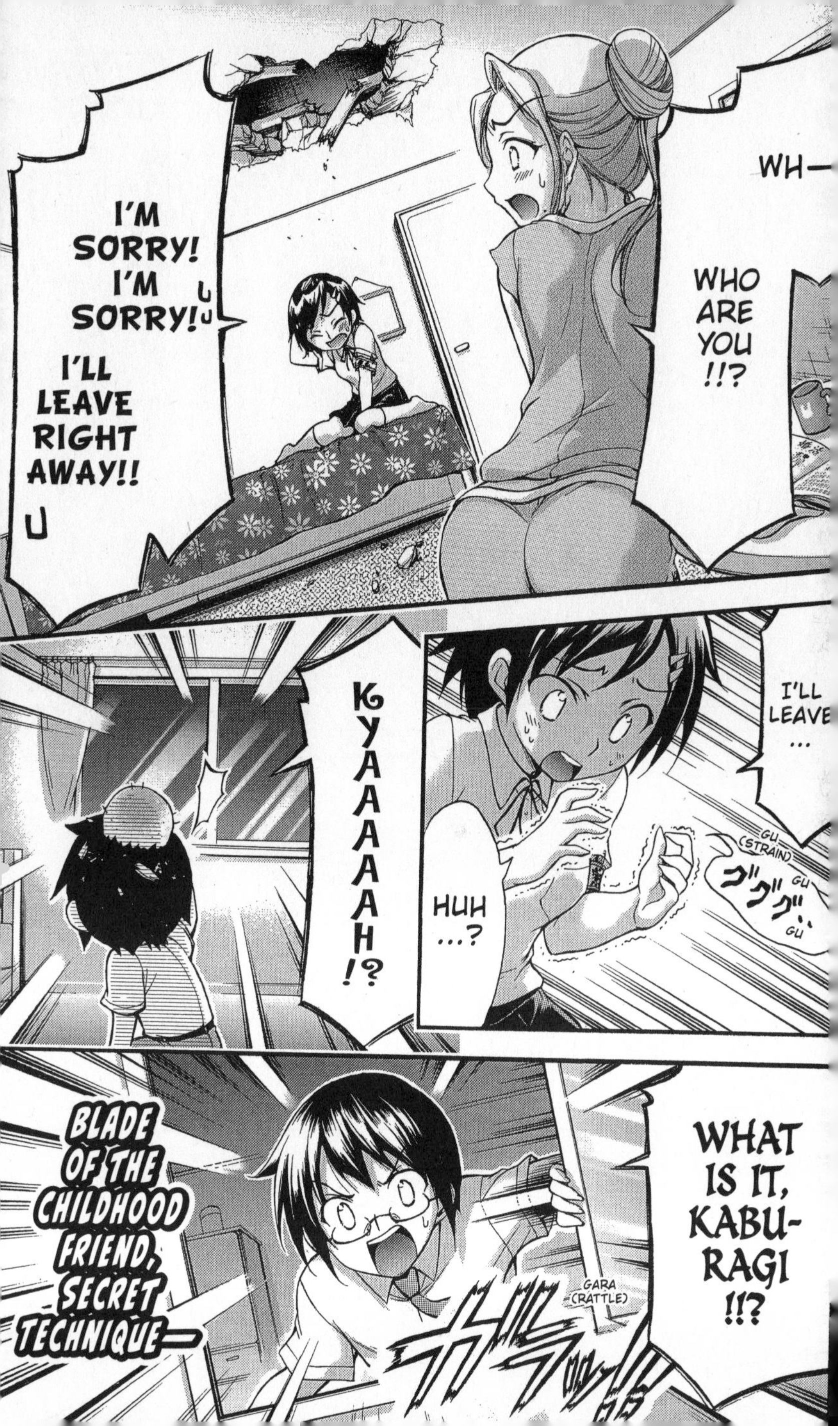
WH—
WHO ARE YOU!!?
I'M SORRY! I'M SORRY!
I'LL LEAVE RIGHT AWAY!!
I'LL LEAVE ...
GU (STRAIN)
GU
GU
HUH ...?
KYAAAAAAAH!?
WHAT IS IT, KABURAGI!!?
GARA (RATTLE)
BLADE OF THE CHILDHOOD FRIEND, SECRET TECHNIQUE—

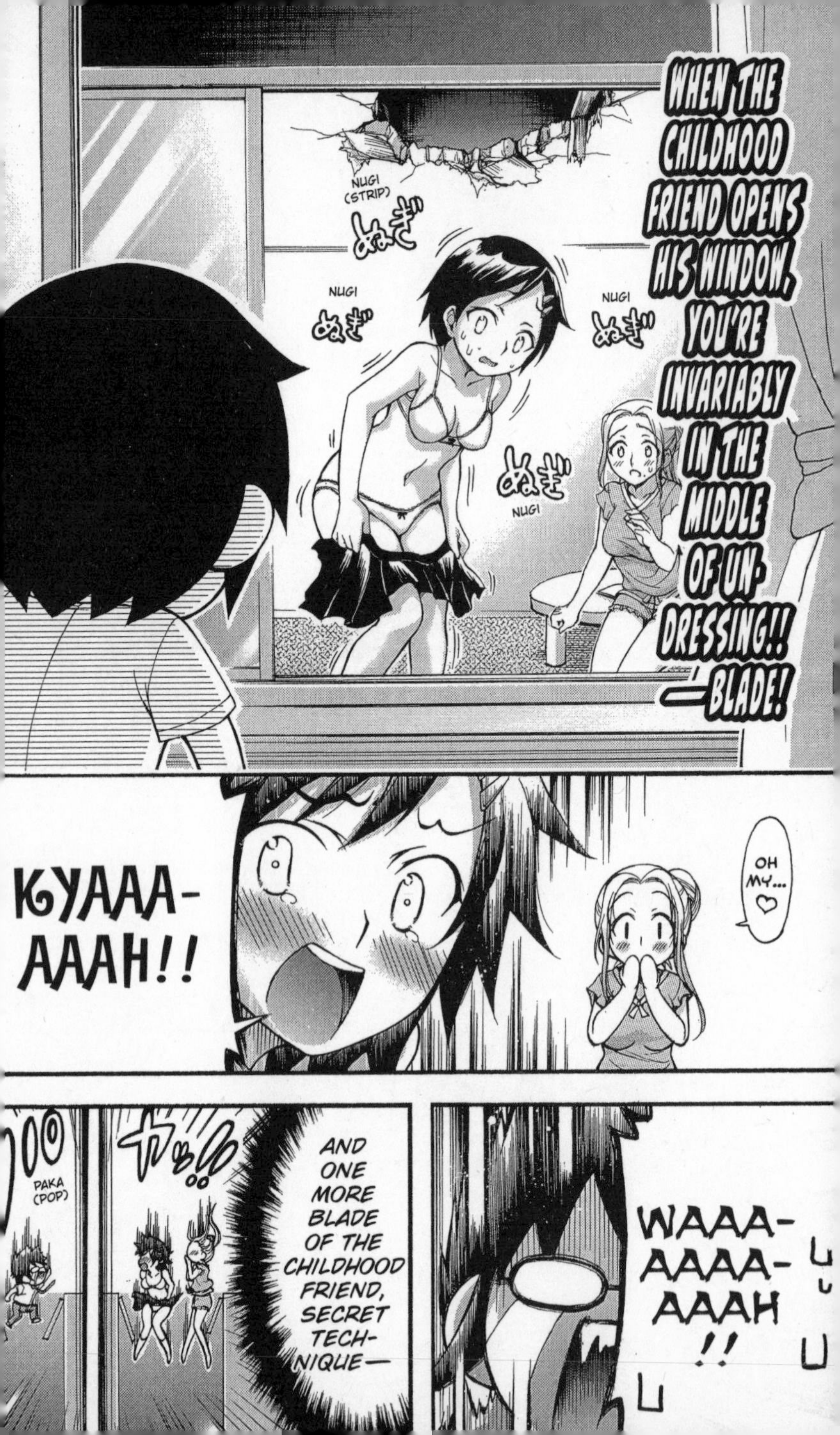
WHEN THE CHILDHOOD FRIEND OPENS HIS WINDOW, YOU'RE INVARIABLY IN THE MIDDLE OF UN-DRESSING!! —BLADE!
ぬぎ NUGI (STRIP)
ぬぎ NUGI
ぬぎ NUGI
ぬぎ NUGI
OH MY... ♡
KYAAAA-AAAH!!
WAAAA-AAAA-AAAH!!
AND ONE MORE BLADE OF THE CHILDHOOD FRIEND, SECRET TECH-NIQUE—
PAKA (POP)

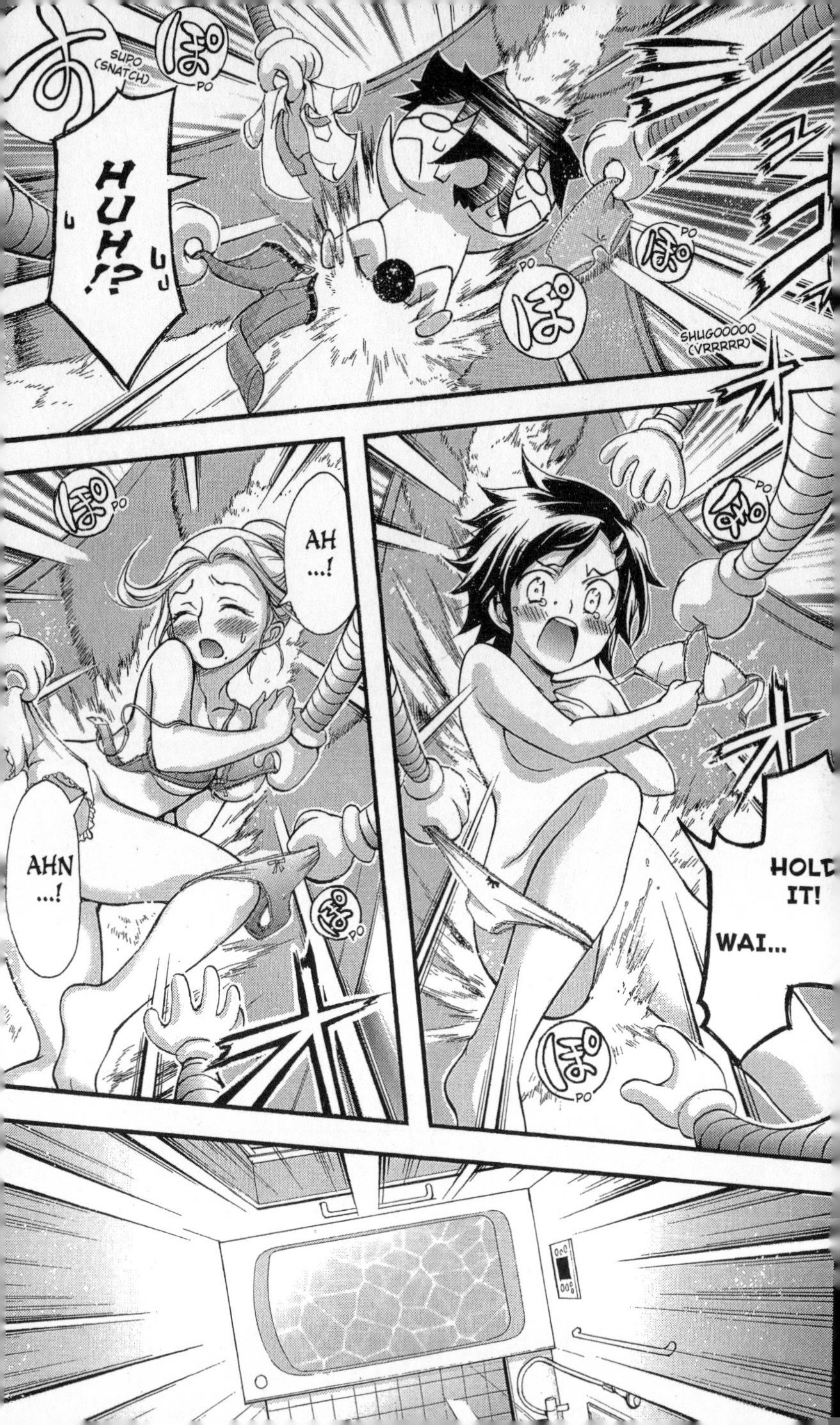

ぽ PO
ぽ PO
SHUGOOOOO (VRRRRR)
SUPO (SNATCH)
ぽ PO
あ
HUH!?
ぽ PO
HOLD IT!
WAI...
ぽ PO
ぽ PO
AH ...!
AHN ...!
ぽ PO

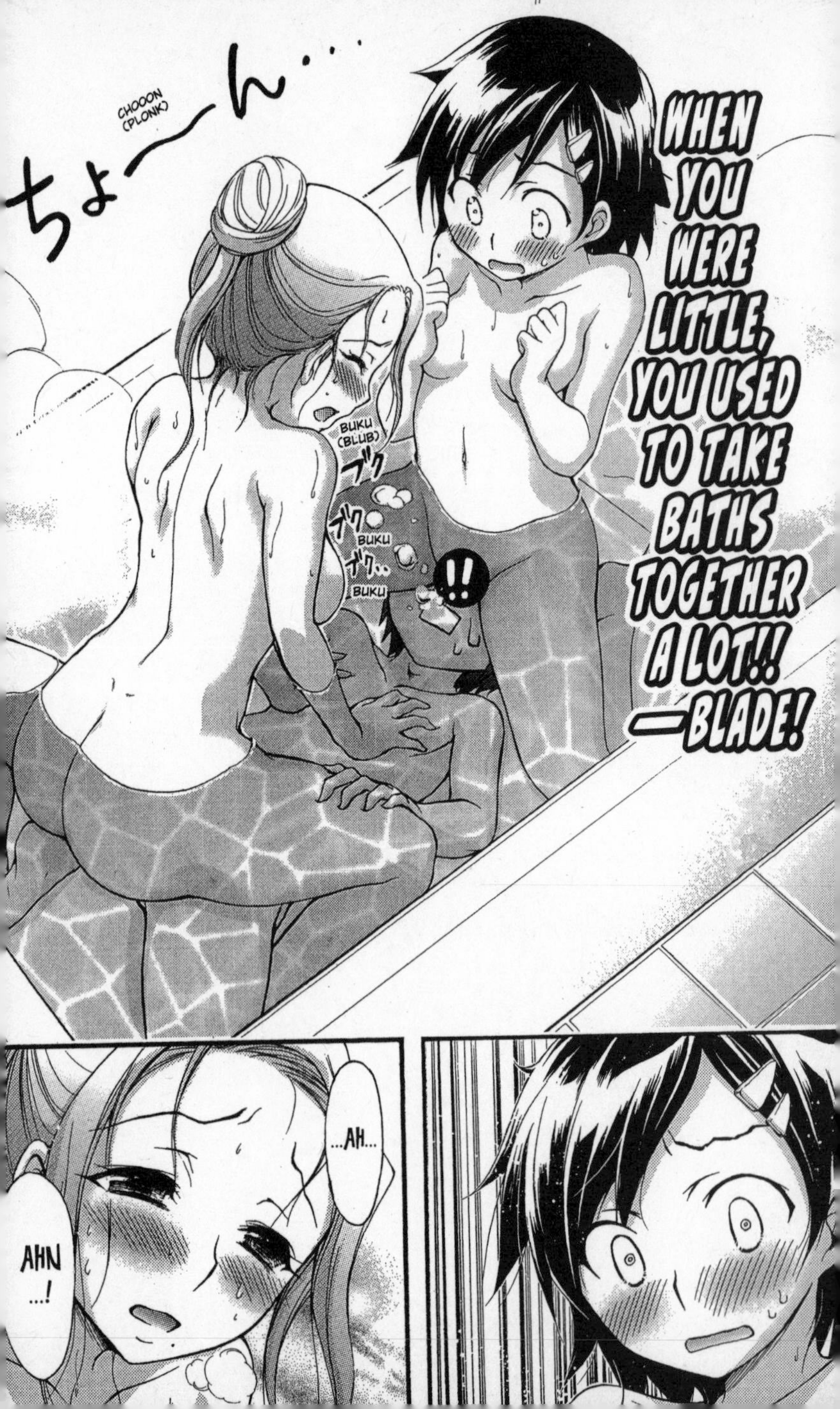
WHEN YOU WERE LITTLE, YOU USED TO TAKE BATHS TOGETHER A LOT!! —BLADE!
ちょ〜ん…
CHOOON (PLONK)
ブク
BUKU (BLUB)
ブク
BUKU
ブク..
BUKU
!!
...AH...
AHN ...!

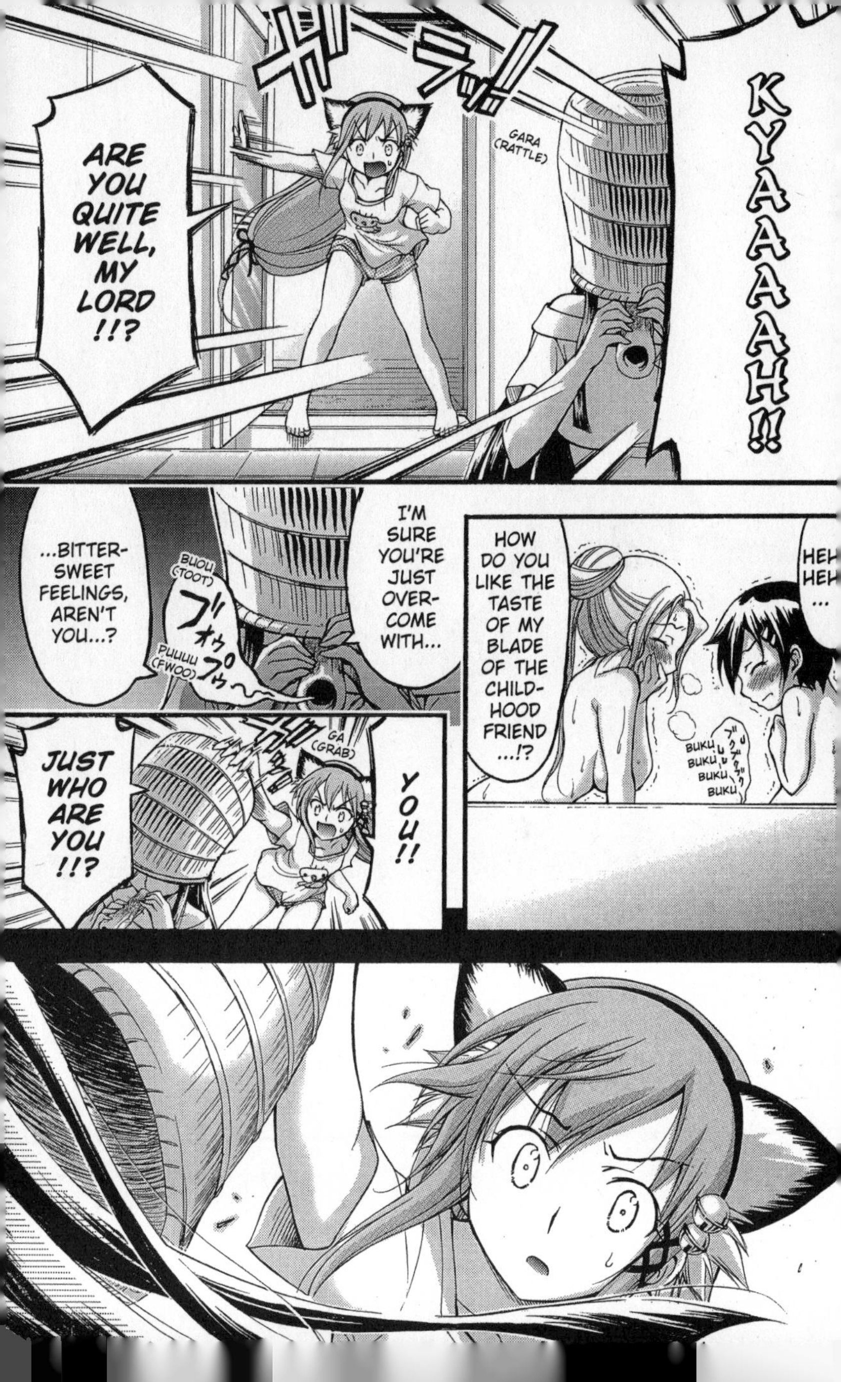
KYAAAAAH!!
GARA (RATTLE)
ARE YOU QUITE WELL, MY LORD!!?
HEH HEH...
HOW DO YOU LIKE THE TASTE OF MY BLADE OF THE CHILDHOOD FRIEND...!?
BUKU BUKU BUKU BUKU
I'M SURE YOU'RE JUST OVERCOME WITH...
BUOU (TOOT)
PUUUU (FWOO)
...BITTERSWEET FEELINGS, AREN'T YOU...?
YOU!!
GA (GRAB)
JUST WHO ARE YOU!!?

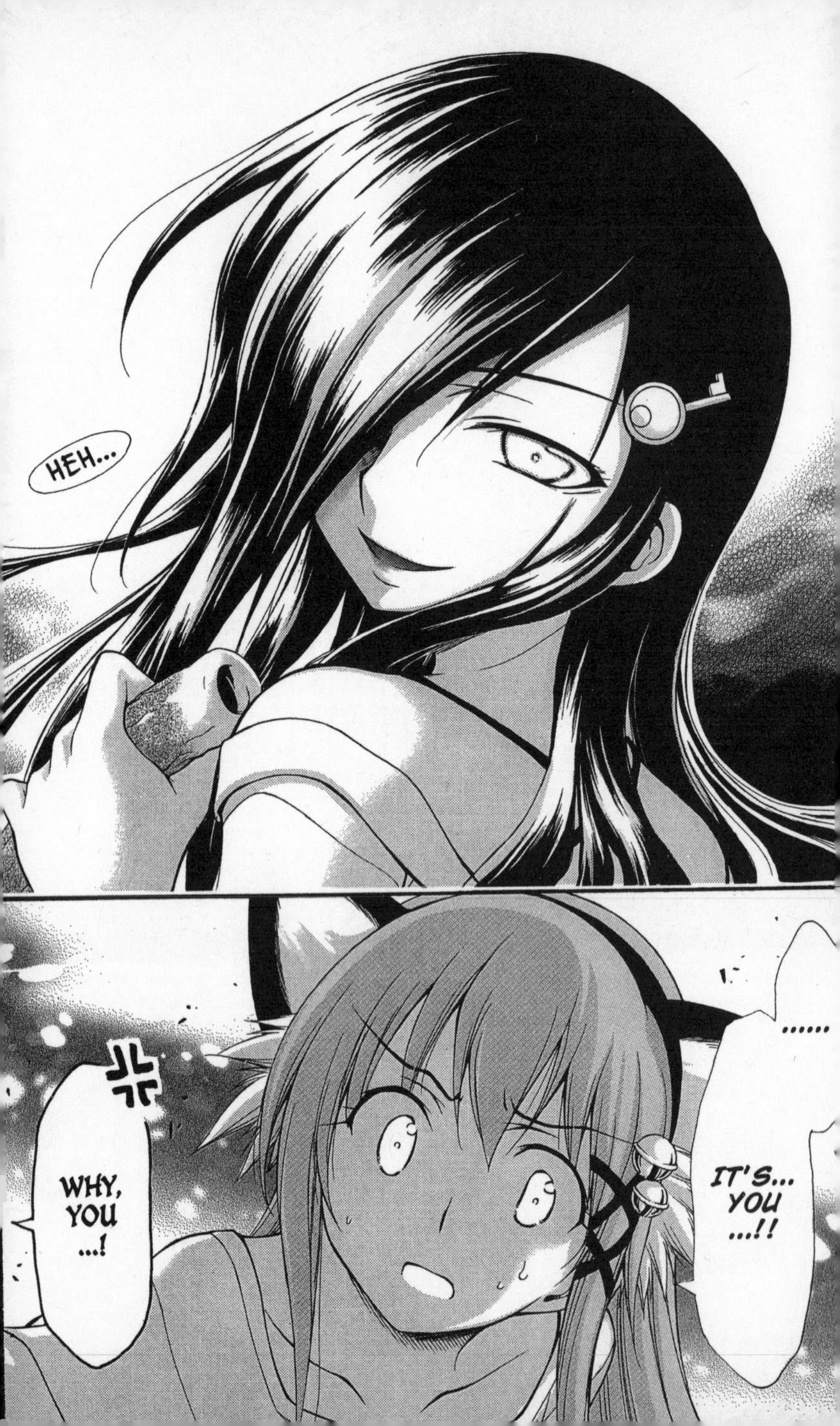
HEH...
......
IT'S... YOU ...!!
WHY, YOU ...!

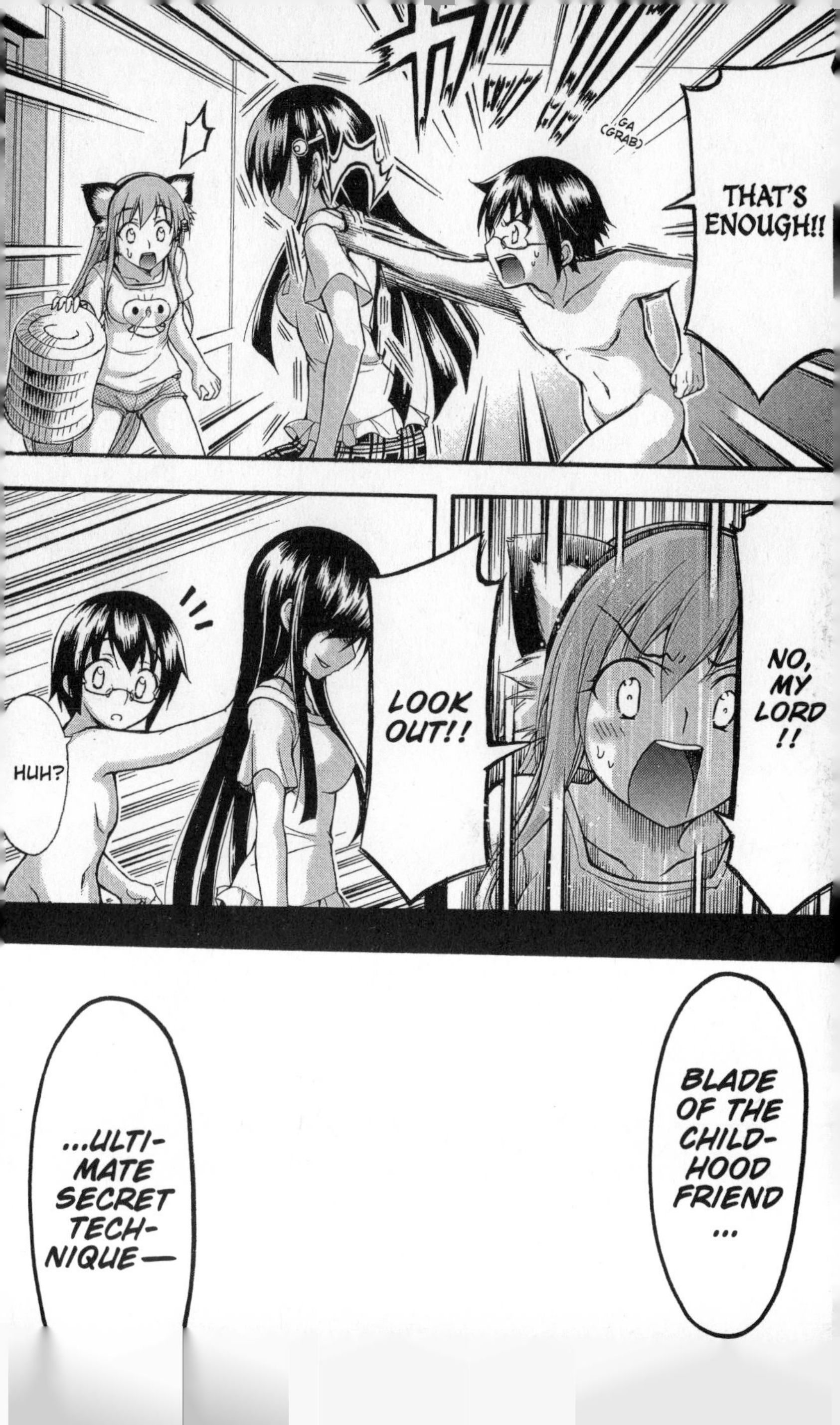
GA (GRAB)
THAT'S ENOUGH!!
NO, MY LORD!!
LOOK OUT!!
HUH?
BLADE OF THE CHILDHOOD FRIEND...
...ULTIMATE SECRET TECHNIQUE—

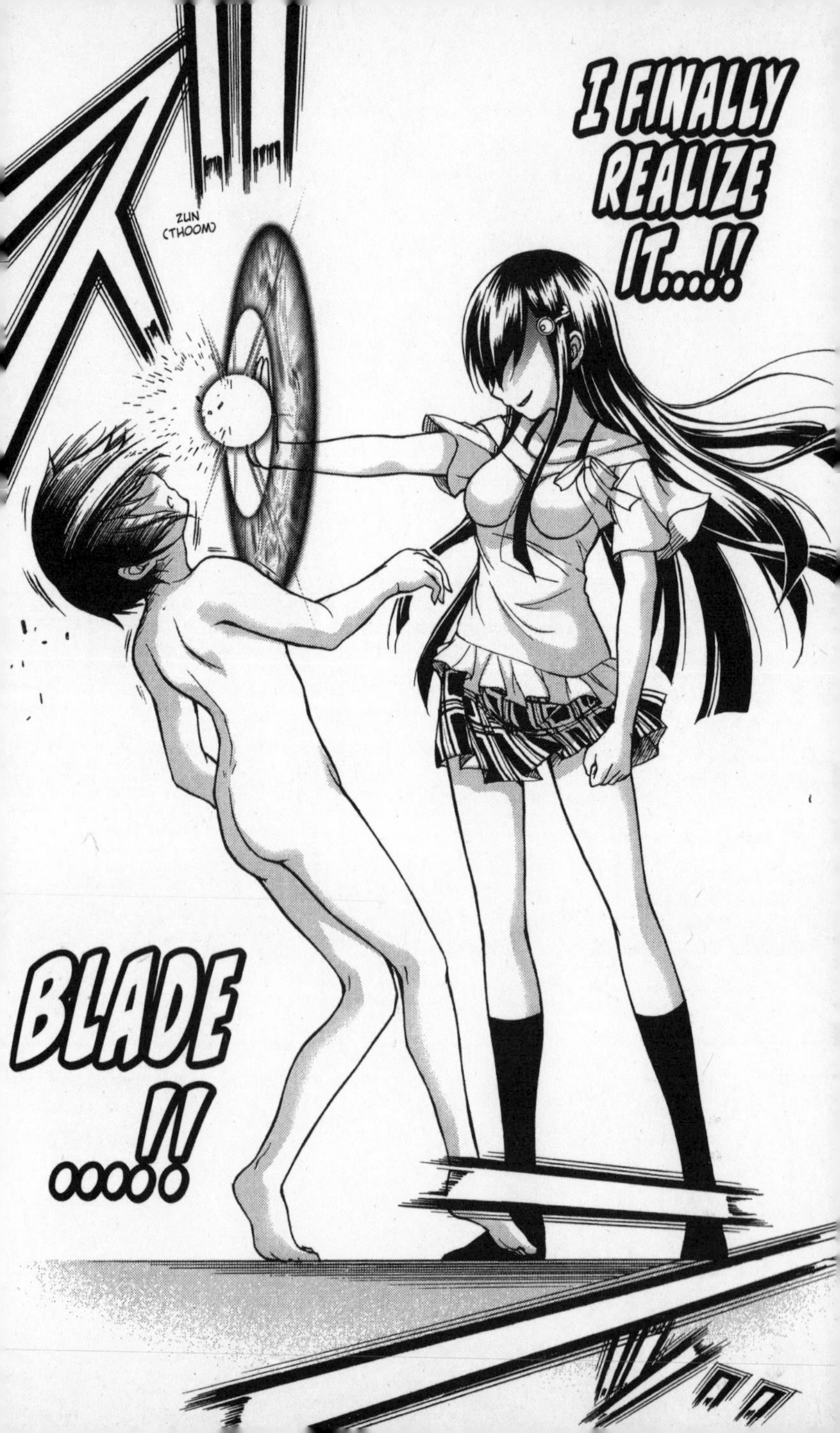
I FINALLY REALIZE IT...!!
ZUN (THOOM)
BLADE ....!!

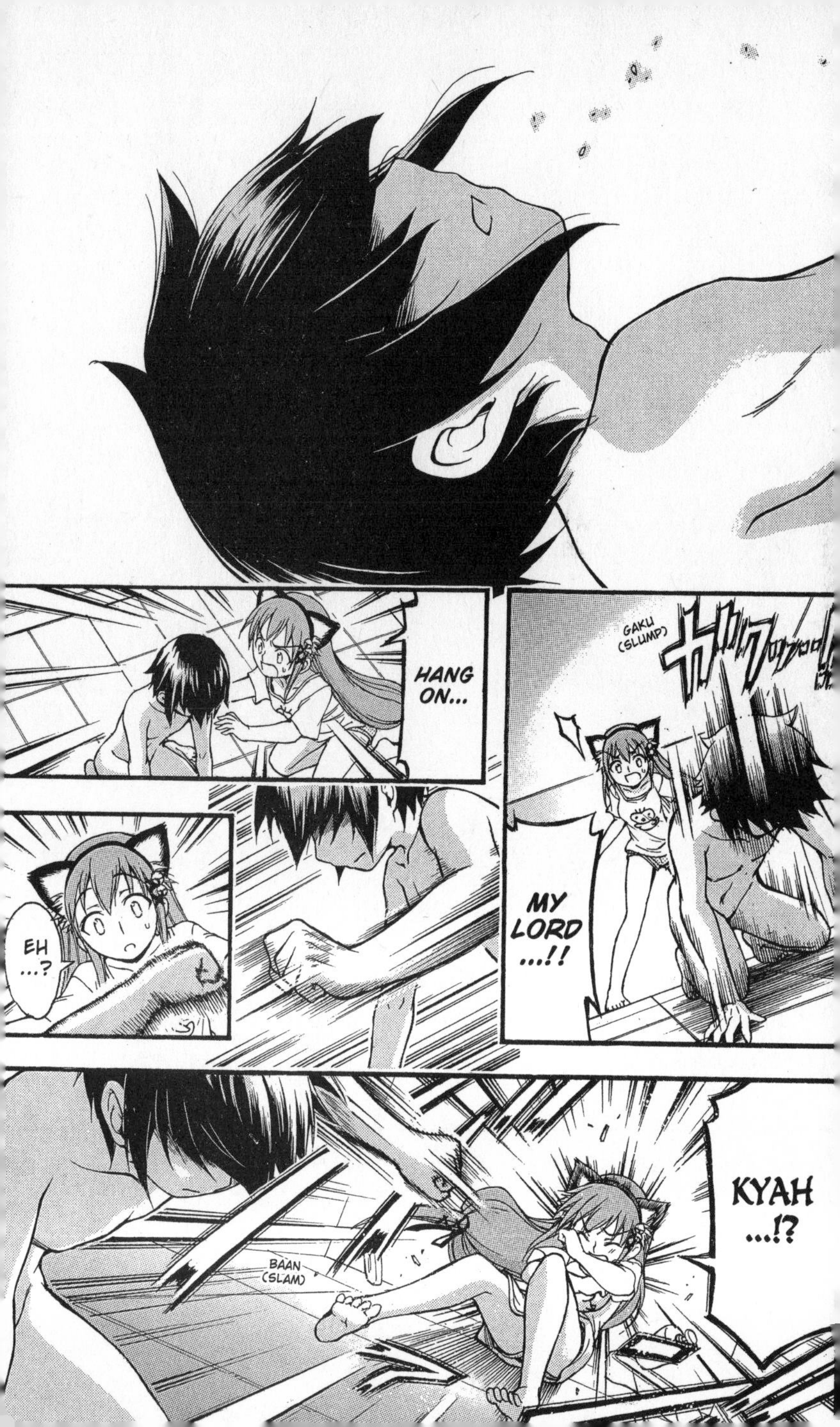
GAKU (SLUMP)
MY LORD ...!!
HANG ON...
EH ...?
KYAH ...!?
BAAN (SLAM)

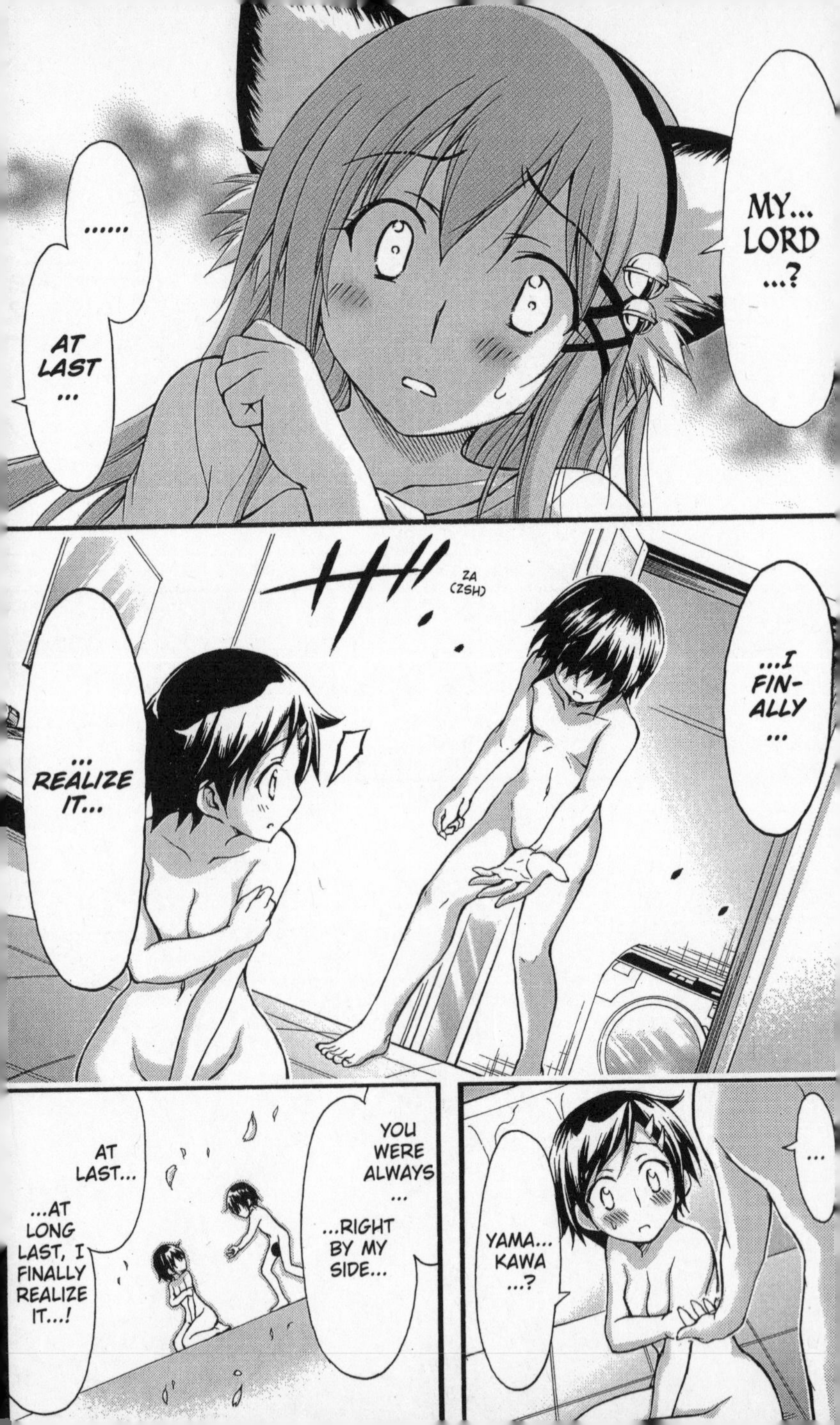
MY... LORD ...?
......
AT LAST ...
ZA (ZSH)
...I FIN-ALLY ...
... REALIZE IT...
...
YAMA... KAWA ...?
YOU WERE ALWAYS ...
...RIGHT BY MY SIDE...
AT LAST...
...AT LONG LAST, I FINALLY REALIZE IT...!

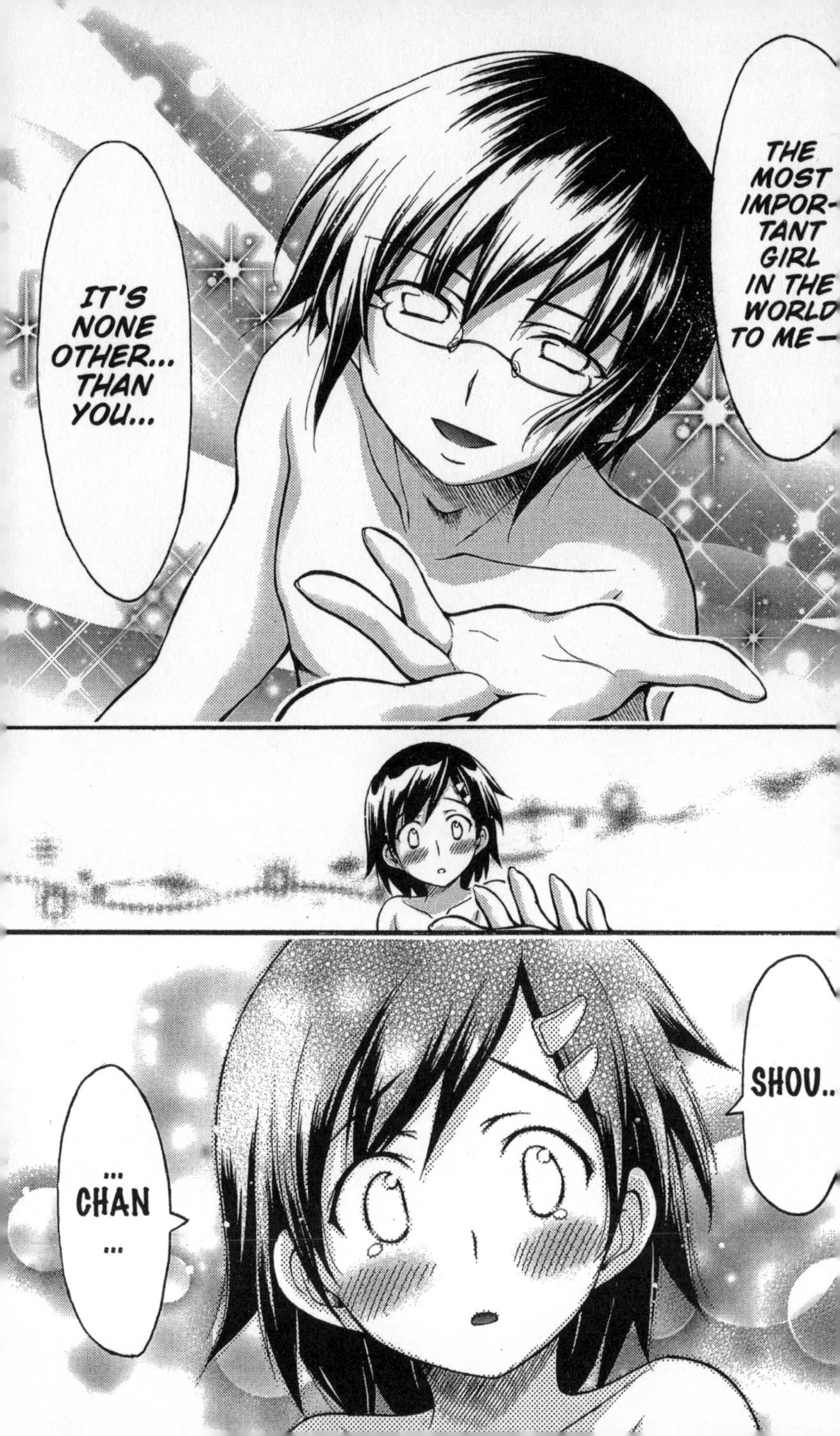
THE MOST IMPOR-TANT GIRL IN THE WORLD TO ME—
IT'S NONE OTHER... THAN YOU...
SHOU..
...CHAN...

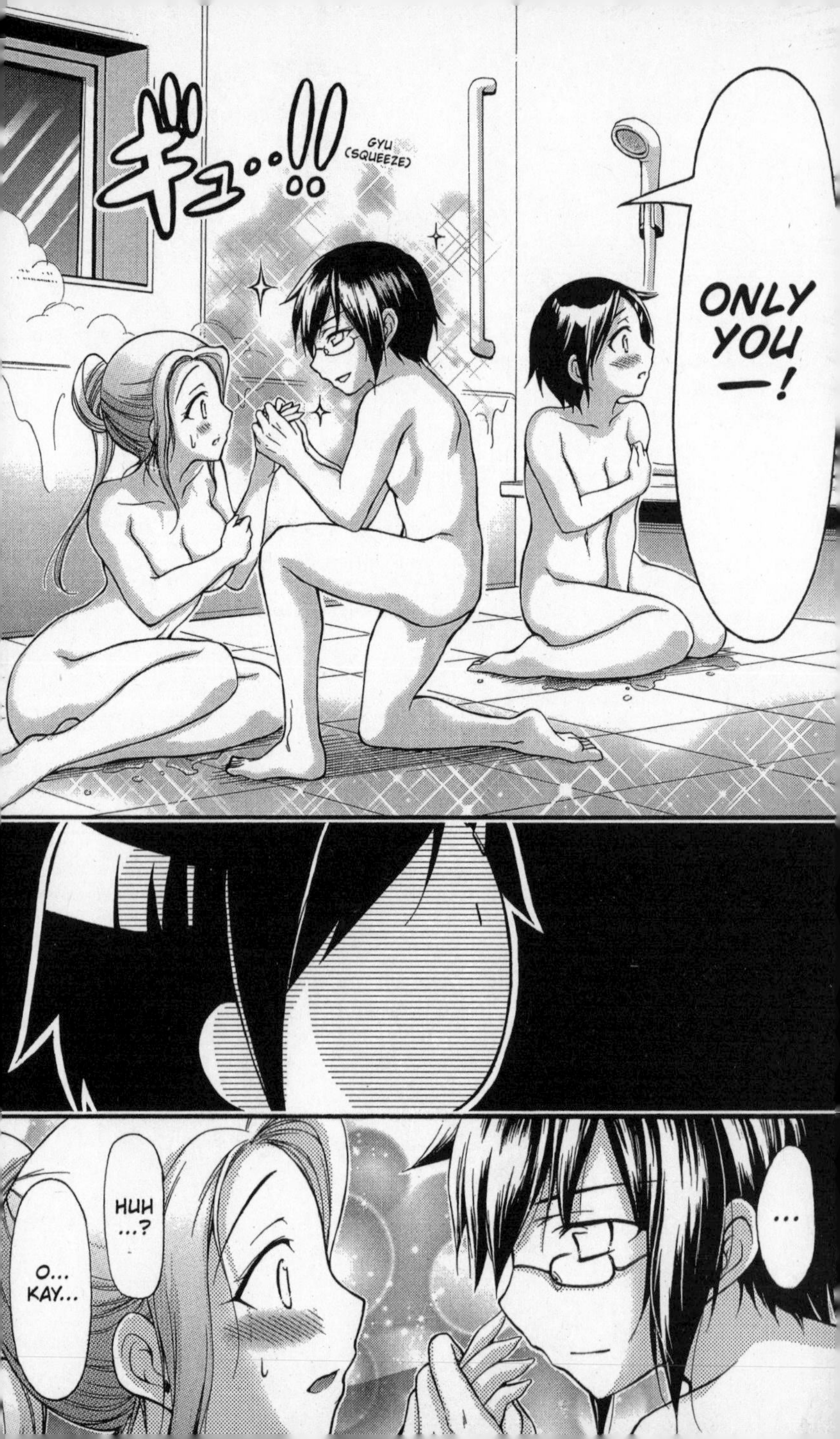
ONLY YOU—!
ギュ…!!
GYU (SQUEEZE)
...
HUH ...?
O... KAY...

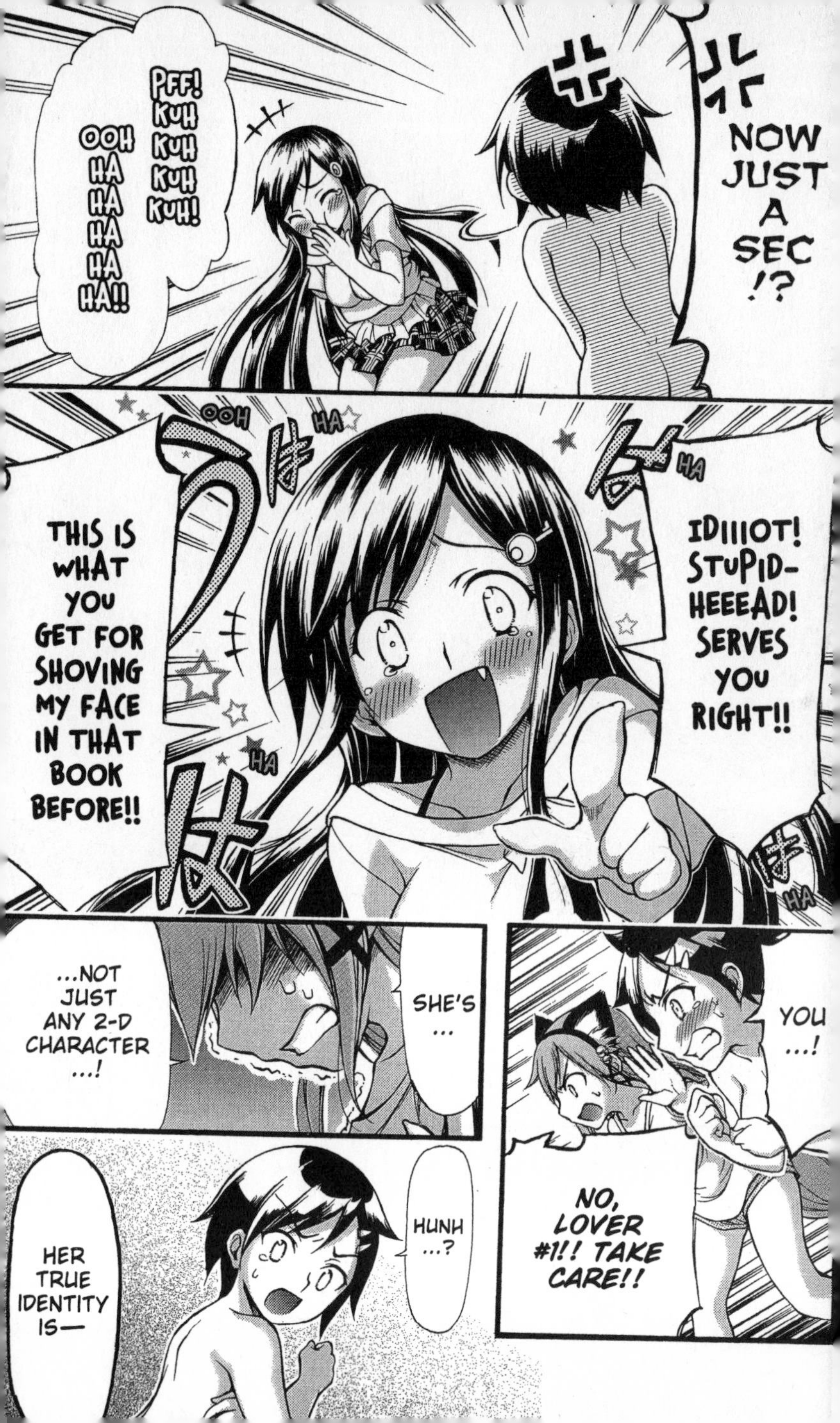
NOW JUST A SEC!?
PFF! KUH KUH KUH KUH!
OOH HA HA HA HA HA!!
OOH
HA
HA
HA
HA
IDIIIOT! STUPID-HEEEAD! SERVES YOU RIGHT!!
THIS IS WHAT YOU GET FOR SHOVING MY FACE IN THAT BOOK BEFORE!!
YOU ...!
NO, LOVER #1!! TAKE CARE!!
SHE'S ...
...NOT JUST ANY 2-D CHARACTER ...!
HUNH ...?
HER TRUE IDENTITY IS—

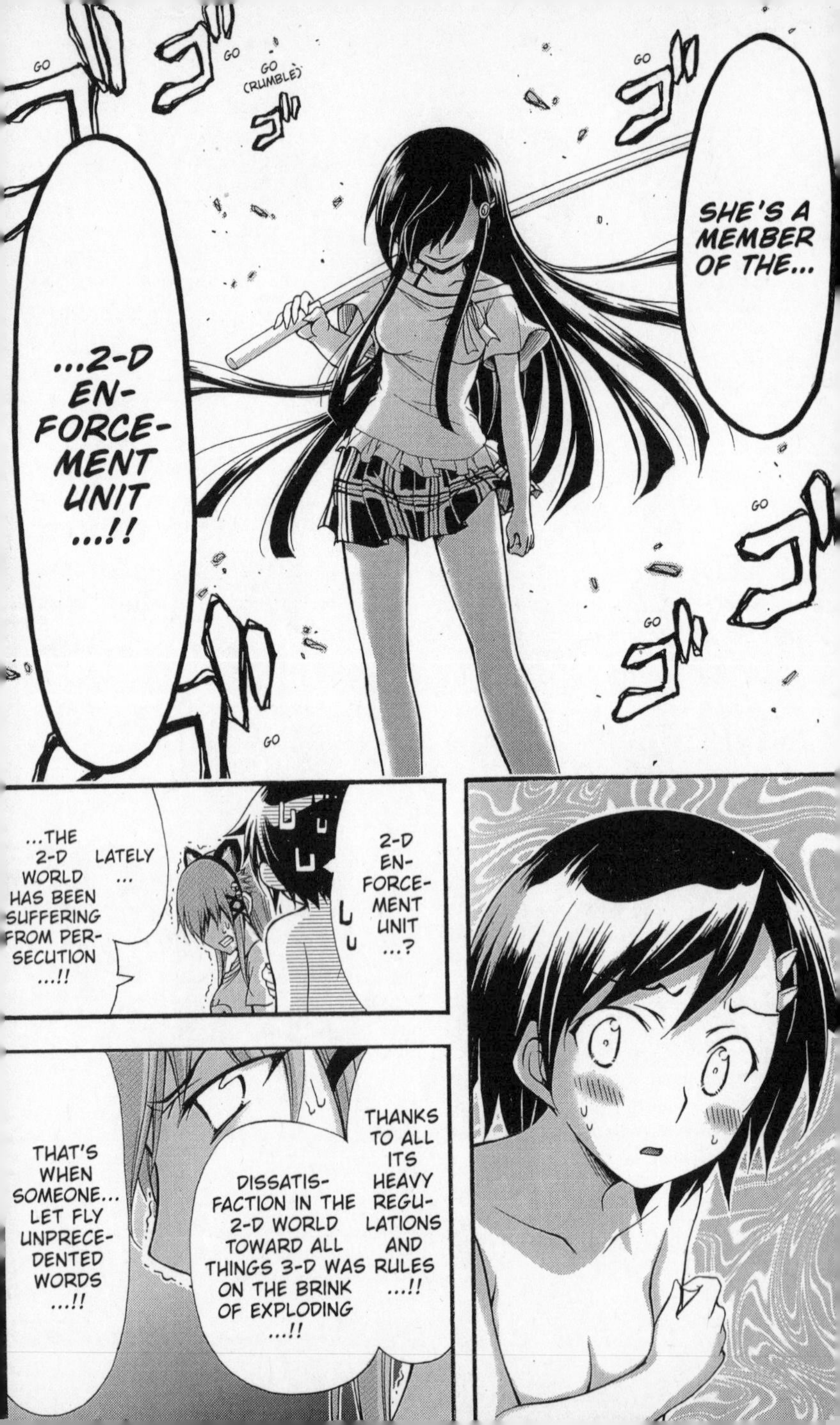
GO
SHE'S A MEMBER OF THE...
GO
GO (RUMBLE)
GO
GO
...2-D ENFORCEMENT UNIT ...!!
GO
GO
GO
2-D ENFORCEMENT UNIT ...?
LATELY ...
...THE 2-D WORLD HAS BEEN SUFFERING FROM PERSECUTION ...!!
THANKS TO ALL ITS HEAVY REGULATIONS AND RULES ...!!
DISSATISFACTION IN THE 2-D WORLD TOWARD ALL THINGS 3-D WAS ON THE BRINK OF EXPLODING ...!!
THAT'S WHEN SOMEONE... LET FLY UNPRECEDENTED WORDS ...!!

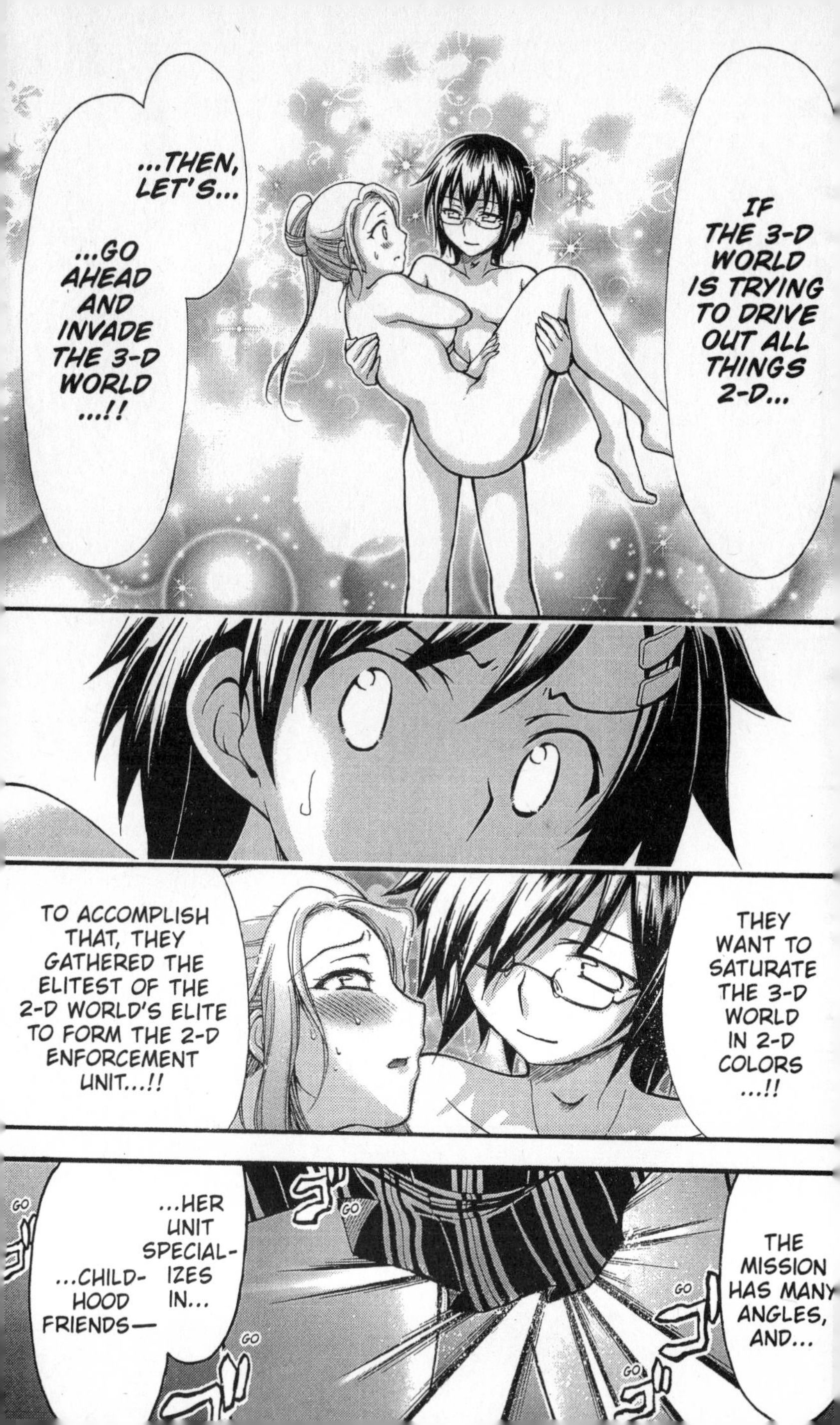
IF THE 3-D WORLD IS TRYING TO DRIVE OUT ALL THINGS 2-D...
...THEN, LET'S...
...GO AHEAD AND INVADE THE 3-D WORLD ...!!
THEY WANT TO SATURATE THE 3-D WORLD IN 2-D COLORS ...!!
TO ACCOMPLISH THAT, THEY GATHERED THE ELITEST OF THE 2-D WORLD'S ELITE TO FORM THE 2-D ENFORCEMENT UNIT...!!
GO
GO
THE MISSION HAS MANY ANGLES, AND...
GO
...HER UNIT SPECIAL-IZES IN...
...CHILD-HOOD FRIENDS—
GO
GO

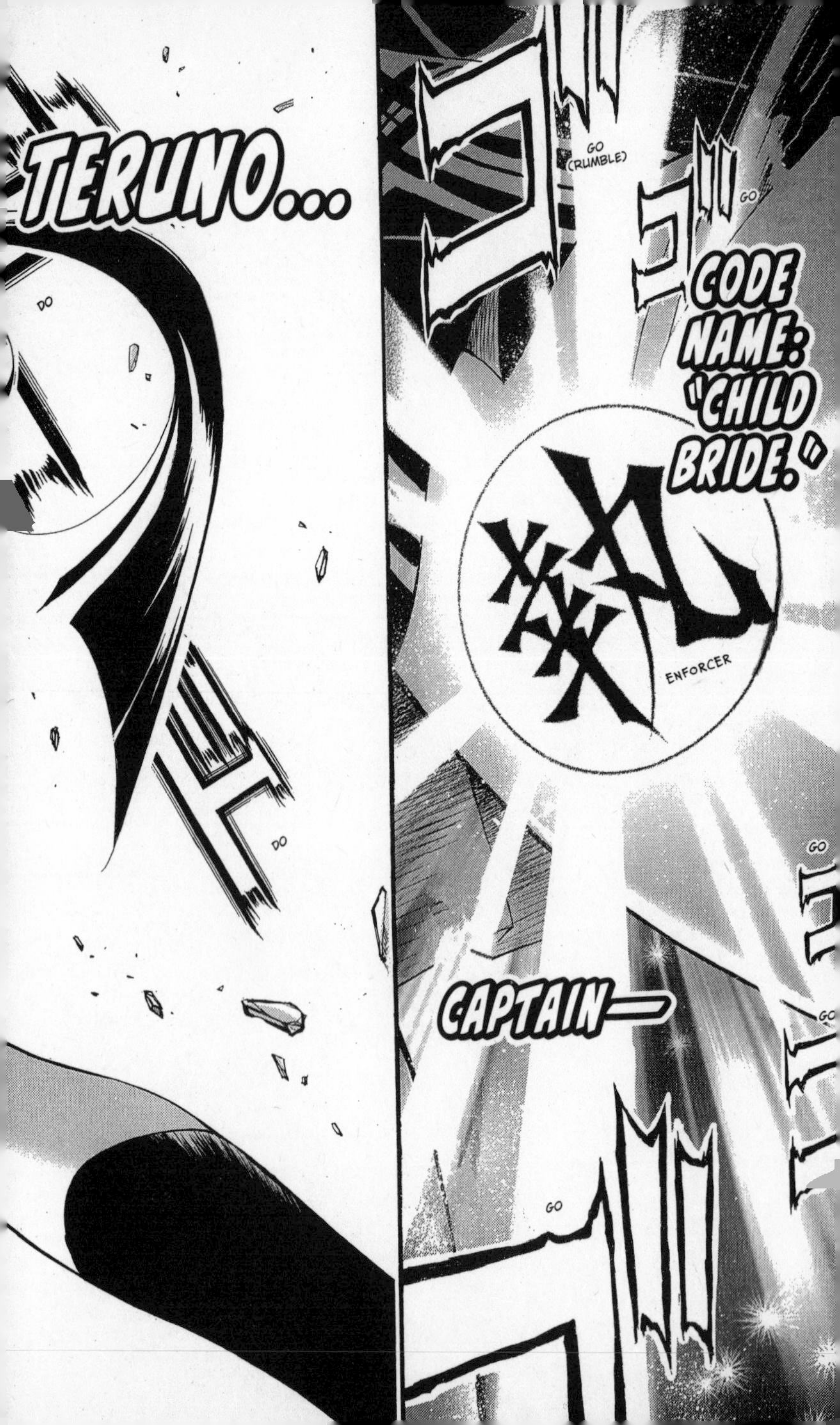
GO
(RUMBLE)
GO
CODE NAME: "CHILD BRIDE."
ENFORCER
GO
CAPTAIN—
GO
GO
TERUNO...
DO
DO

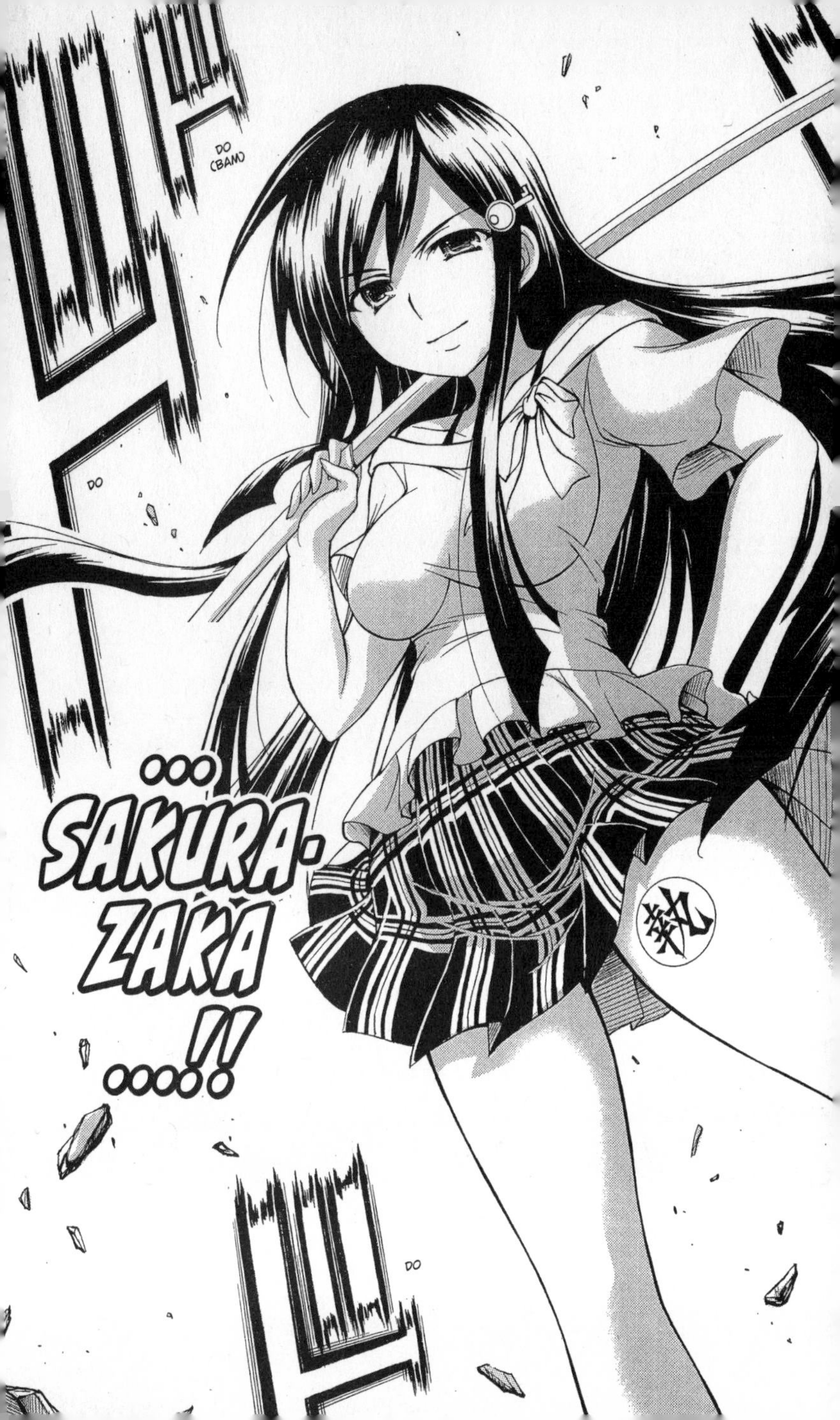
DO (BAM)
DO
...SAKURA-ZAKA...!!
DO

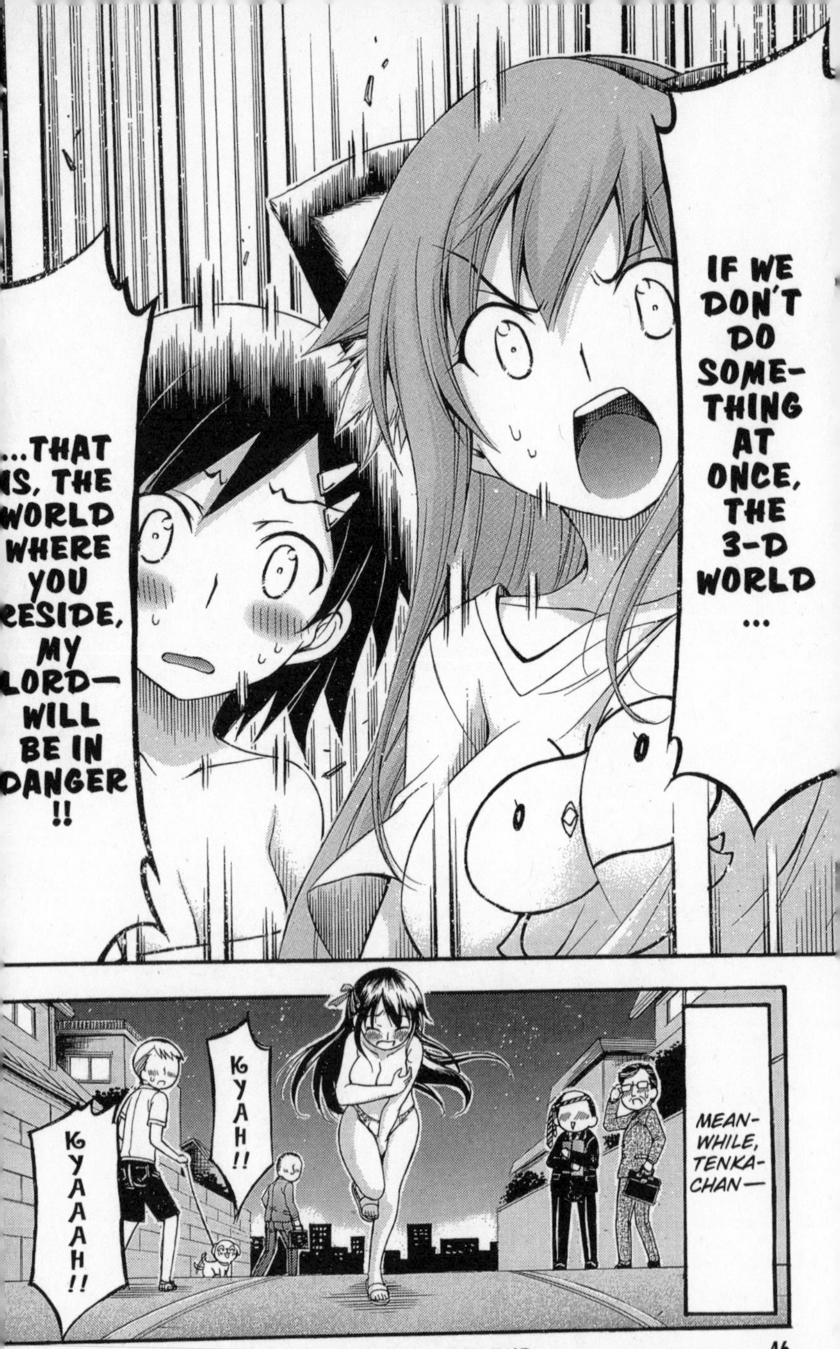
IF WE DON'T DO SOME-THING AT ONCE, THE 3-D WORLD...
...THAT IS, THE WORLD WHERE YOU RESIDE, MY LORD—WILL BE IN DANGER!!
MEAN-WHILE, TENKA-CHAN—
KYAH!!
KYAAAAH!!

14TH OFFENSE • THE END

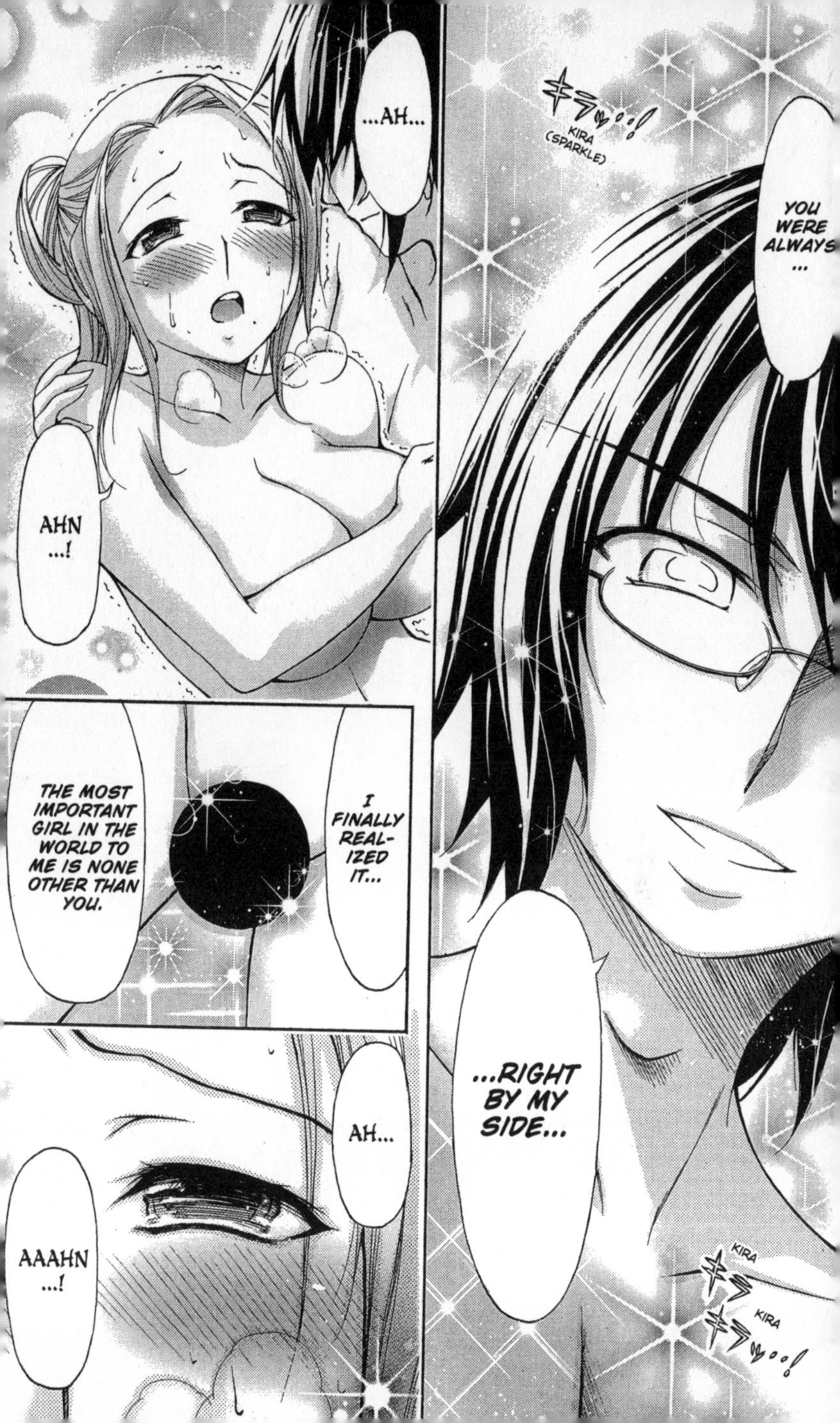
KIRA (SPARKLE)
YOU WERE ALWAYS ...
...RIGHT BY MY SIDE...
KIRA
KIRA
...AH...
AHN ...!
I FINALLY REAL-IZED IT...
THE MOST IMPORTANT GIRL IN THE WORLD TO ME IS NONE OTHER THAN YOU.
AH...
AAAHN ...!

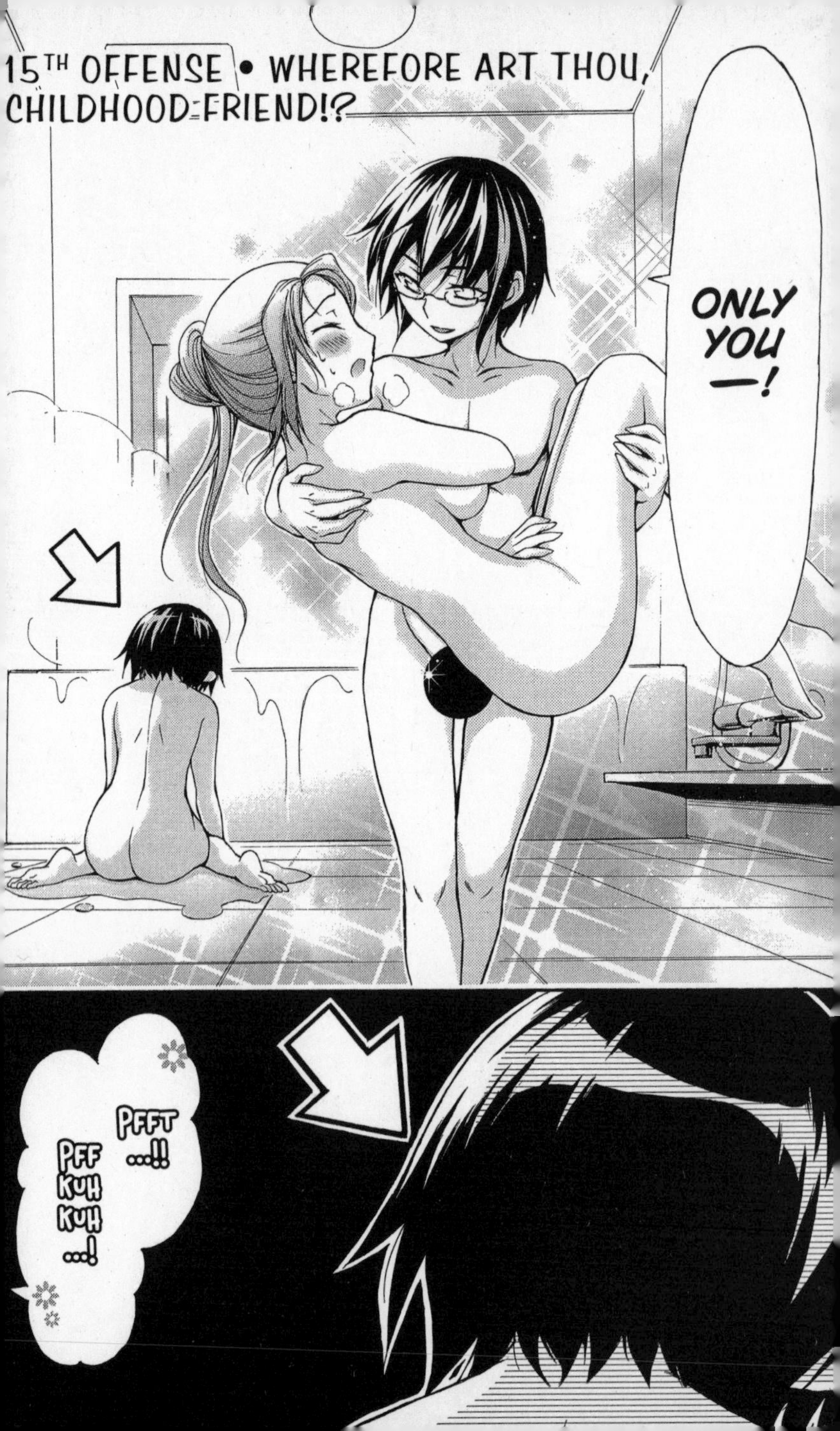
15TH OFFENSE • WHEREFORE ART THOU, CHILDHOOD-FRIEND!?
ONLY YOU —!
PFFT ...!!
PFF KUH KUH ...!

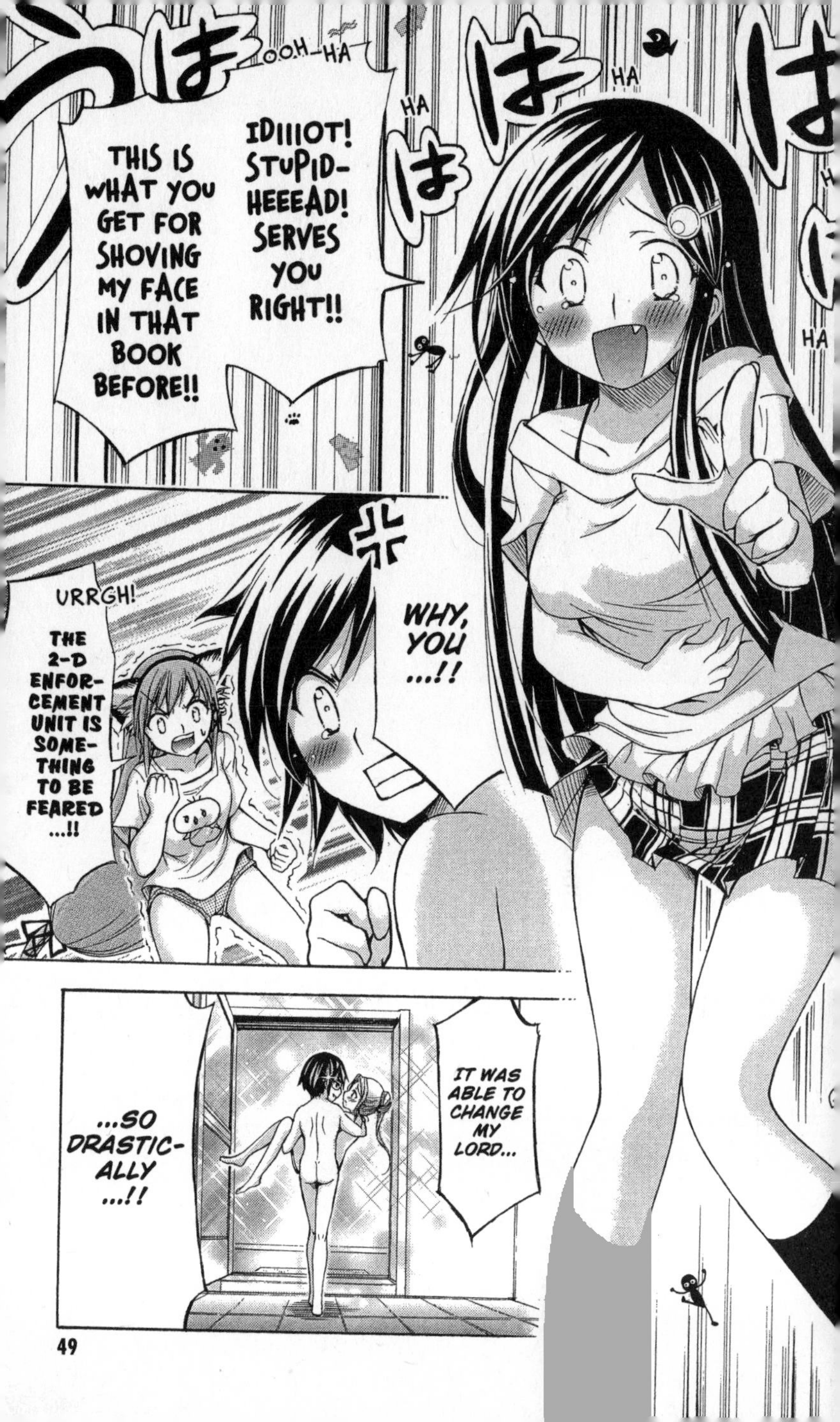
OOH-HA
HA
HA
HA
HA
IDIIIOT! STUPID-HEEEAD! SERVES YOU RIGHT!!
THIS IS WHAT YOU GET FOR SHOVING MY FACE IN THAT BOOK BEFORE!!
WHY, YOU ...!!
URRGH!
THE 2-D ENFORCEMENT UNIT IS SOMETHING TO BE FEARED ...!!
IT WAS ABLE TO CHANGE MY LORD...
...SO DRASTICALLY ...!!

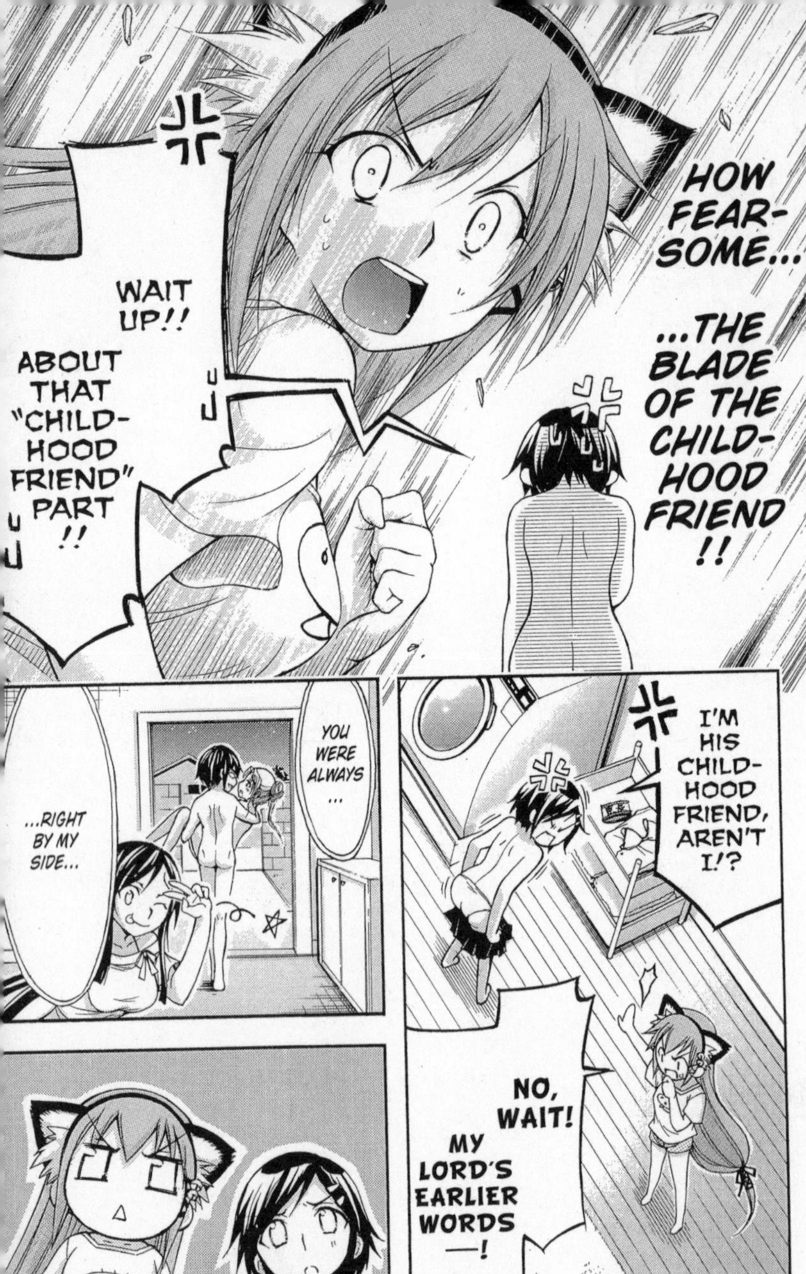
HOW FEAR-SOME...
...THE BLADE OF THE CHILD-HOOD FRIEND!!
WAIT UP!!
ABOUT THAT "CHILD-HOOD FRIEND" PART!!
I'M HIS CHILD-HOOD FRIEND, AREN'T I!?
NO, WAIT!
MY LORD'S EARLIER WORDS—!
YOU WERE ALWAYS...
...RIGHT BY MY SIDE...

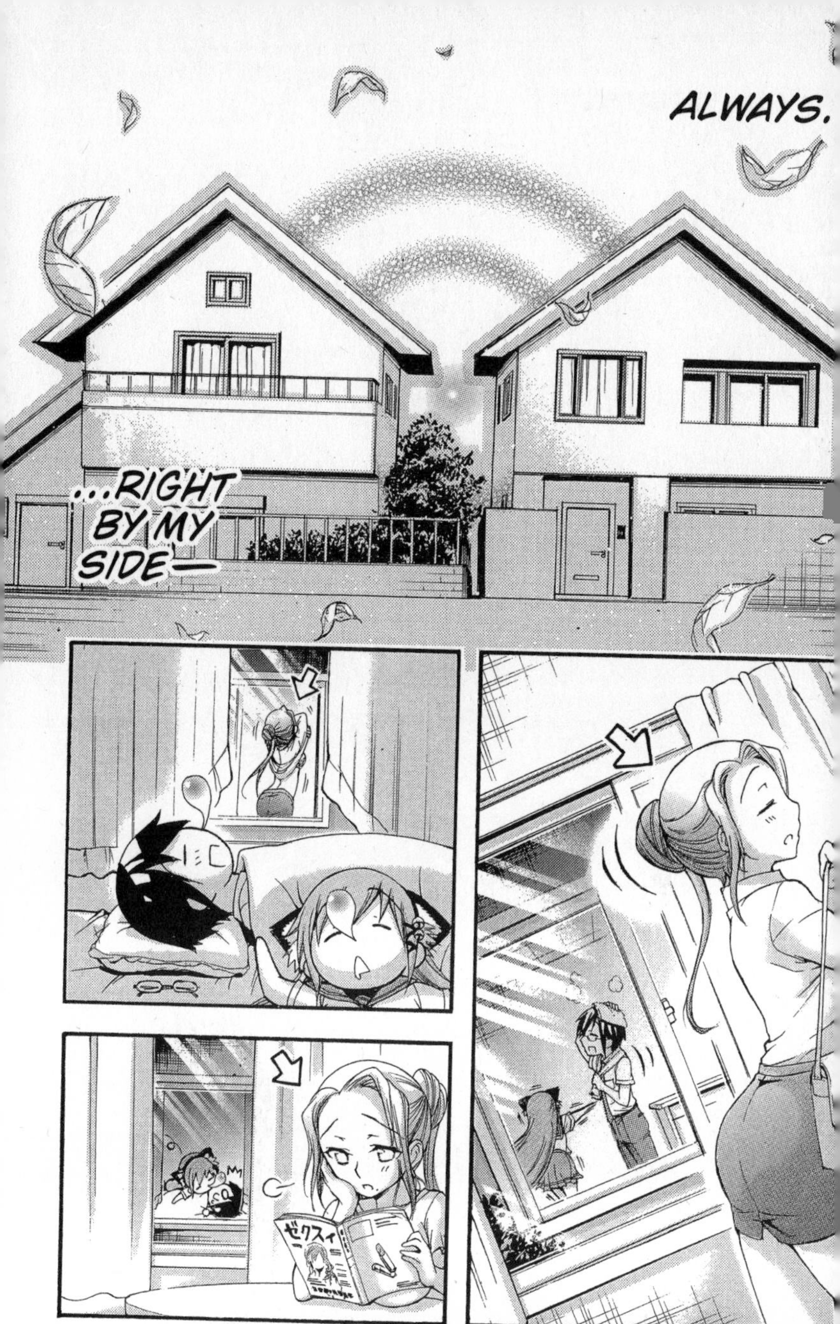
ALWAYS.
...RIGHT BY MY SIDE—
ゼクスィ

MAGAZINE: ZEXY

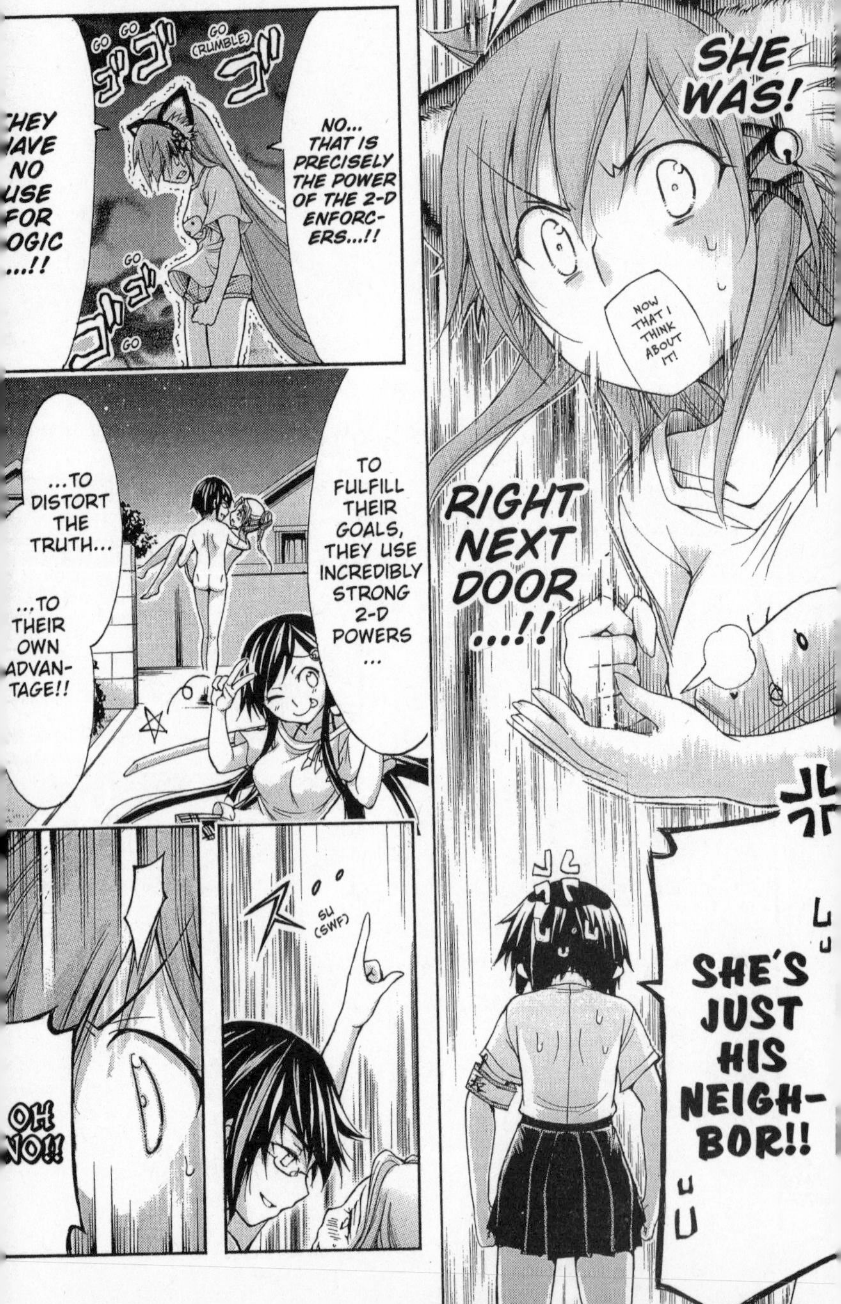
SHE WAS!
NOW THAT I THINK ABOUT IT!
RIGHT NEXT DOOR...!!
SHE'S JUST HIS NEIGHBOR!!
GO GO GO (RUMBLE)
NO... THAT IS PRECISELY THE POWER OF THE 2-D ENFORCERS...!!
THEY AVE NO USE FOR OGIC...!!
GO GO
TO FULFILL THEIR GOALS, THEY USE INCREDIBLY STRONG 2-D POWERS...
...TO DISTORT THE TRUTH...
...TO THEIR OWN ADVANTAGE!!
SU (SWF)
OH NO!!

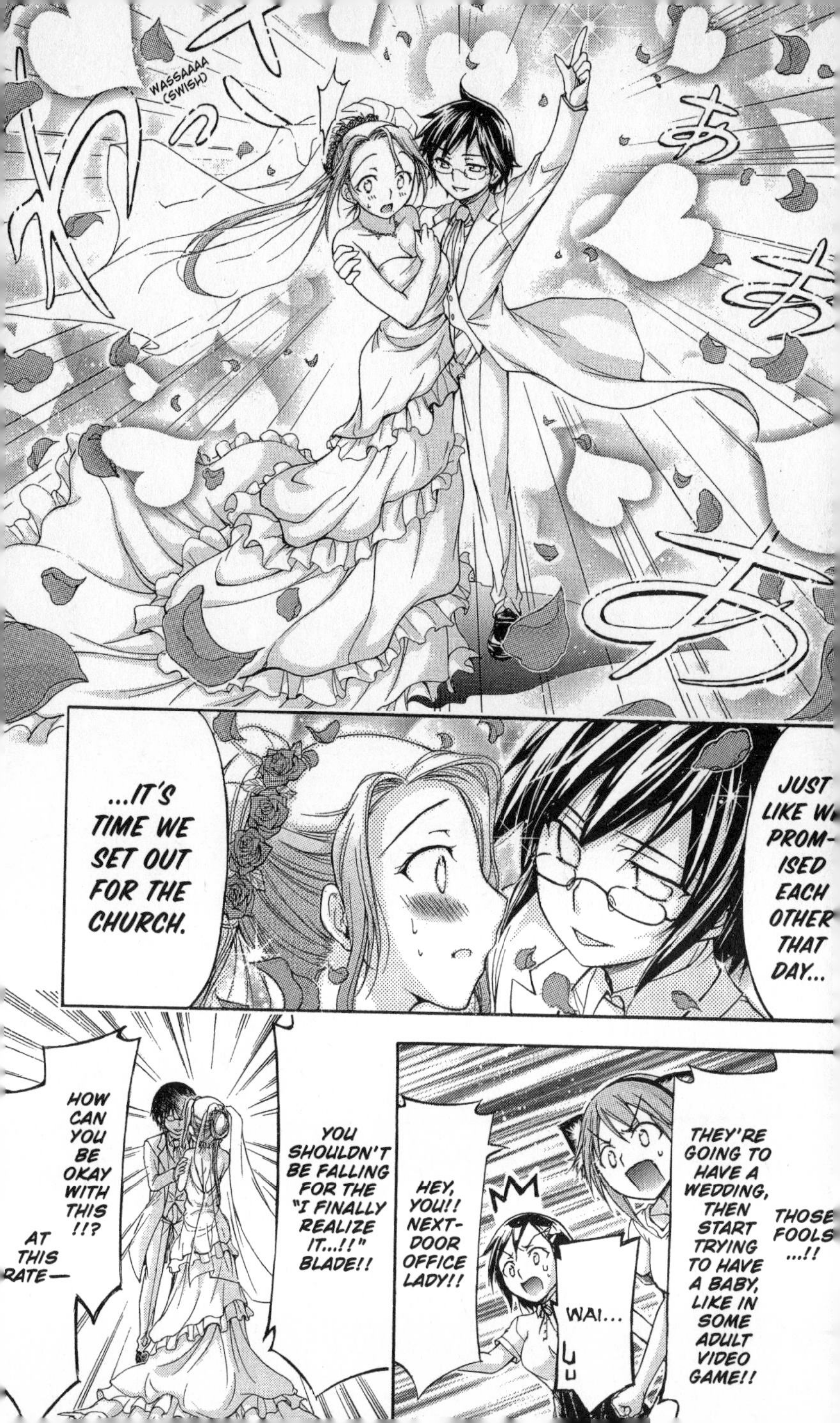
WASSAAAA (SWISH)
JUST LIKE W PROMISED EACH OTHER THAT DAY...
...IT'S TIME WE SET OUT FOR THE CHURCH.
THOSE FOOLS...!!
THEY'RE GOING TO HAVE A WEDDING, THEN START TRYING TO HAVE A BABY, LIKE IN SOME ADULT VIDEO GAME!!
HEY, YOU!! NEXT-DOOR OFFICE LADY!!
WAI...UU
YOU SHOULDN'T BE FALLING FOR THE "I FINALLY REALIZE IT...!!" BLADE!!
HOW CAN YOU BE OKAY WITH THIS!!?
AT THIS RATE—

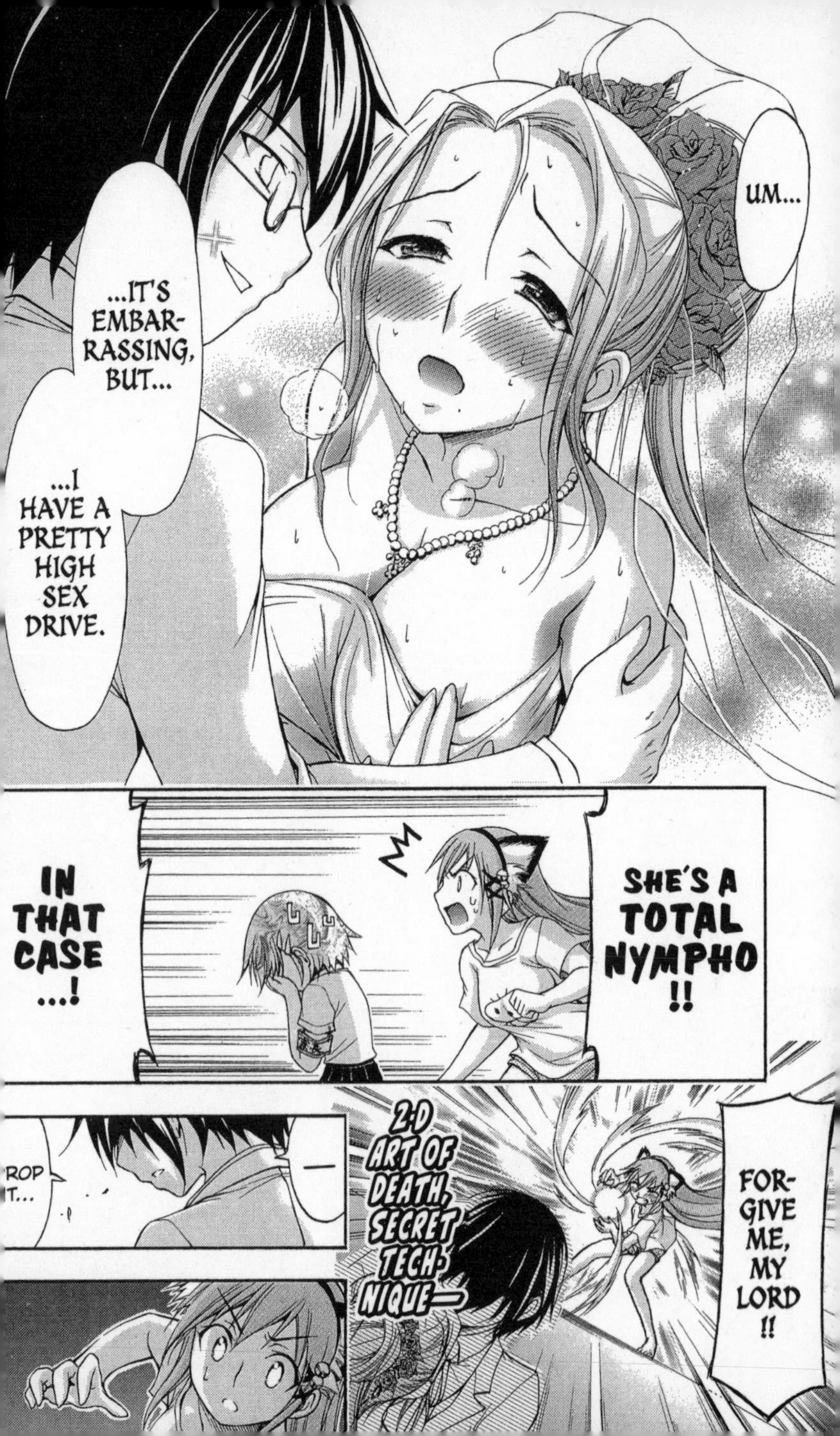
UM...
...IT'S EMBARRASSING, BUT...
...I HAVE A PRETTY HIGH SEX DRIVE.
SHE'S A TOTAL NYMPHO!!
IN THAT CASE...!
FORGIVE ME, MY LORD!!
2-D ART OF DEATH, SECRET TECHNIQUE—
—
ROP T...

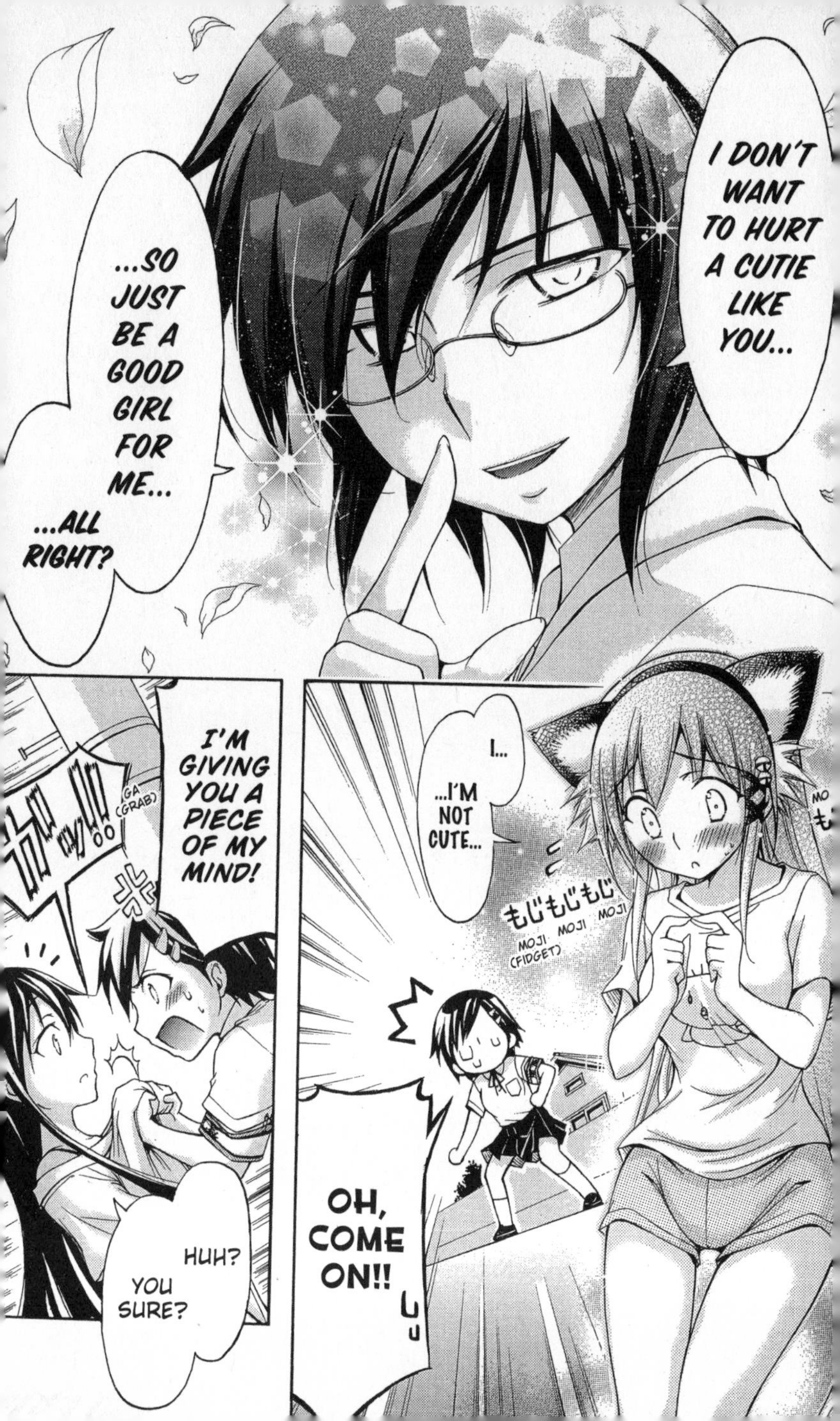

I DON'T WANT TO HURT A CUTIE LIKE YOU...
...SO JUST BE A GOOD GIRL FOR ME...
...ALL RIGHT?
I...
...I'M NOT CUTE...
MO も
もじもじもじ
MOJI MOJI MOJI (FIDGET)
OH, COME ON!!
GA (GRAB)
I'M GIVING YOU A PIECE OF MY MIND!
HUH? YOU SURE?

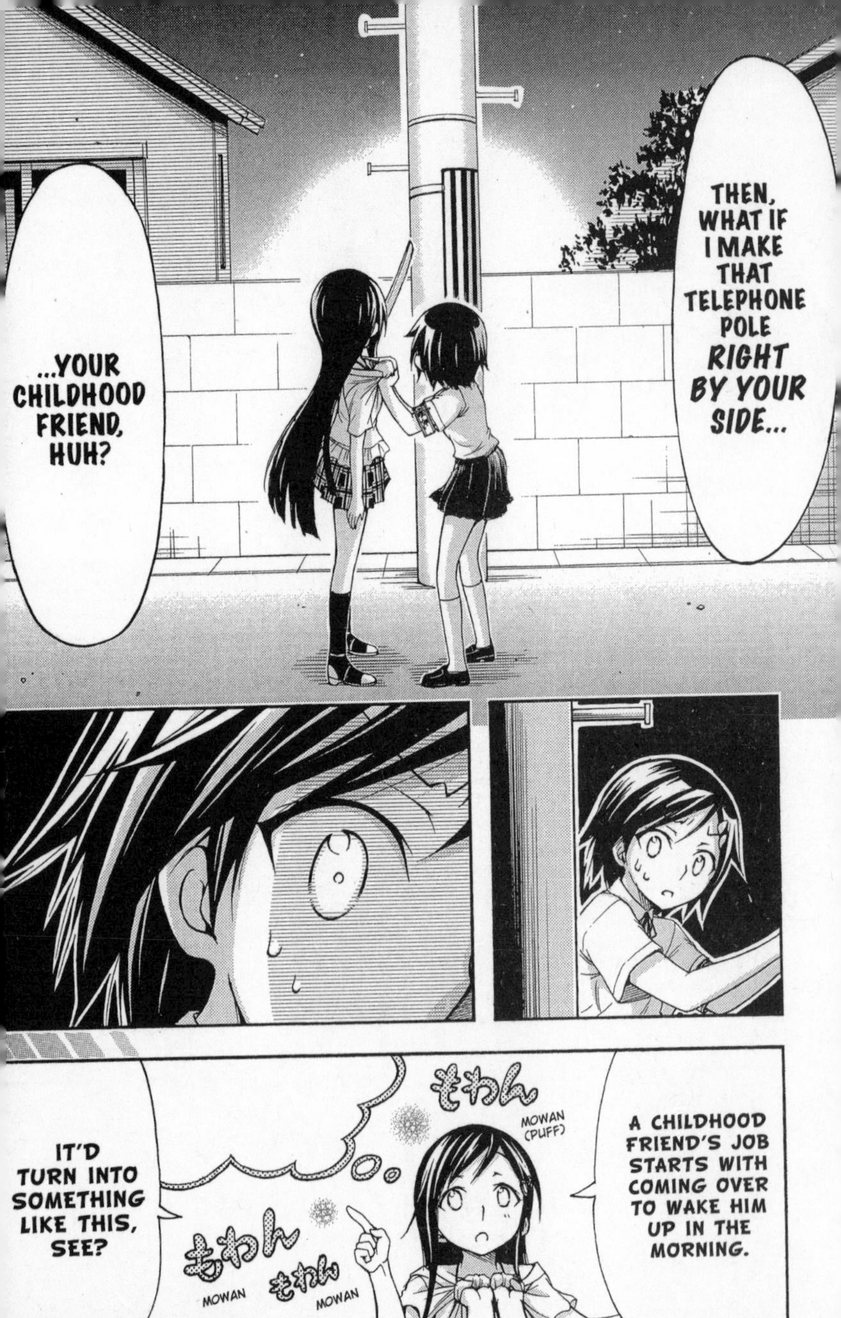
THEN, WHAT IF I MAKE THAT TELEPHONE POLE RIGHT BY YOUR SIDE...
...YOUR CHILDHOOD FRIEND, HUH?
A CHILDHOOD FRIEND'S JOB STARTS WITH COMING OVER TO WAKE HIM UP IN THE MORNING.
もわん
MOWAN (PUFF)
もわん
MOWAN
もわん
MOWAN
IT'D TURN INTO SOMETHING LIKE THIS, SEE?

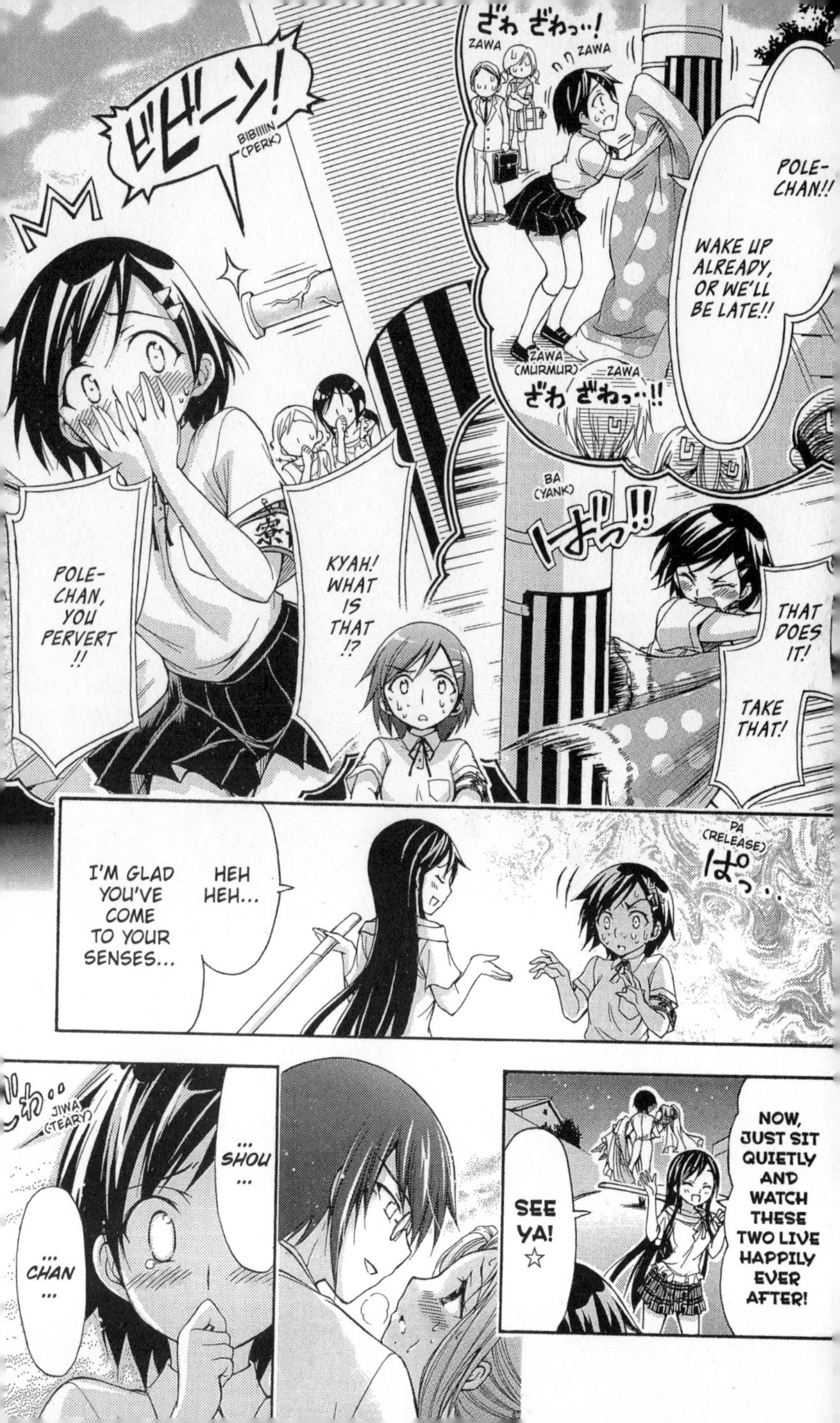
ざわ ざわっ…!
ZAWA
ZAWA
POLE-CHAN!!
WAKE UP ALREADY, OR WE'LL BE LATE!!
ZAWA (MURMUR)
ZAWA
ざわ ざわっ…!!
BA (YANK)
ぱっ!!
THAT DOES IT!
TAKE THAT!
ビビーン!
BIBIIIIN (PERK)
KYAH! WHAT IS THAT!?
POLE-CHAN, YOU PERVERT!!
PA (RELEASE)
ぱっ…
HEH HEH...
I'M GLAD YOU'VE COME TO YOUR SENSES...
NOW, JUST SIT QUIETLY AND WATCH THESE TWO LIVE HAPPILY EVER AFTER!
SEE YA! ☆
...SHOU...
JIWA (TEARY)
...CHAN...

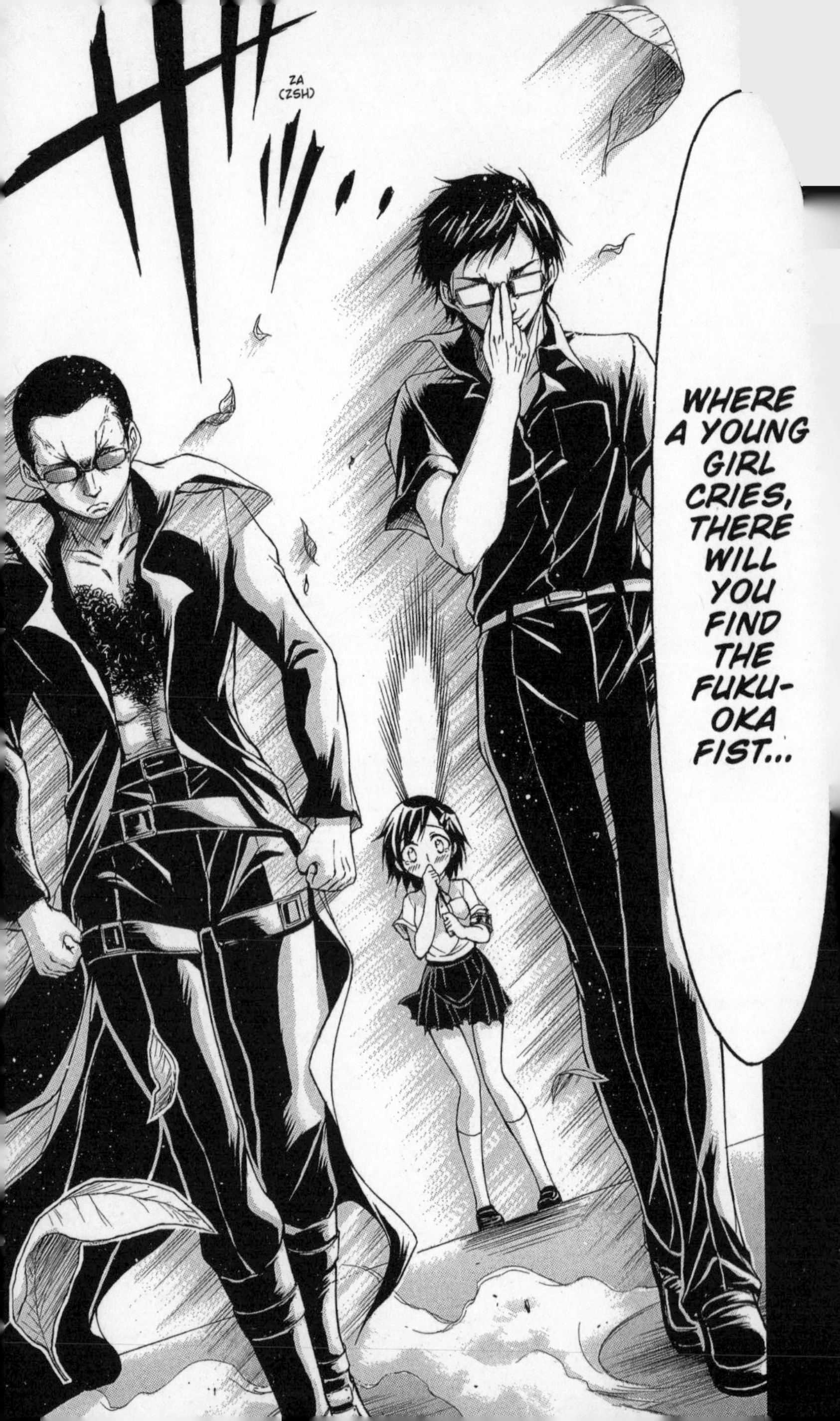
ZA
(ZSH)
WHERE A YOUNG GIRL CRIES, THERE WILL YOU FIND THE FUKU-OKA FIST...

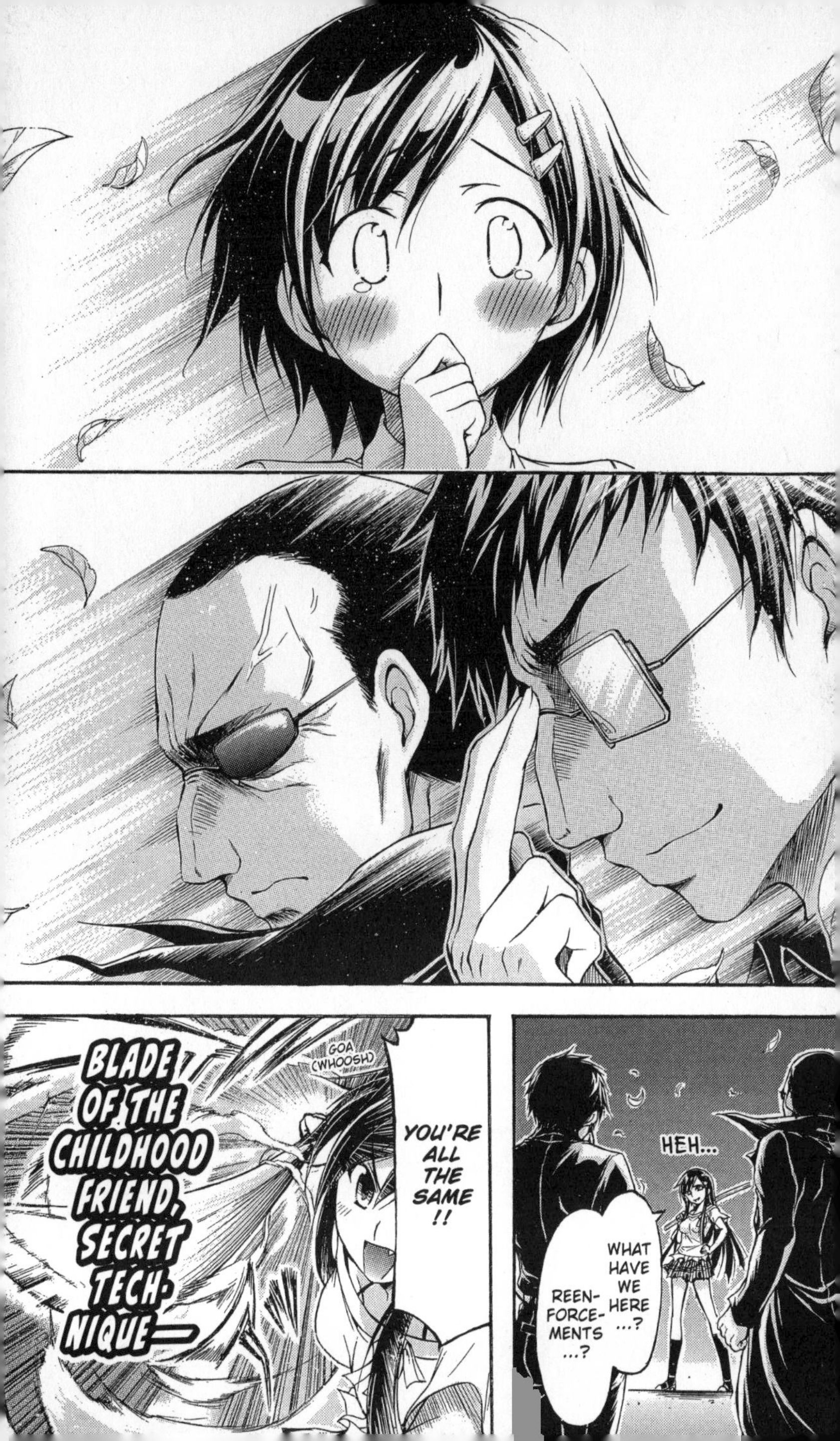
HEH...
WHAT HAVE WE HERE ...?
REEN-FORCE-MENTS ...?
GOA (WHOOSH)
YOU'RE ALL THE SAME !!
BLADE OF THE CHILDHOOD FRIEND, SECRET TECH-NIQUE—

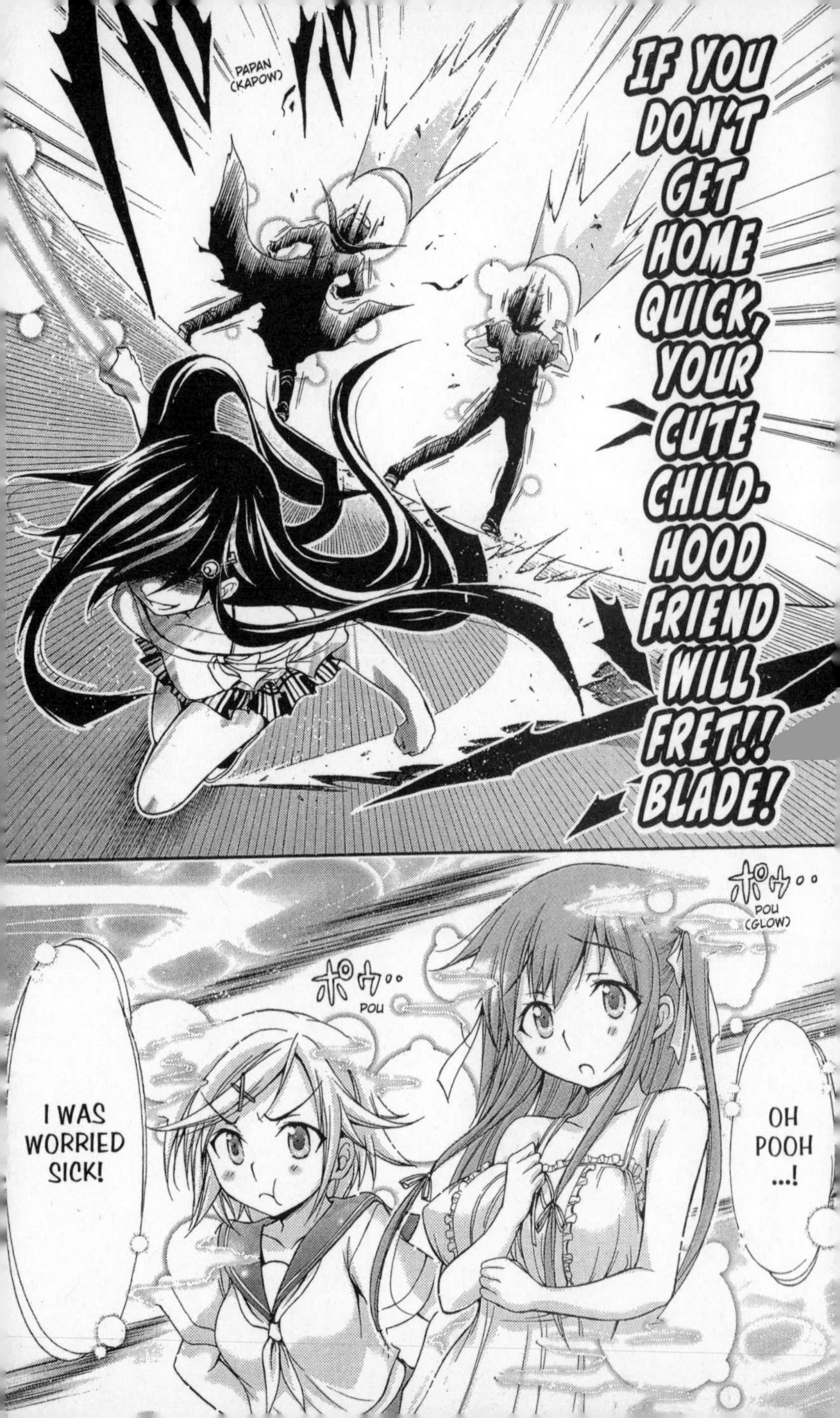
IF YOU DON'T GET HOME QUICK, YOUR CUTE CHILD-HOOD FRIEND WILL FRET!! BLADE!
PAPAN (KAPOW)
POU (GLOW)
OH POOH ...!
POU
I WAS WORRIED SICK!

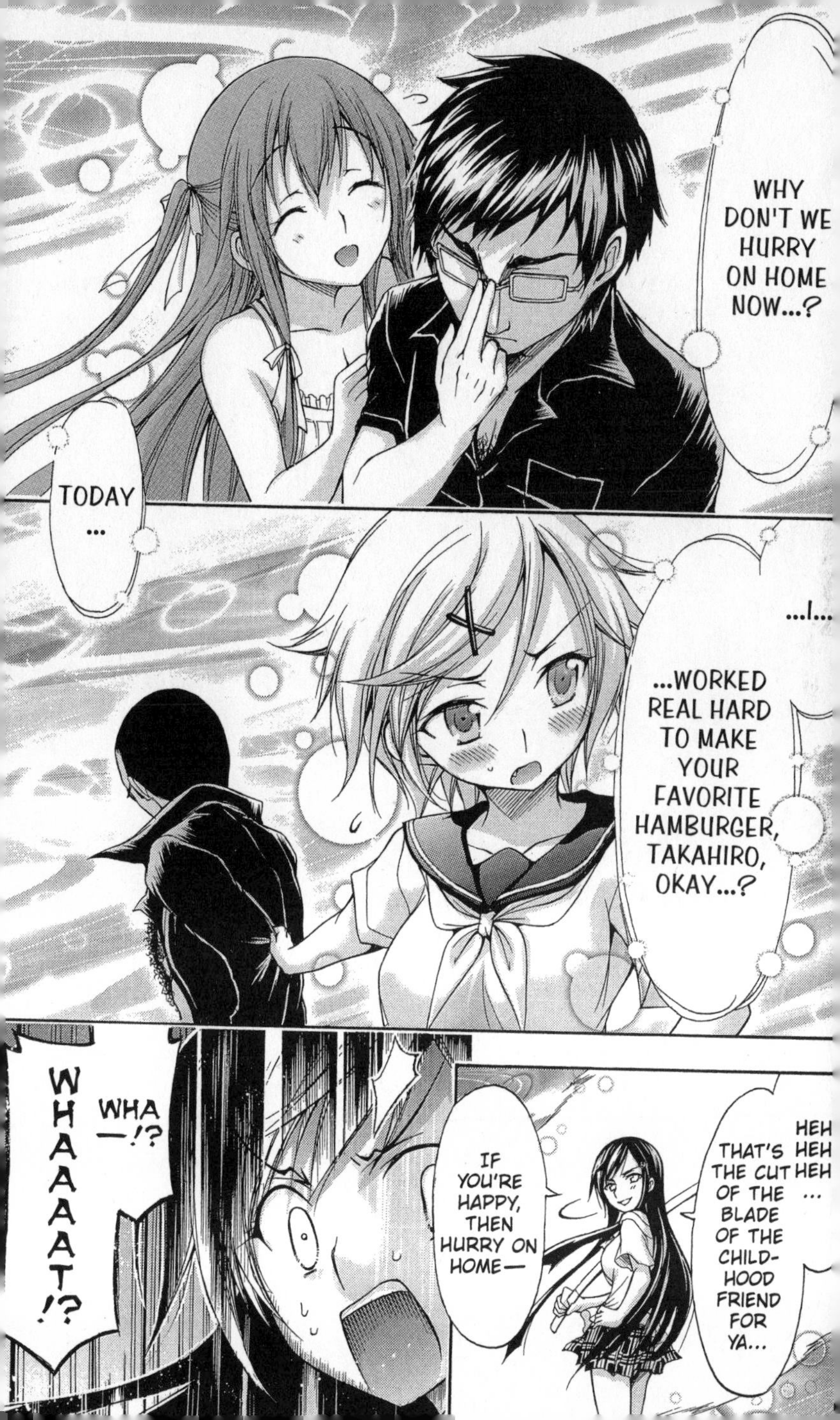
WHY DON'T WE HURRY ON HOME NOW...?
TODAY ...
...I...
...WORKED REAL HARD TO MAKE YOUR FAVORITE HAMBURGER, TAKAHIRO, OKAY...?
HEH HEH HEH HEH ...
THAT'S THE CUT OF THE BLADE OF THE CHILD-HOOD FRIEND FOR YA...
IF YOU'RE HAPPY, THEN HURRY ON HOME—
WHA—!?
WHAAAAT!?

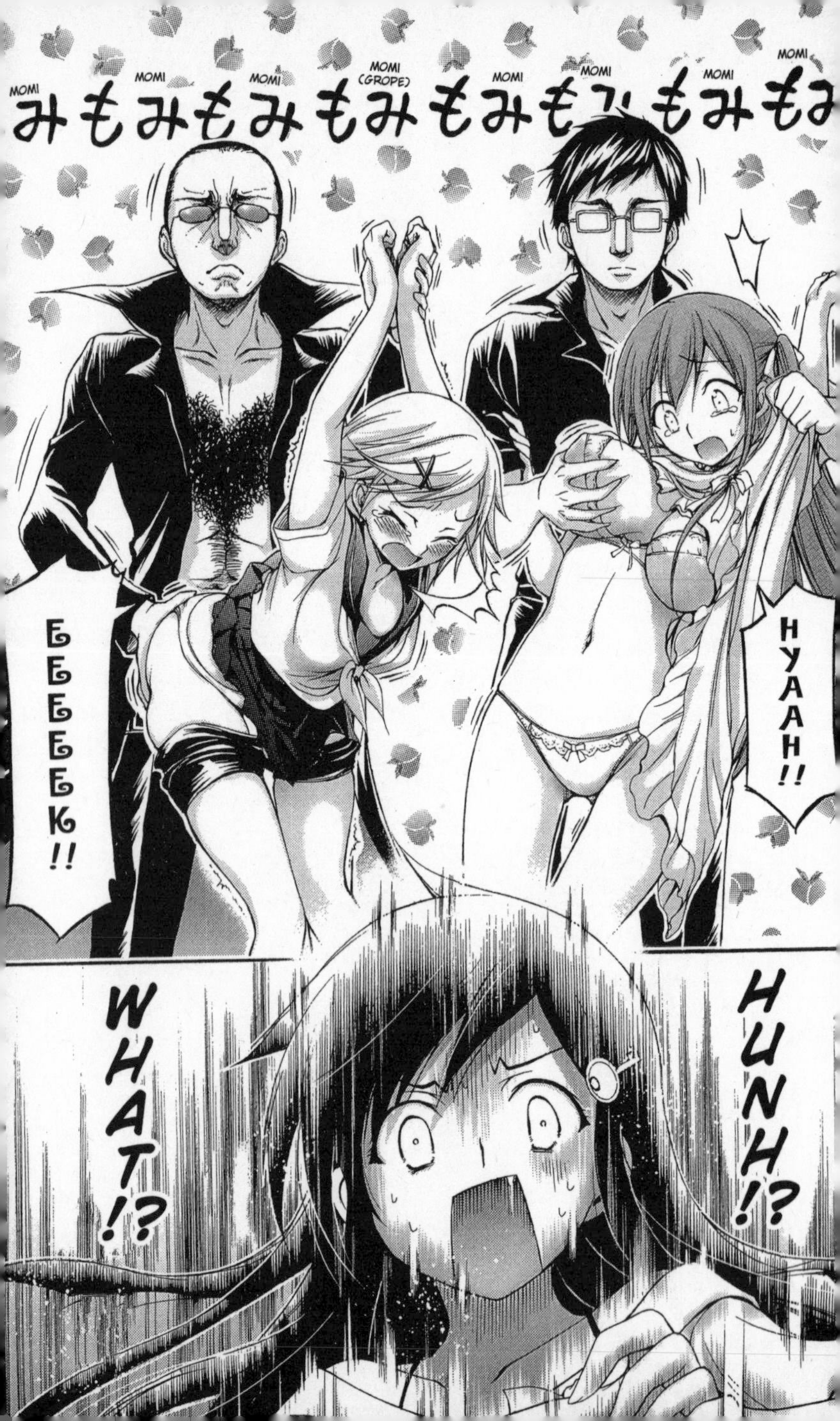
MOMI MOMI MOMI MOMI (GROPE) MOMI MOMI MOMI MOMI
みもみもみもみもみもみもみもみもみ
HYAAAH!!
EEEEEEK!!
HUNH!?
WHAT!?

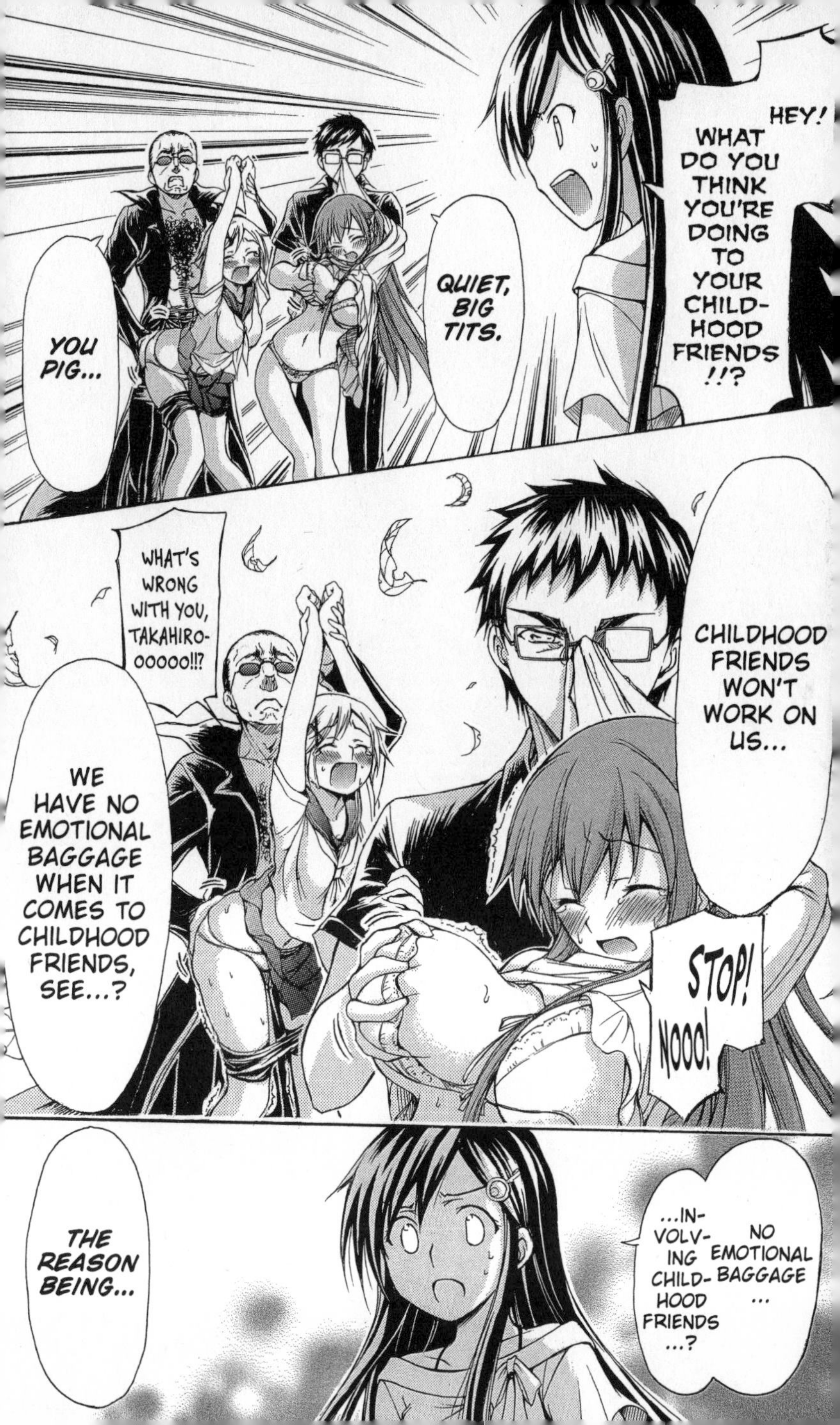
HEY! WHAT DO YOU THINK YOU'RE DOING TO YOUR CHILDHOOD FRIENDS!!?
QUIET, BIG TITS.
YOU PIG...
CHILDHOOD FRIENDS WON'T WORK ON US...
WHAT'S WRONG WITH YOU, TAKAHIRO-OOOOO!!?
STOP! NOOO!
WE HAVE NO EMOTIONAL BAGGAGE WHEN IT COMES TO CHILDHOOD FRIENDS, SEE...?
NO EMOTIONAL BAGGAGE ... ...INVOLVING CHILDHOOD FRIENDS ...?
THE REASON BEING...

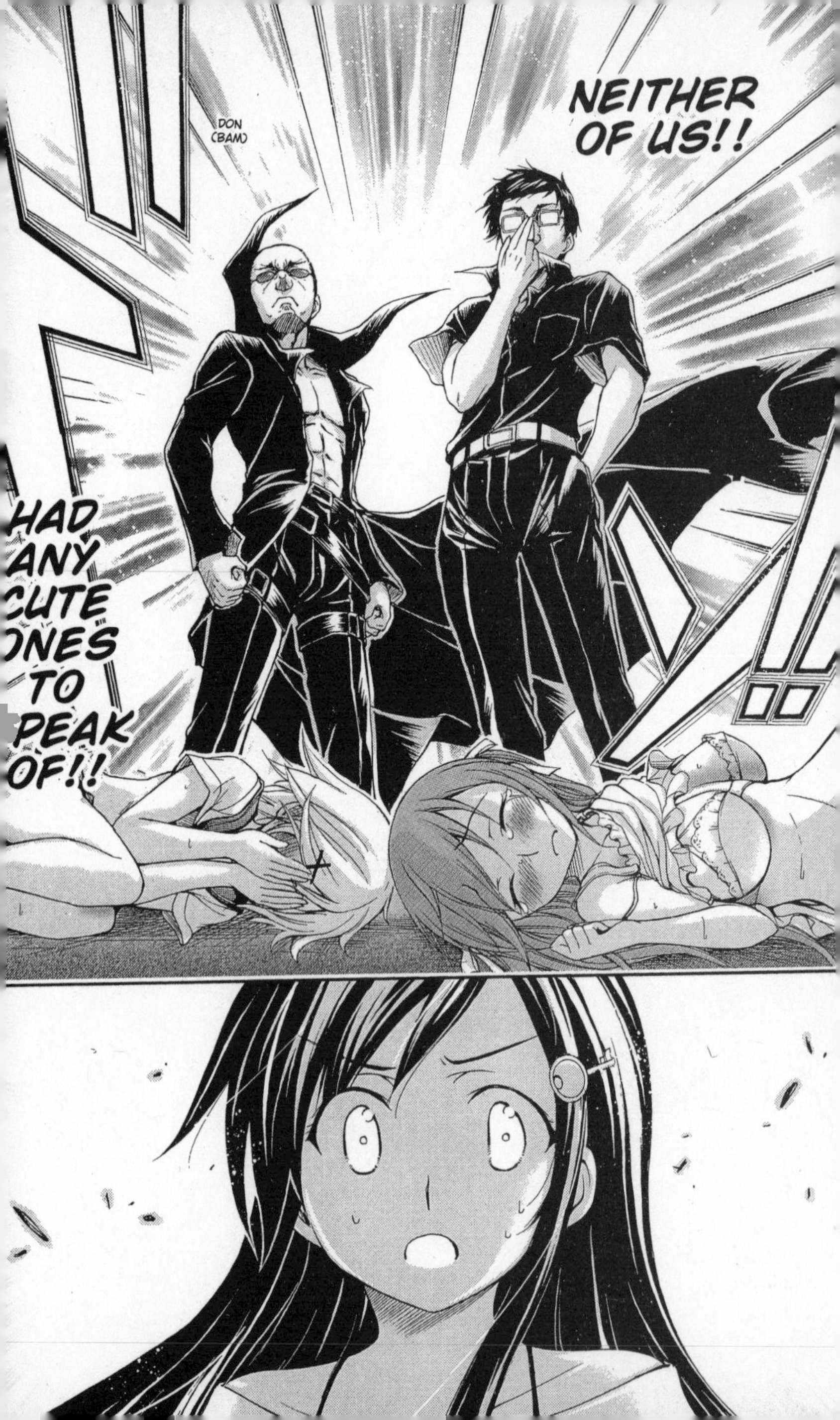
NEITHER OF US!!
DON (BAM)
HAD ANY CUTE ONES TO PEAK OF!!

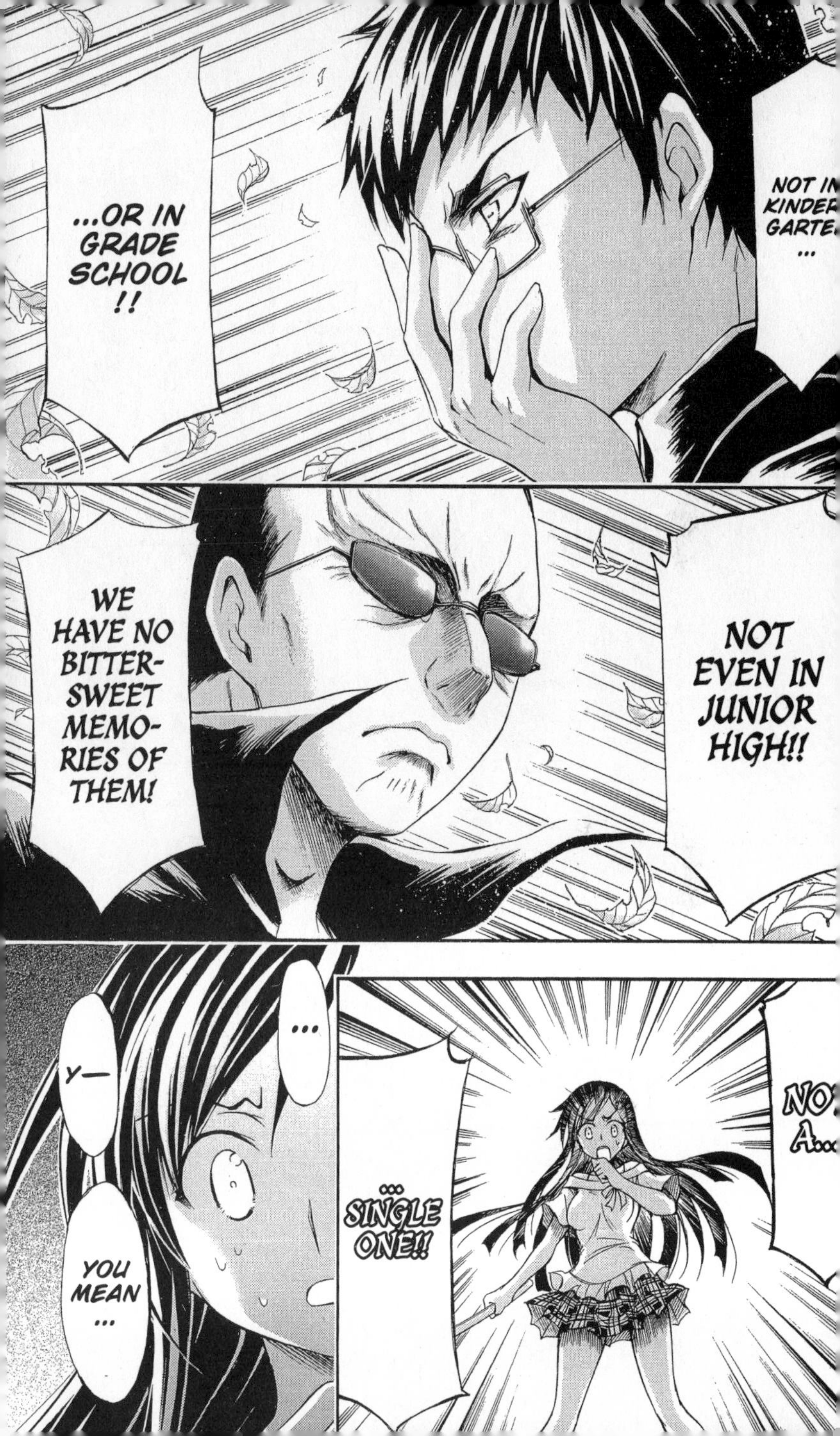
NOT IN KINDER GARTE ...
...OR IN GRADE SCHOOL !!
NOT EVEN IN JUNIOR HIGH!!
WE HAVE NO BITTER-SWEET MEMORIES OF THEM!
NOT A...
...SINGLE ONE!!
...
Y—
YOU MEAN ...

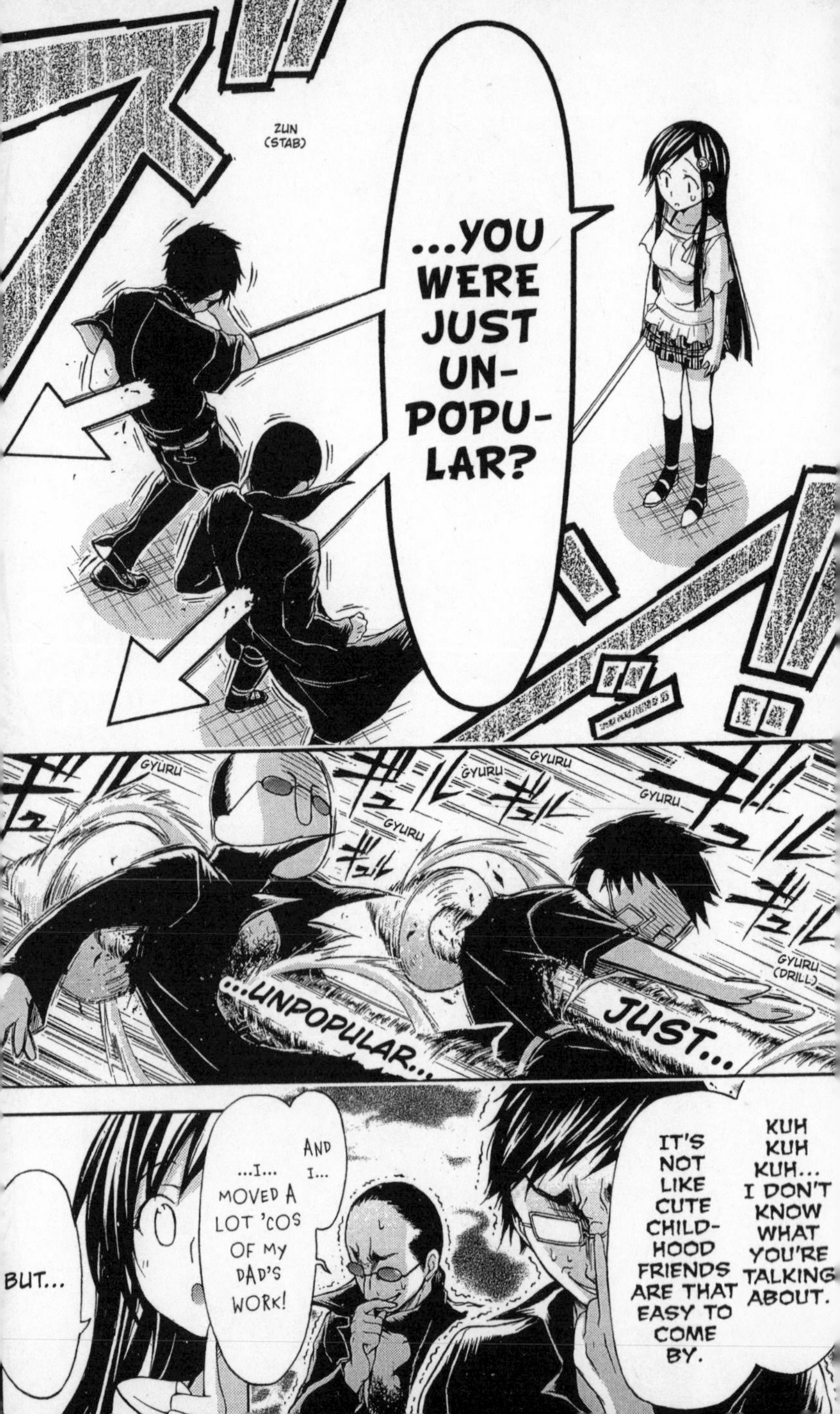
...YOU WERE JUST UN-POPULAR?
ZUN (STAB)
GYURU
GYURU
GYURU
GYURU
GYURU
GYURU (DRILL)
JUST...
...UNPOPULAR...
KUH KUH KUH... I DON'T KNOW WHAT YOU'RE TALKING ABOUT.
IT'S NOT LIKE CUTE CHILD-HOOD FRIENDS ARE THAT EASY TO COME BY.
AND I...
...I... MOVED A LOT 'COS OF MY DAD'S WORK!
BUT...

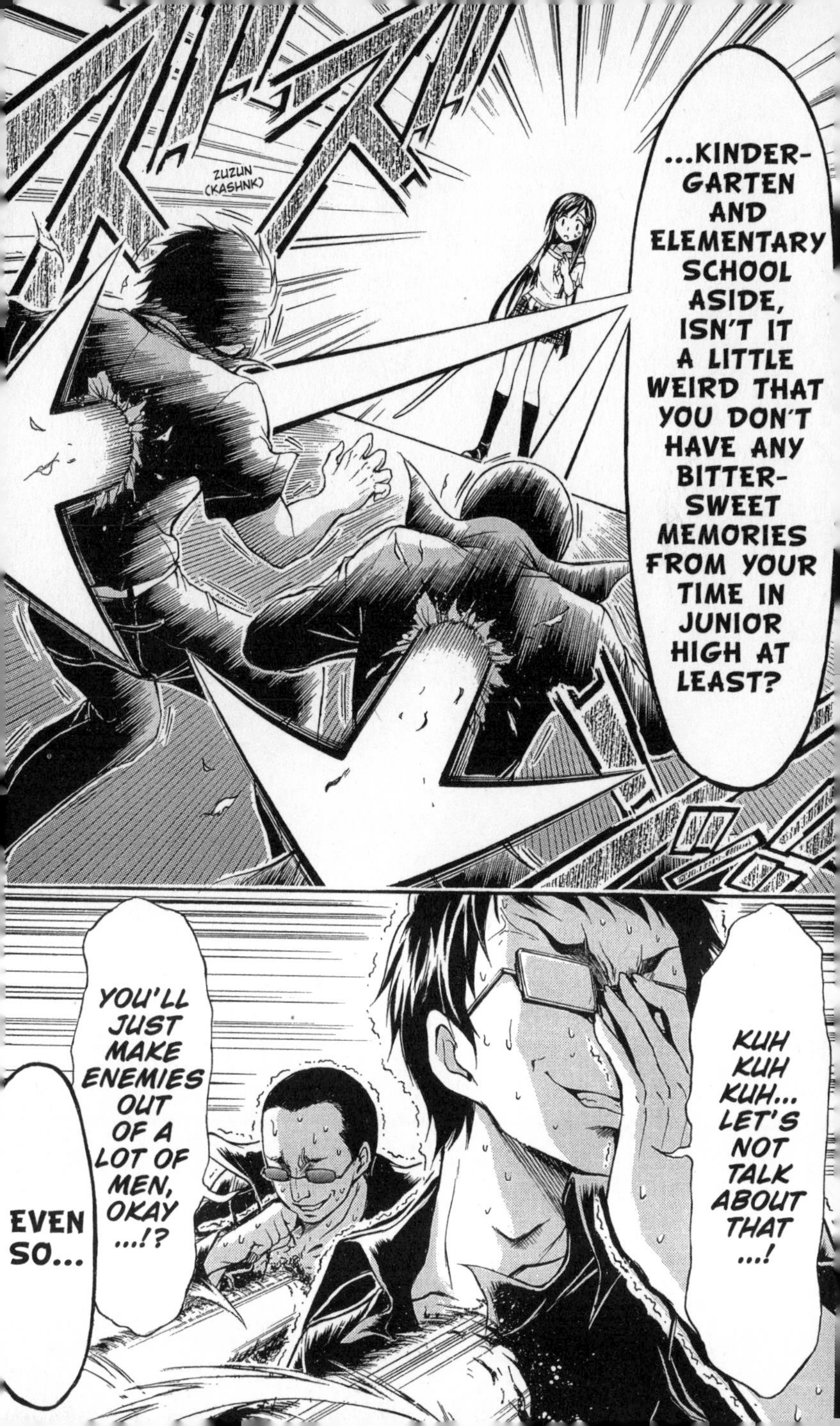
...KINDER-GARTEN AND ELEMENTARY SCHOOL ASIDE, ISN'T IT A LITTLE WEIRD THAT YOU DON'T HAVE ANY BITTER-SWEET MEMORIES FROM YOUR TIME IN JUNIOR HIGH AT LEAST?
ZUZUN (KASHNK)
KUH KUH KUH... LET'S NOT TALK ABOUT THAT ...!
YOU'LL JUST MAKE ENEMIES OUT OF A LOT OF MEN, OKAY ...!?
EVEN SO...

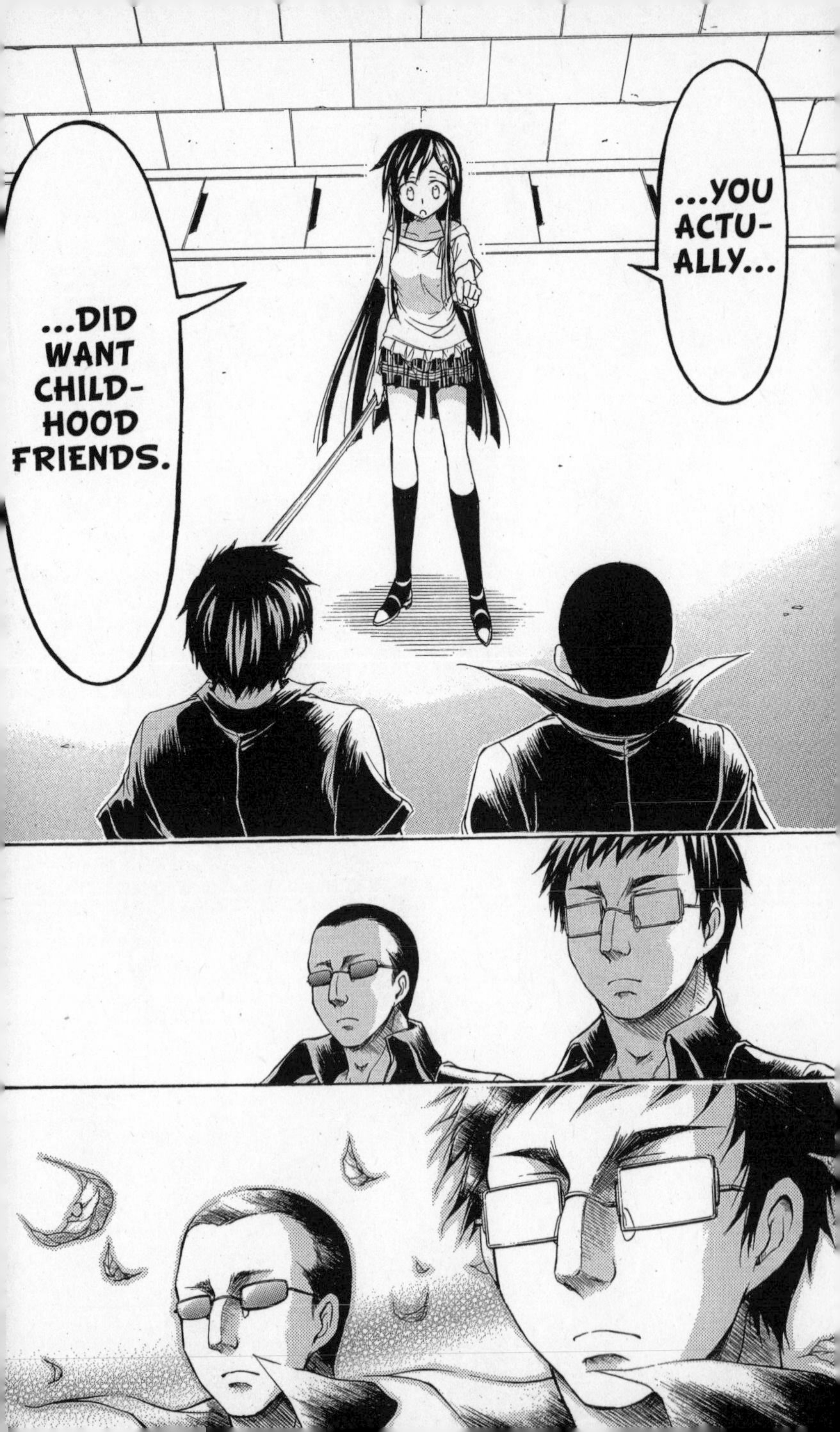
...YOU ACTU-ALLY...
...DID WANT CHILD-HOOD FRIENDS.

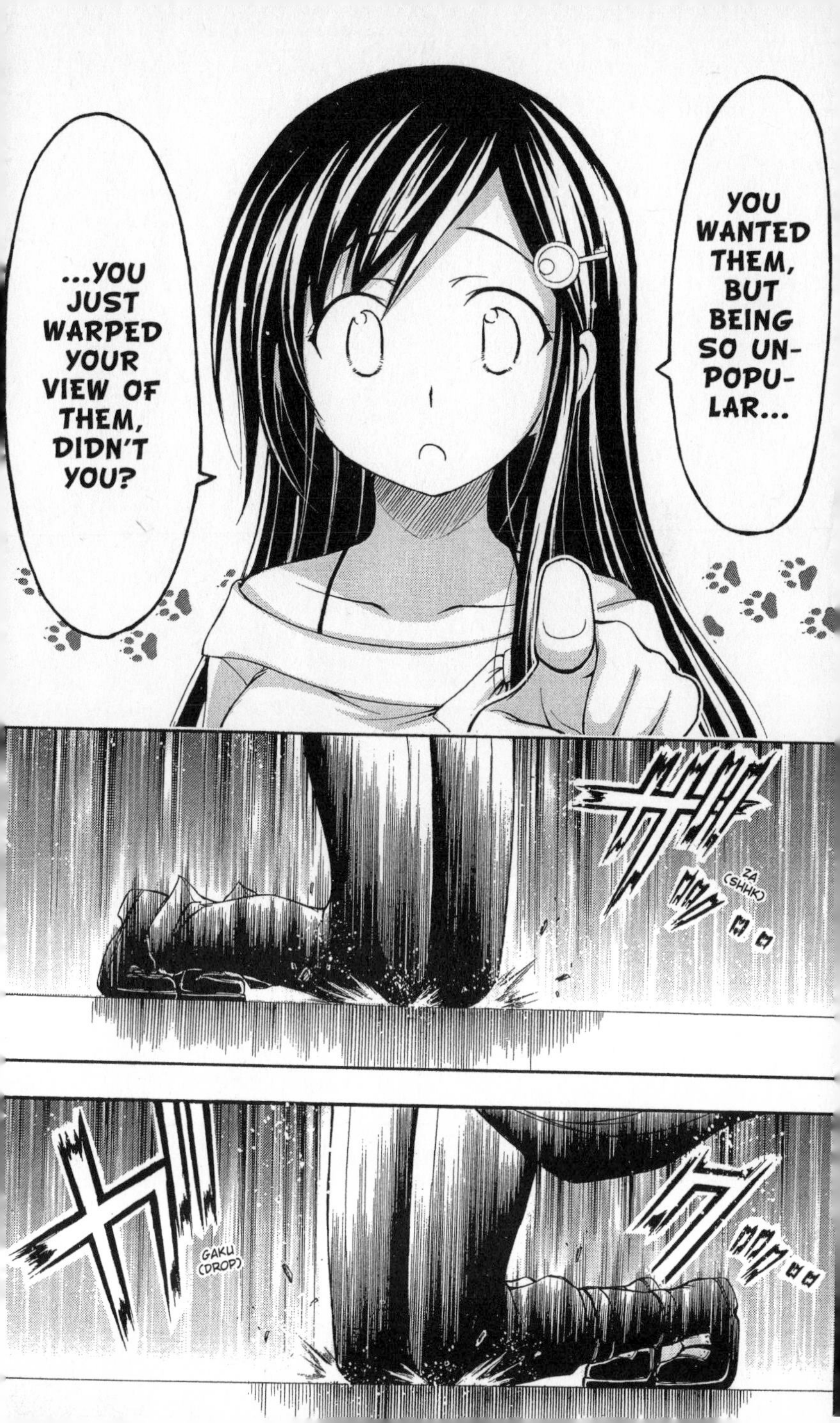
YOU WANTED THEM, BUT BEING SO UN-POPU-LAR...
...YOU JUST WARPED YOUR VIEW OF THEM, DIDN'T YOU?
ZA (SHHK)
GAKU (DROP)

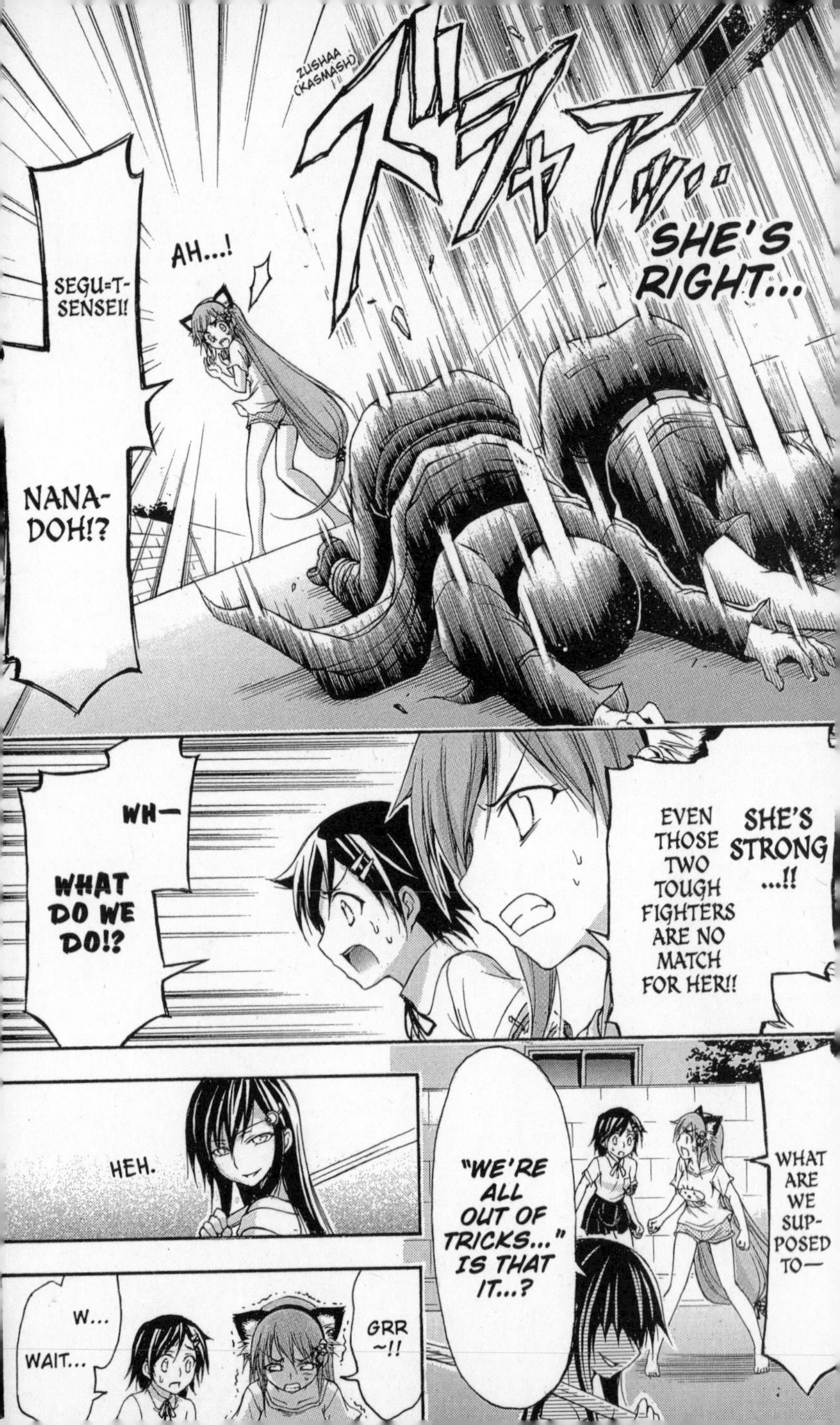
ZUSHAA (KASMASH)
SHE'S RIGHT...
AH...!
SEGU=T-SENSEI!
NANA-DOH!?
SHE'S STRONG ...!!
EVEN THOSE TWO TOUGH FIGHTERS ARE NO MATCH FOR HER!!
WH—
WHAT DO WE DO!?
WHAT ARE WE SUP-POSED TO—
"WE'RE ALL OUT OF TRICKS..." IS THAT IT...?
HEH.
GRR ~!!
W... WAIT...

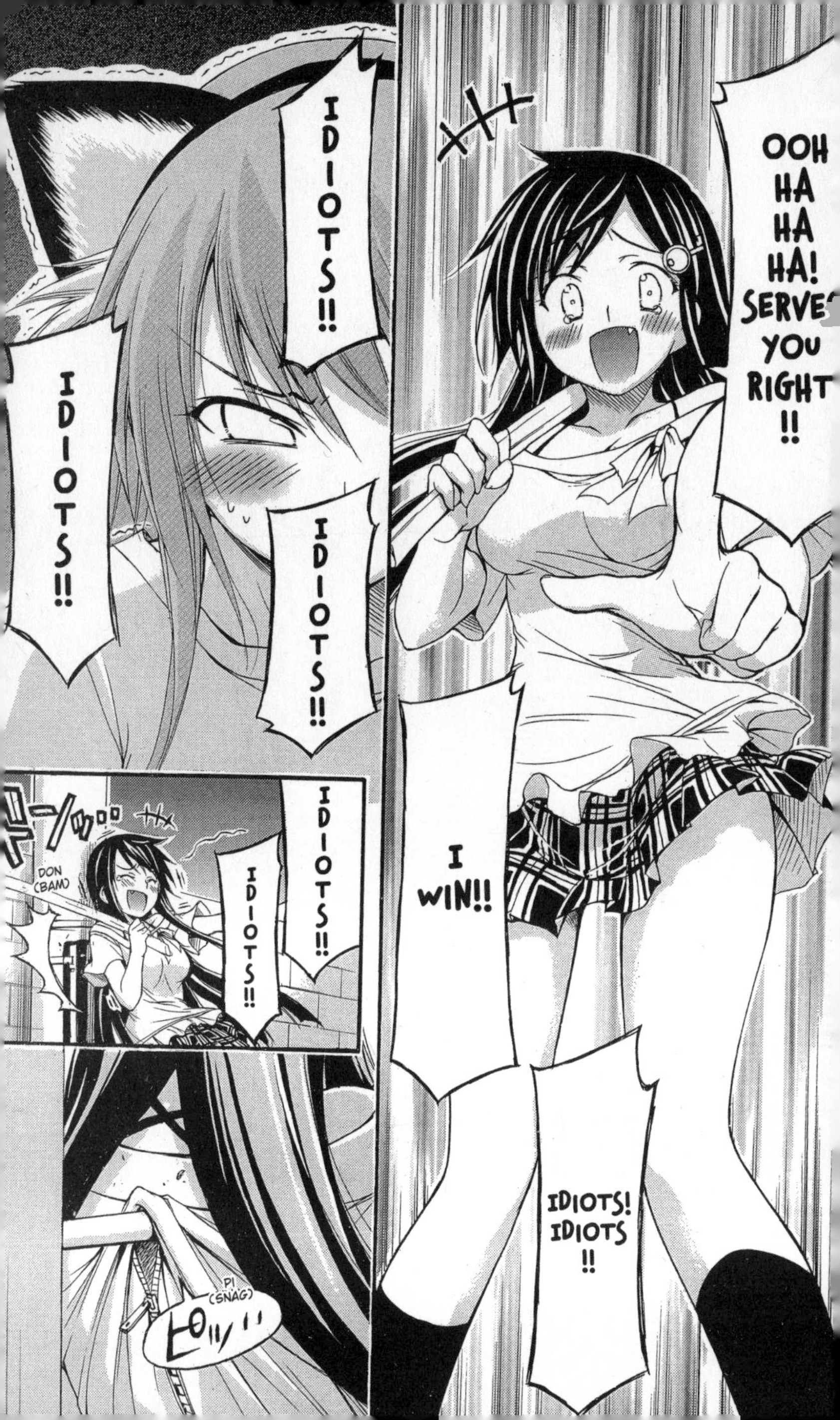
OOH HA HA HA! SERVES YOU RIGHT!!
I WIN!!
IDIOTS! IDIOTS!!
IDIOTS!!
IDIOTS!!
IDIOTS!!
DON (BAM)
IDIOTS!!
IDIOTS!!
PI (SNAG)

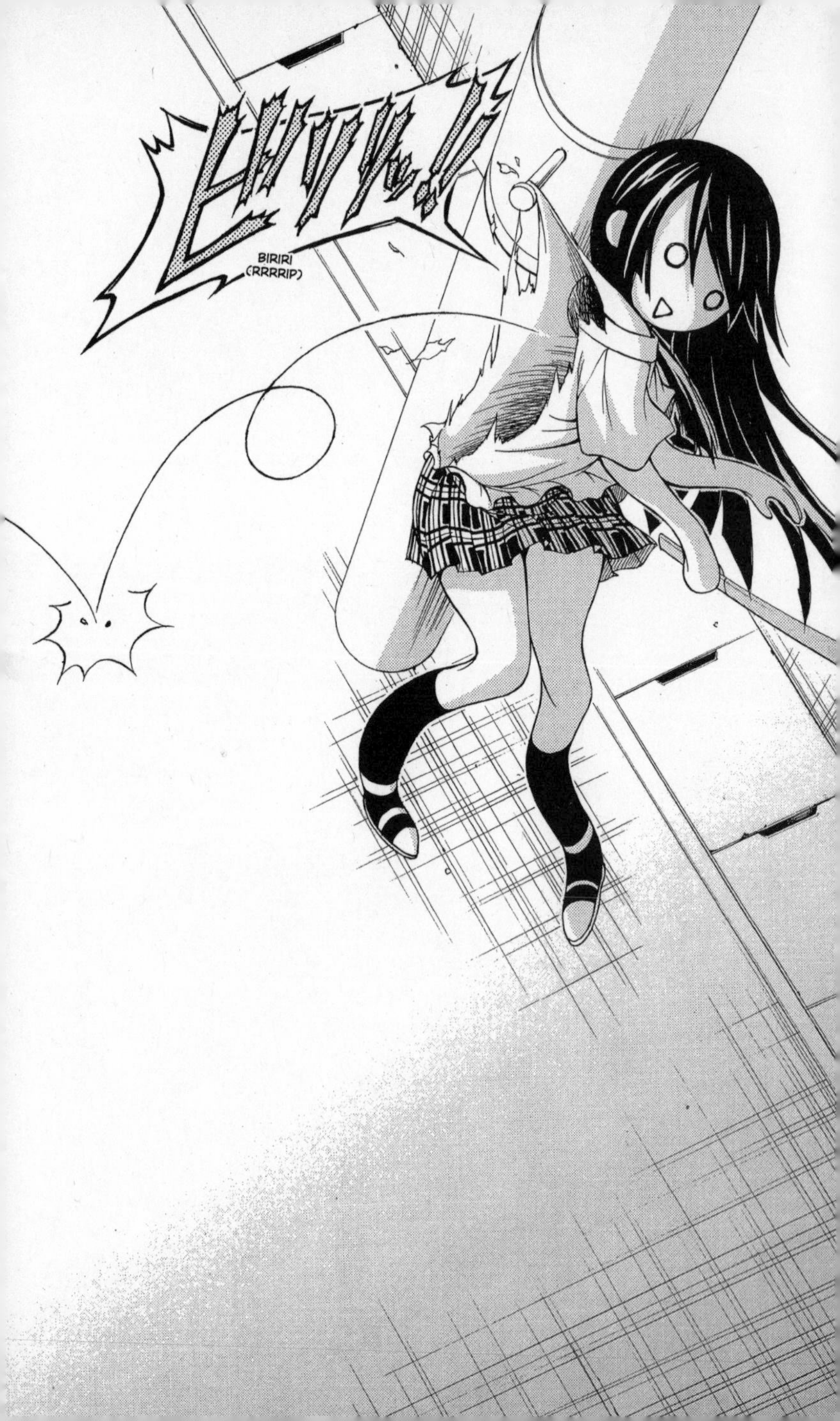
BIRIRI
(RRRRIP)

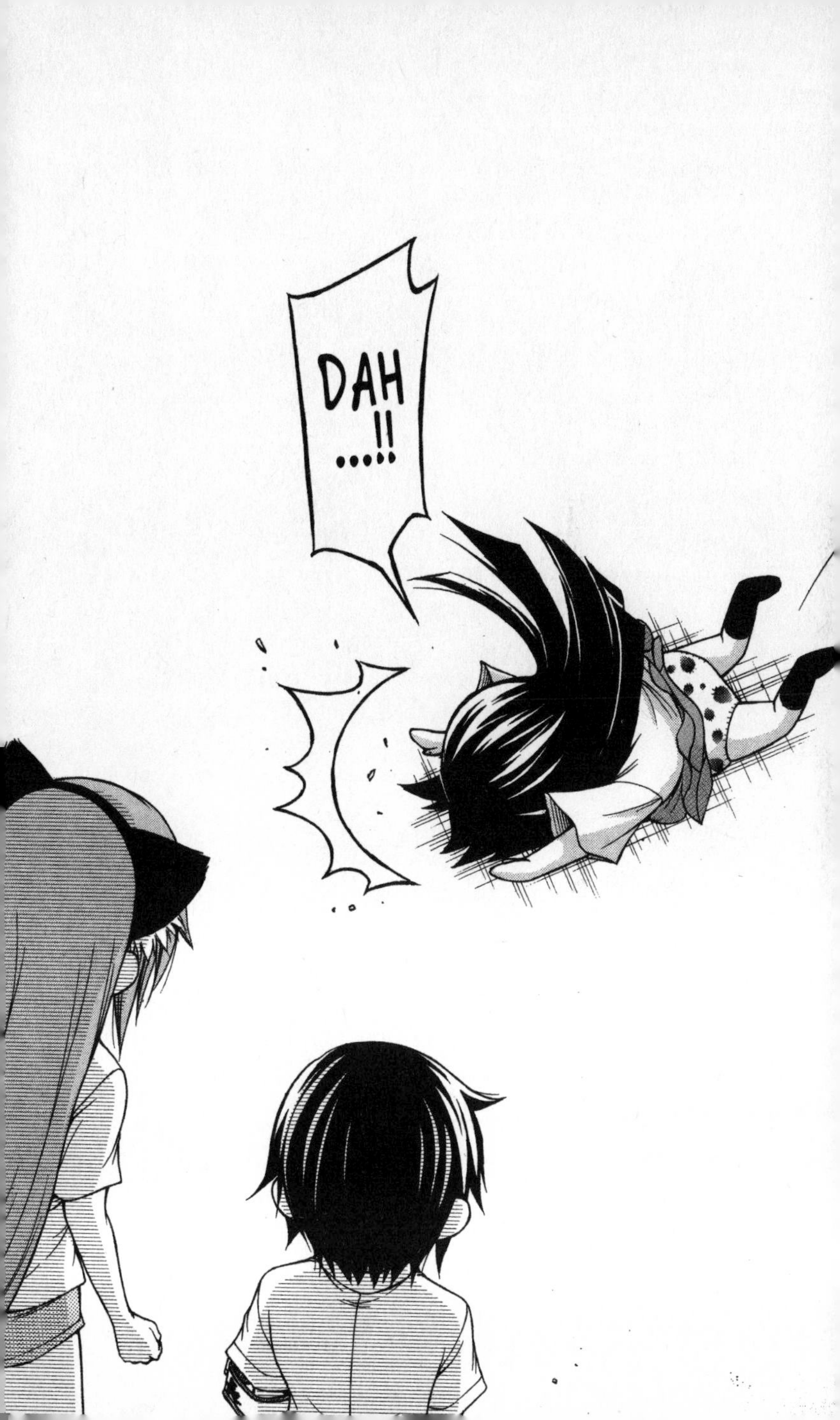
DAH ...!!

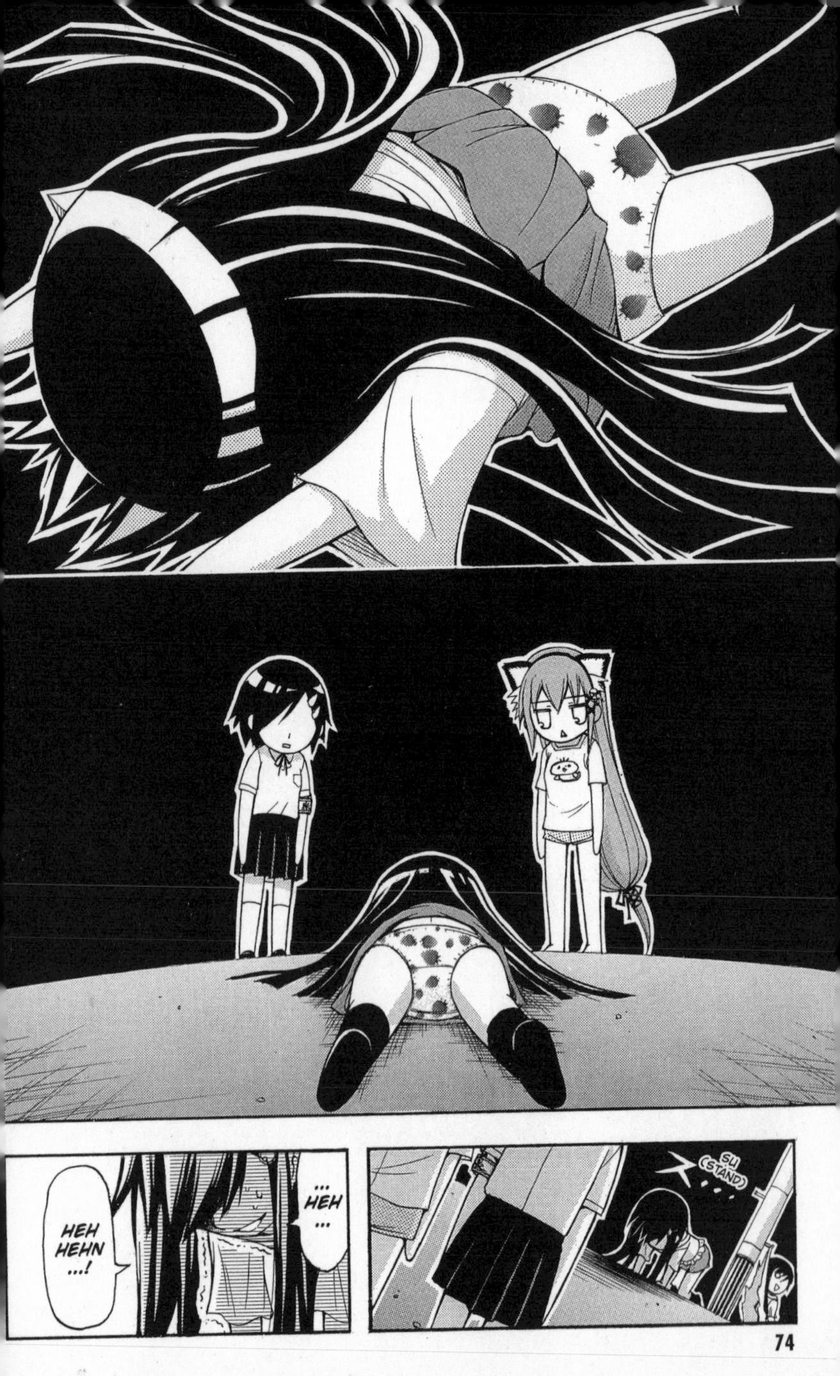
SU (STAND)
... HEH ...
HEH HEHN ...!

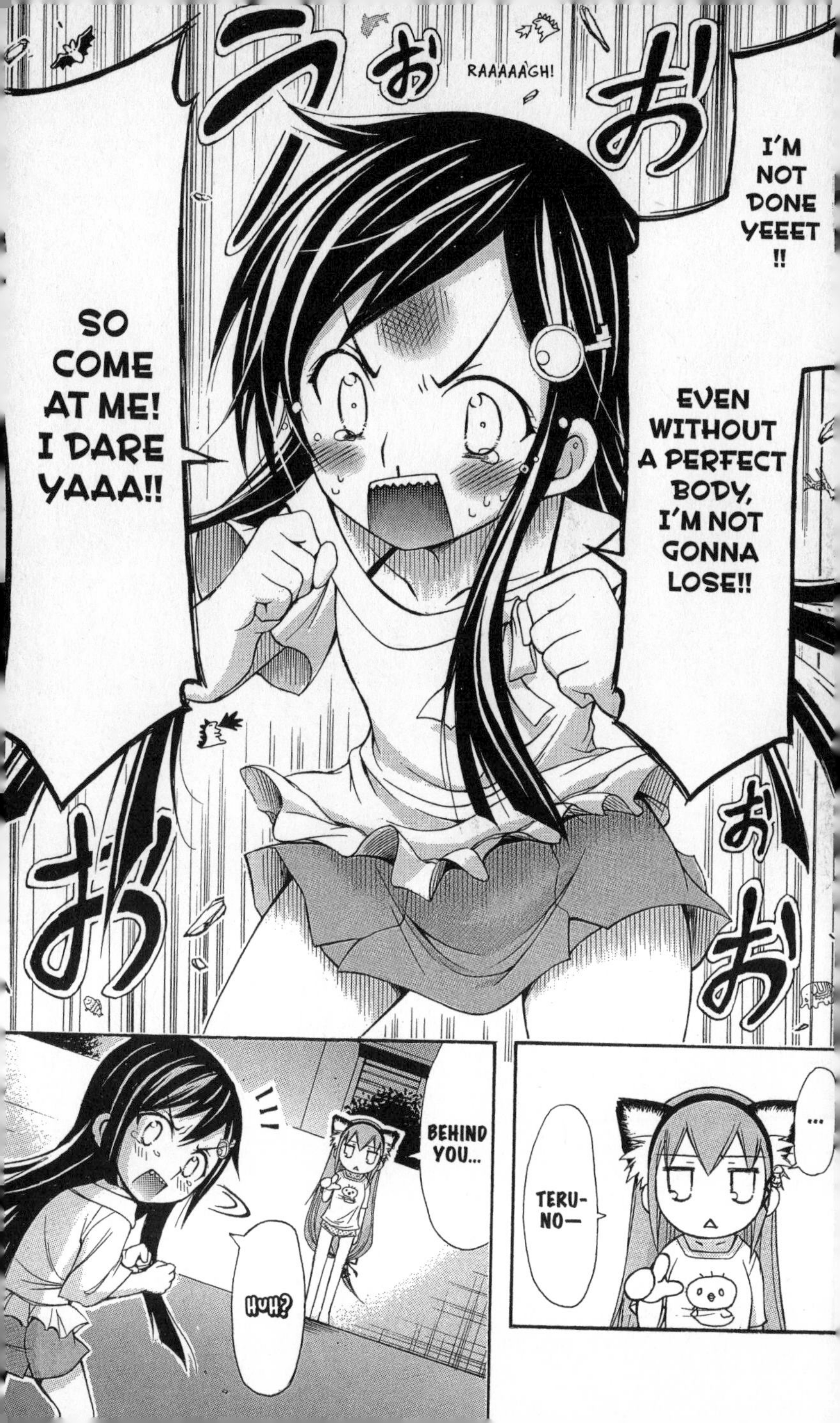
RAAAAAGH!
I'M NOT DONE YEEET !!
EVEN WITHOUT A PERFECT BODY, I'M NOT GONNA LOSE!!
SO COME AT ME! I DARE YAAA!!
...
TERU-NO—
BEHIND YOU...
HUH?

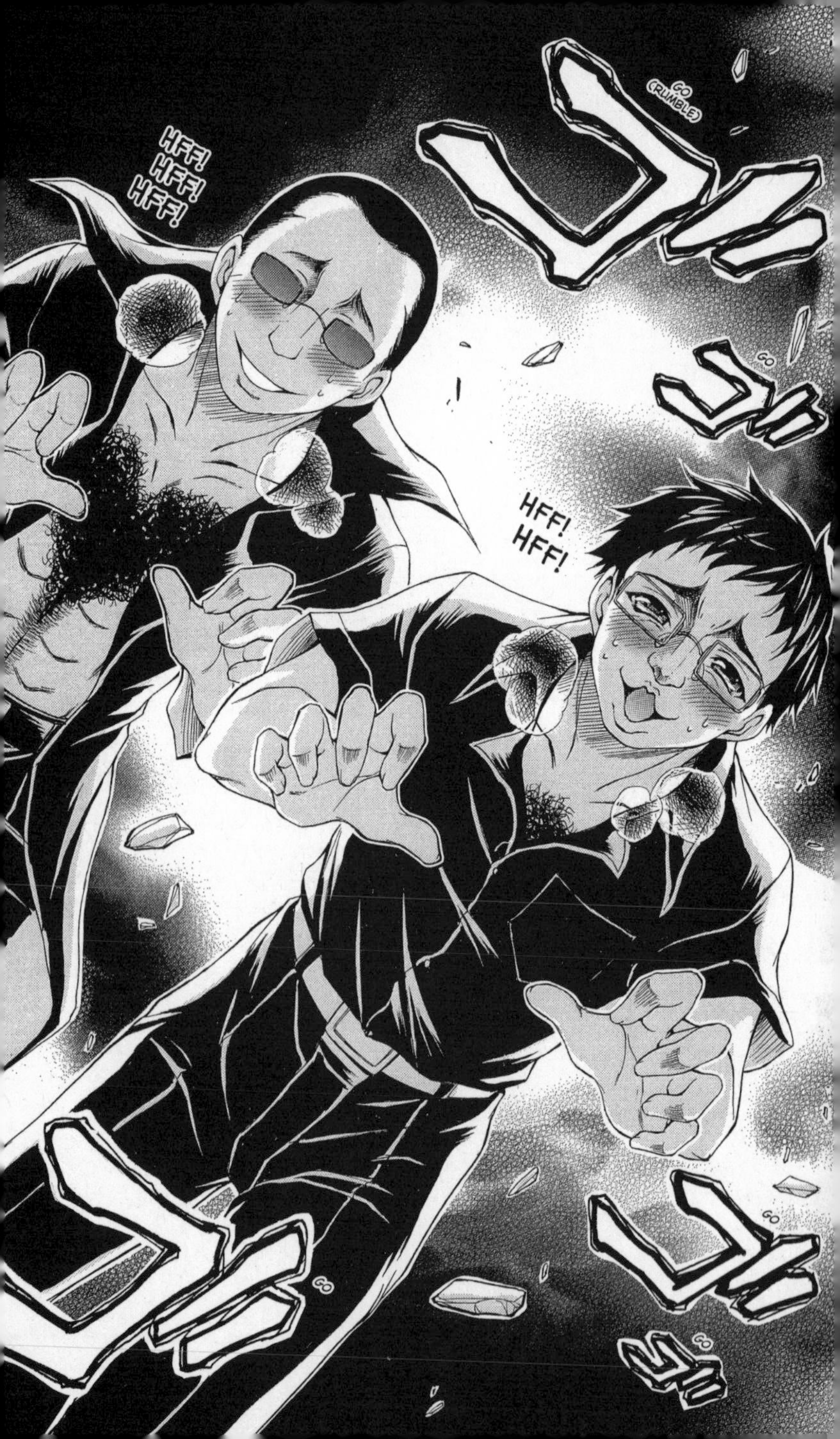
GO (RUMBLE)
GO
HFF! HFF! HFF!
HFF! HFF!
GO
GO
GO

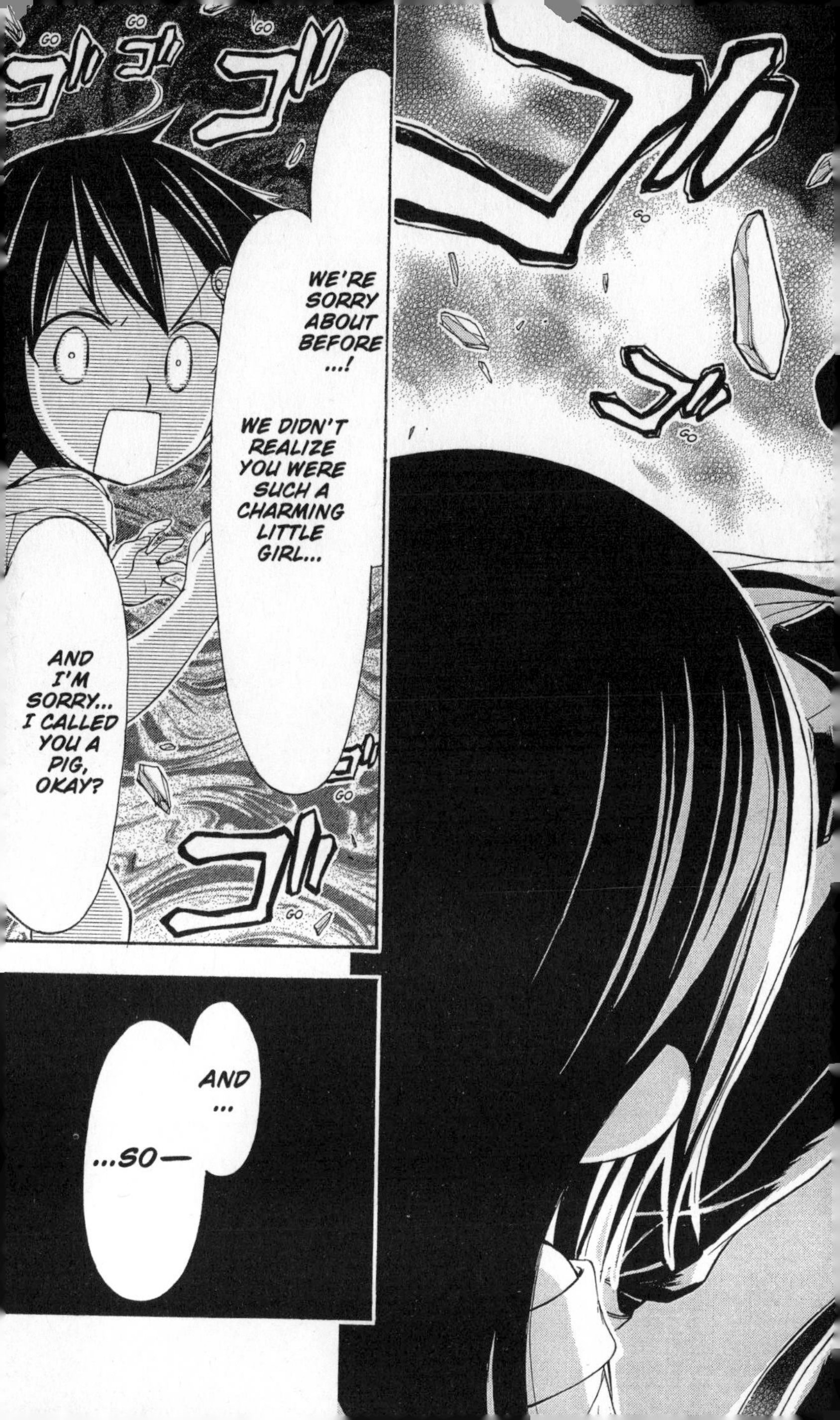
GO
GO
GO
GO
GO
WE'RE SORRY ABOUT BEFORE ...!
WE DIDN'T REALIZE YOU WERE SUCH A CHARMING LITTLE GIRL...
AND I'M SORRY... I CALLED YOU A PIG, OKAY?
GO
GO
AND ...
...SO—

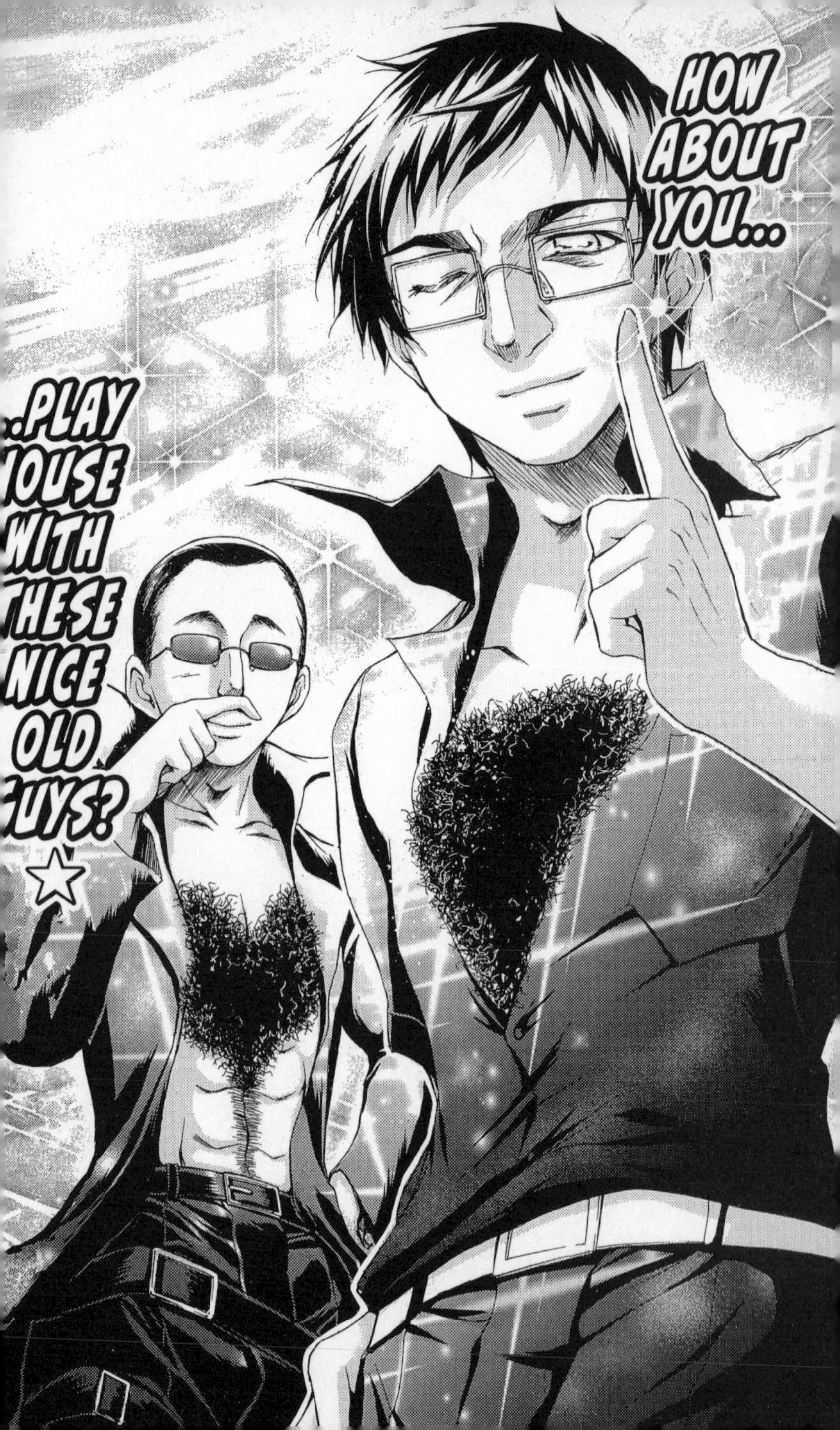
HOW ABOUT YOU...
.PLAY IOUSE WITH THESE NICE OLD UYS? ☆

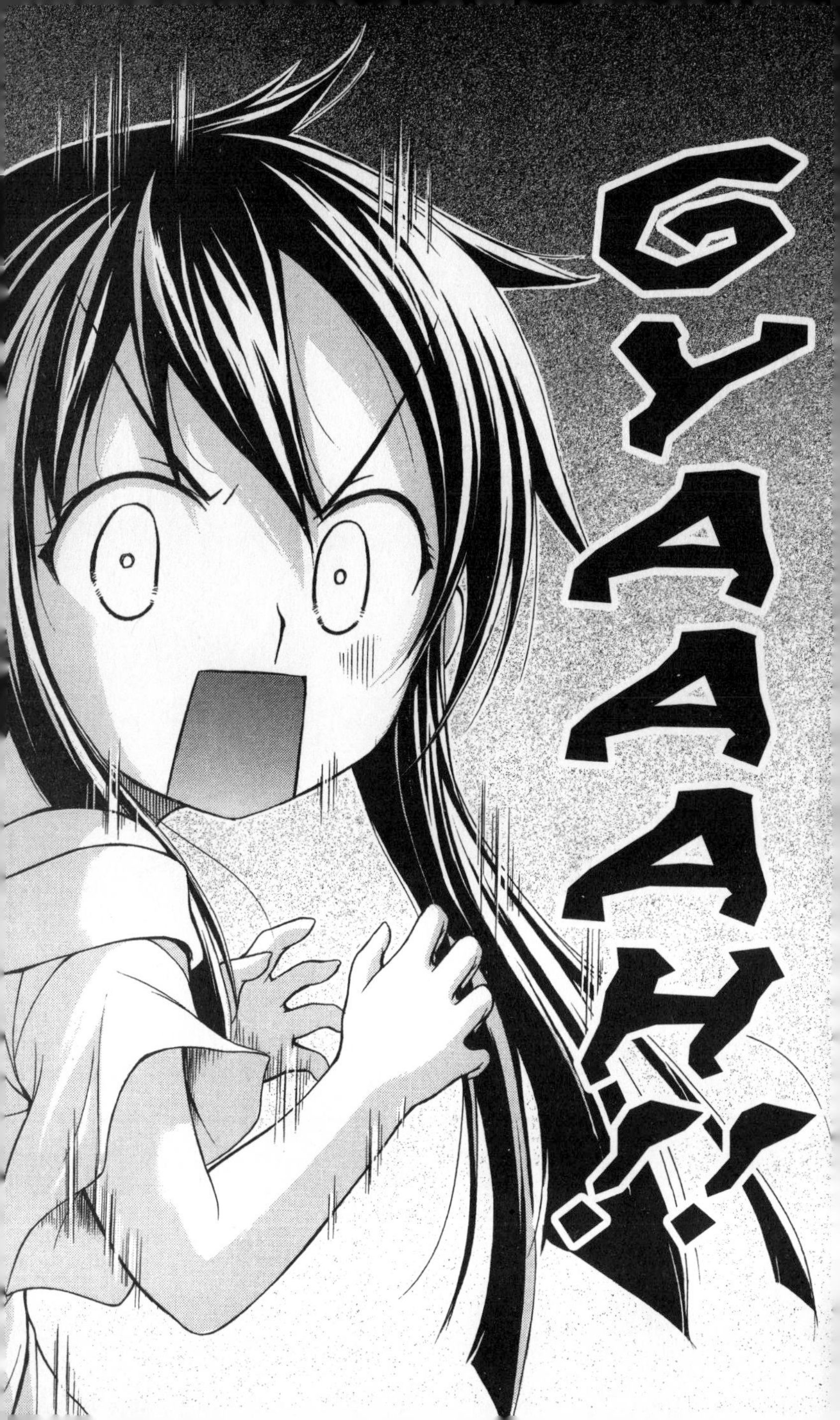
GYAAAH!!

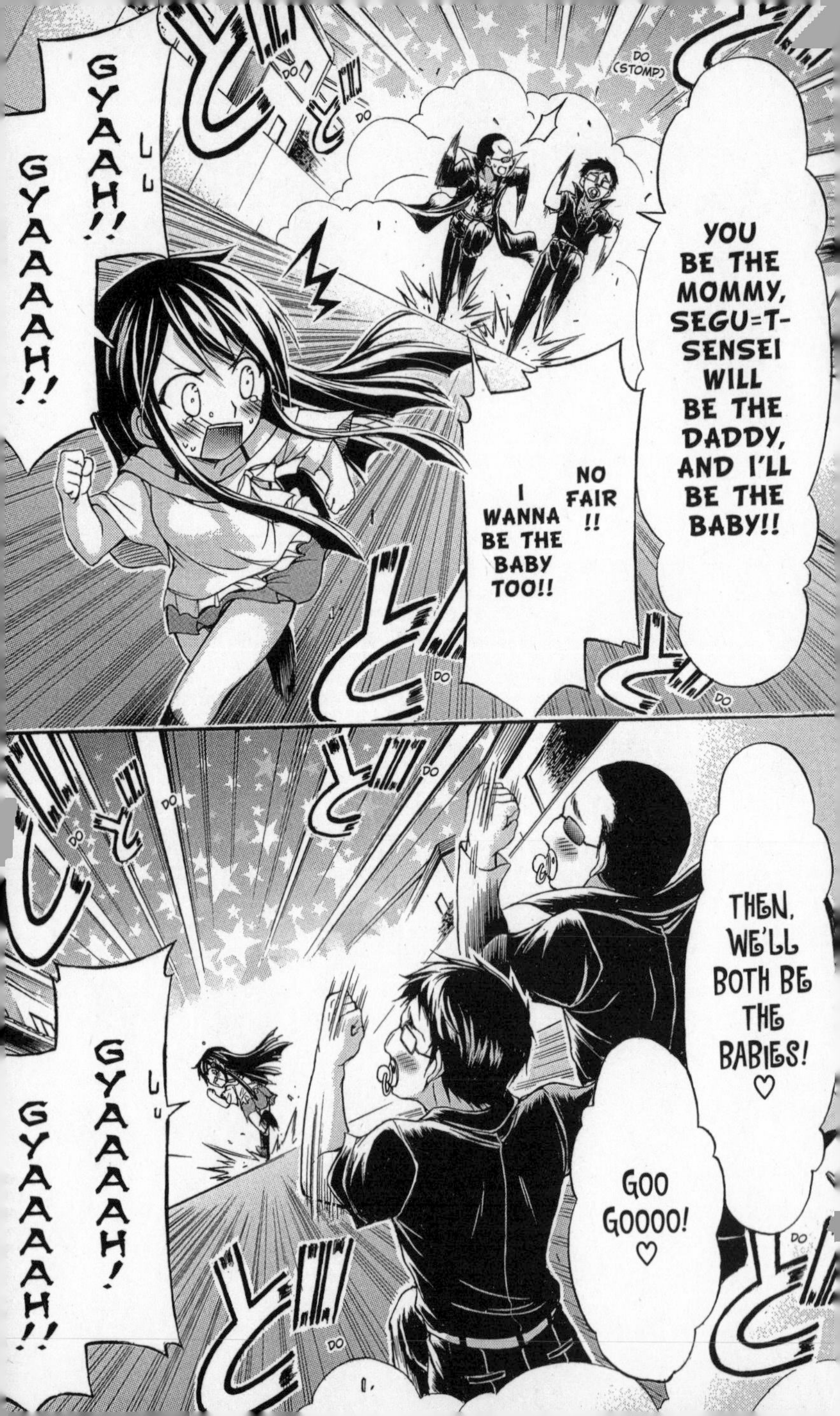
DO
DO (STOMP)
DO
YOU BE THE MOMMY, SEGU=T-SENSEI WILL BE THE DADDY, AND I'LL BE THE BABY!!
NO FAIR!!
I WANNA BE THE BABY TOO!!
DO
DO
GYAAH!! GYAAAAAAH!!
DO
DO
DO
THEN, WE'LL BOTH BE THE BABIES! ♡
GOO GOOOO! ♡
DO
DO
GYAAAAH! GYAAAAAH!!

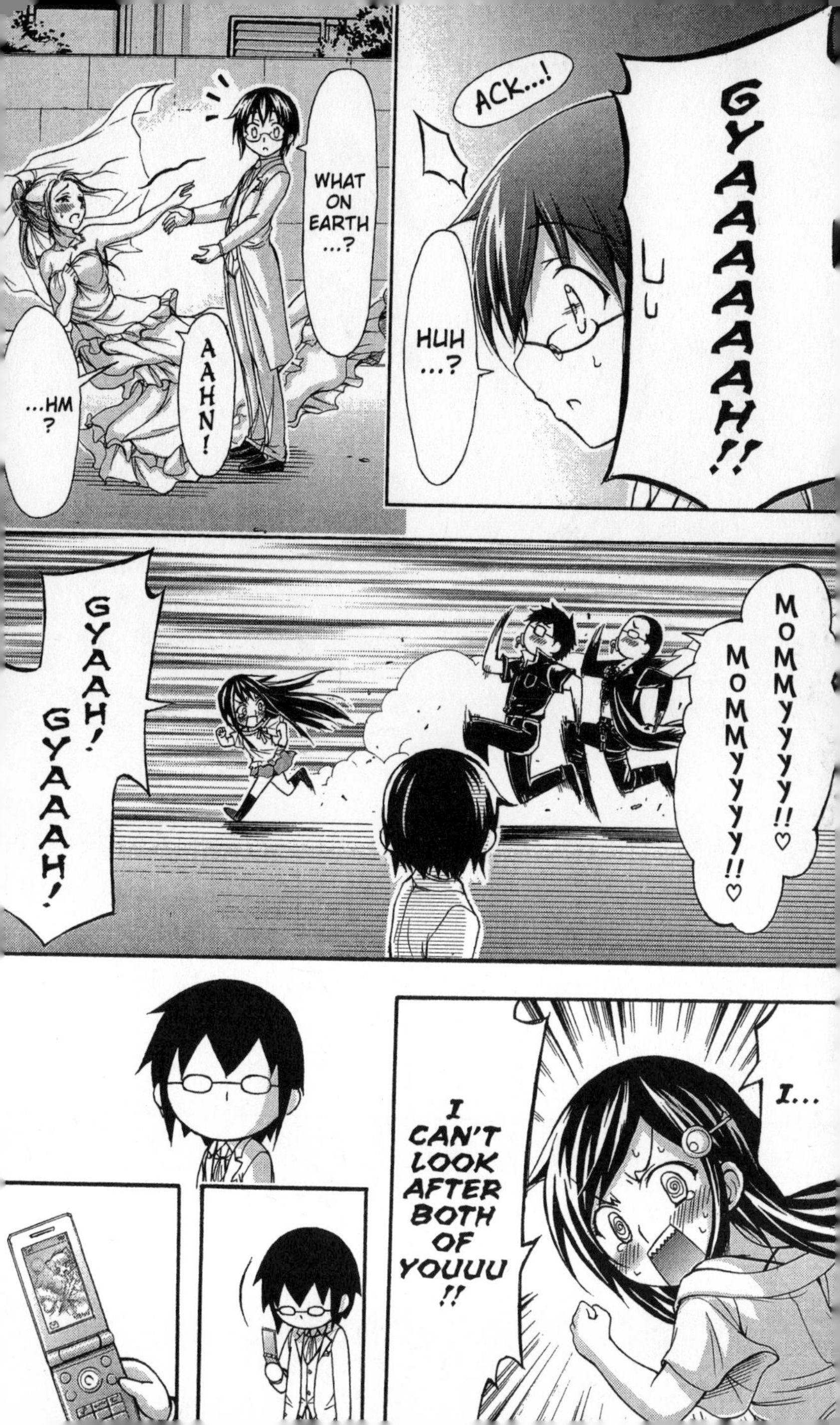
GYAAAAAAH!!
ACK...!
HUH...?
WHAT ON EARTH...?
AAHN!
...HM?
MOMMYYYY!!♡
MOMMYYYYY!!♡
GYAAH! GYAAAH!
I...
I CAN'T LOOK AFTER BOTH OF YOUUU!!

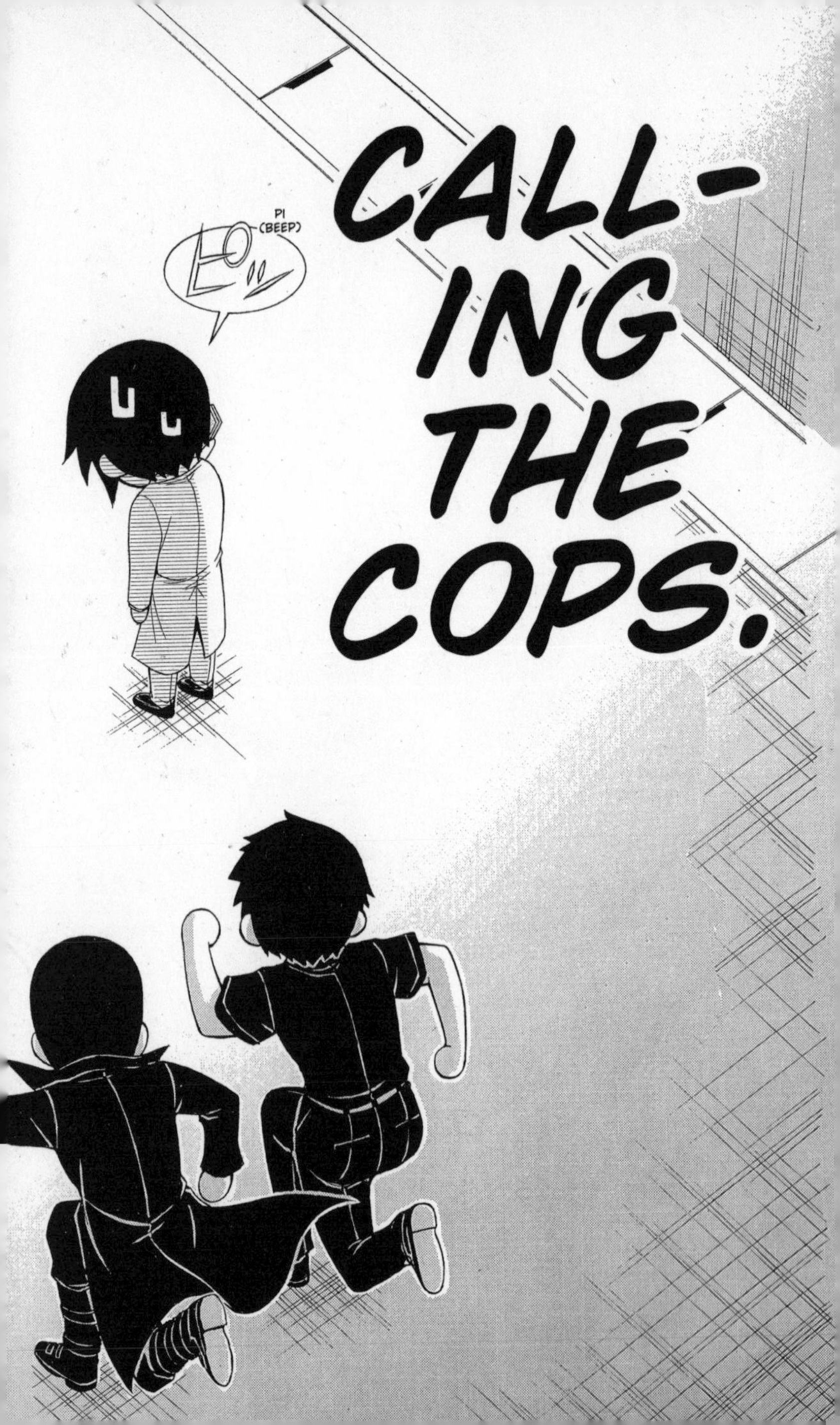
PI
(BEEP)
CALL-
ING
THE
COPS.

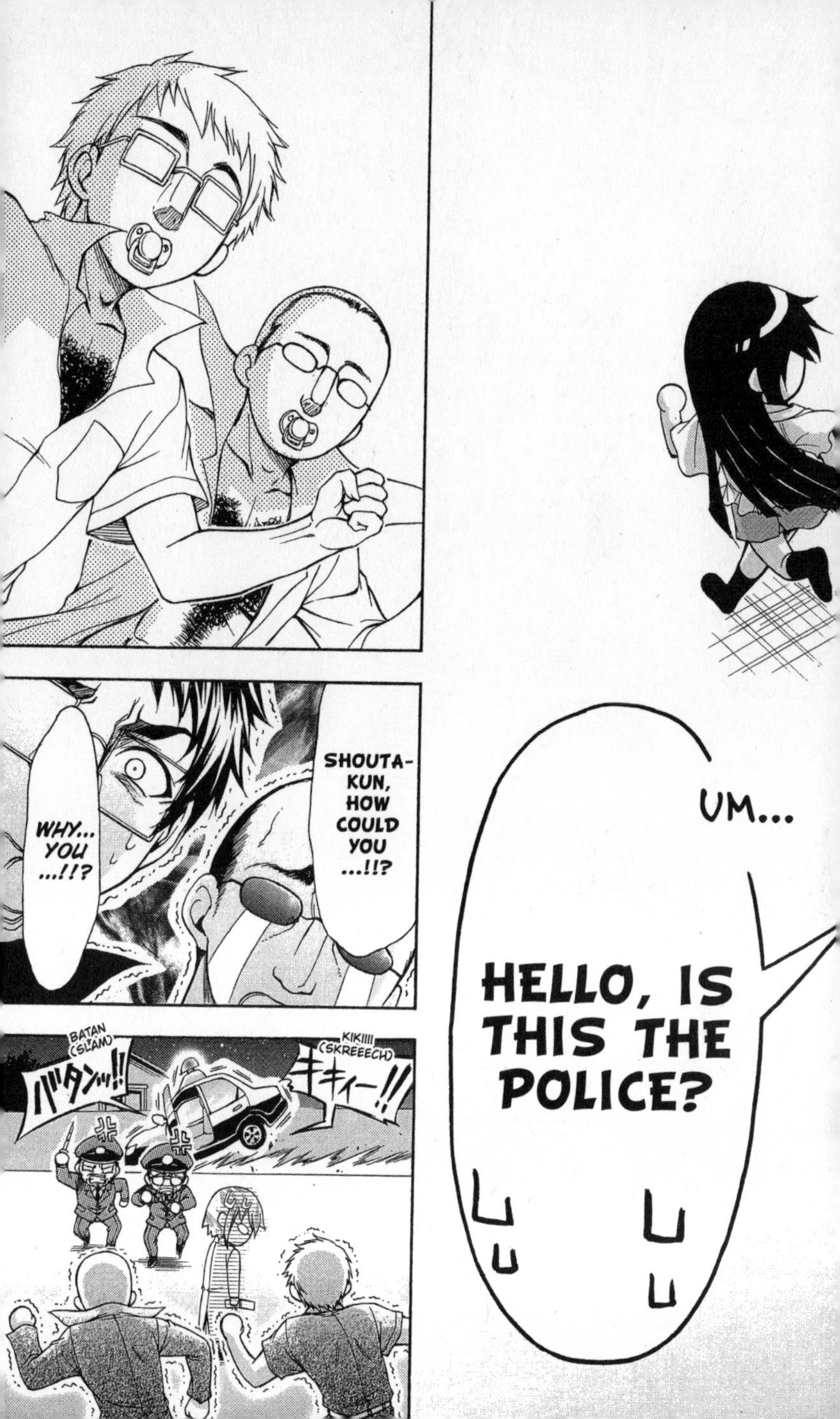
UM...
HELLO, IS THIS THE POLICE?
SHOUTA-KUN, HOW COULD YOU ...!!?
WHY... YOU ...!!?
KIKIIII (SKREEECH)
キキィー!!
BATAN (SLAM)
バタンッ!!

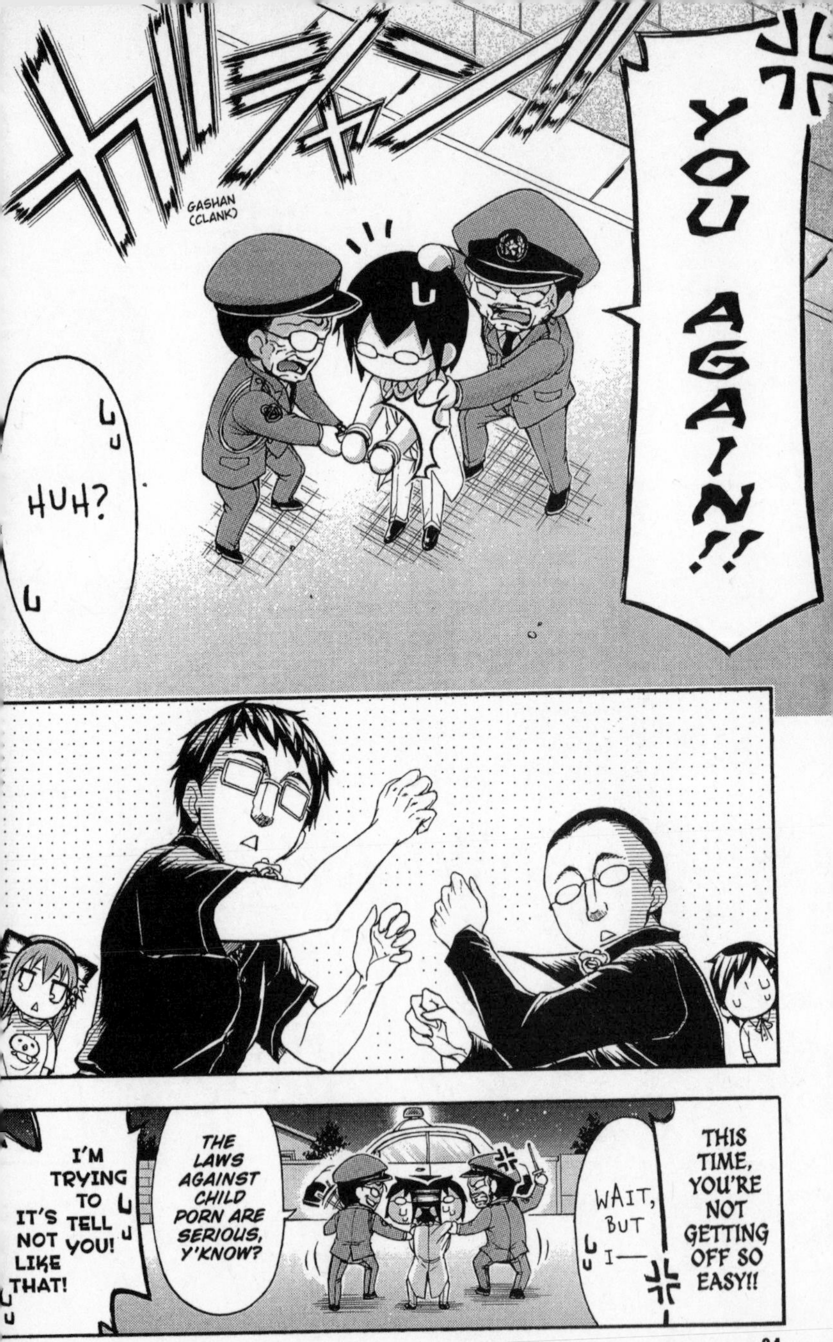
YOU AGAIN!!
GASHAN (CLANK)
HUH?
THIS TIME, YOU'RE NOT GETTING OFF SO EASY!!
WAIT, BUT I—
THE LAWS AGAINST CHILD PORN ARE SERIOUS, Y'KNOW?
I'M TRYING TO TELL YOU!
IT'S NOT LIKE THAT!

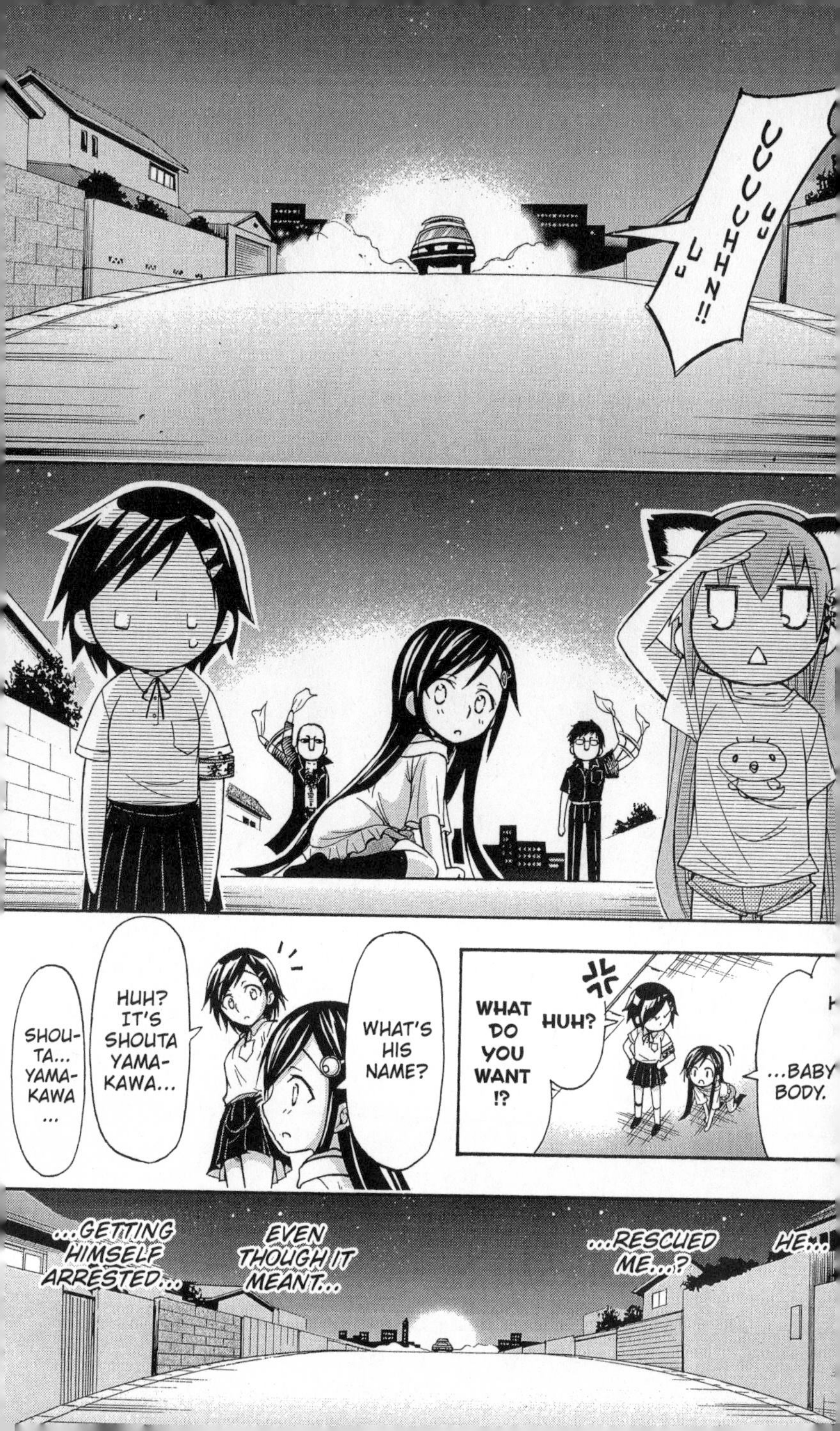
UUUUHHN!!
...BABY BODY.
HUH?
WHAT DO YOU WANT!?
WHAT'S HIS NAME?
HUH? IT'S SHOUTA YAMAKAWA...
SHOUTA... YAMAKAWA...
HE...
...RESCUED ME...?
EVEN THOUGH IT MEANT...
...GETTING HIMSELF ARRESTED...

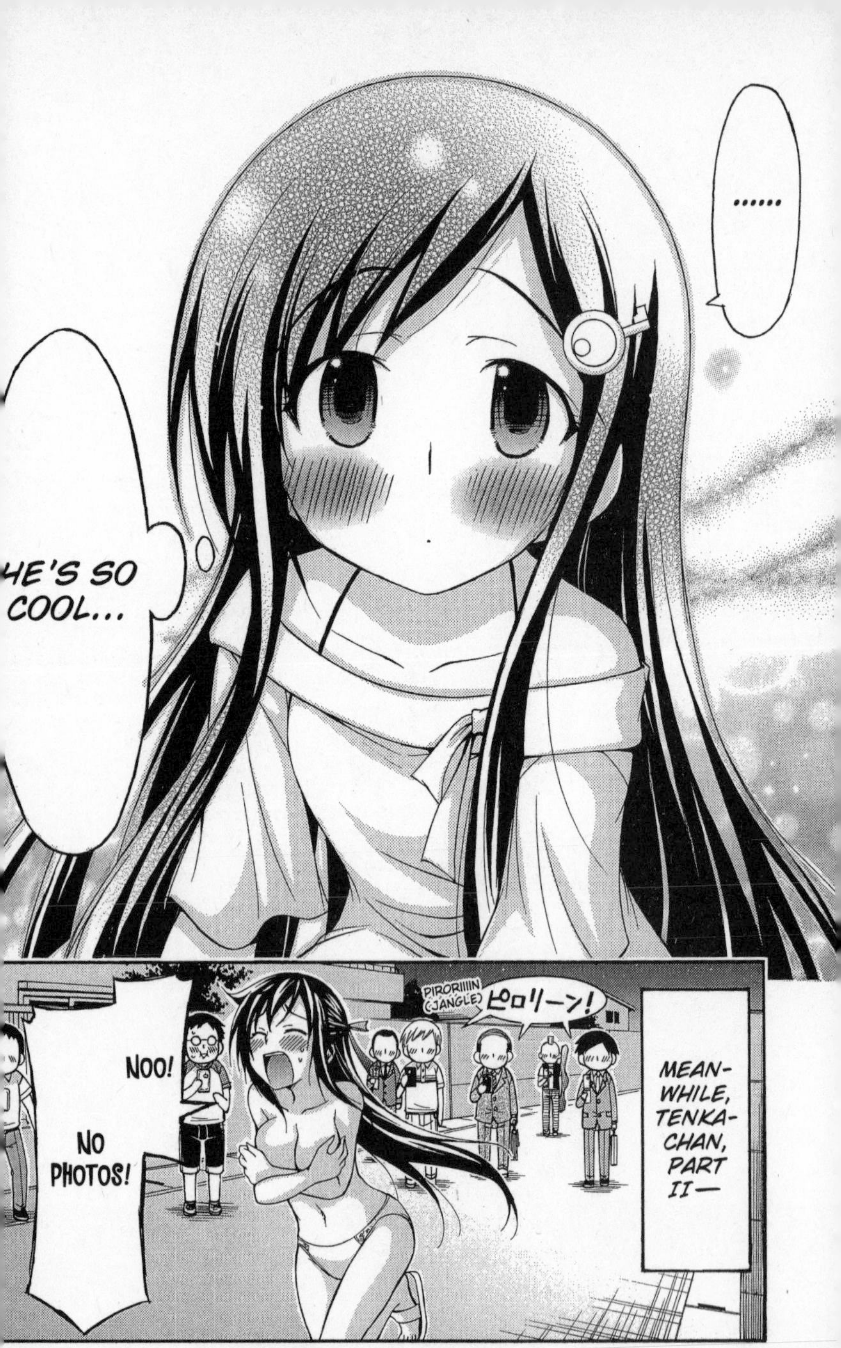
......
HE'S SO COOL...
MEAN-WHILE, TENKA-CHAN, PART II—
PIRORIIIIN (JANGLE) ピロリーン!
NOO!
NO PHOTOS!

15TH OFFENSE • THE END

GOU-DERE
SORA NAGIHARA

16TH OFFENSE • THE PERSON CALLED SHOUTA YAMAKAWA

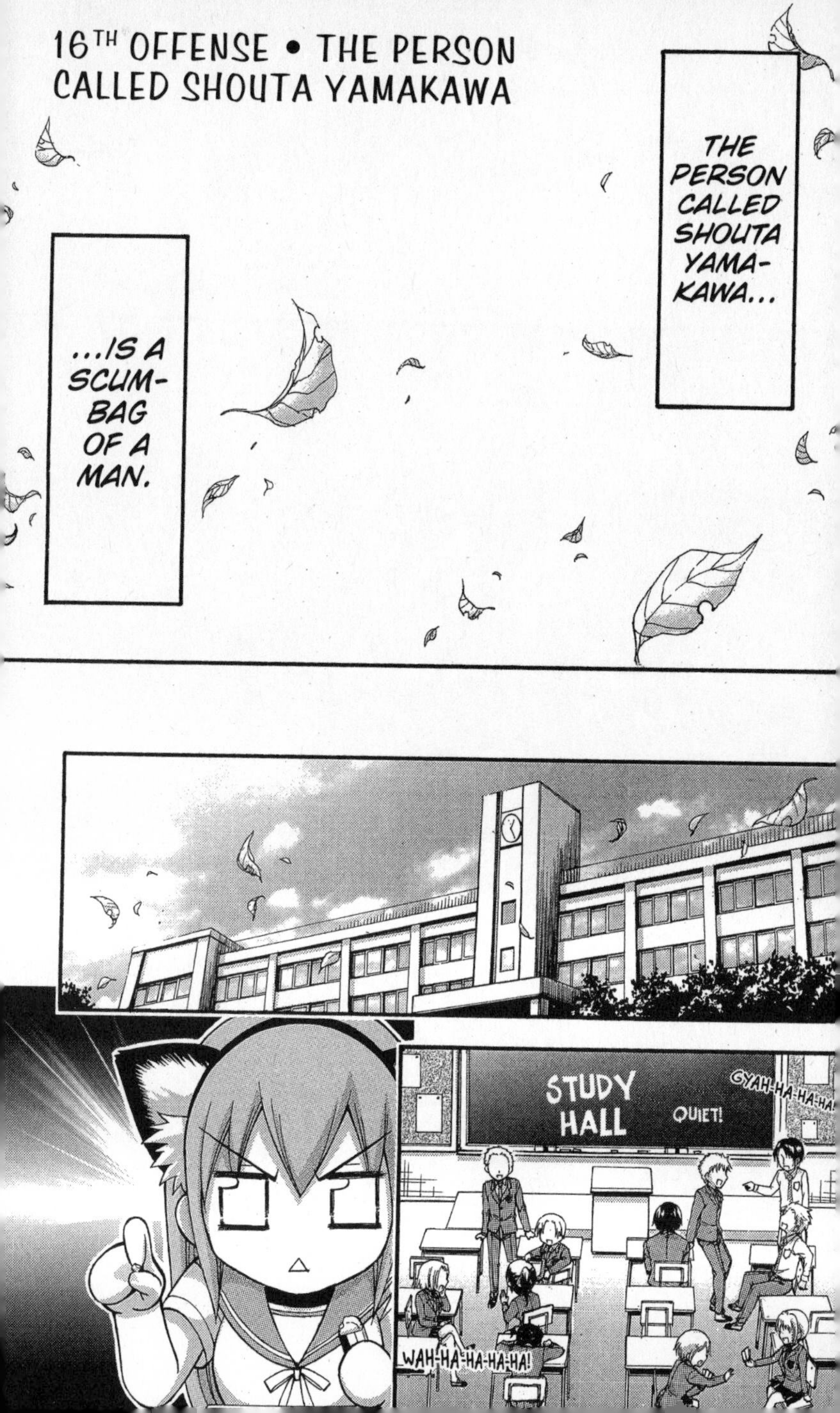
THE PERSON CALLED SHOUTA YAMA-KAWA...
...IS A SCUM-BAG OF A MAN.
STUDY HALL
QUIET!
GYAH-HA-HA-HA!
WAH-HA-HA-HA-HA!

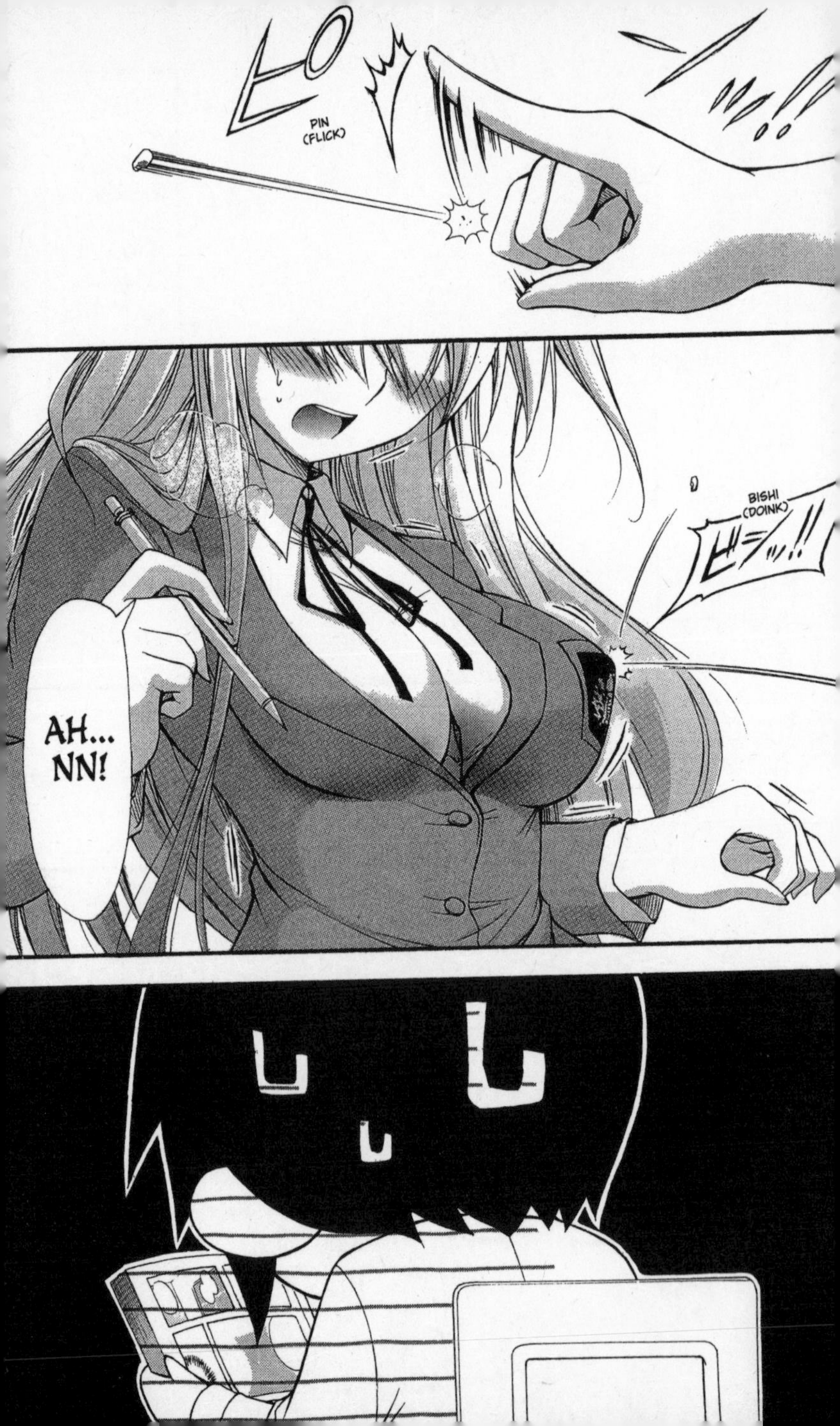
PIN (FLICK)
BISHI (DOINK)
AH... NN!

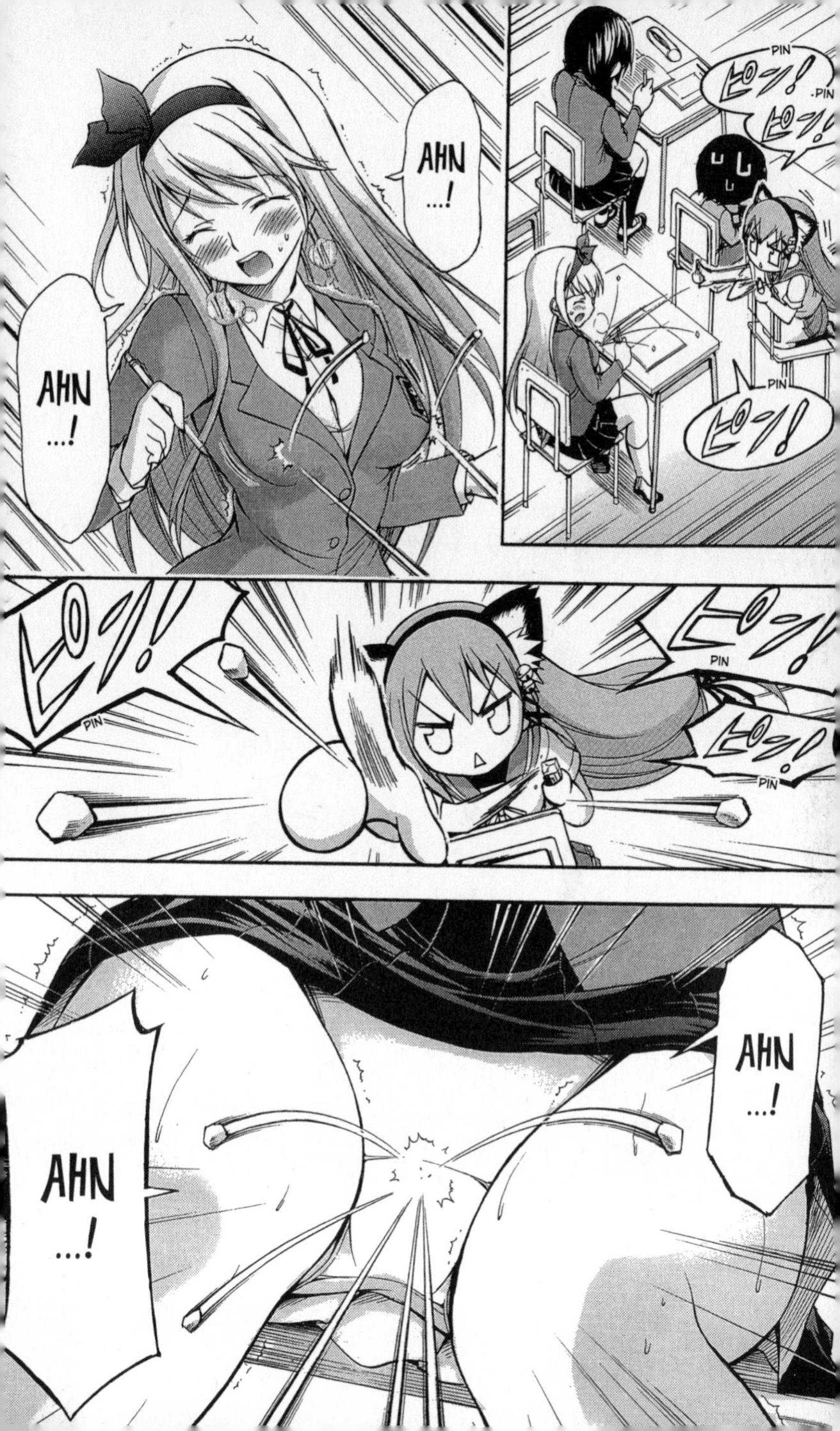

PIN
PIN
PIN
AHN ...!
AHN ...!
PIN
PIN
PIN
AHN ...!
AHN ...!

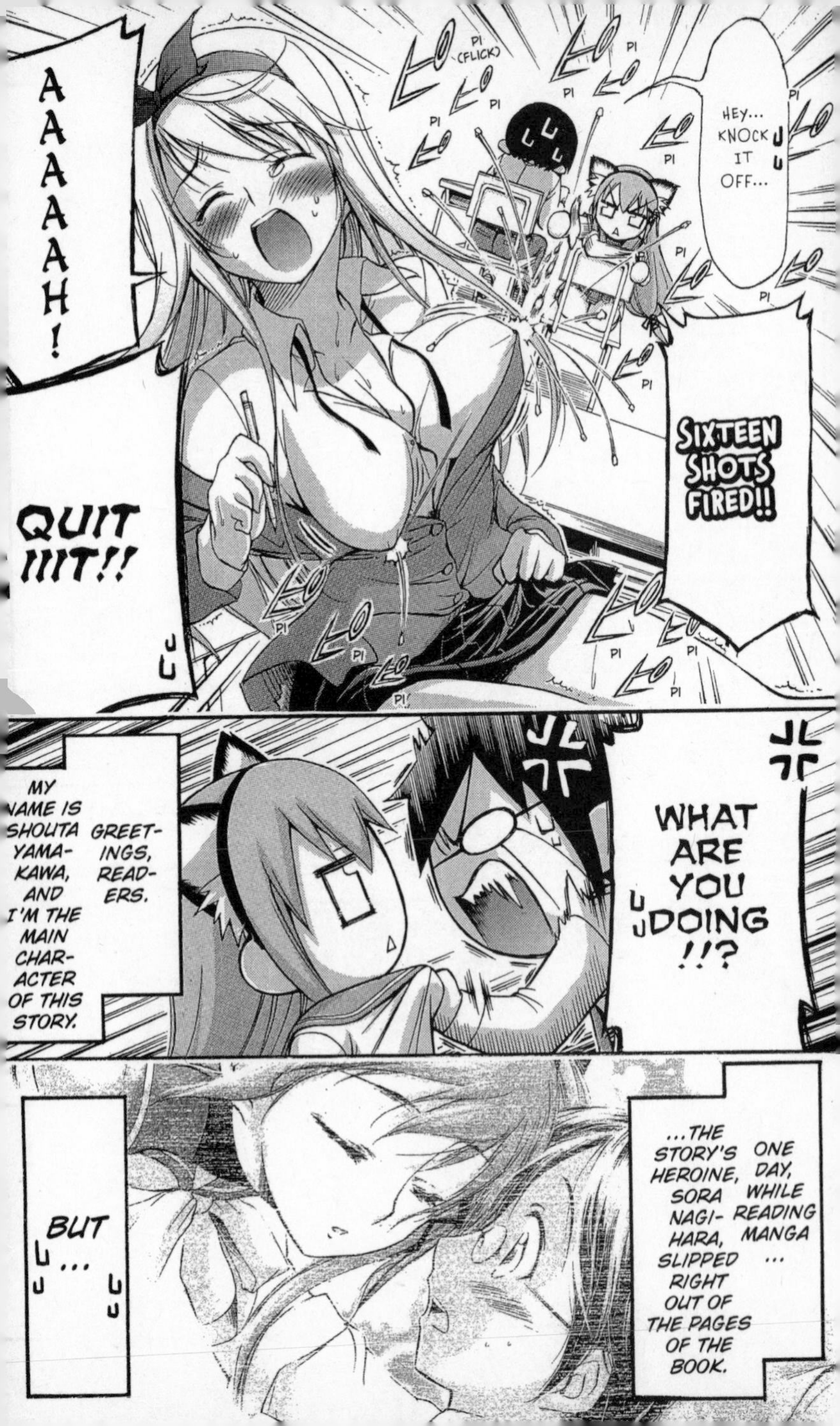
PI (FLICK)
HEY... KNOCK IT OFF...
SIXTEEN SHOTS FIRED!!
AAAAAAH!
QUIT IIIT!!
WHAT ARE YOU DOING!!?
GREETINGS, READERS.
MY NAME IS SHOUTA YAMAKAWA, AND I'M THE MAIN CHARACTER OF THIS STORY.
ONE DAY, WHILE READING MANGA...
...THE STORY'S HEROINE, SORA NAGIHARA, SLIPPED RIGHT OUT OF THE PAGES OF THE BOOK.
BUT...

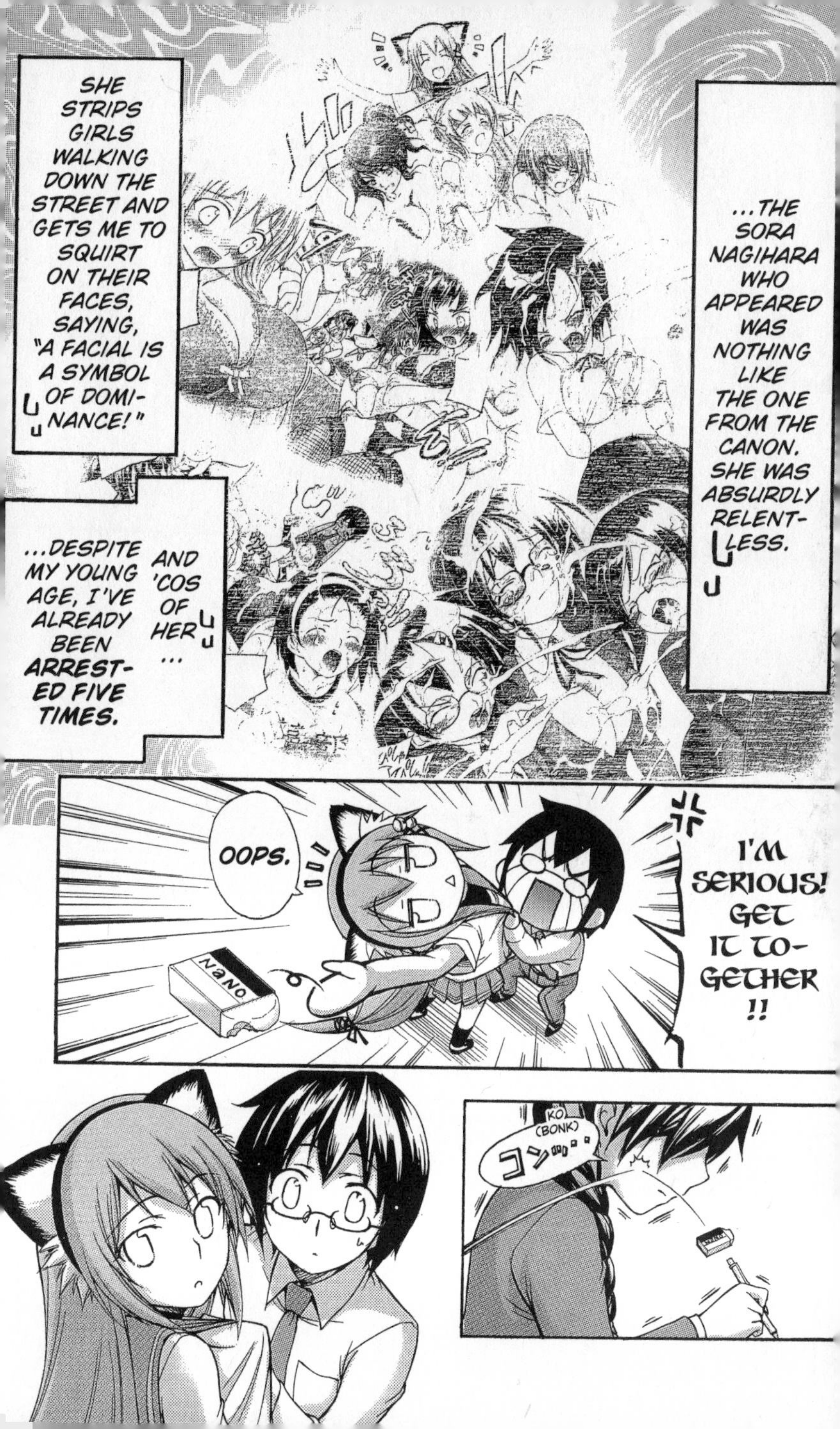
...THE SORA NAGIHARA WHO APPEARED WAS NOTHING LIKE THE ONE FROM THE CANON. SHE WAS ABSURDLY RELENT-LESS.
SHE STRIPS GIRLS WALKING DOWN THE STREET AND GETS ME TO SQUIRT ON THEIR FACES, SAYING, "A FACIAL IS A SYMBOL OF DOMI-NANCE!"
AND 'COS OF HER...
...DESPITE MY YOUNG AGE, I'VE ALREADY BEEN ARREST-ED FIVE TIMES.
I'M SERIOUS! GET IT TO-GETHER!!
OOPS.
KO (BONK)

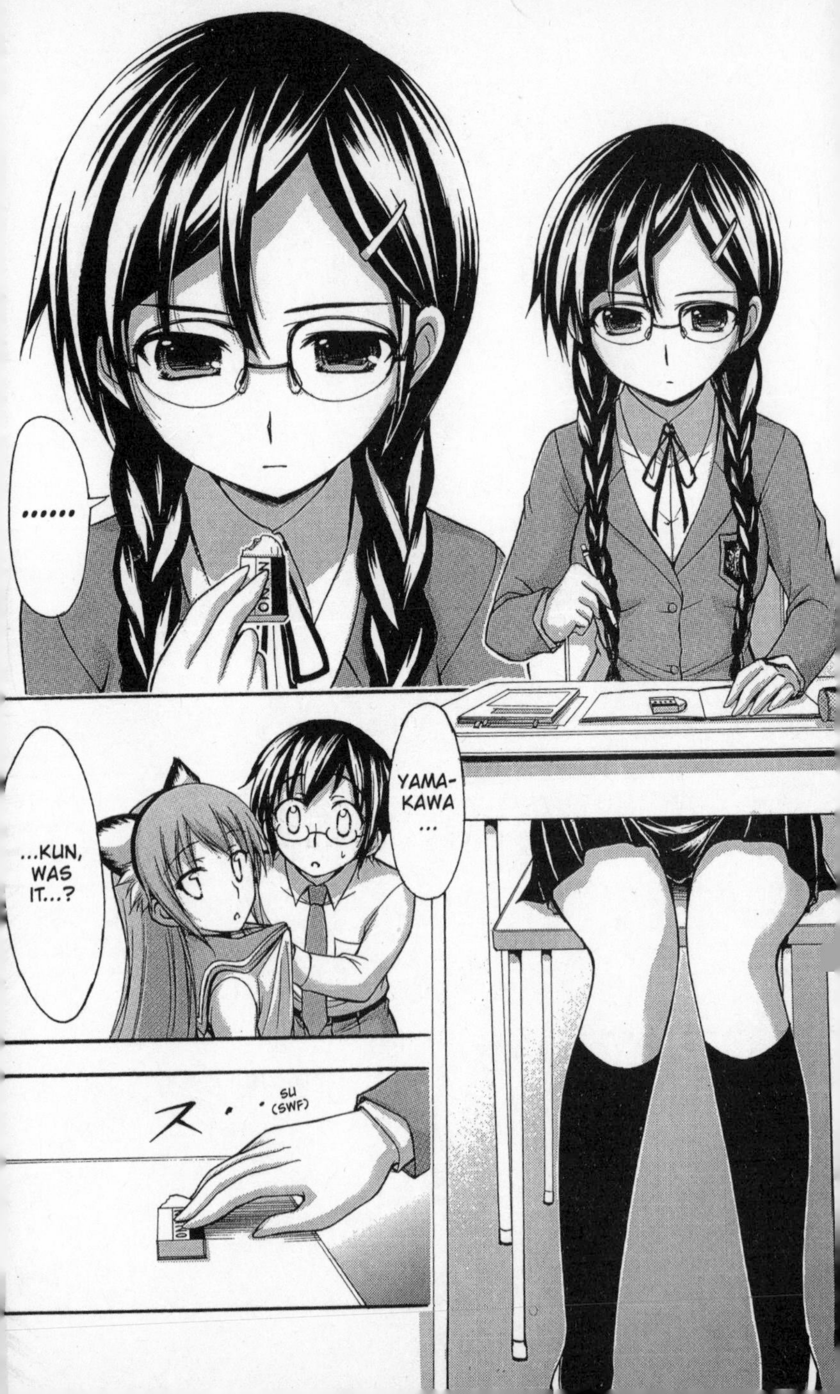

......
YAMA-KAWA ...
...KUN, WAS IT...?
ス・・
SU (SWF)

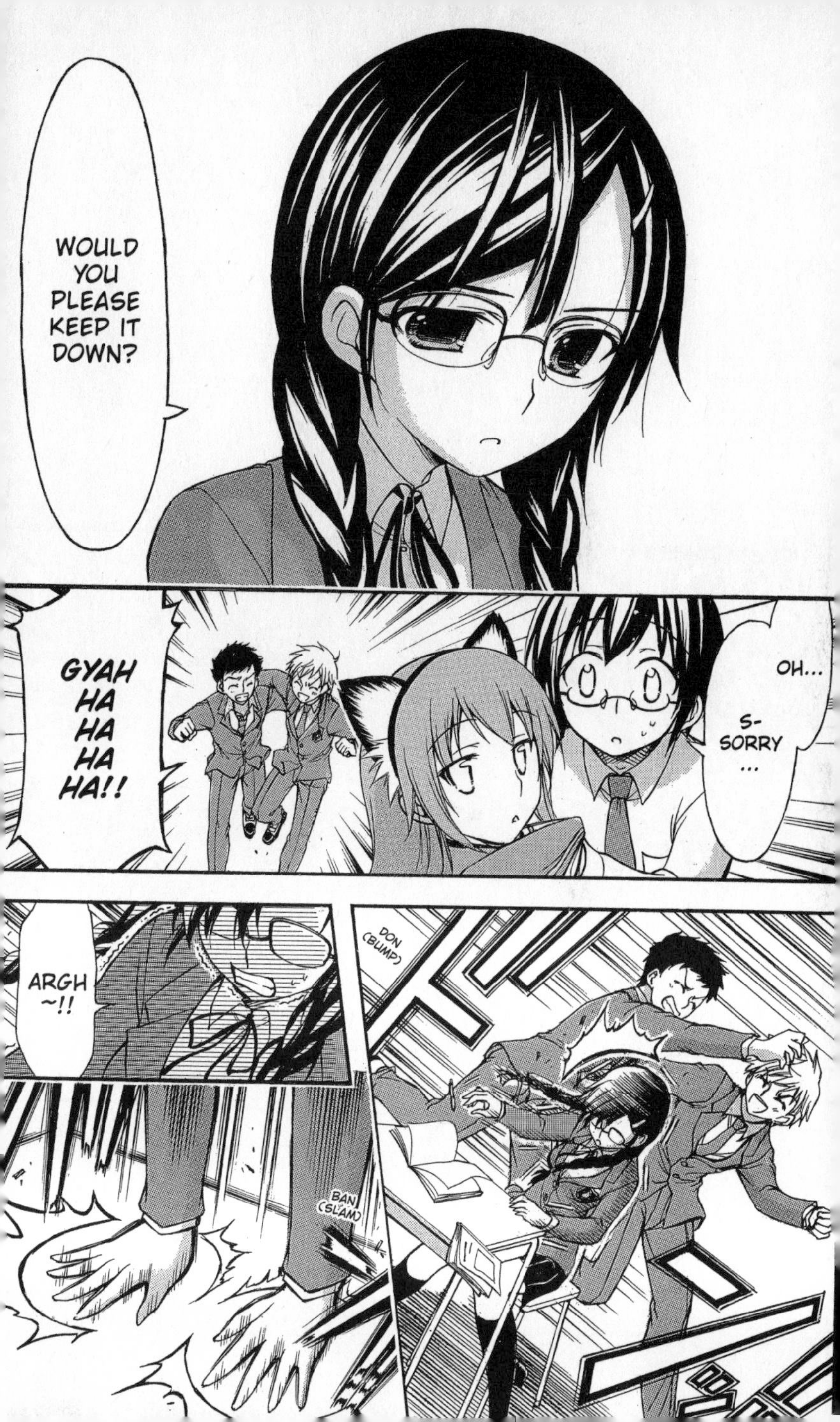
WOULD YOU PLEASE KEEP IT DOWN?
OH...
S-SORRY ...
GYAH HA HA HA HA!!
DON (BUMP)
BAN (SLAM)
ARGH ~!!

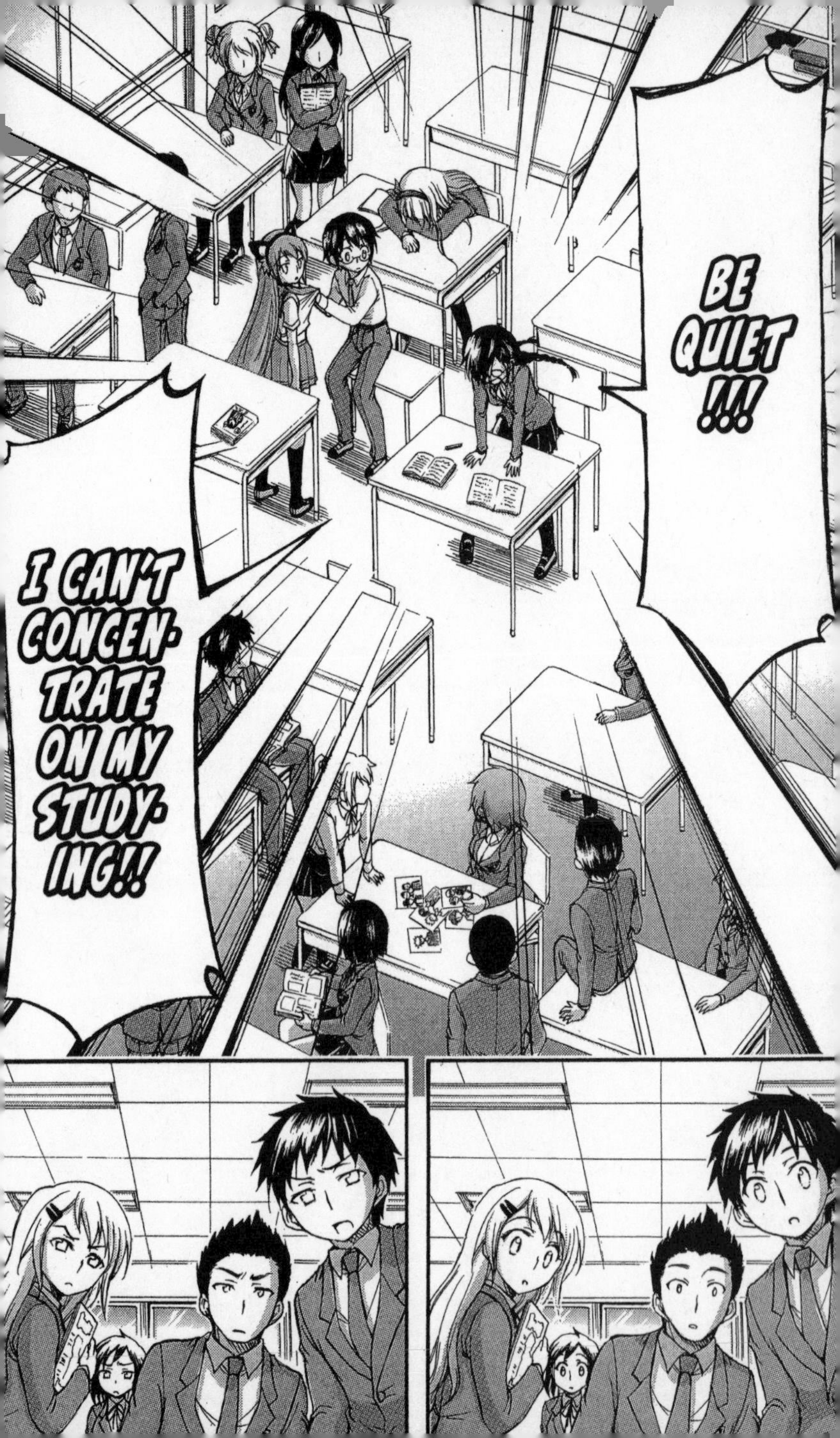
BE QUIET!!!
I CAN'T CONCEN-TRATE ON MY STUDY-ING!!

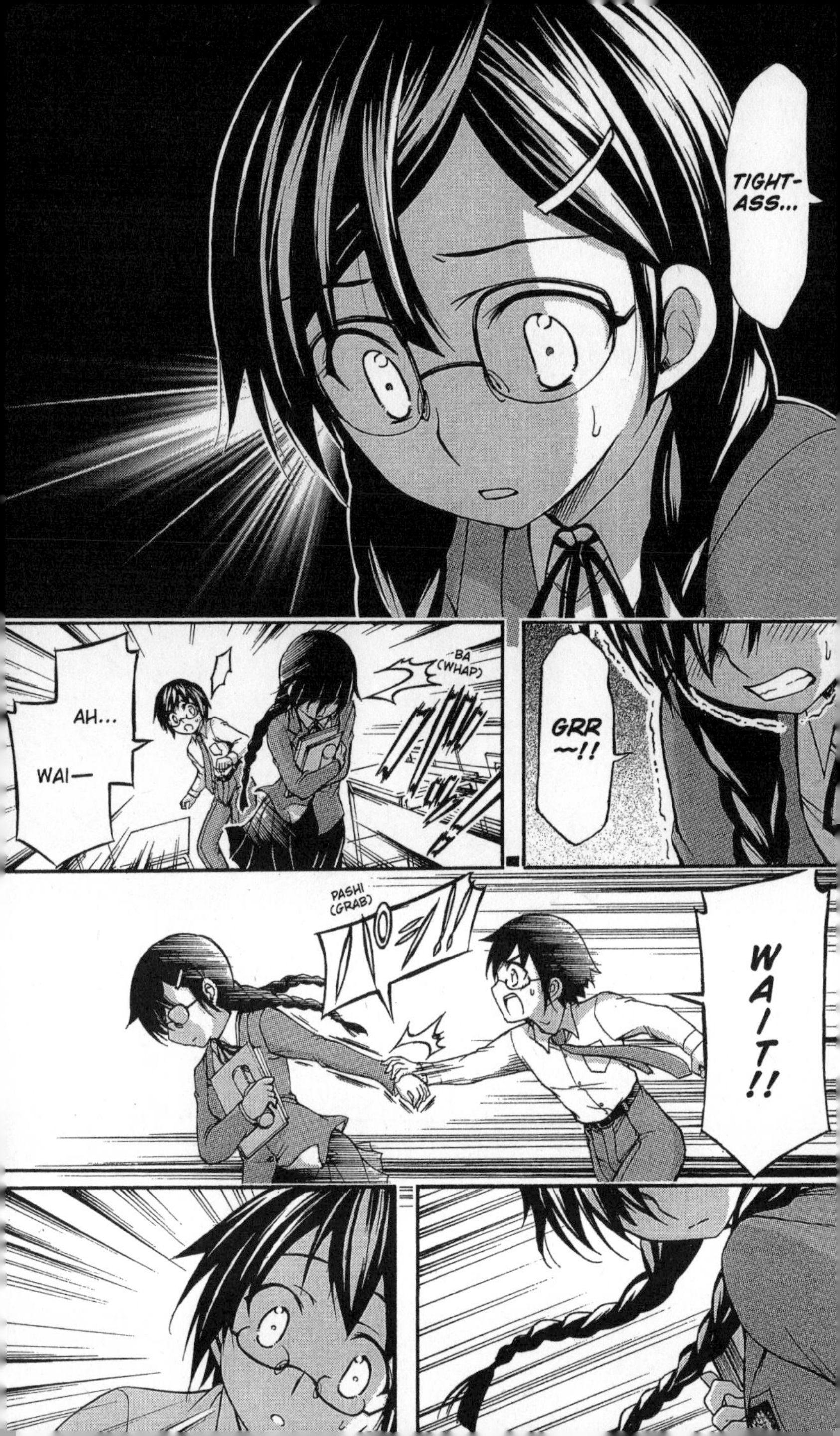
TIGHT-ASS...
GRR ~!!
BA (WHAP)
AH... WAI—
WAIT!!
PASHI (GRAB)

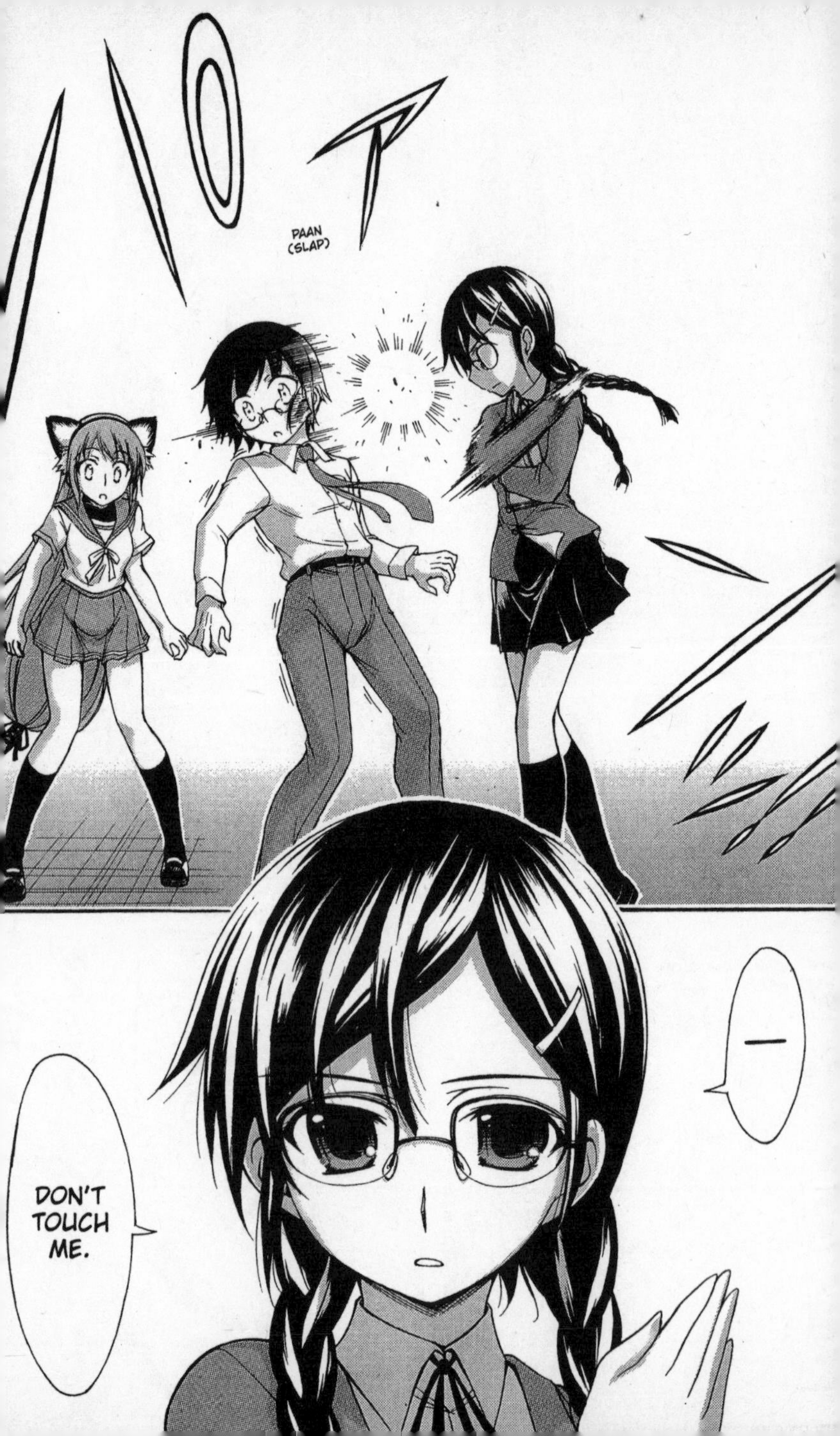
PAAN (SLAP)
—
DON'T TOUCH ME.

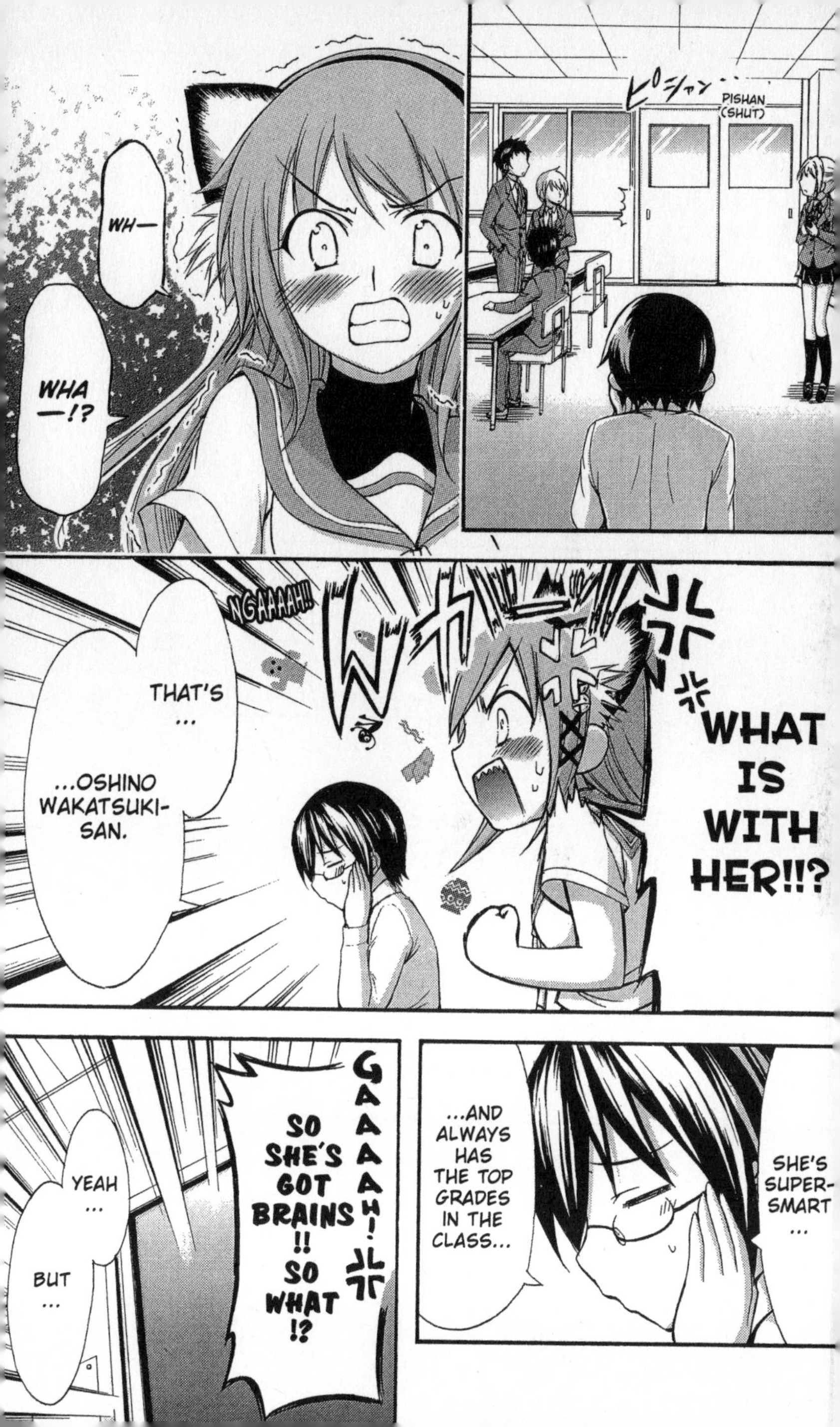
ピシャン
PISHAN (SHUT)
WH—
WHA—!?
WHAT IS WITH HER!!?
NGAAAAH!!
THAT'S ...
...OSHINO WAKATSUKI-SAN.
SHE'S SUPER-SMART ...
...AND ALWAYS HAS THE TOP GRADES IN THE CLASS...
GAAAAAH!
SO SHE'S GOT BRAINS!! SO WHAT!?
YEAH ...
BUT ...

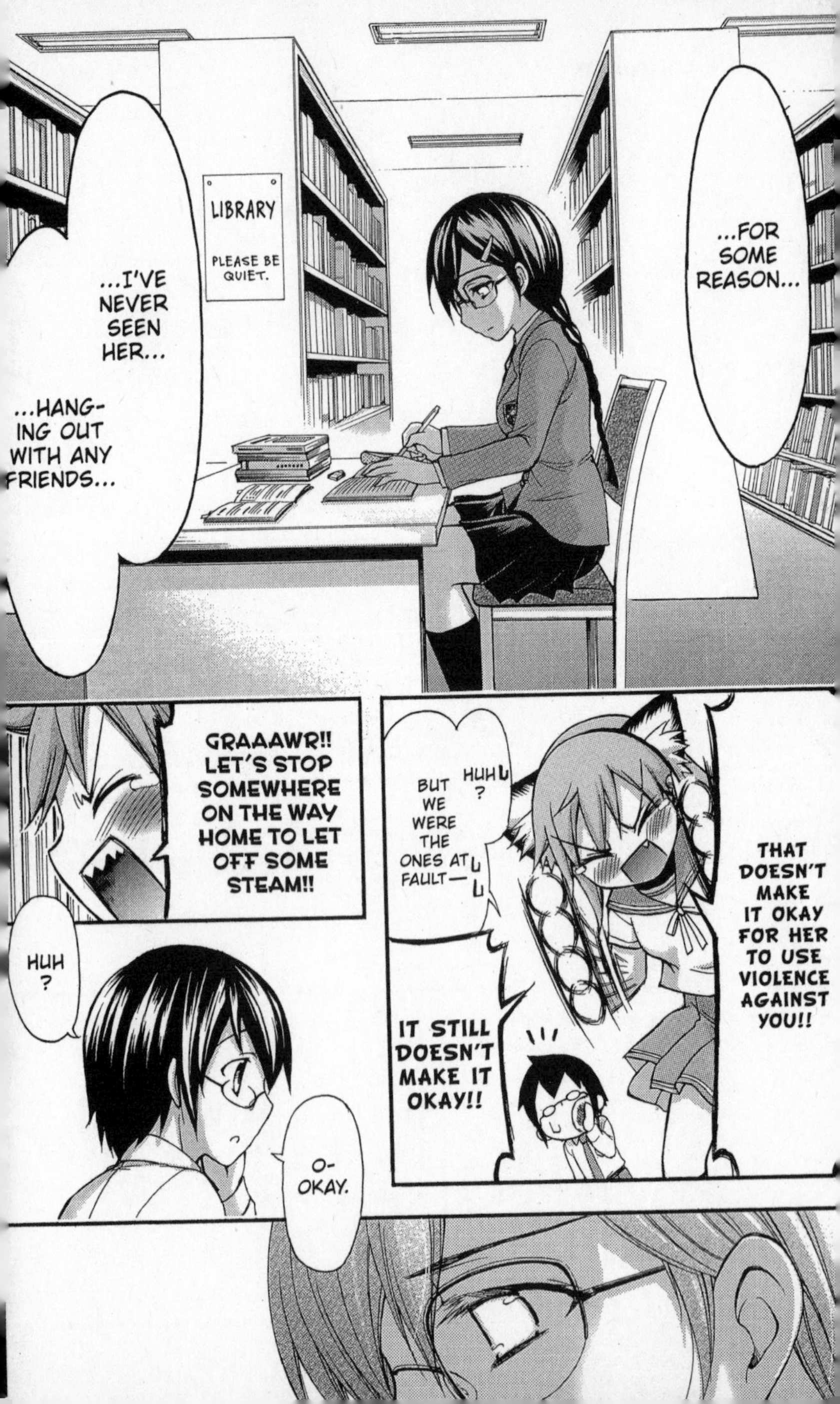
...FOR SOME REASON...
LIBRARY
PLEASE BE QUIET.
...I'VE NEVER SEEN HER...
...HANG-ING OUT WITH ANY FRIENDS...
THAT DOESN'T MAKE IT OKAY FOR HER TO USE VIOLENCE AGAINST YOU!!
HUH?
BUT WE WERE THE ONES AT FAULT—
IT STILL DOESN'T MAKE IT OKAY!!
GRAAAWR!! LET'S STOP SOMEWHERE ON THE WAY HOME TO LET OFF SOME STEAM!!
HUH?
O-OKAY.

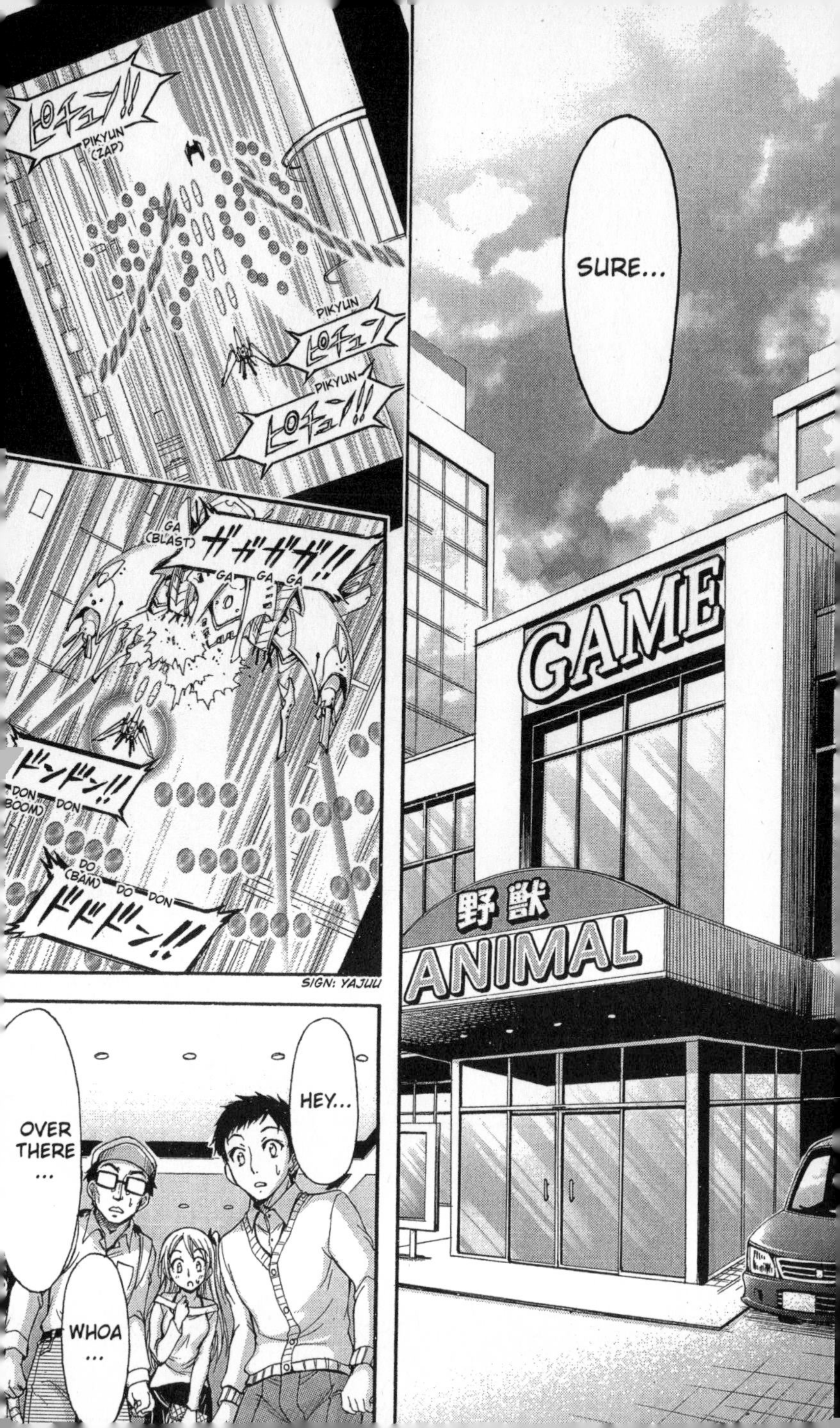
SURE...
GAME
野獣
ANIMAL
ピキュン!!
PIKYUN (ZAP)
PIKYUN
ピキュン
PIKYUN
ピキュン!!
GA (BLAST)
ガガガガ!!
GA GA GA
ドンドン!!
DON (BOOM) DON
DO (BAM) DO DON
ドドドン!!
SIGN: YAJUU
HEY...
OVER THERE ...
WHOA ...

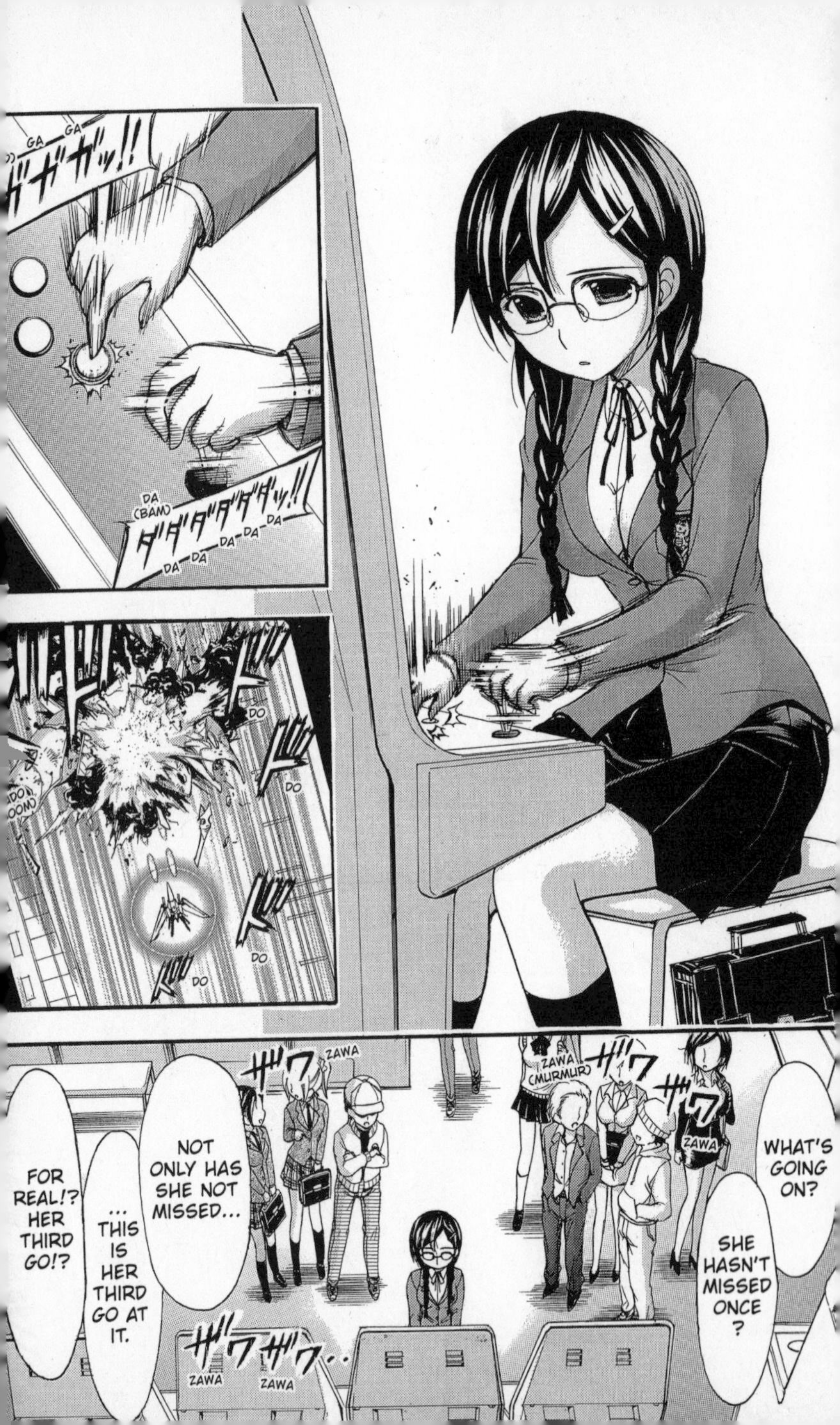
GA GA
ガガガッ!!
DA (BAM)
ダダダダダッ!!
DA DA DA DA DA
DO DO DO DO
ZAWA (MURMUR)
ザワ
ザワ
ZAWA
ZAWA
WHAT'S GOING ON?
SHE HASN'T MISSED ONCE?
NOT ONLY HAS SHE NOT MISSED...
... THIS IS HER THIRD GO AT IT.
FOR REAL!? HER THIRD GO!?
ザワザワ..
ZAWA ZAWA

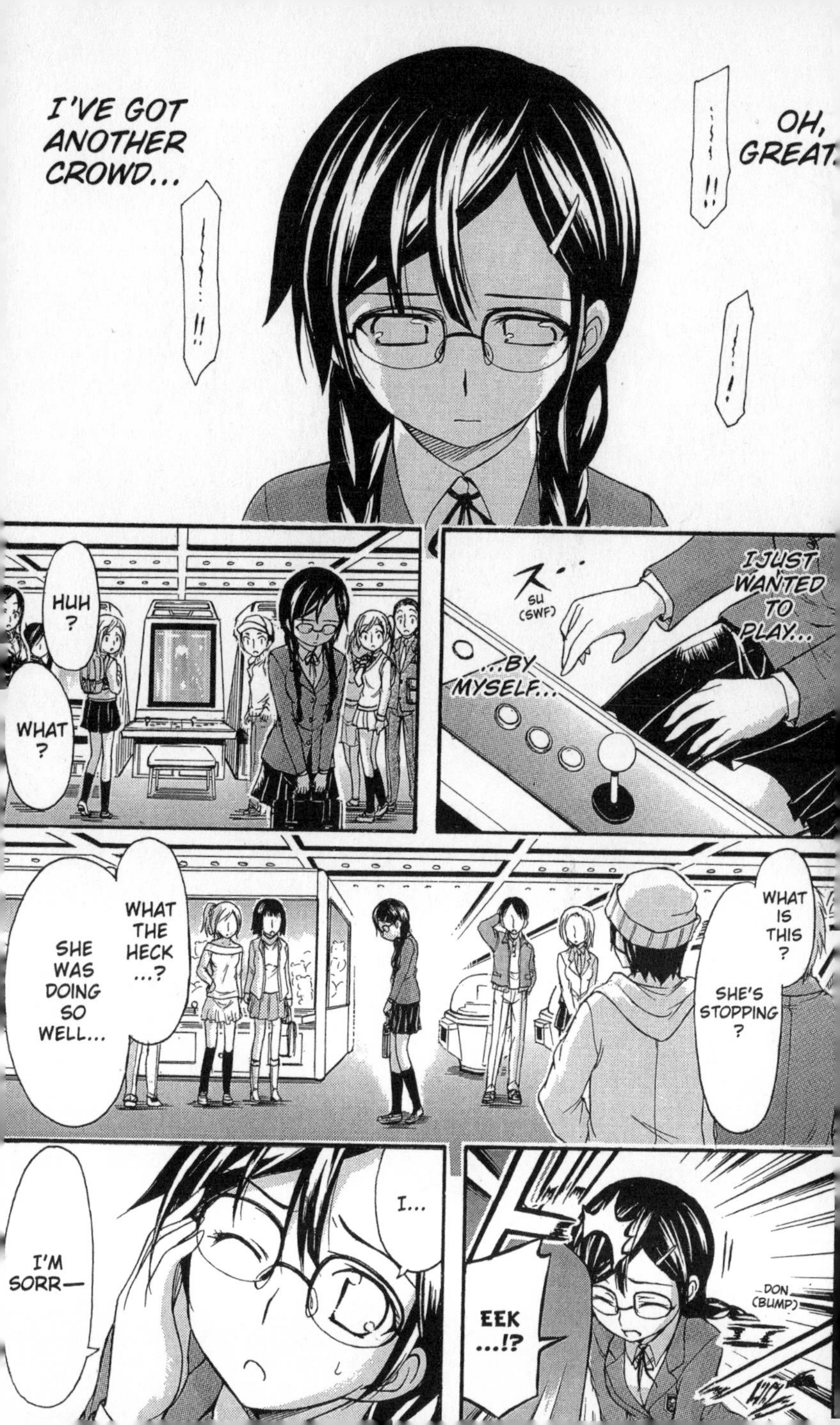
OH, GREAT.
......!!
I'VE GOT ANOTHER CROWD...
......!!
......!
I JUST WANTED TO PLAY...
ス
SU (SWF)
...BY MYSELF...
HUH?
WHAT?
WHAT IS THIS?
SHE'S STOPPING?
WHAT THE HECK...?
SHE WAS DOING SO WELL...
DON (BUMP)
EEK...!?
I...
I'M SORR—

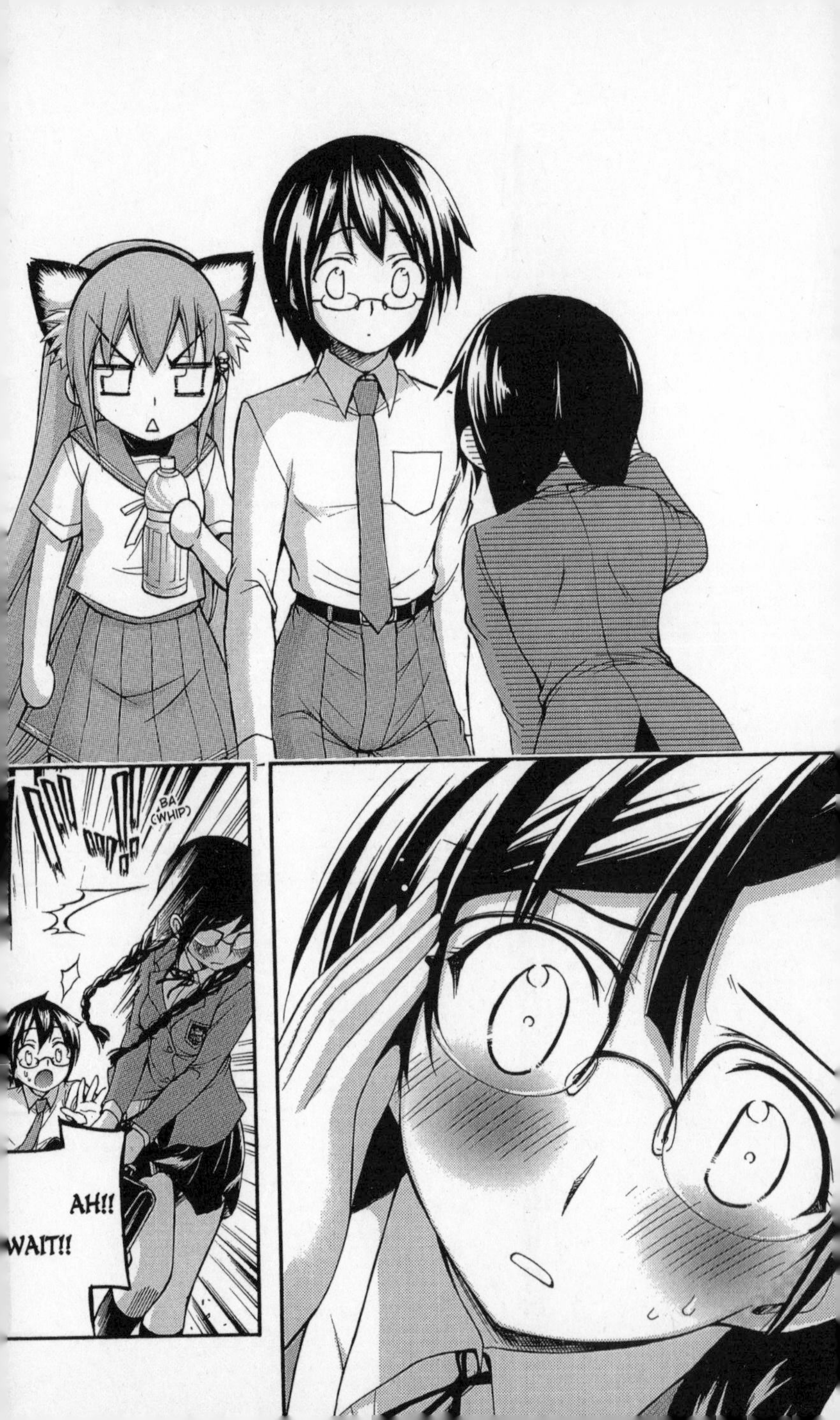
BA
(WHIP)
AH!!
WAIT!!

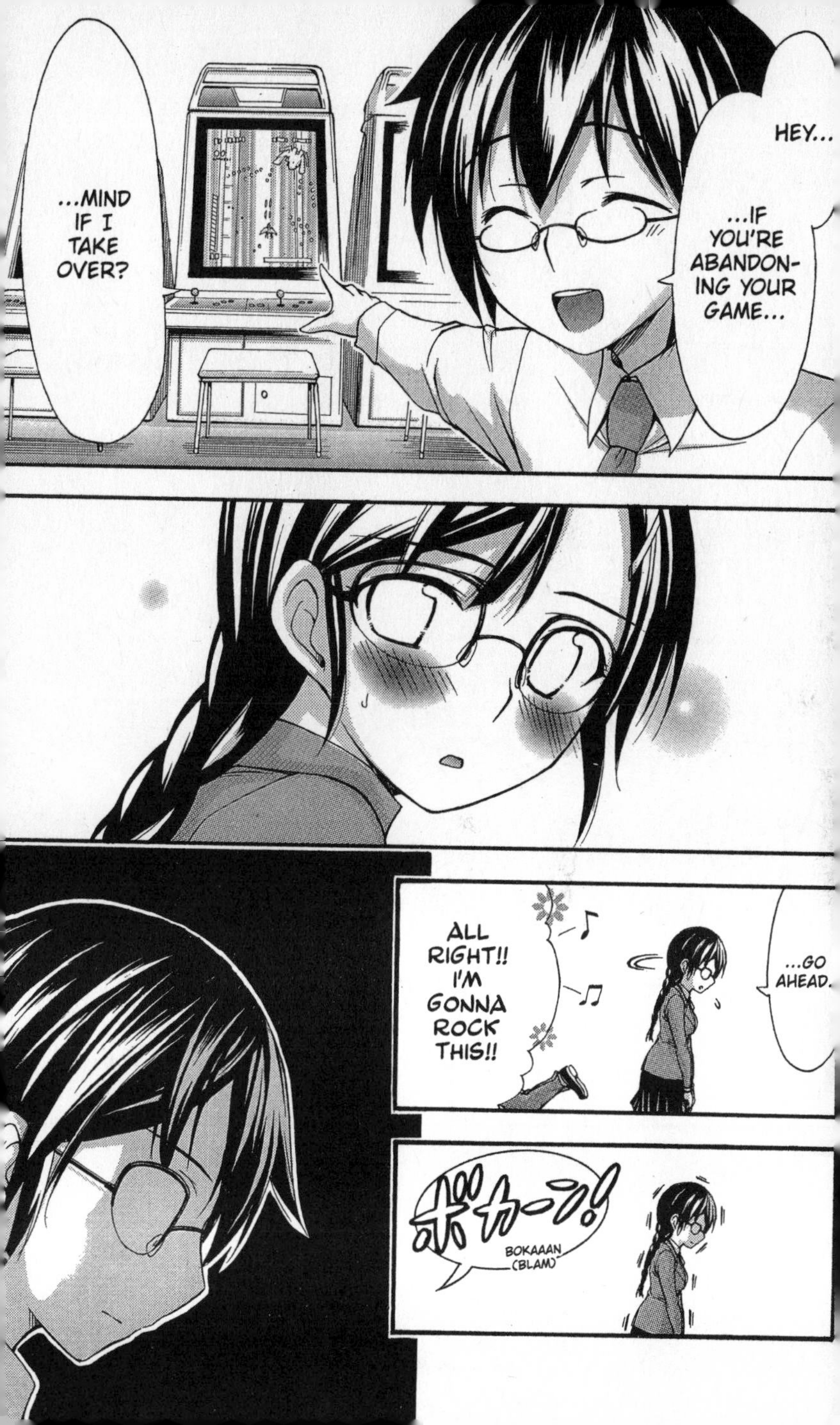
HEY...
...IF YOU'RE ABANDONING YOUR GAME...
...MIND IF I TAKE OVER?
...GO AHEAD.
ALL RIGHT!! I'M GONNA ROCK THIS!!
ボカーン!
BOKAAAN (BLAM)

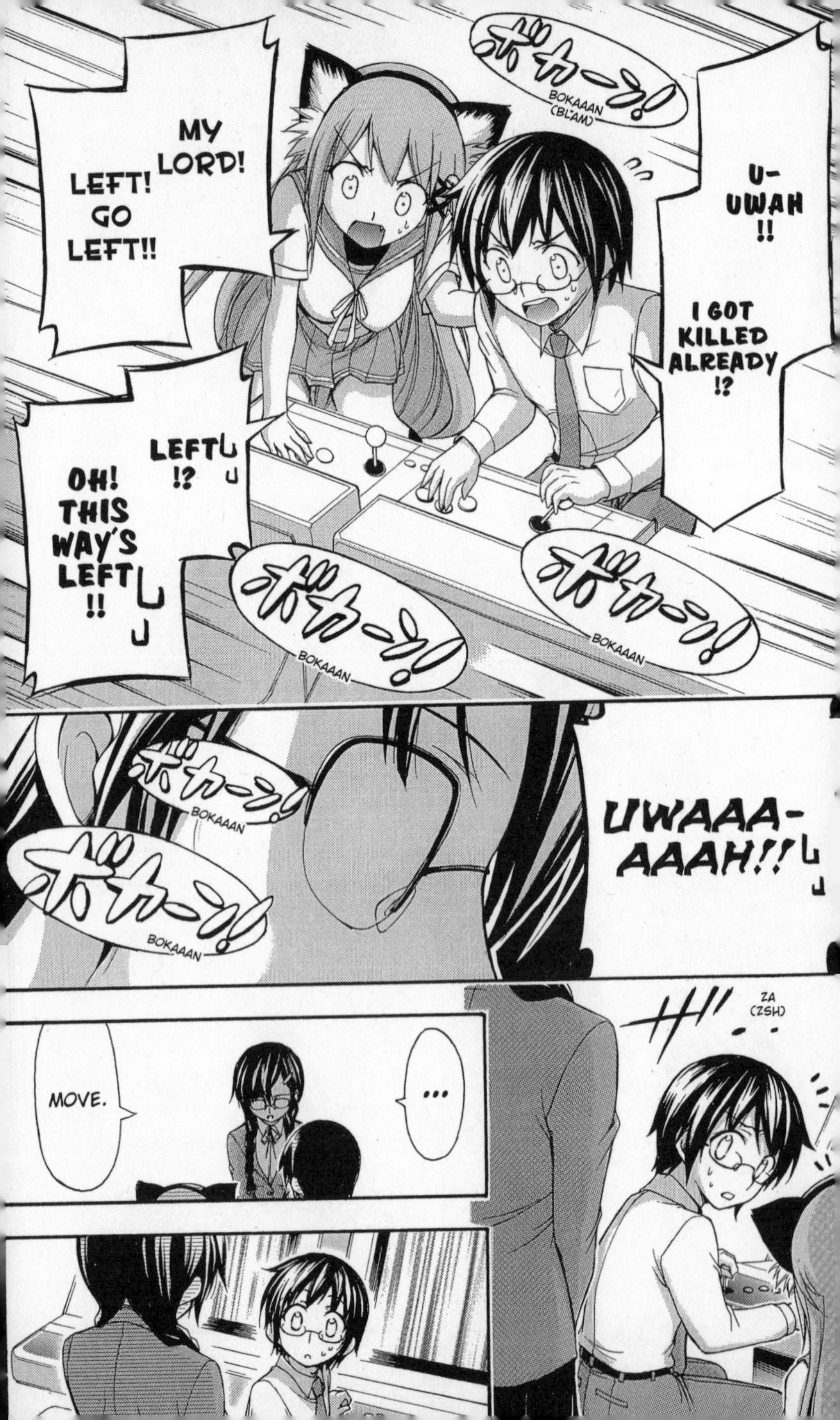
BOKAAAN (BLAM)
U-UWAH!!
I GOT KILLED ALREADY!?
MY LORD!
LEFT! GO LEFT!!
LEFT!?
OH! THIS WAY'S LEFT!!
BOKAAAN
BOKAAAN
UWAAA-AAAH!!
BOKAAAN
BOKAAAN
ZA (ZSH)
...
MOVE.

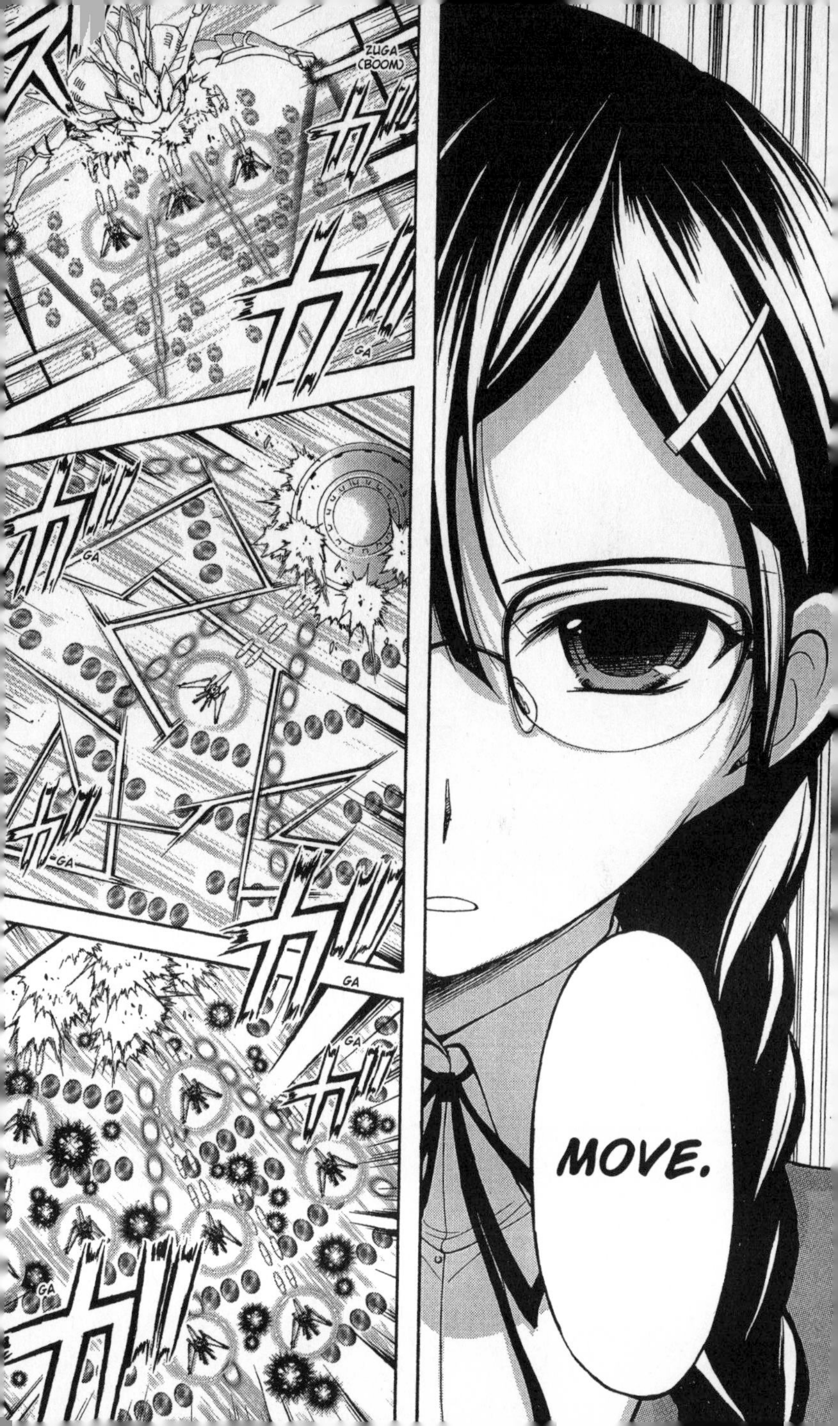
MOVE.
ZUGA
(BOOM)
GA
GA
GA
GA
GA
GA

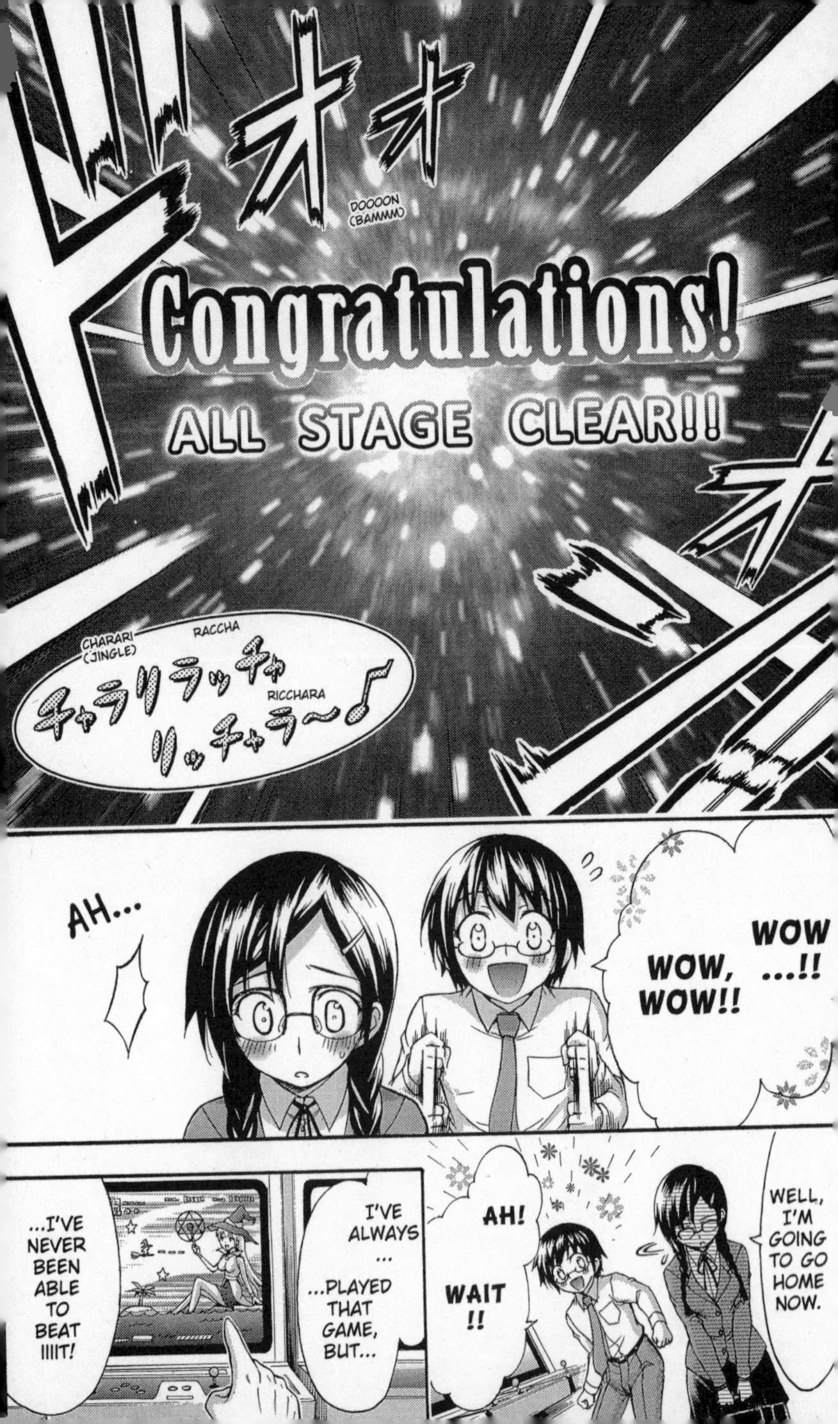
DOOOON (BAMMM)
Congratulations!
ALL STAGE CLEAR!!
CHARARI (JINGLE)
RACCHA
RICCHARA
チャラリラッチャ
リッチャラ〜♪
WOW ...!!
WOW, WOW!!
AH...
WELL, I'M GOING TO GO HOME NOW.
AH!
WAIT!!
I'VE ALWAYS ...
...PLAYED THAT GAME, BUT...
...I'VE NEVER BEEN ABLE TO BEAT IIIIT!

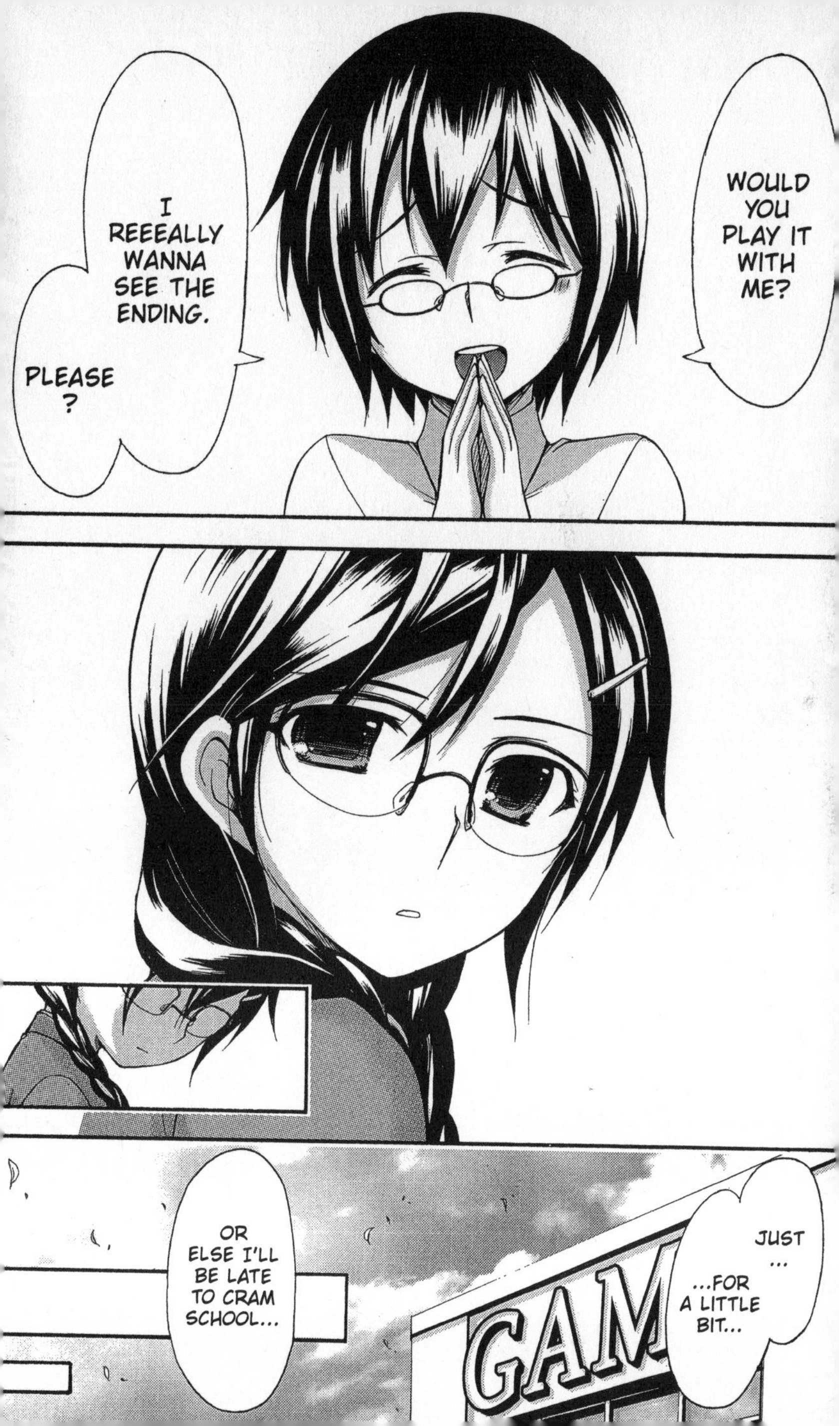
WOULD YOU PLAY IT WITH ME?
I REEEALLY WANNA SEE THE ENDING.
PLEASE?
JUST...
...FOR A LITTLE BIT...
OR ELSE I'LL BE LATE TO CRAM SCHOOL...
GAM

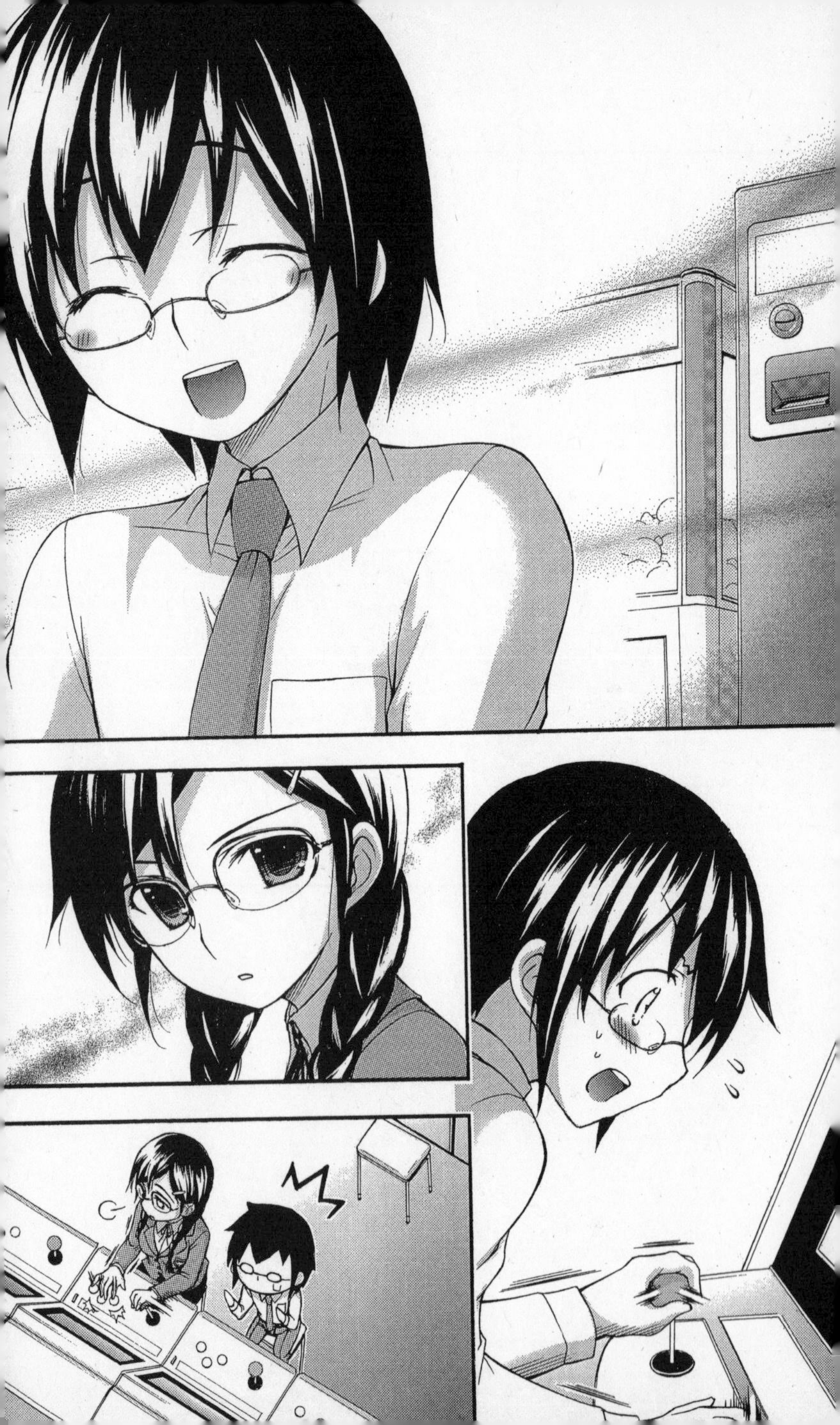

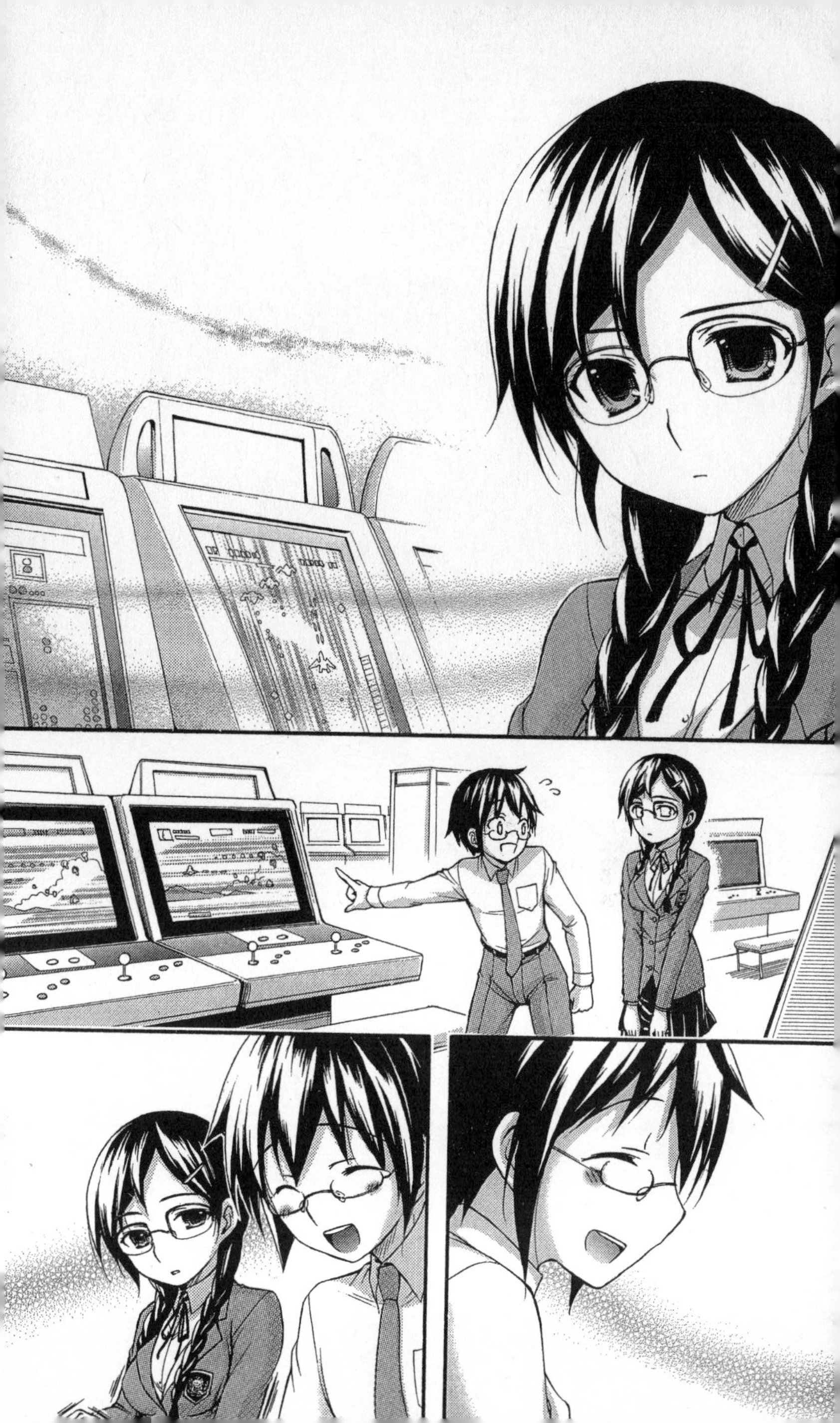

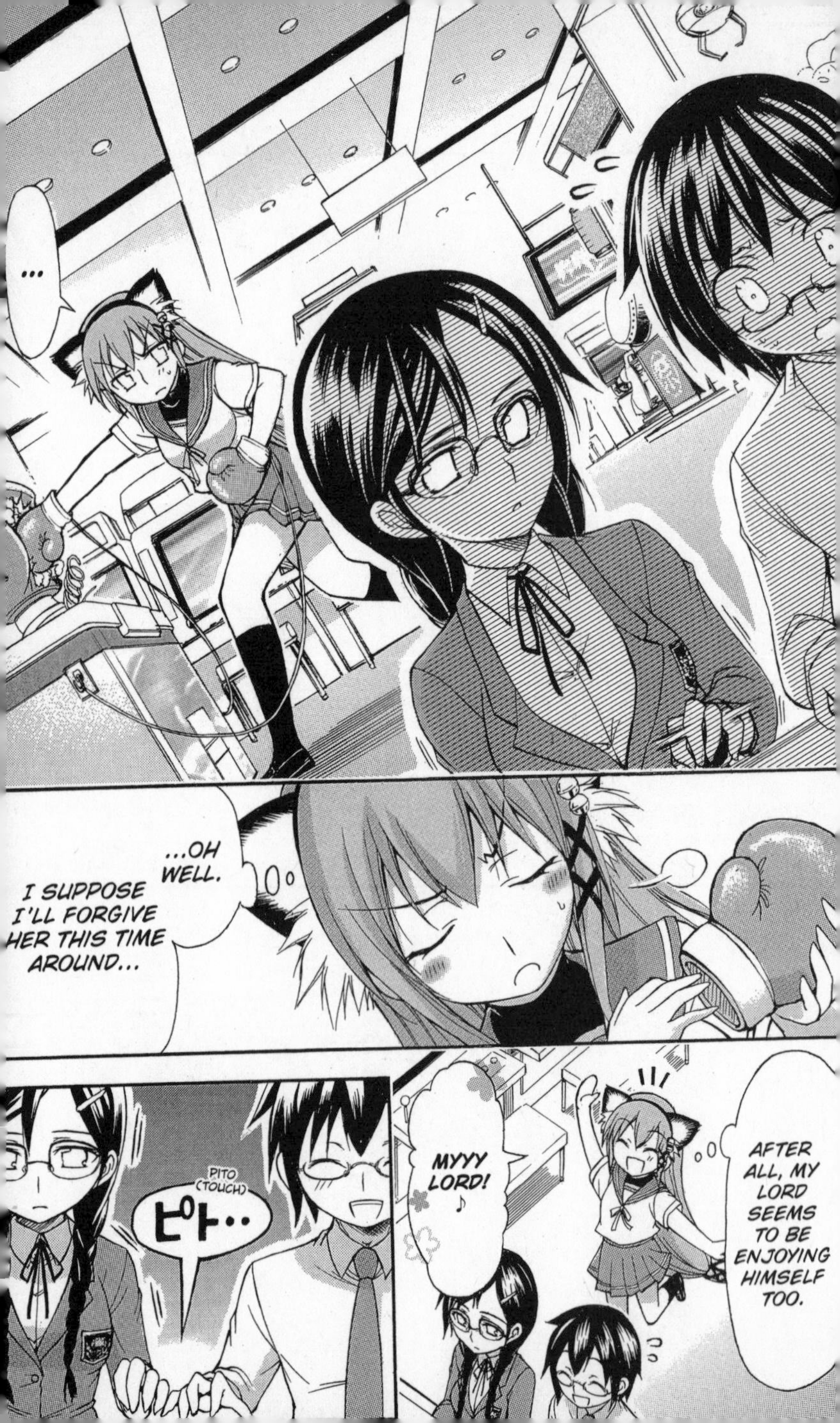
...
...OH WELL.
I SUPPOSE I'LL FORGIVE HER THIS TIME AROUND...
AFTER ALL, MY LORD SEEMS TO BE ENJOYING HIMSELF TOO.
MYYY LORD! ♪
PITO (TOUCH)
ピト‥

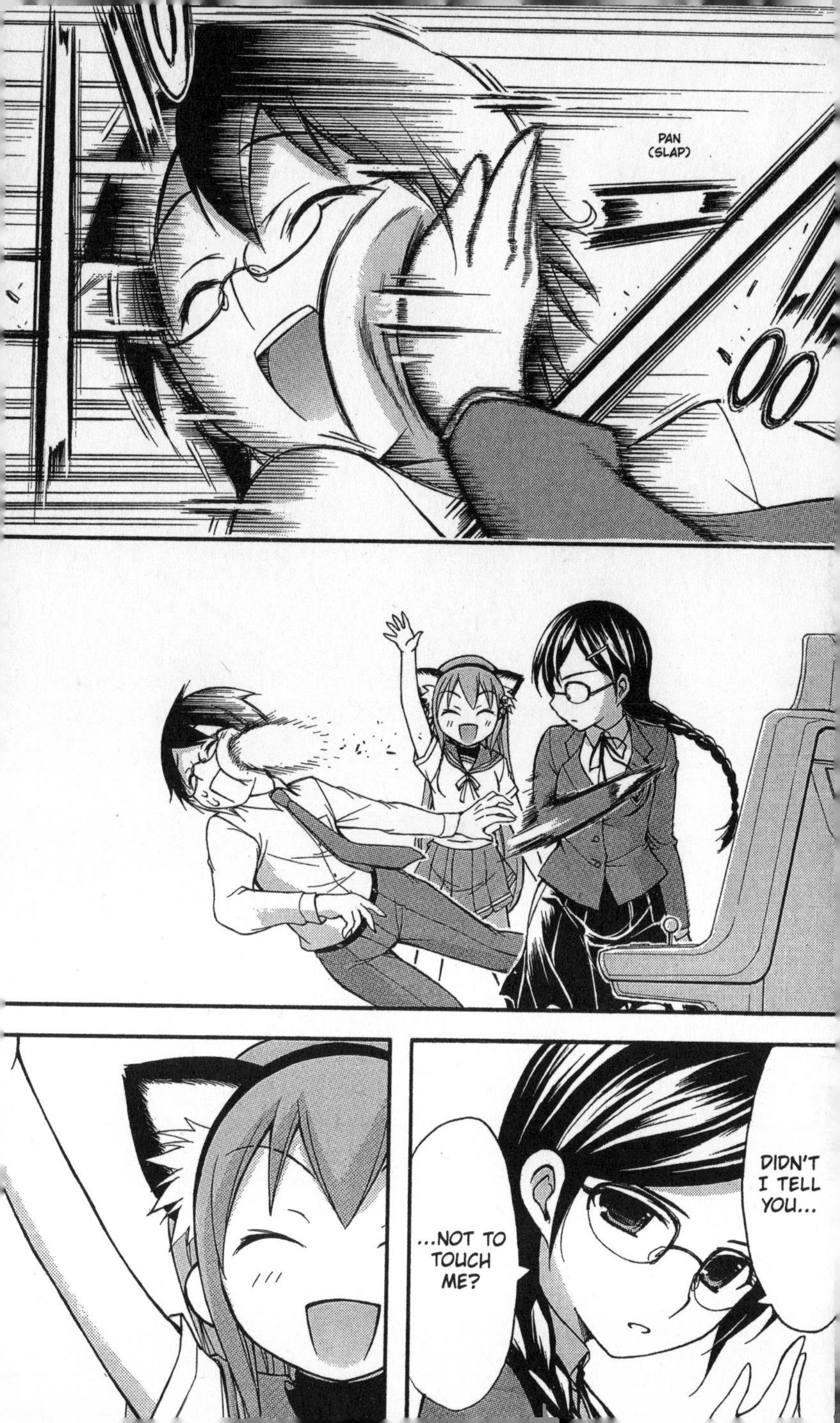
PAN
(SLAP)
DIDN'T I TELL YOU...
...NOT TO TOUCH ME?

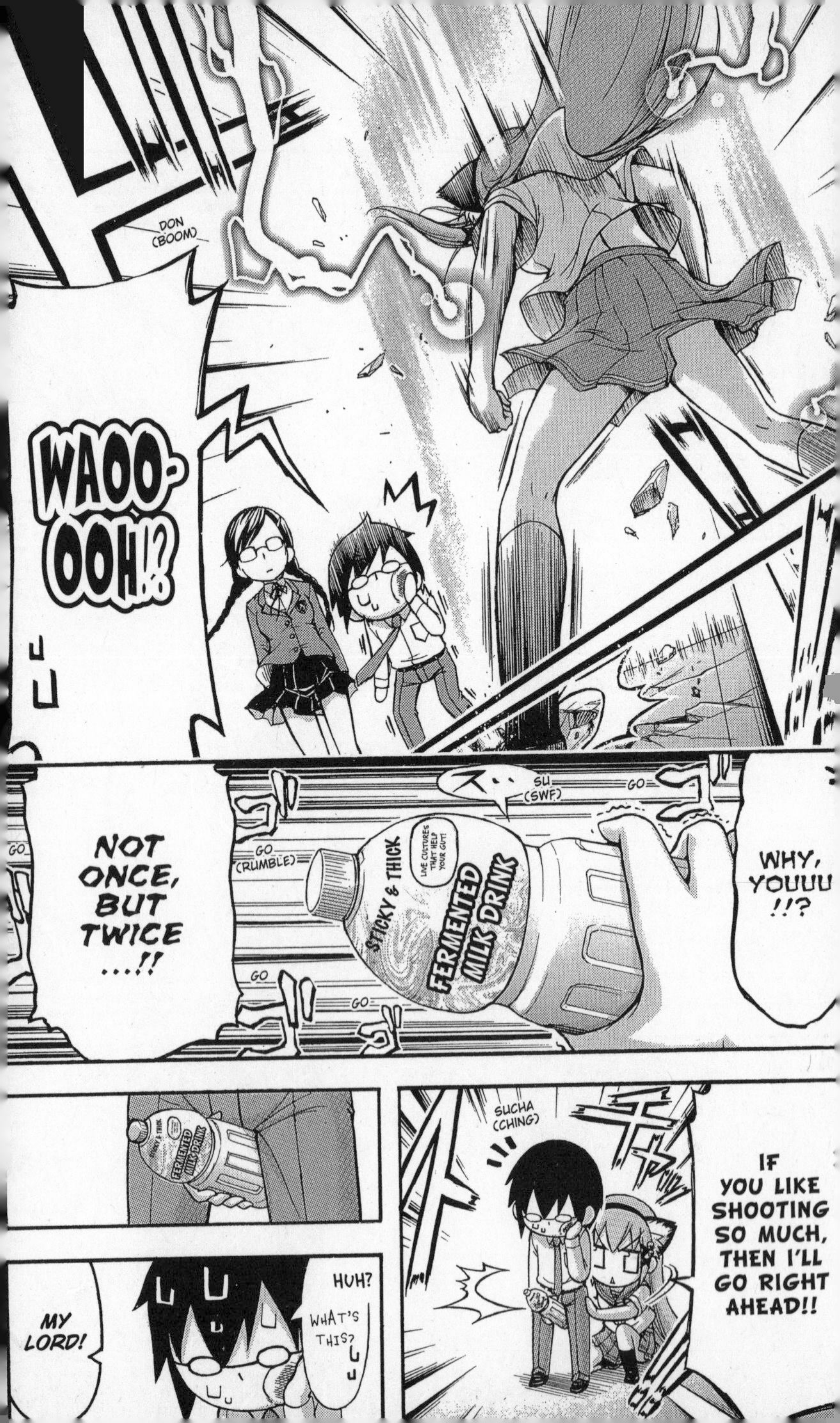
DON (BOOM)
WAOO-OOH!?
SU (SWF)
GO
WHY, YOUUU!!?
FERMENTED MILK DRINK
STICKY & THICK
LIVE CULTURES THAT HELP YOUR GUT!
GO (RUMBLE)
GO
GO
NOT ONCE, BUT TWICE...!!
SUCHA (CHING)
IF YOU LIKE SHOOTING SO MUCH, THEN I'LL GO RIGHT AHEAD!!
FERMENTED MILK DRINK
STICKY & THICK
HUH?
WHAT'S THIS?
MY LORD!

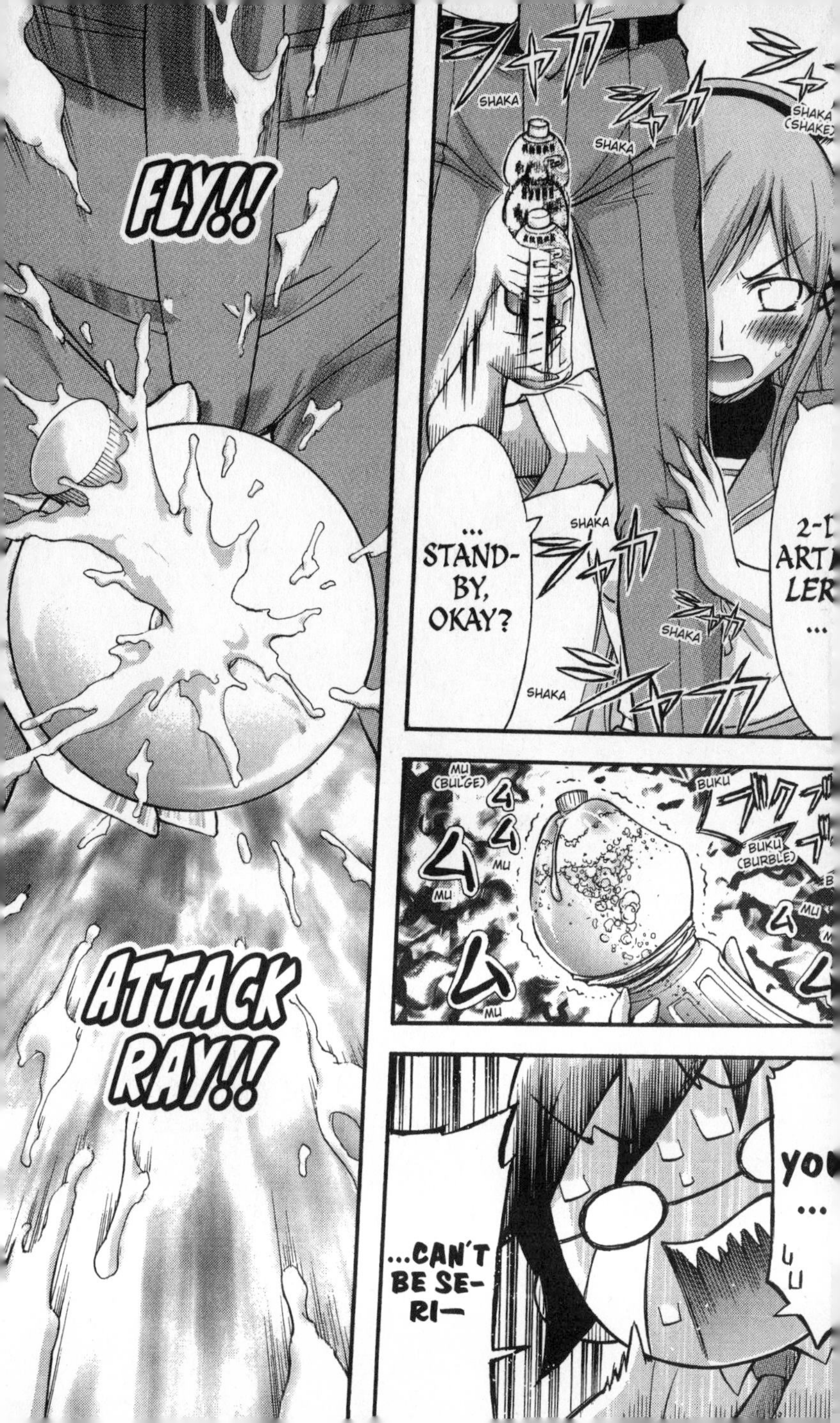
SHAKA (SHAKE)
SHAKA
SHAKA
2-D ARTI LER …
… STAND-BY, OKAY?
SHAKA
SHAKA
SHAKA
BUKU
BUKU (BURBLE)
MU
MU (BULGE)
MU
MU
MU
YOU …
UU
…CAN'T BE SE-RI—
FLY!!
ATTACK RAY!!

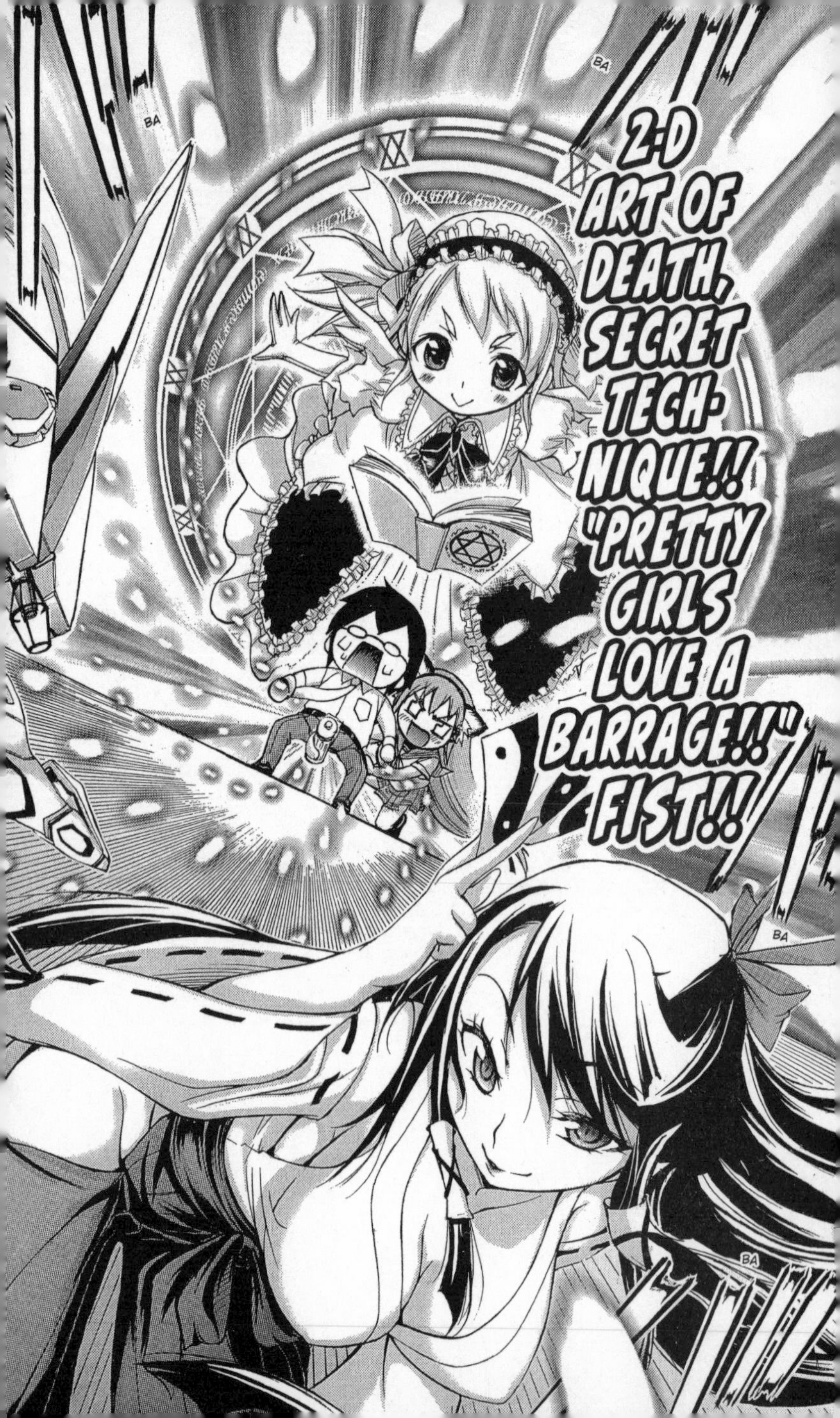
2-D ART OF DEATH, SECRET TECH-NIQUE!! "PRETTY GIRLS LOVE A BARRAGE!!" FIST!!
BA
BA
BA
BA

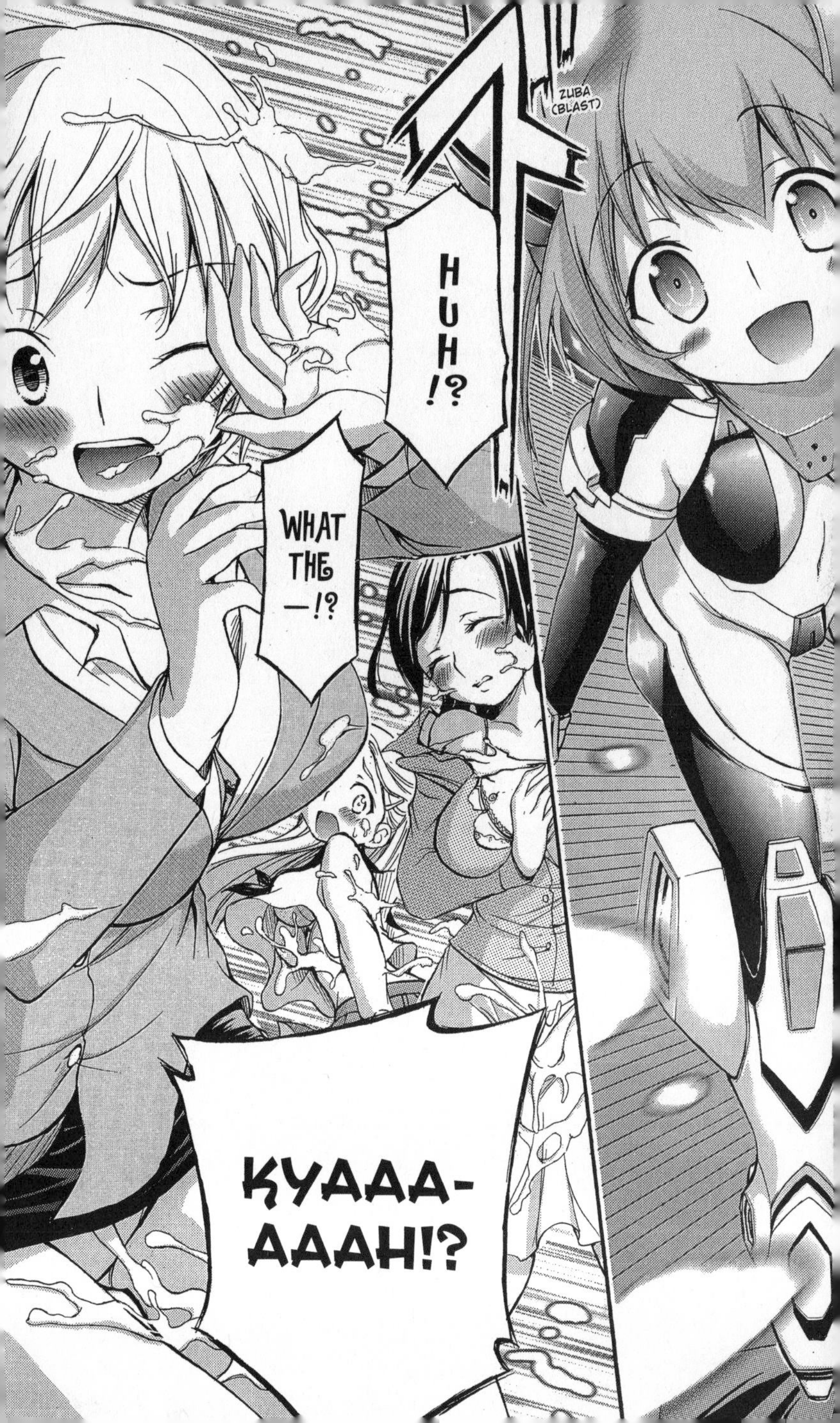
ZUBA (BLAST)
HUH!?
WHAT THE—!?
KYAAA-AAAH!?

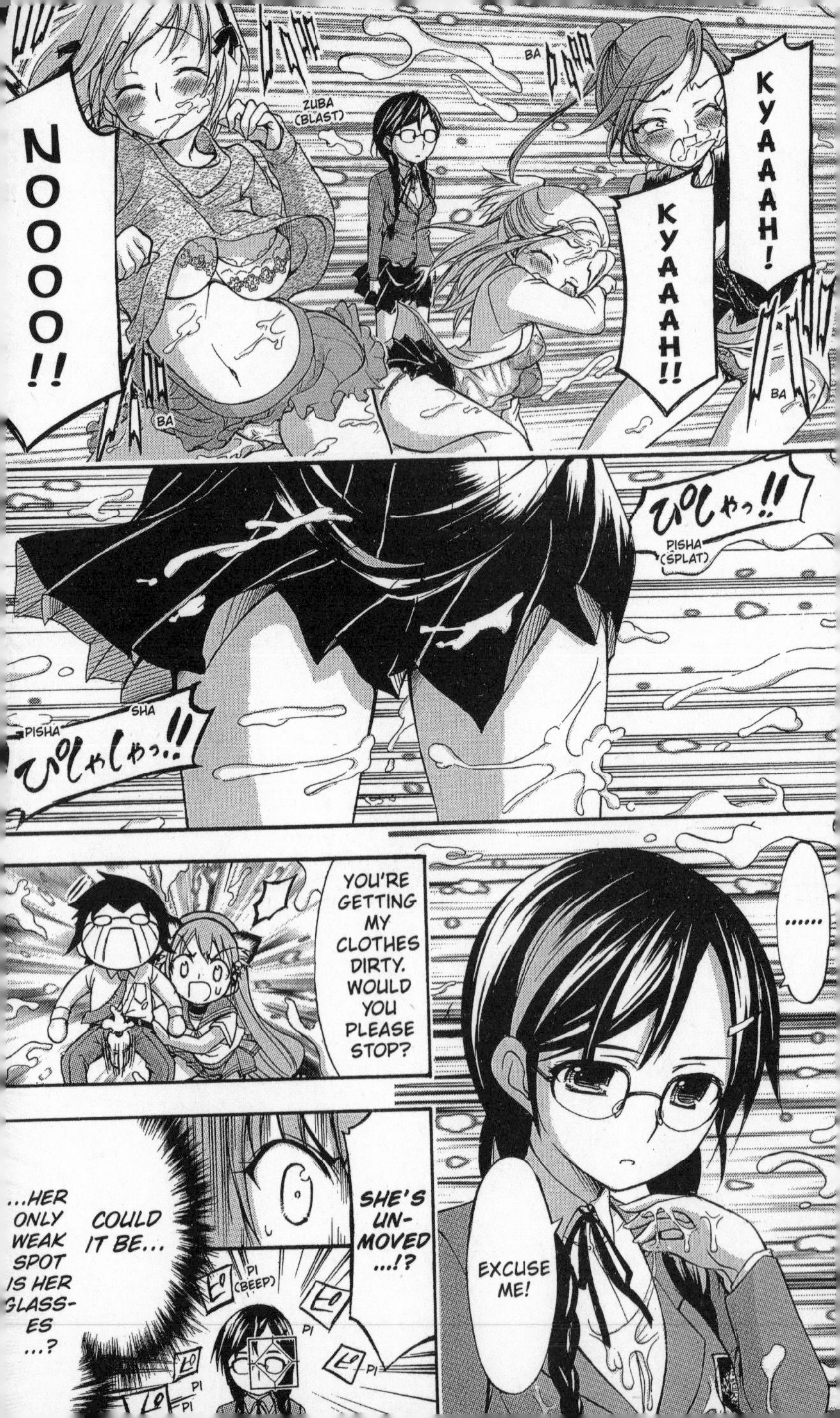
KYAAAH!
KYAAAH!!
BA
BA
ZUBA (BLAST)
NOOOOO!!
BA
ぴしゃっ!!
PISHA (SPLAT)
SHA
PISHA
ぴしゃしゃっ!!
......
EXCUSE ME!
YOU'RE GETTING MY CLOTHES DIRTY. WOULD YOU PLEASE STOP?
SHE'S UN-MOVED...!?
COULD IT BE...
...HER ONLY WEAK SPOT IS HER GLASS-ES...?
PI (BEEP)
PI
PI
PI
PI

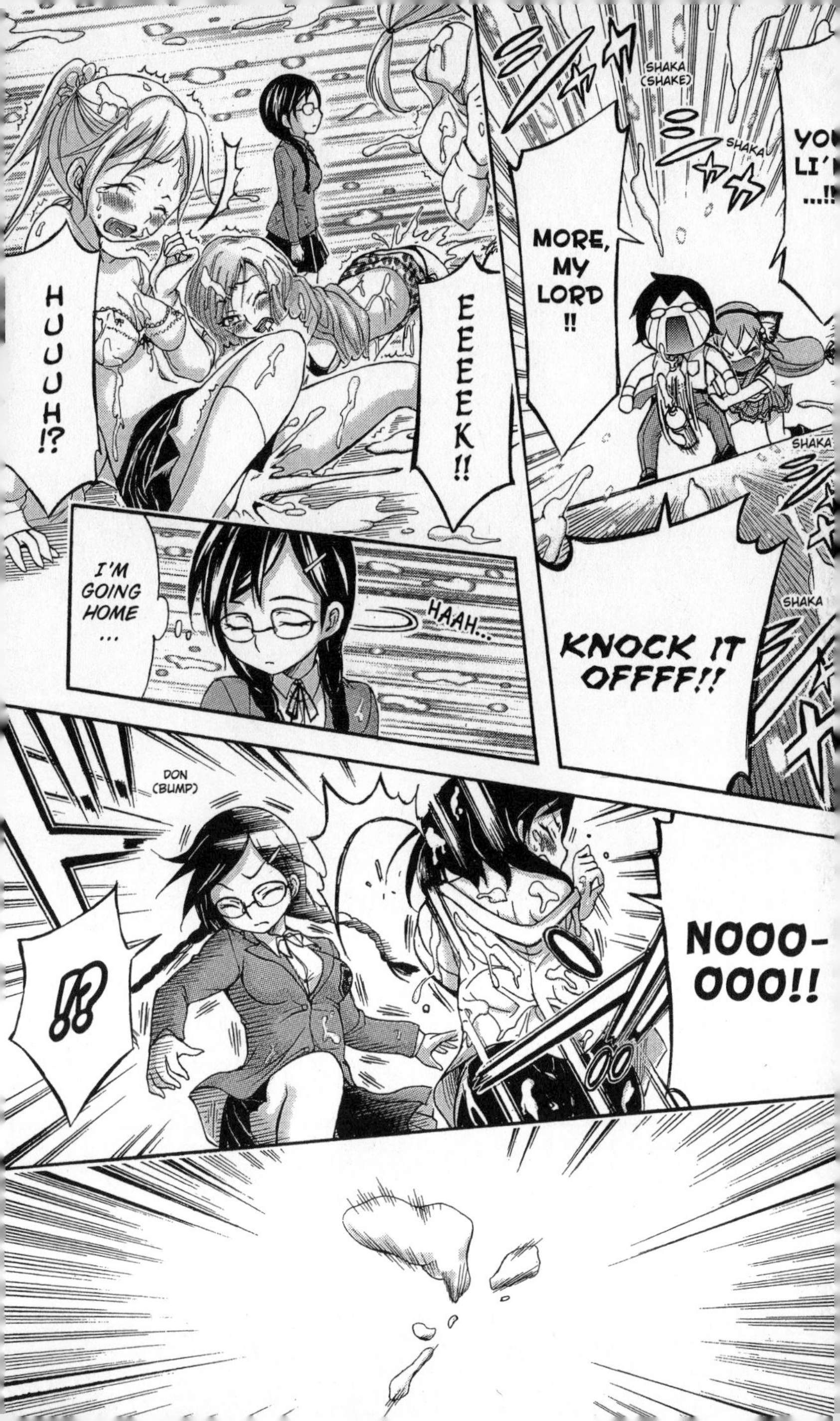
SHAKA (SHAKE)
SHAKA
MORE, MY LORD!!
SHAKA
SHAKA
KNOCK IT OFFFF!!
EEEEEK!!
HUUUH!?
I'M GOING HOME...
HAAH...
DON (BUMP)
NOOO-OOO!!
!!?

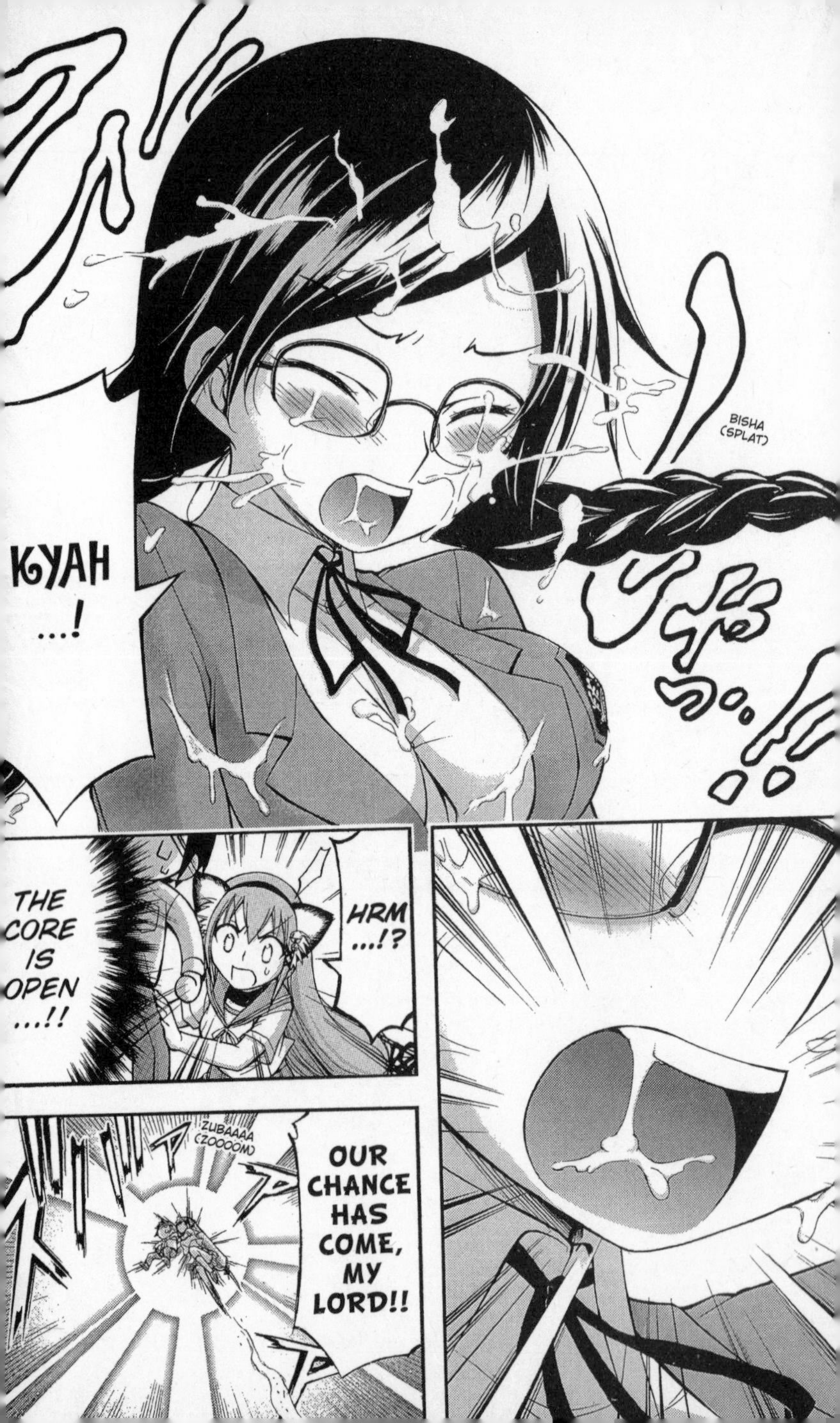
BISHA (SPLAT)
KYAH ...!
HRM ...!?
THE CORE IS OPEN ...!!
OUR CHANCE HAS COME, MY LORD!!
ZUBAAAA (ZOOOOM)

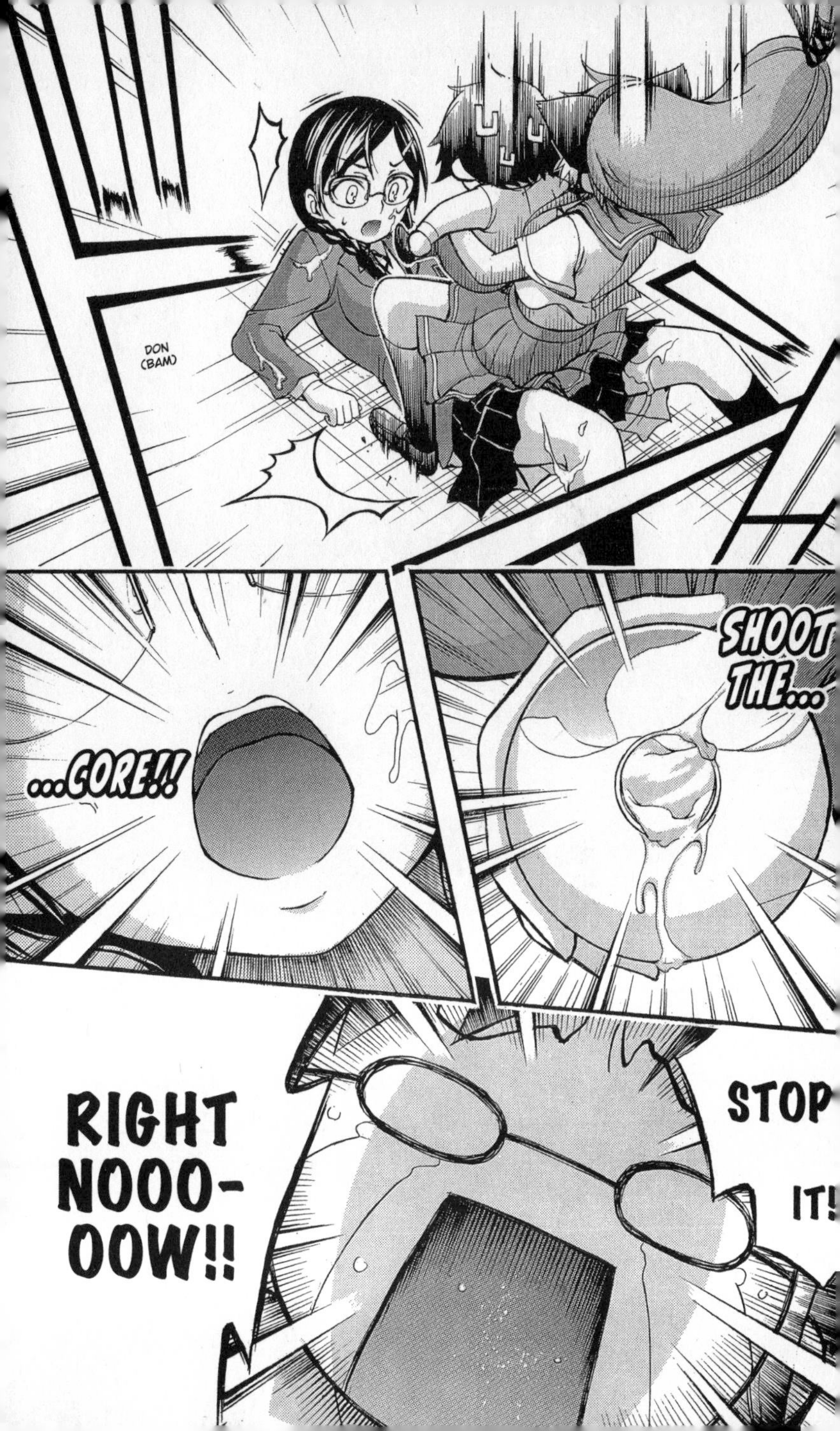
DON
(BAM)
SHOOT THE...
...CORE!!
STOP IT!
RIGHT NOOOO-OOW!!

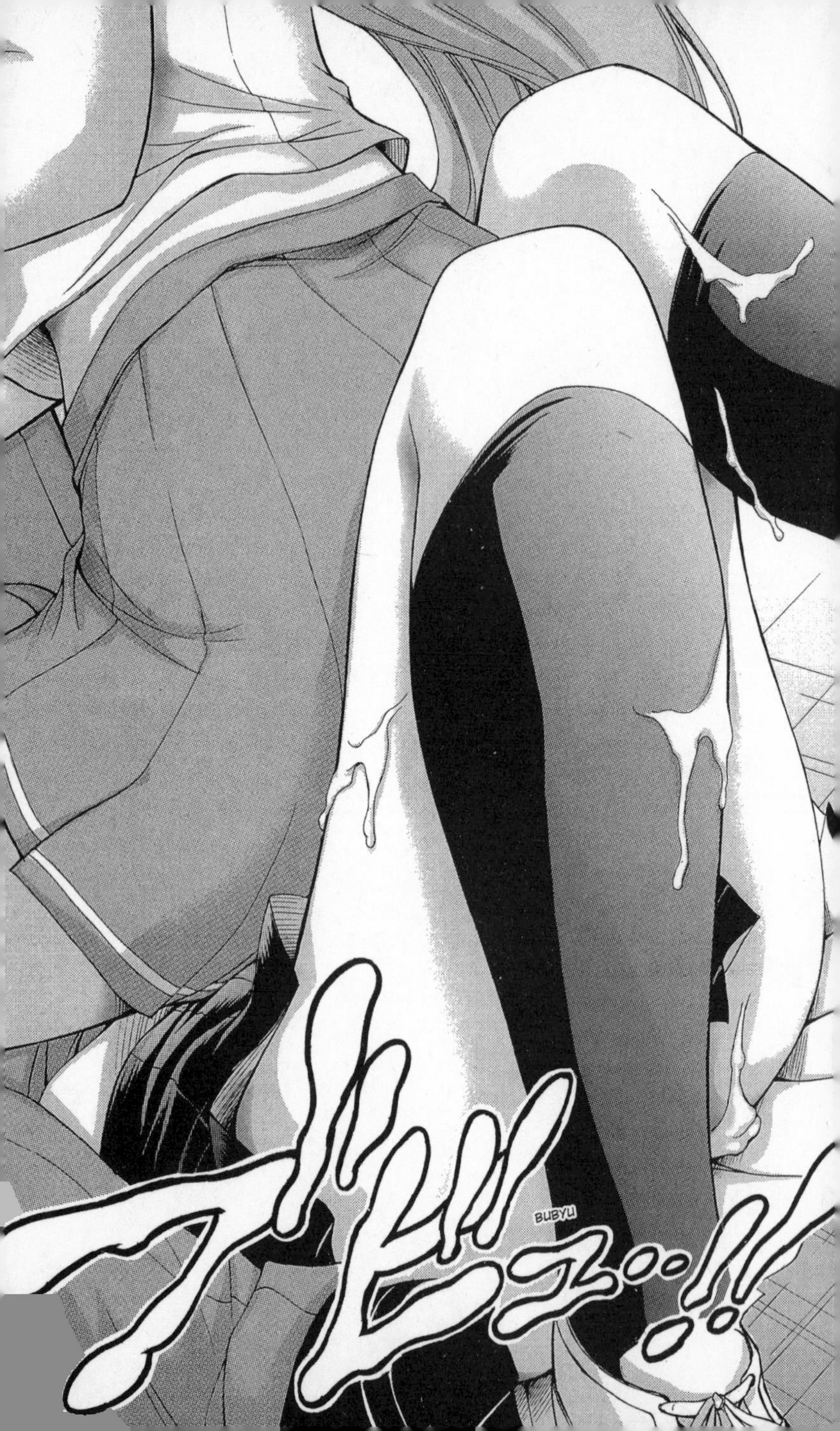
BUBYU

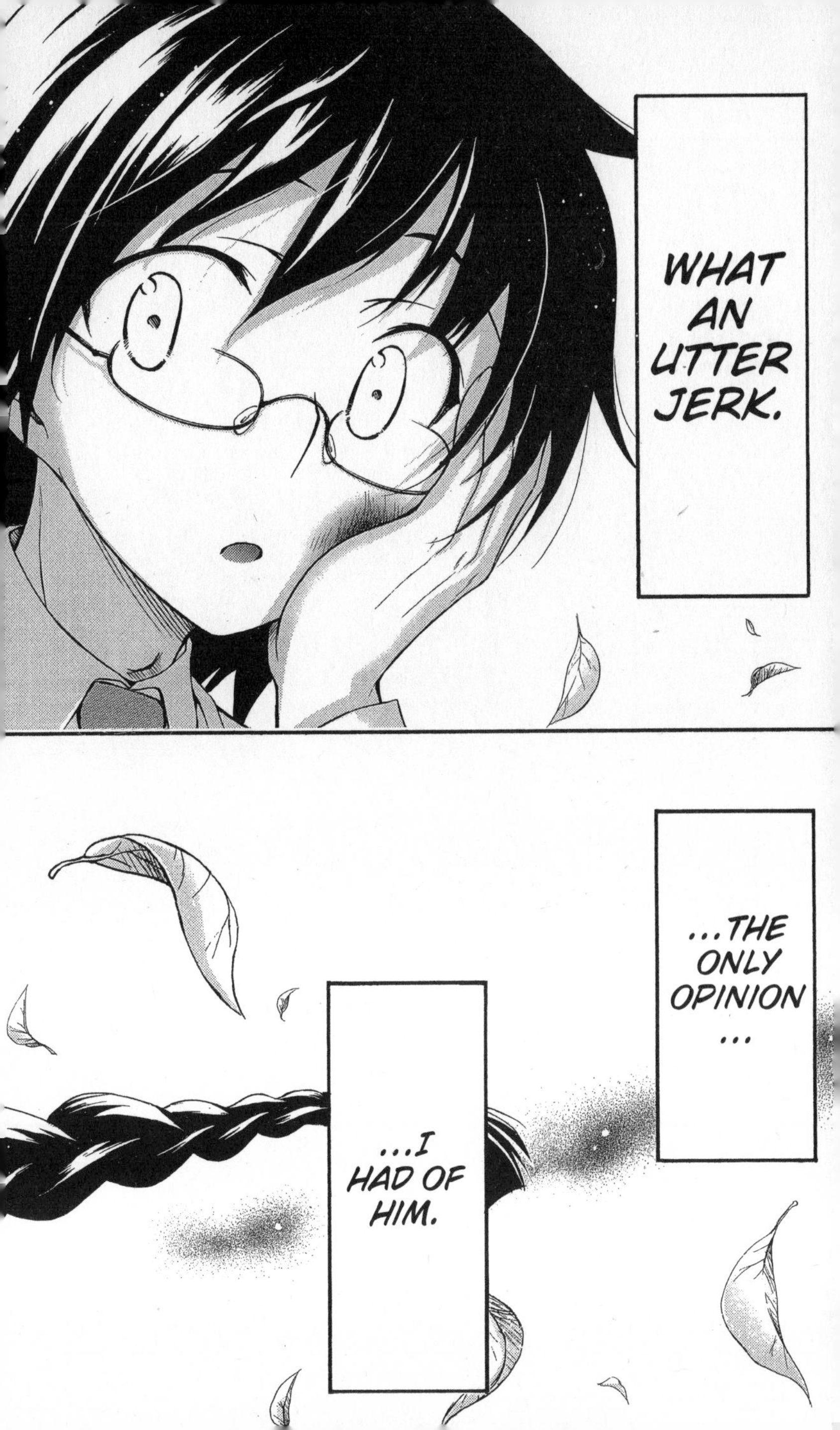
WHAT AN UTTER JERK.
...THE ONLY OPINION ...
...I HAD OF HIM.

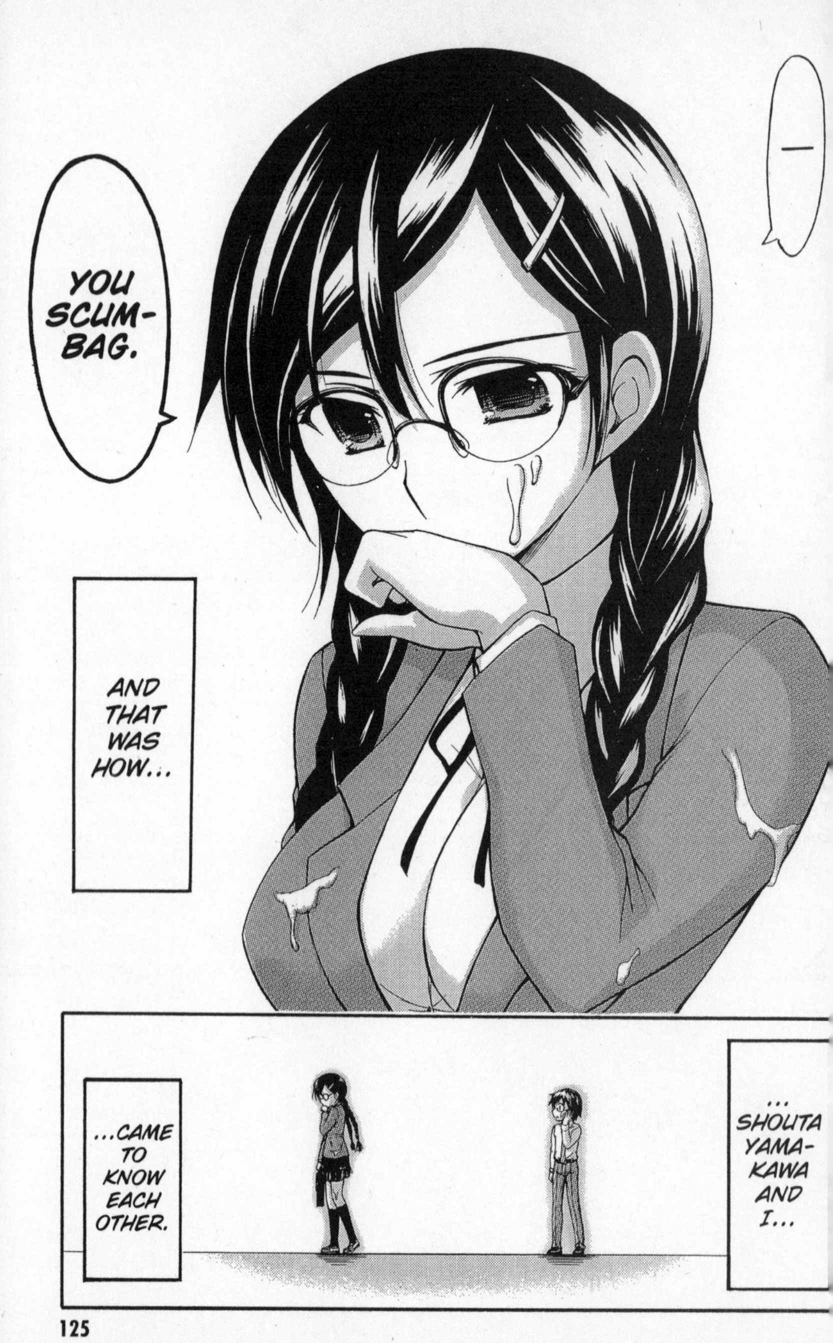
—
YOU SCUM-BAG.
AND THAT WAS HOW...
...SHOUTA YAMA-KAWA AND I...
...CAME TO KNOW EACH OTHER.

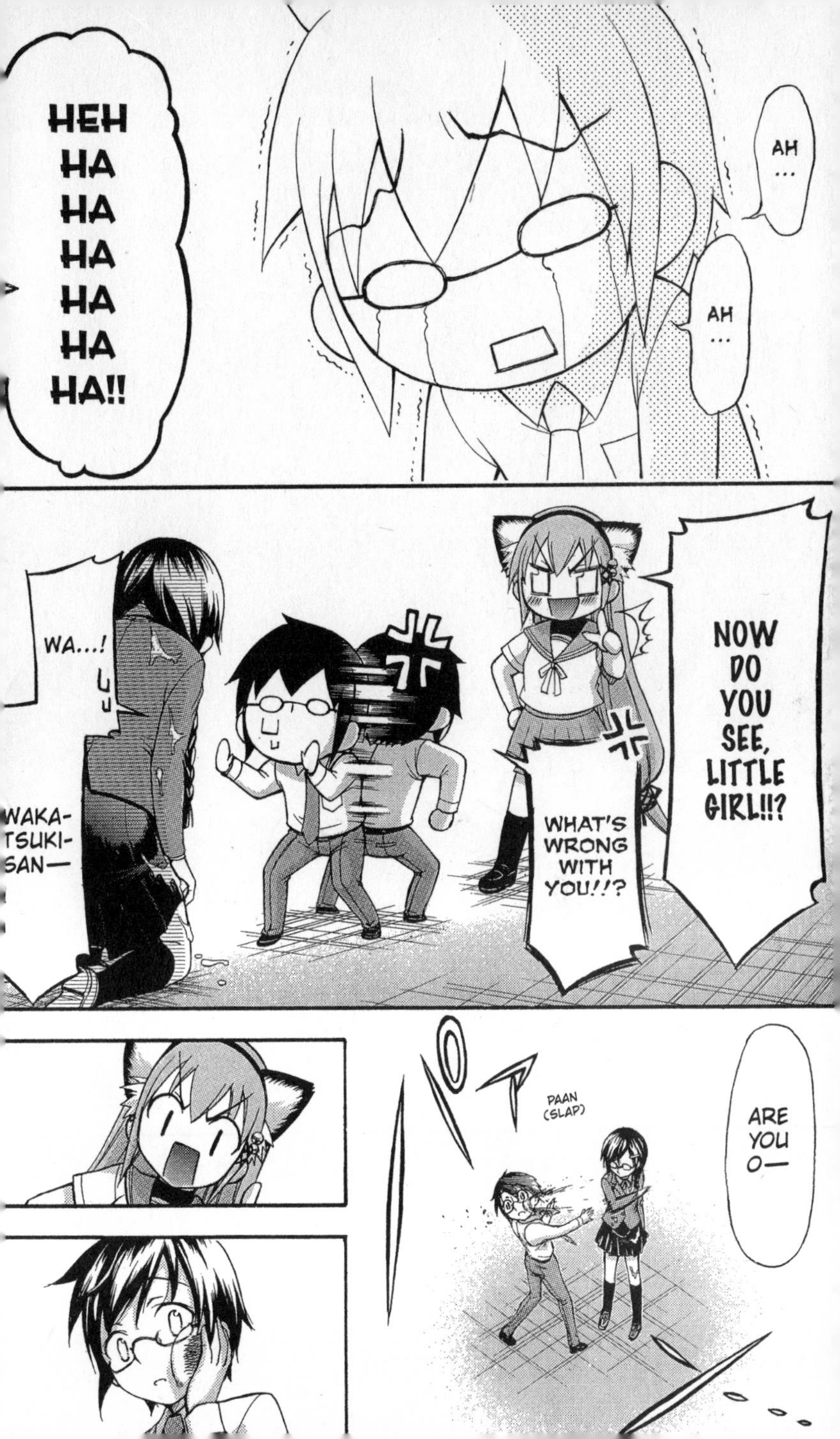

AH ...
AH ...
HEH HA HA HA HA HA HA!!
NOW DO YOU SEE, LITTLE GIRL!!?
WHAT'S WRONG WITH YOU!!?
WA...!
WAKA-TSUKI-SAN—
ARE YOU O—
PAAN (SLAP)

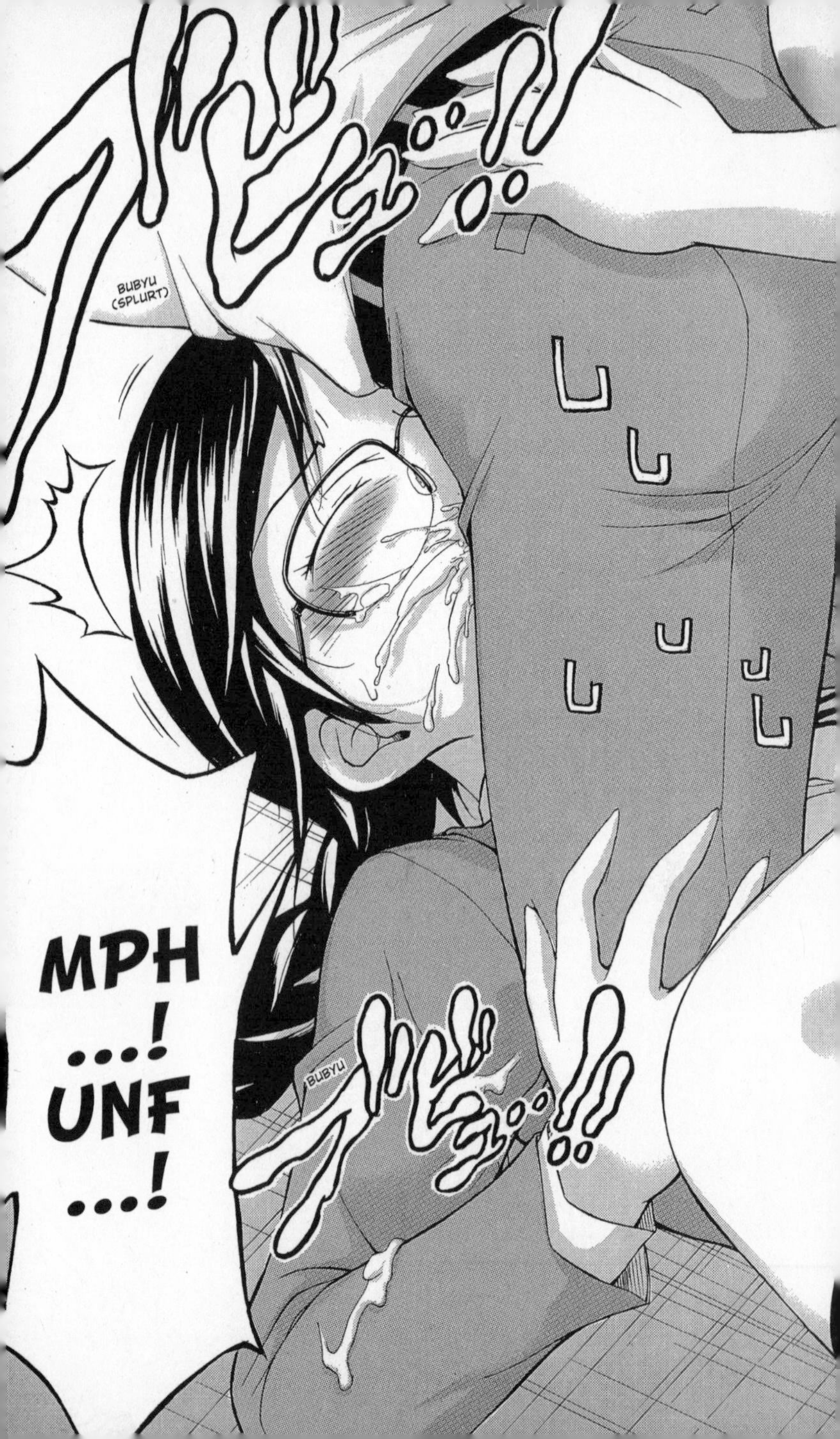
BUBYU
(SPLURT)
BUBYU
MPH
...!
UNF
...!

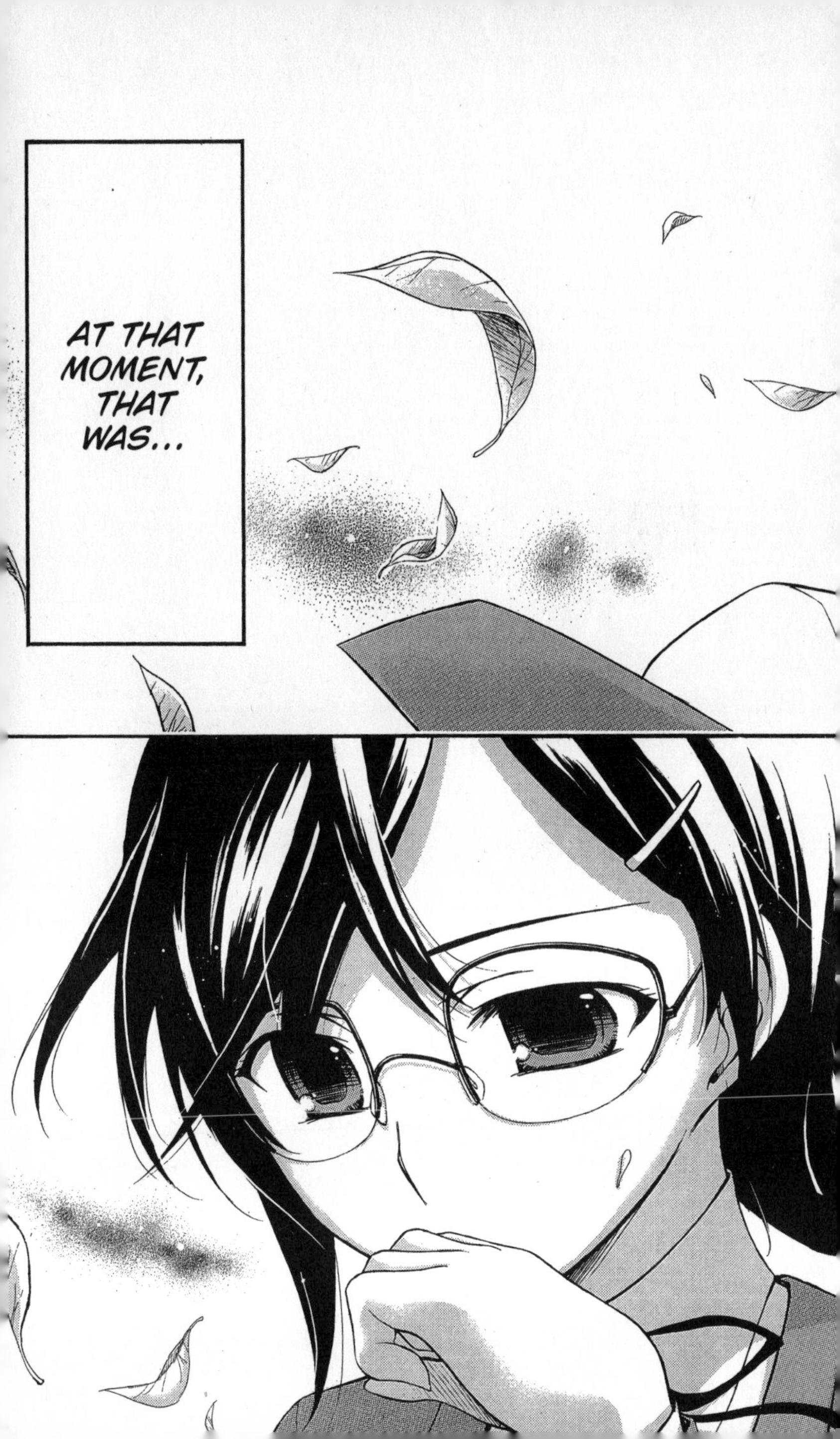
AT THAT MOMENT, THAT WAS...

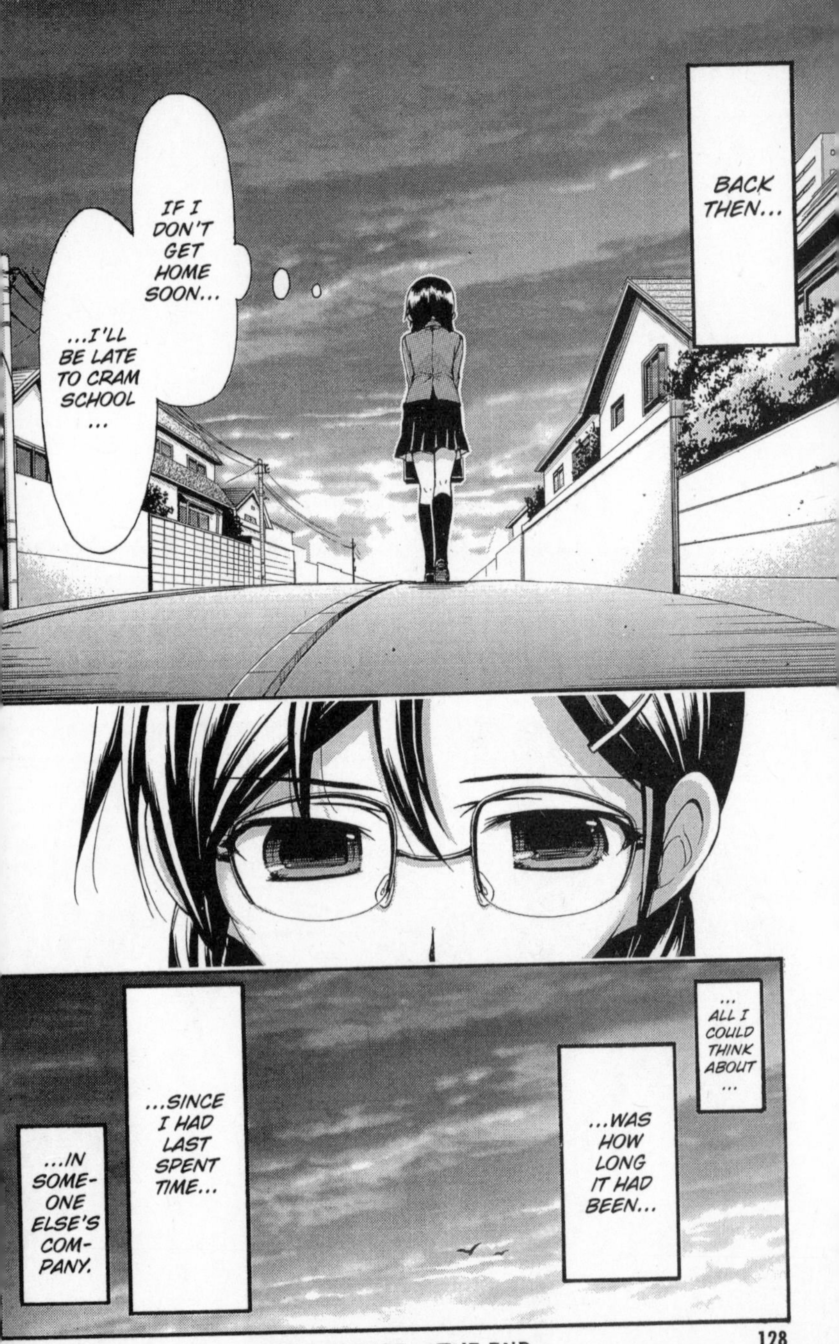
BACK THEN...
IF I DON'T GET HOME SOON...
...I'LL BE LATE TO CRAM SCHOOL...
...ALL I COULD THINK ABOUT...
...WAS HOW LONG IT HAD BEEN...
...SINCE I HAD LAST SPENT TIME...
...IN SOME-ONE ELSE'S COM-PANY.

16TH OFFENSE • THE END

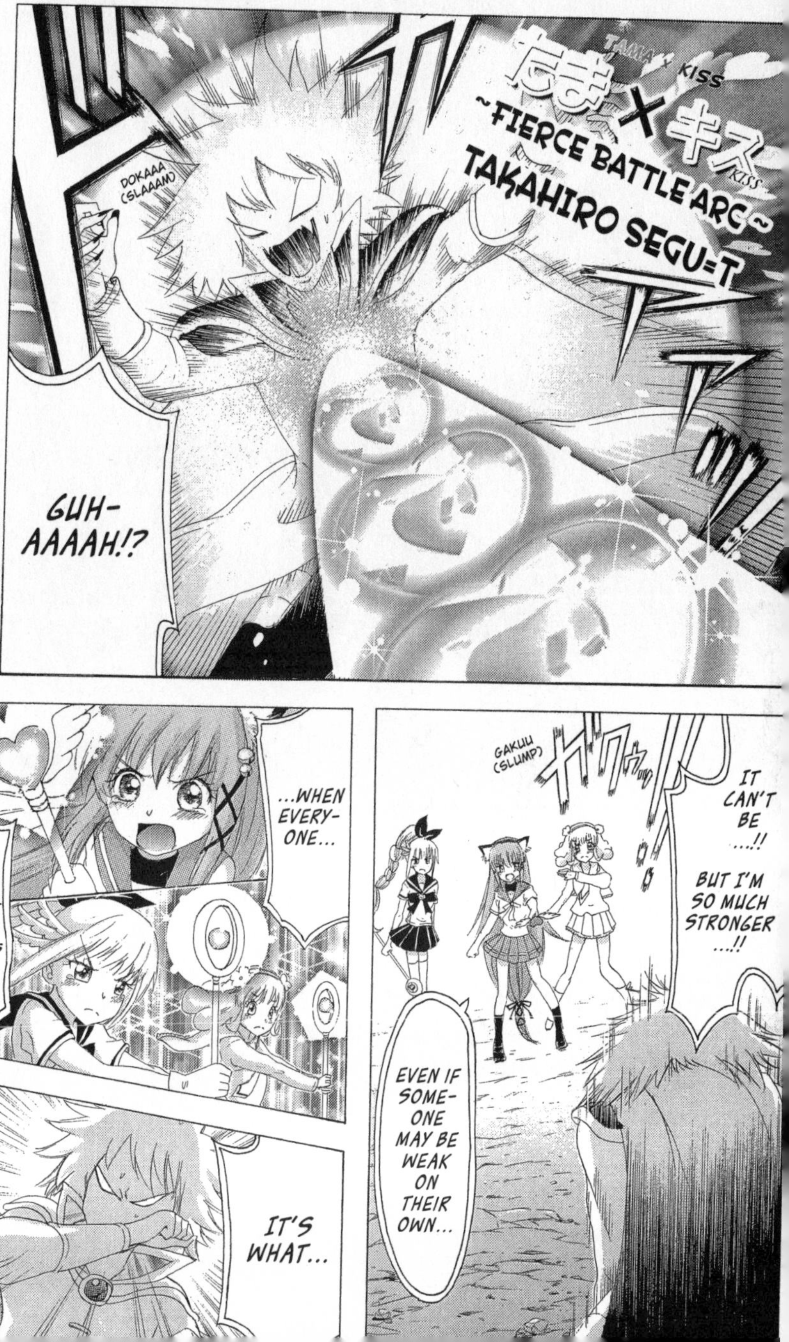
たま×キス
TAMA x KISS
~FIERCE BATTLE ARC~
TAKAHIRO SEGU=T
DOKAAA (SLAAAM)
GUH-AAAAH!?
GAKUU (SLUMP)
IT CAN'T BE ...!!
BUT I'M SO MUCH STRONGER ...!!
EVEN IF SOME-ONE MAY BE WEAK ON THEIR OWN...
...WHEN EVERY-ONE...
...COM-BINES THEIR POWERS ...!!
IT'S WHAT...

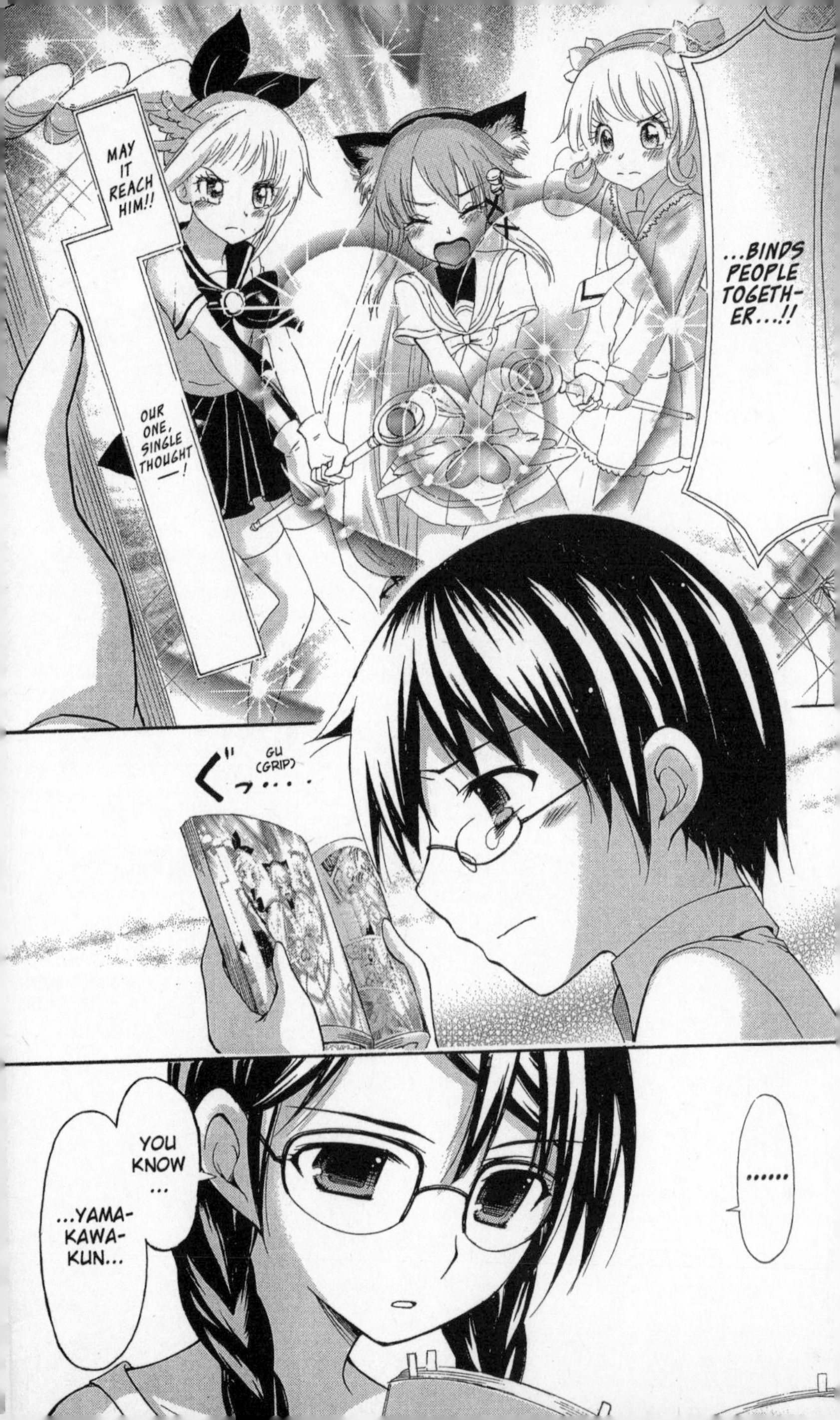

...BINDS PEOPLE TOGETH-ER...!!
MAY IT REACH HIM!!
OUR ONE, SINGLE THOUGHT—!
ぐっ....
GU (GRIP)
......
YOU KNOW ...
...YAMA-KAWA-KUN...

SIGNS: RECEPTION / SHOE RENTAL

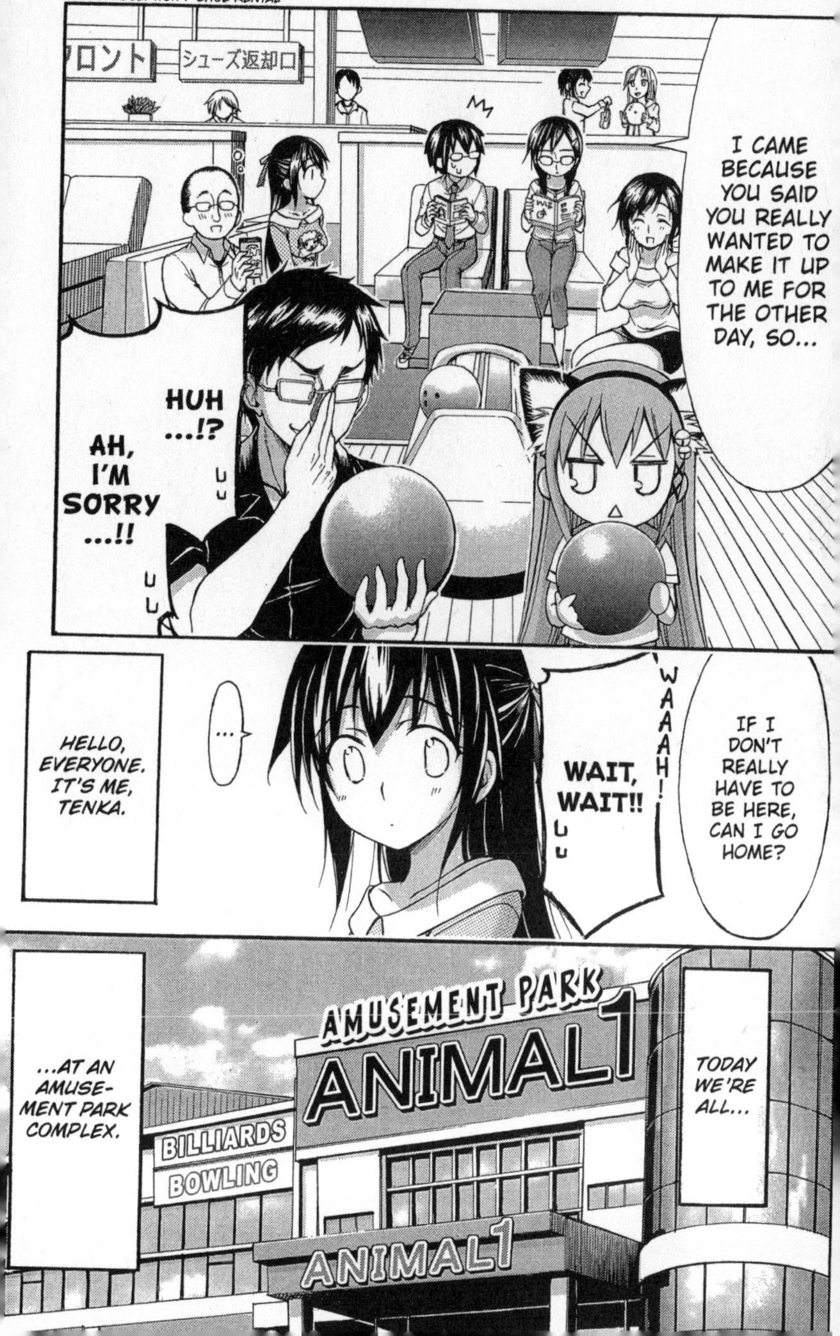
フロント
シューズ返却口
I CAME BECAUSE YOU SAID YOU REALLY WANTED TO MAKE IT UP TO ME FOR THE OTHER DAY, SO...
HUH ...!?
AH, I'M SORRY ...!!
IF I DON'T REALLY HAVE TO BE HERE, CAN I GO HOME?
WAAAAH!
WAIT, WAIT!!
...
HELLO, EVERYONE. IT'S ME, TENKA.
TODAY WE'RE ALL...
AMUSEMENT PARK
ANIMAL1
BILLIARDS
BOWLING
ANIMAL1
...AT AN AMUSE-MENT PARK COMPLEX.

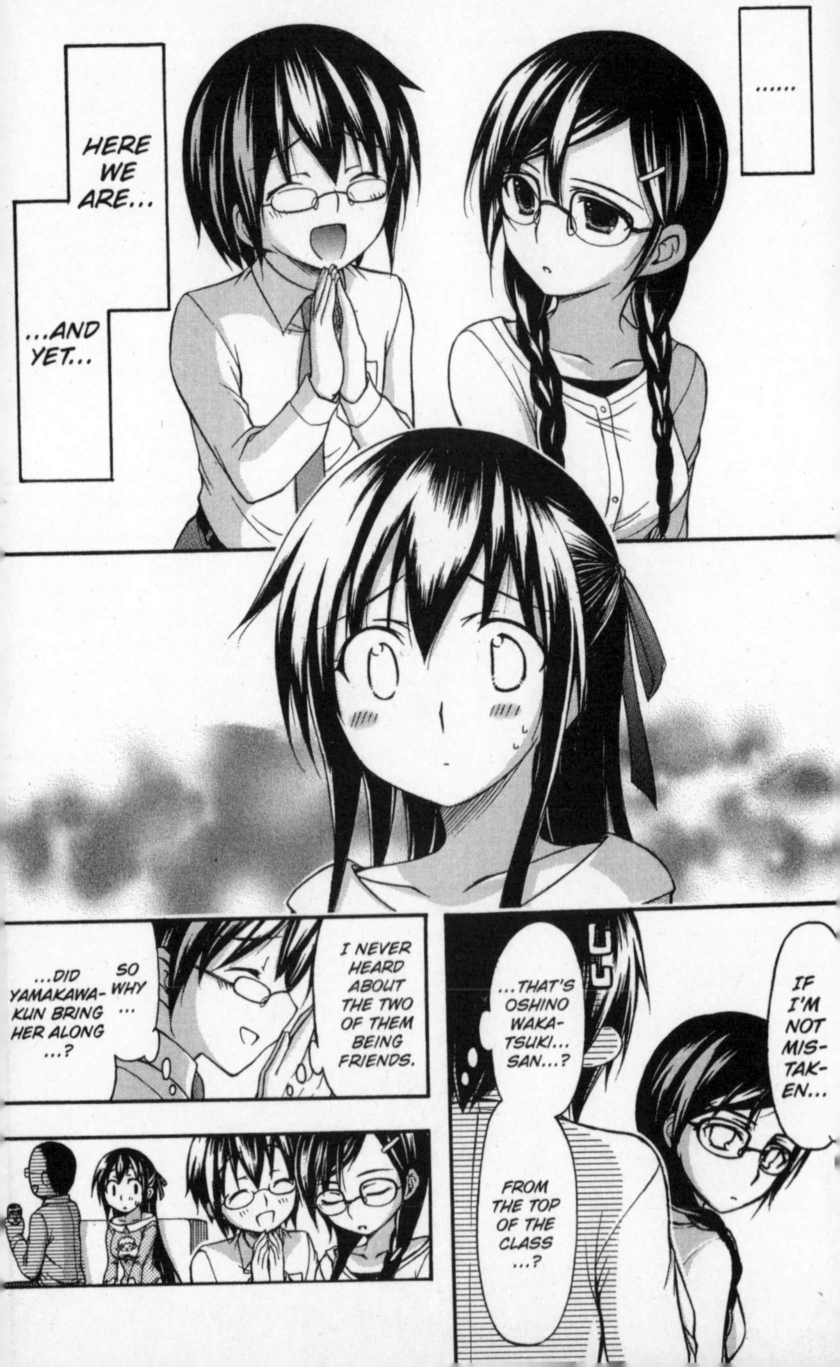
......
HERE WE ARE...
...AND YET...
I NEVER HEARD ABOUT THE TWO OF THEM BEING FRIENDS.
SO WHY ...
...DID YAMAKAWA-KUN BRING HER ALONG ...?
IF I'M NOT MIS-TAK-EN...
...THAT'S OSHINO WAKA-TSUKI... SAN...?
FROM THE TOP OF THE CLASS ...?

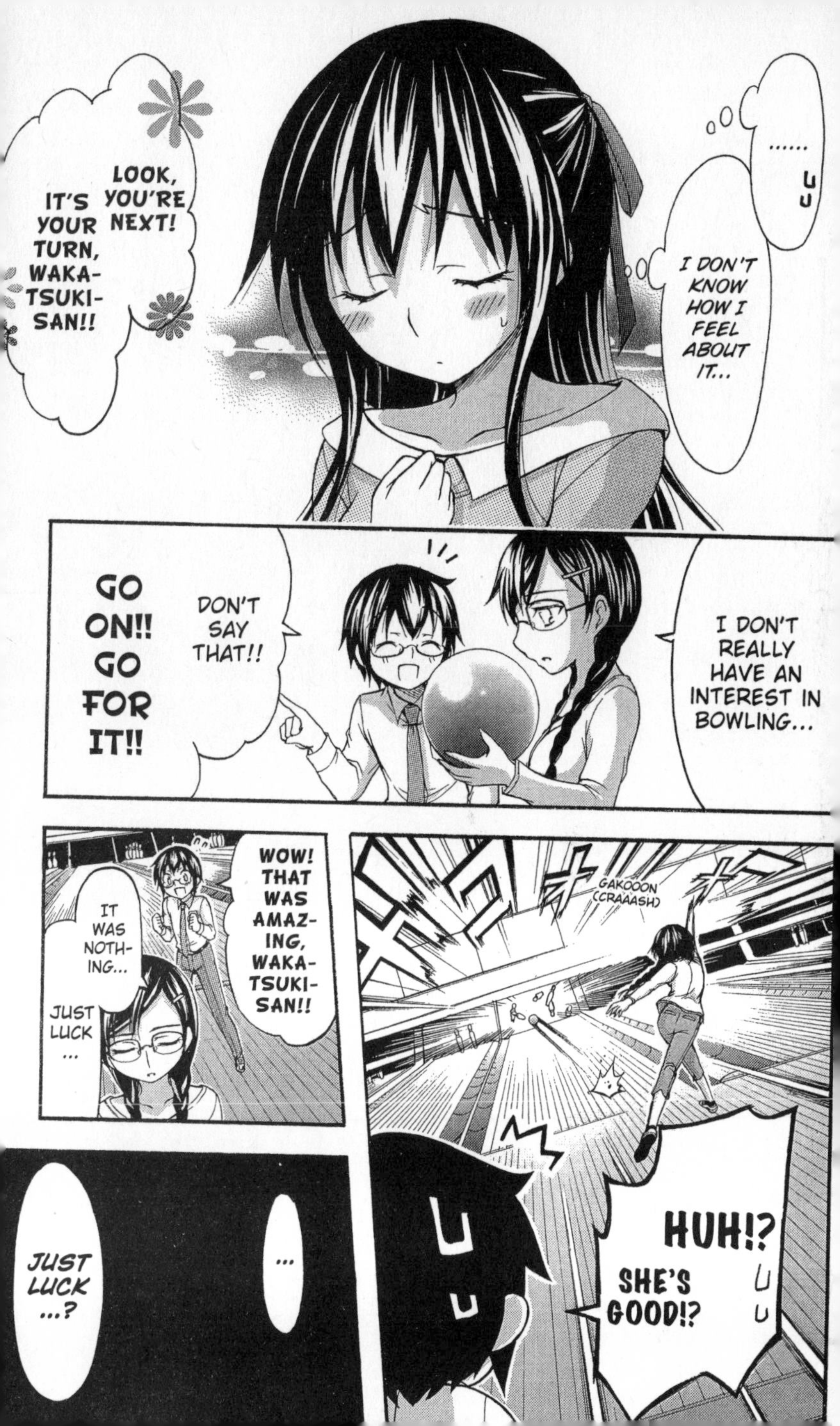
......
uu
I DON'T KNOW HOW I FEEL ABOUT IT...
LOOK, YOU'RE NEXT!
IT'S YOUR TURN, WAKA-TSUKI-SAN!!
I DON'T REALLY HAVE AN INTEREST IN BOWLING...
DON'T SAY THAT!!
GO ON!! GO FOR IT!!
GAKOOON (CRAAASH)
HUH!?
SHE'S GOOD!?
uu
WOW! THAT WAS AMAZ-ING, WAKA-TSUKI-SAN!!
IT WAS NOTH-ING...
JUST LUCK ...
...
JUST LUCK ...?

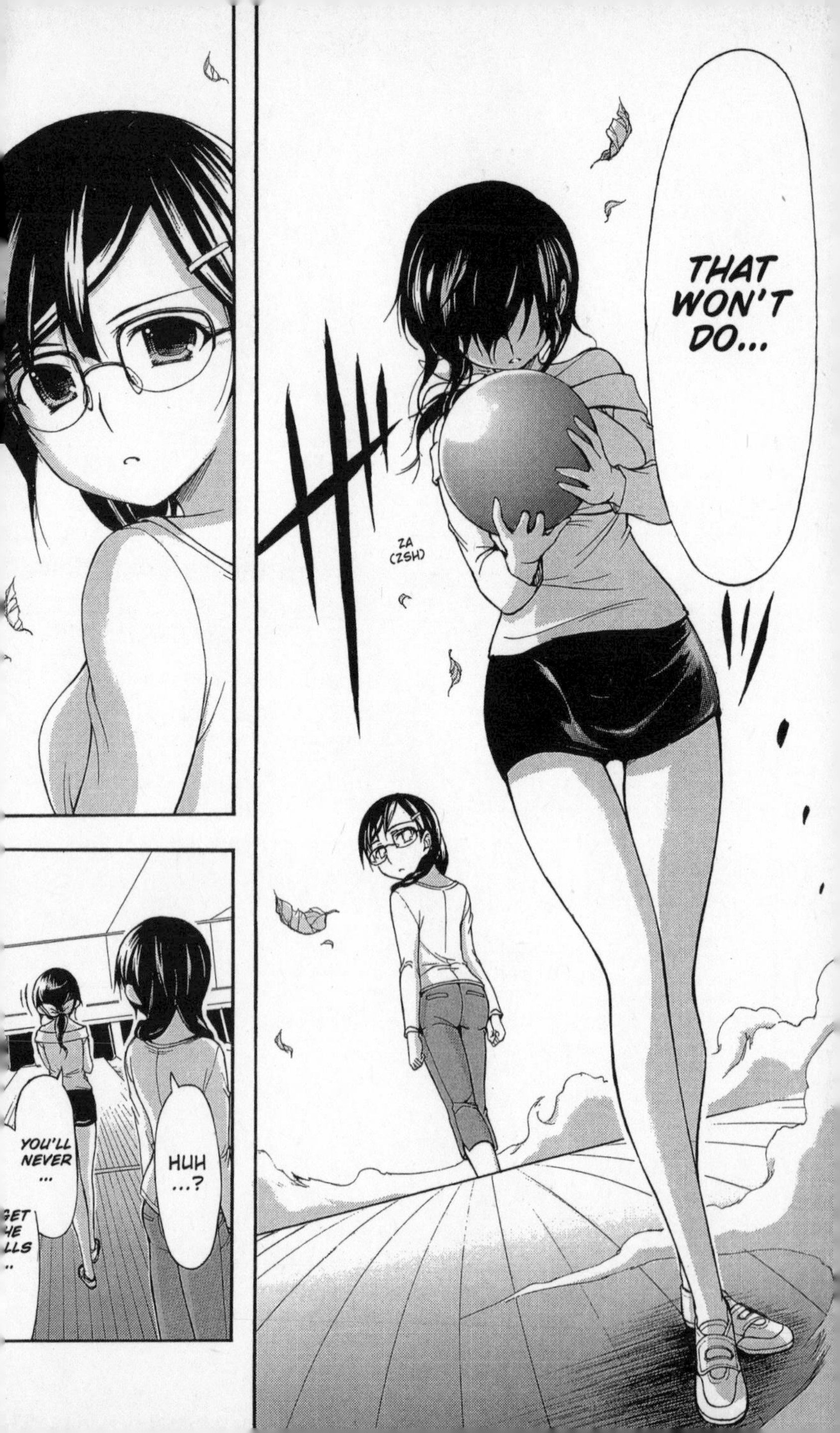
THAT WON'T DO...
ZA (ZSH)
HUH ...?
YOU'LL NEVER ...
GET HE LLS ..

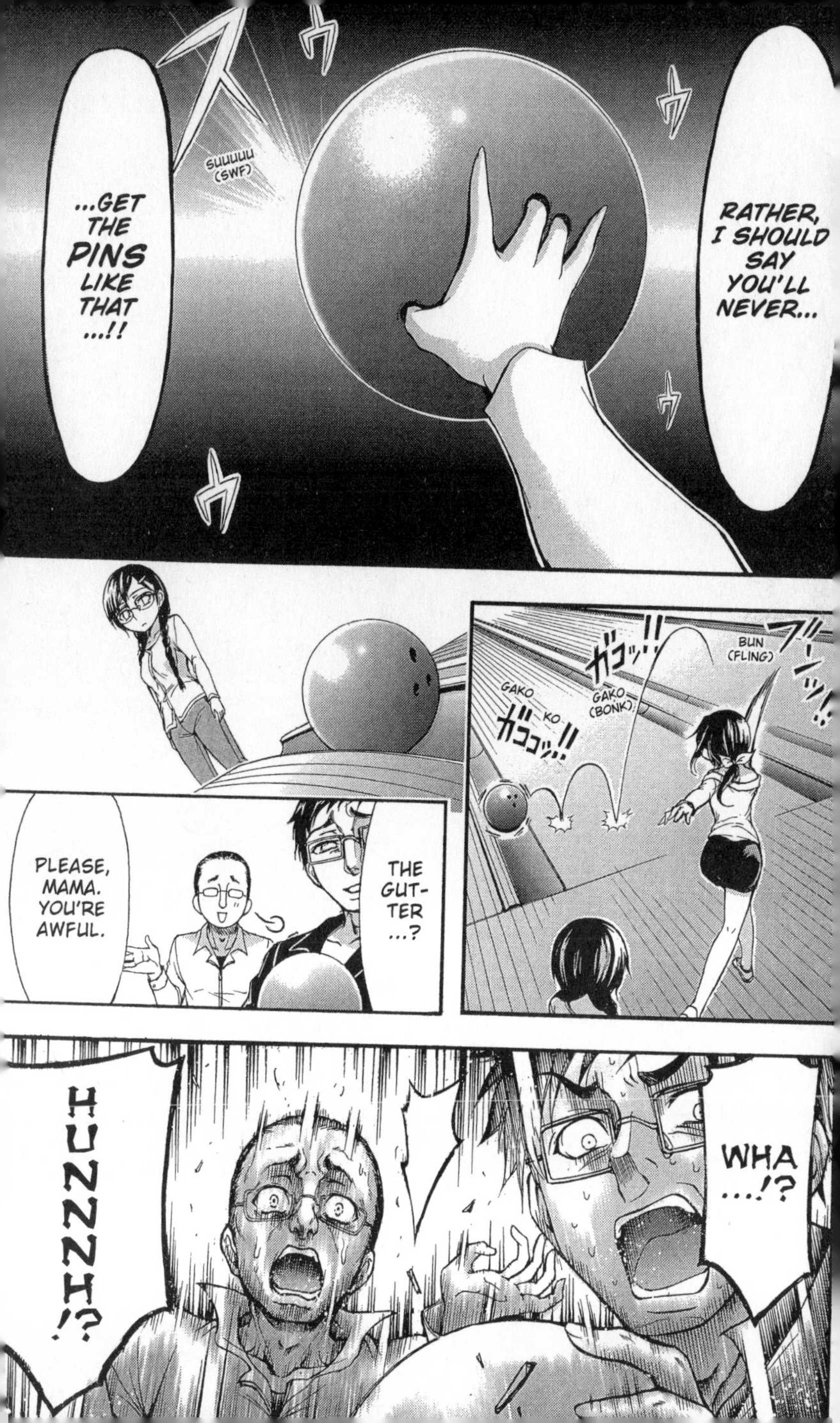
RATHER, I SHOULD SAY YOU'LL NEVER...
SUUUUU (SWF)
...GET THE PINS LIKE THAT...!!
BUN (FLING)
GAKO (BONK)
GAKO
KO
THE GUT-TER...?
PLEASE, MAMA. YOU'RE AWFUL.
WHA...!?
HUNNNH!?

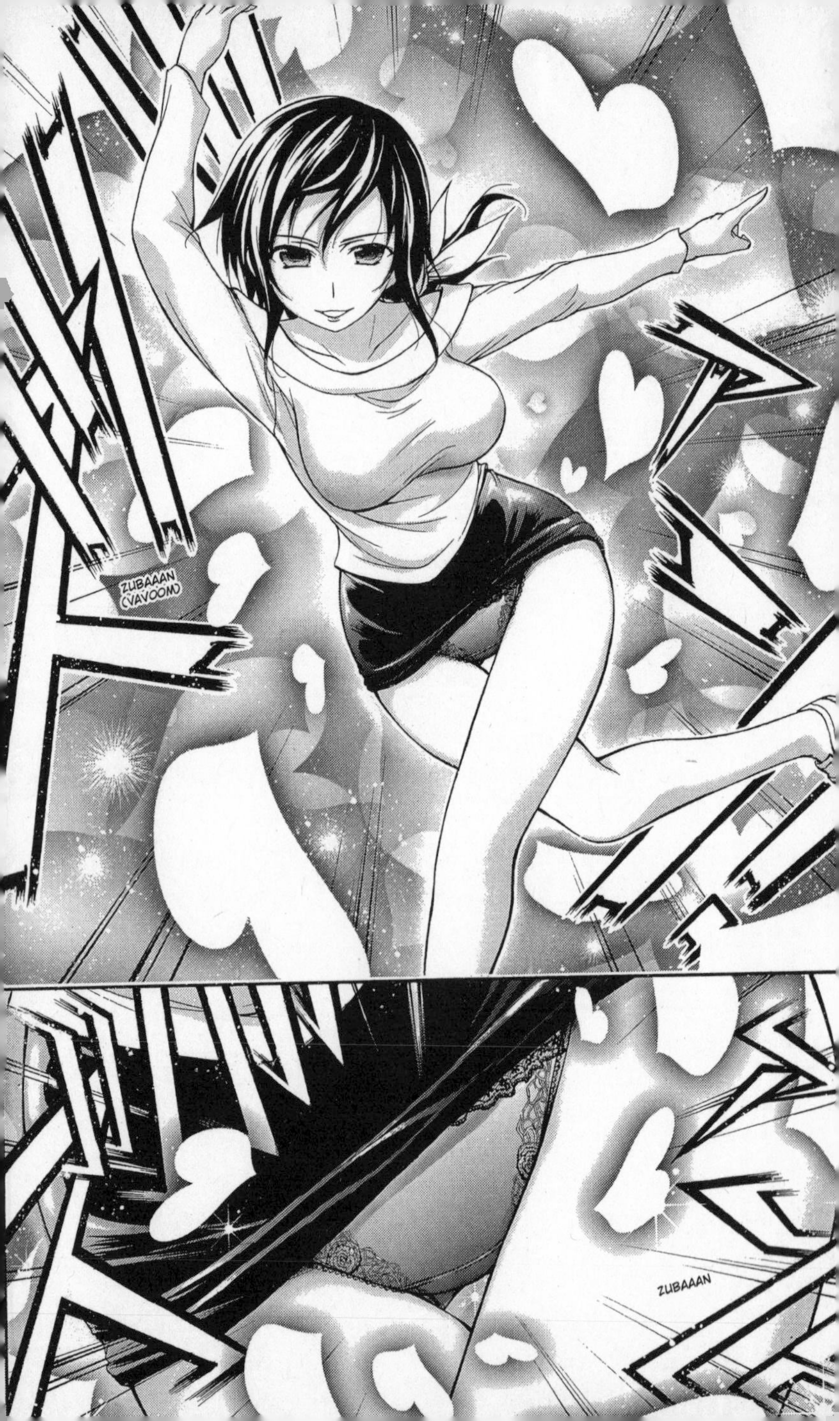
ZUBAAAN
(VAVOOM)
ZUBAAAN

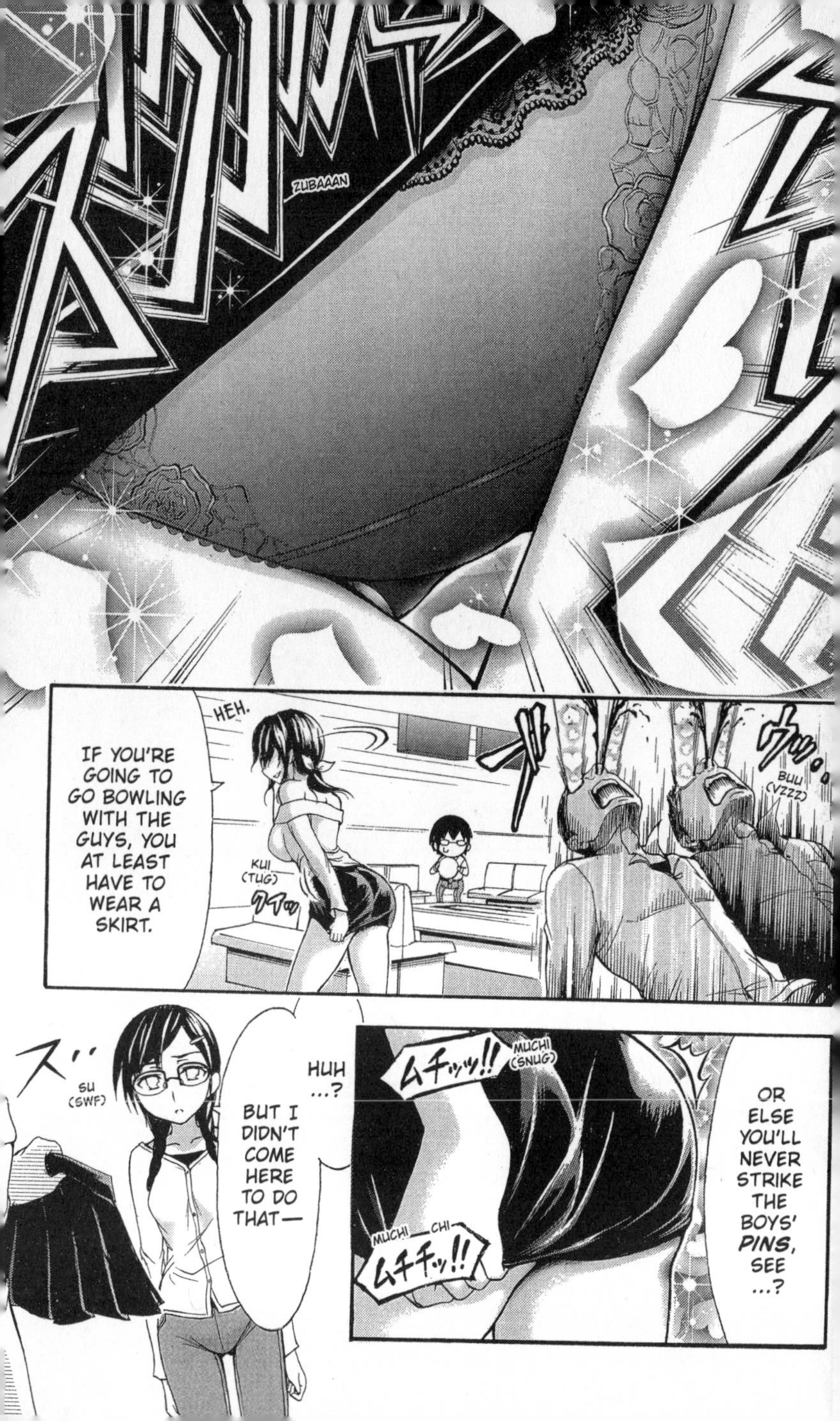
ZUBAAAN
BUU (VZZZ)
HEH.
IF YOU'RE GOING TO GO BOWLING WITH THE GUYS, YOU AT LEAST HAVE TO WEAR A SKIRT.
KUI (TUG)
OR ELSE YOU'LL NEVER STRIKE THE BOYS' *PINS*, SEE ...?
MUCHI (SNUG)
ムチッッ!!
MUCHI CHI
ムチチッ!!
HUH ...?
BUT I DIDN'T COME HERE TO DO THAT—
SU (SWF)

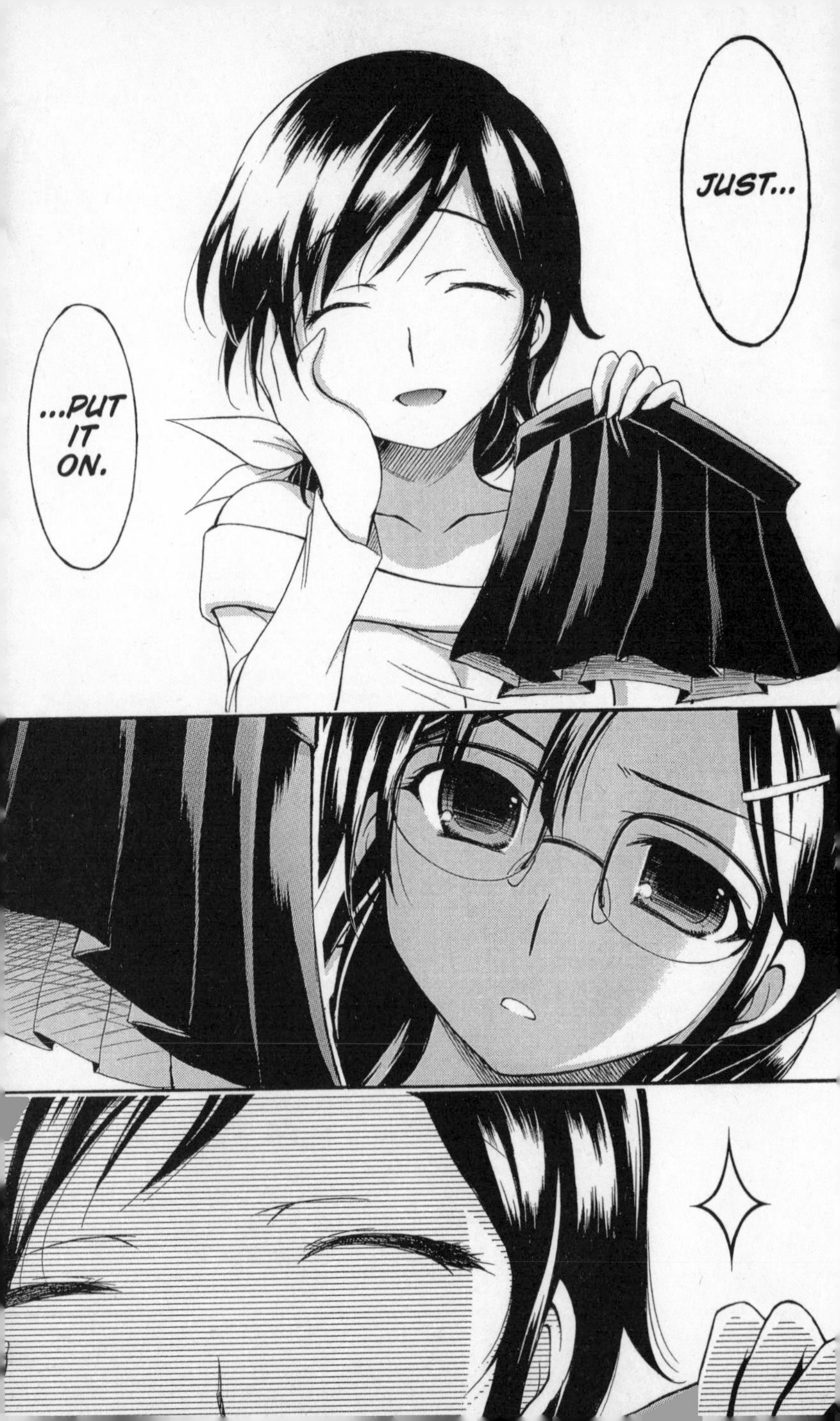
JUST...
...PUT IT ON.

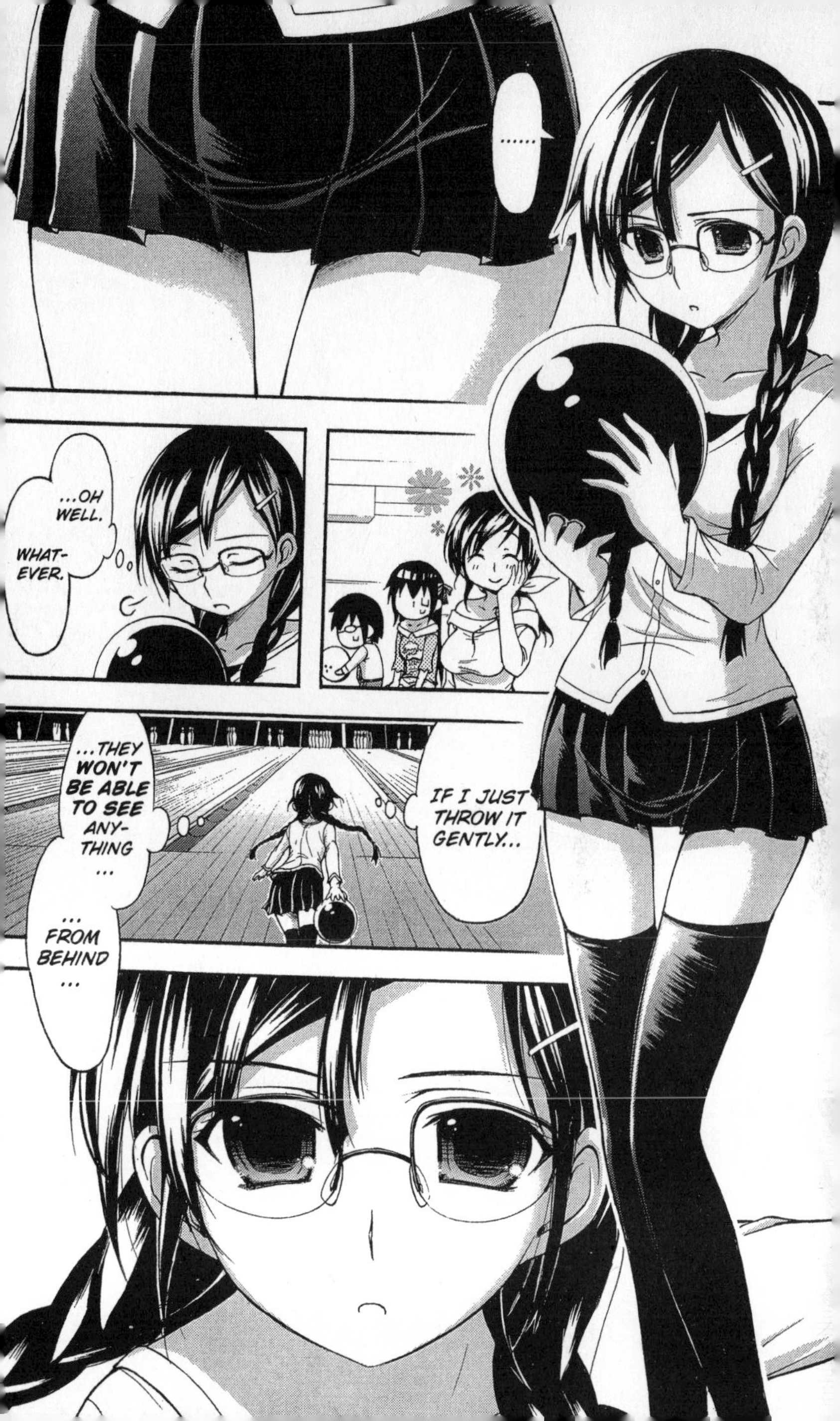
......
...OH WELL.
WHAT-EVER.
IF I JUST THROW IT GENTLY...
...THEY WON'T BE ABLE TO SEE ANY-THING ...
... FROM BEHIND ...

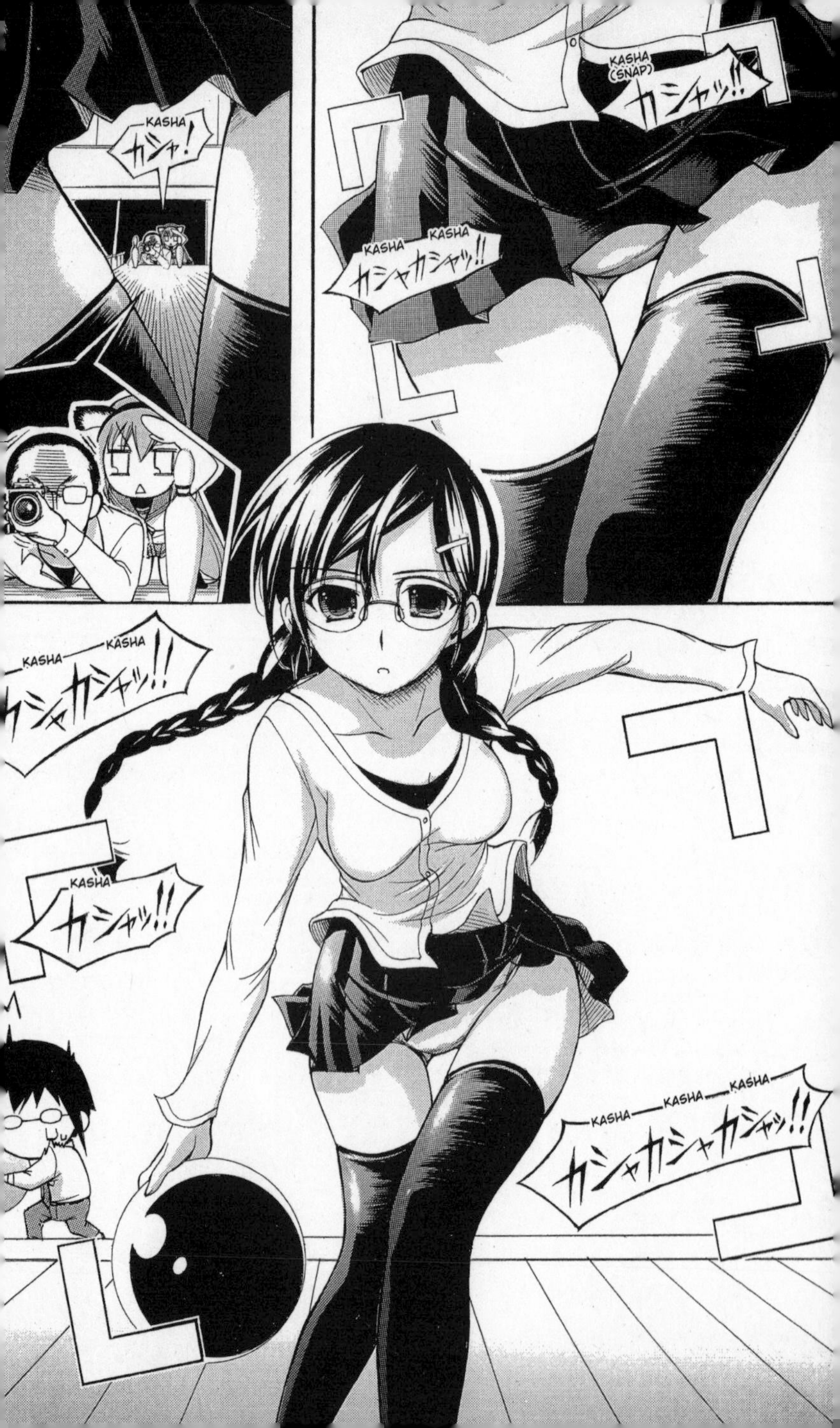
KASHA (SNAP)
カシャッ!!
KASHA KASHA
カシャカシャッ!!
KASHA
カシャ!
KASHA KASHA
カシャカシャッ!!
KASHA
カシャッ!!
KASHA KASHA KASHA
カシャカシャカシャッ!!

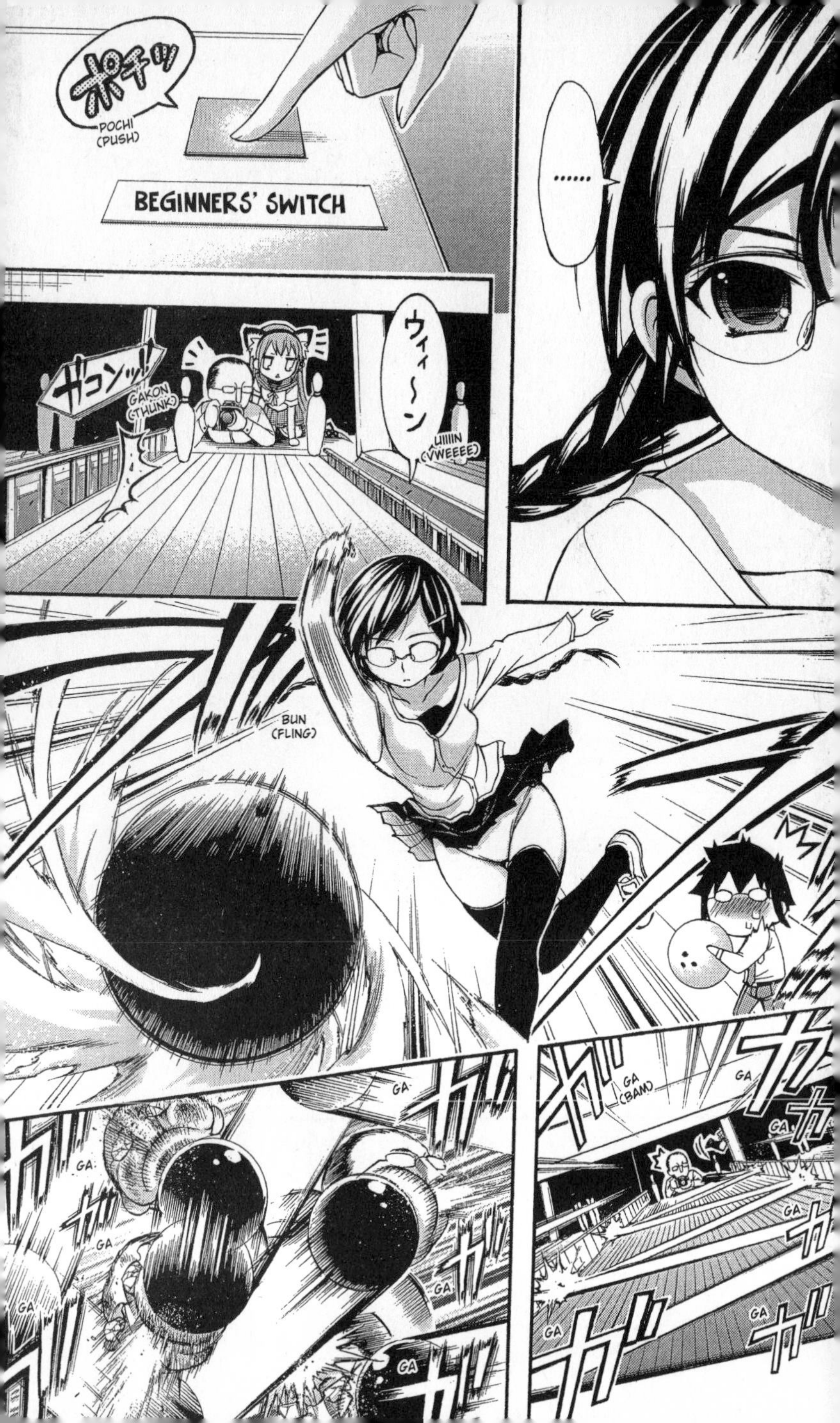
......
ポチッ
POCHI (PUSH)
BEGINNERS' SWITCH
ウィ〜ン
UIIIIN (VWEEEE)
ガコンッ!
GAKON (THUNK)
BUN (FLING)
GA (BAM)
GA
GA
GA
GA
GA
GA
GA
GA
GA
GA
GA

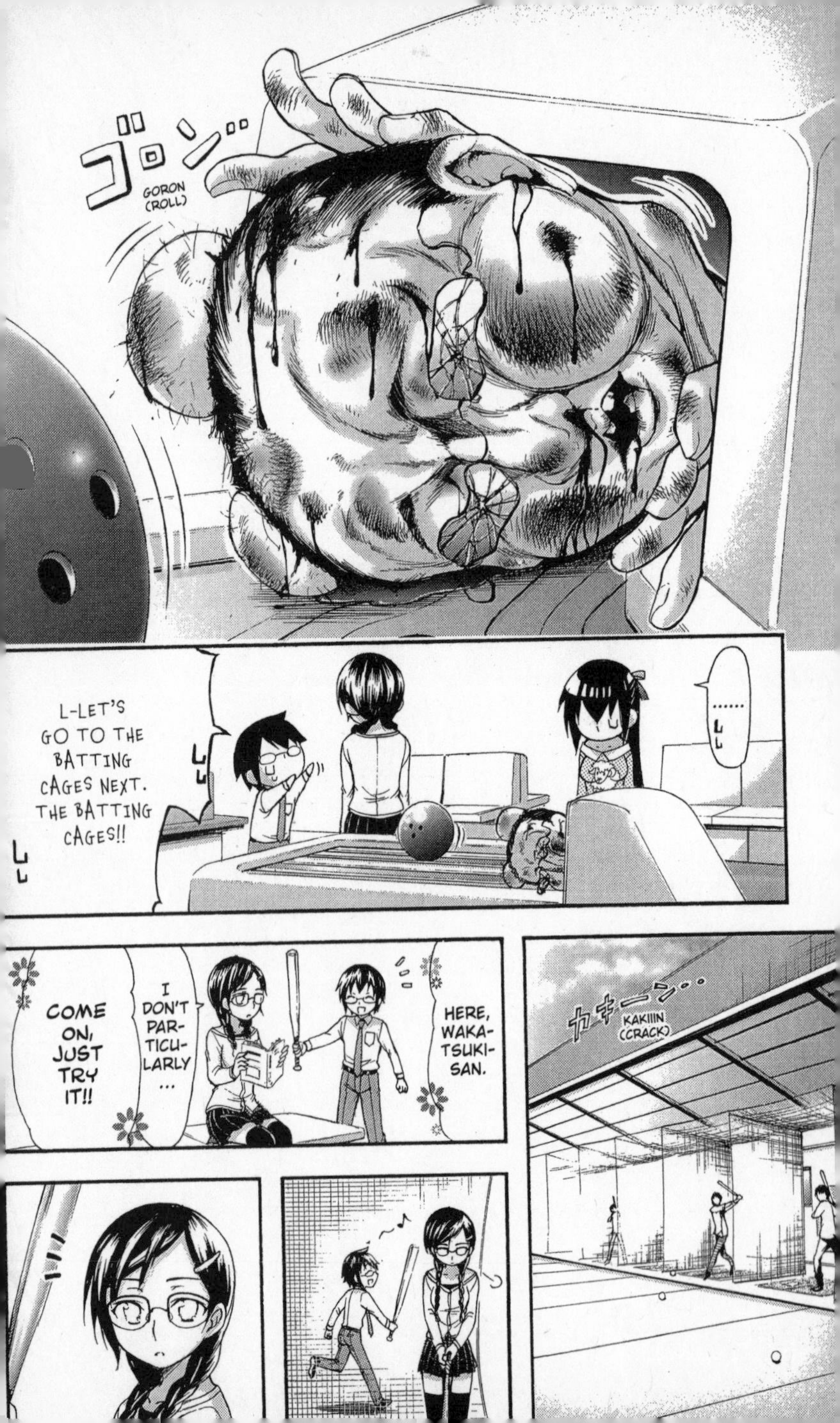
ゴロン
GORON (ROLL)
......
L-LET'S GO TO THE BATTING CAGES NEXT. THE BATTING CAGES!!
カキーン
KAKIIIN (CRACK)
HERE, WAKATSUKI-SAN.
I DON'T PARTICULARLY...
COME ON, JUST TRY IT!!

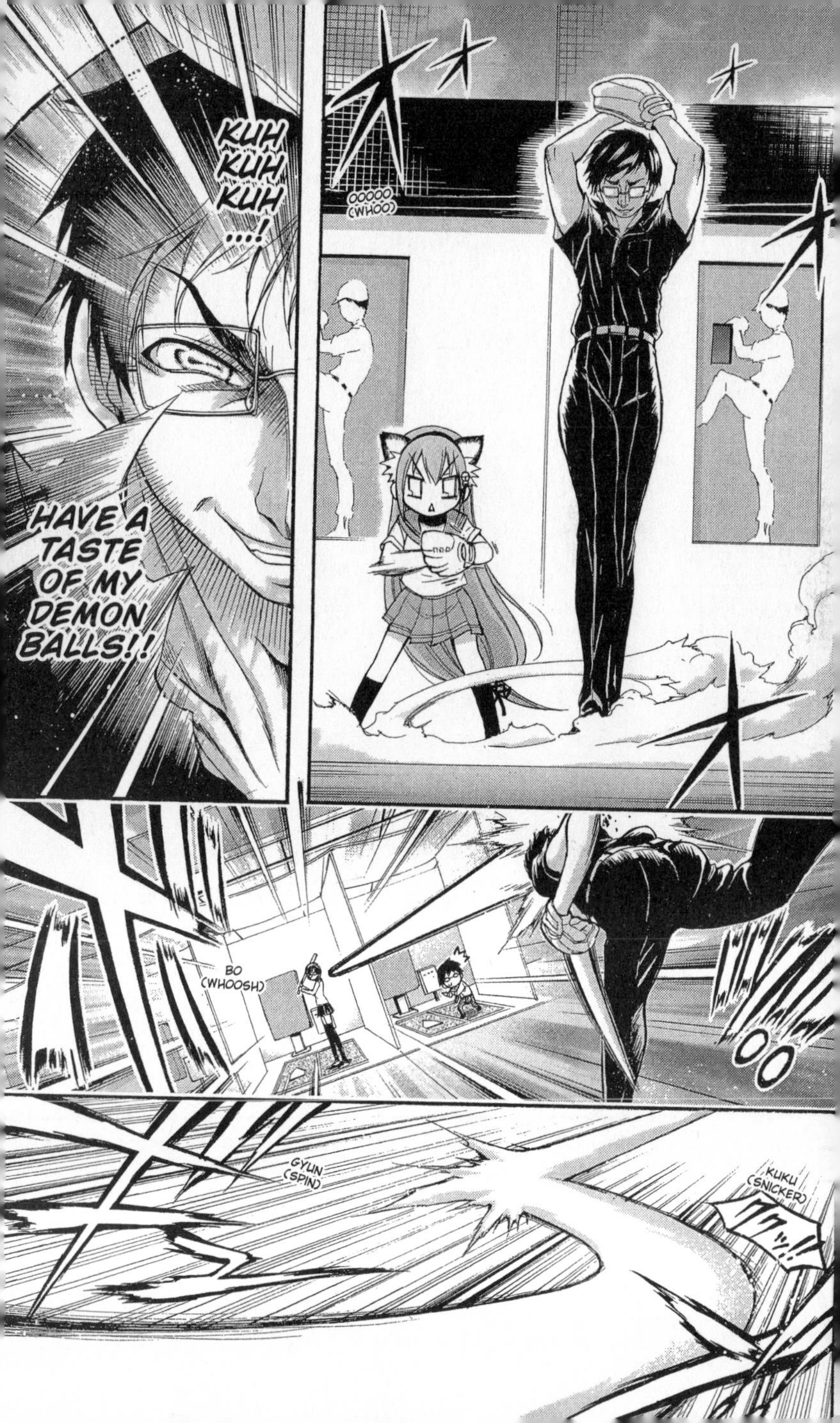
OOOOO (WHOO)
KUH KUH KUH ...!
HAVE A TASTE OF MY DEMON BALLS!!
BO (WHOOSH)
KUKU (SNICKER)
ククッ!!
GYUN (SPIN)

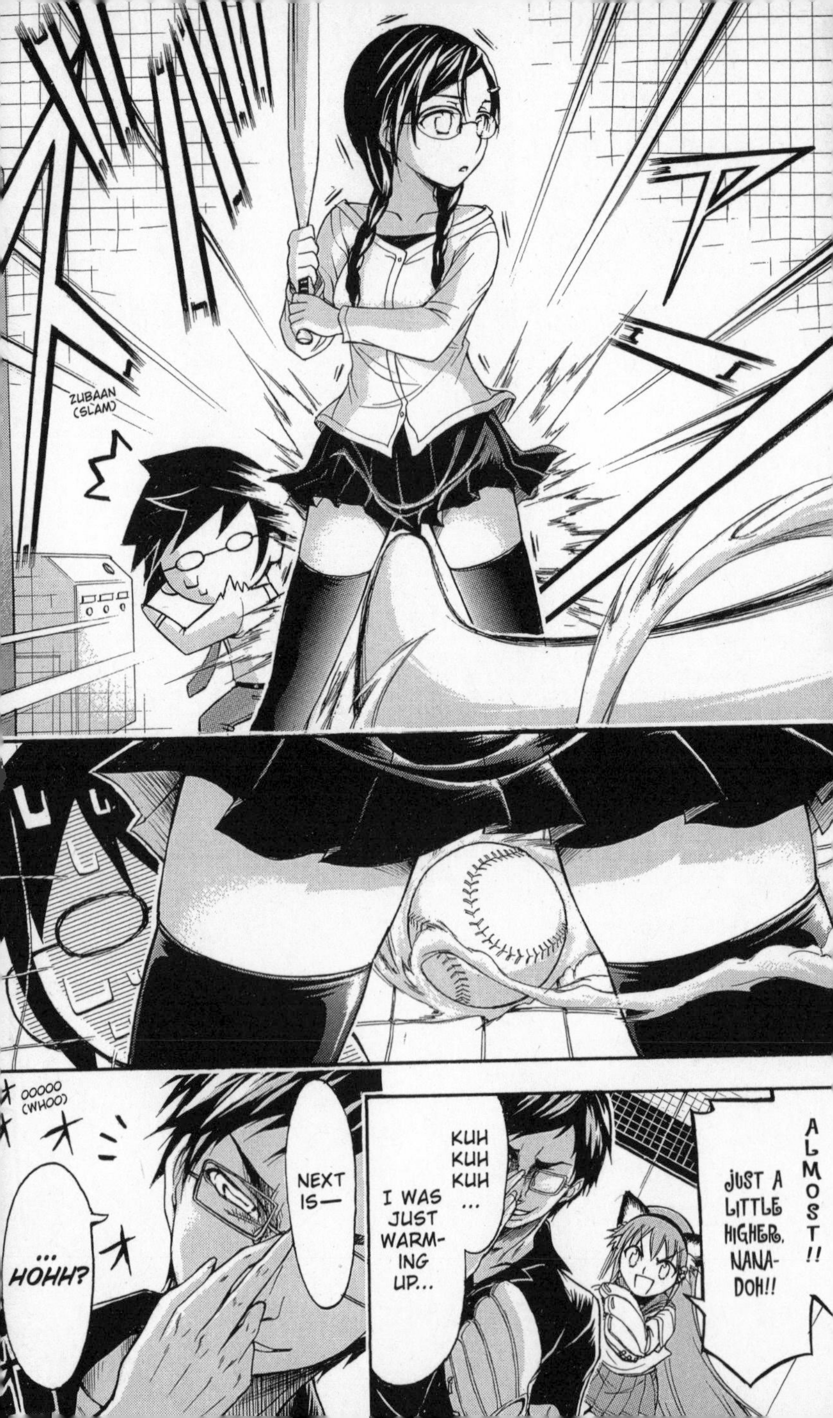
ZUBAAN (SLAM)
ALMOST!!
JUST A LITTLE HIGHER, NANA-DOH!!
KUH KUH KUH ...
I WAS JUST WARMING UP...
NEXT IS—
... HOHH?
OOOOO (WHOO)

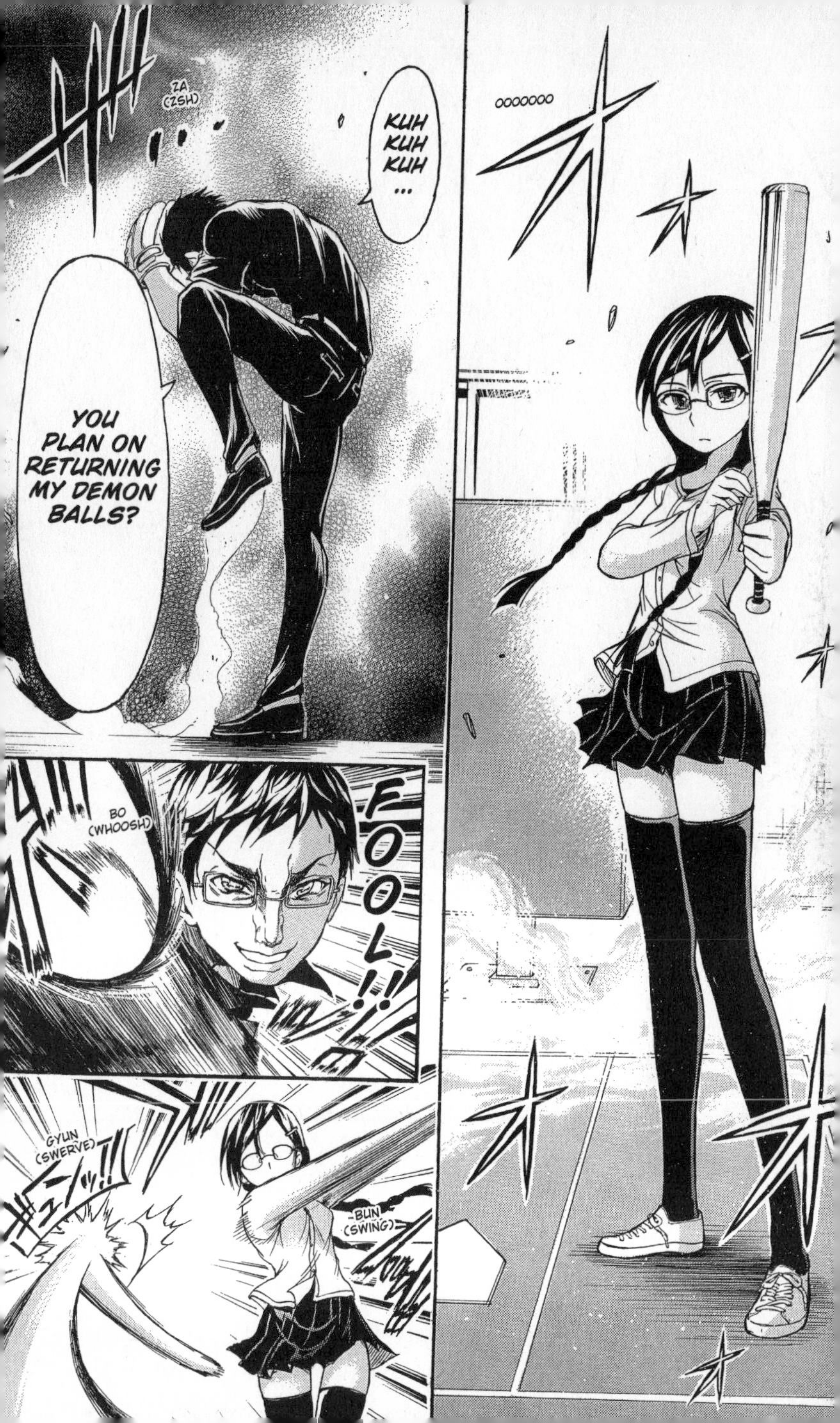
OOOOOOO
KUH KUH KUH ...
ZA (ZSH)
YOU PLAN ON RETURNING MY DEMON BALLS?
FOOOL!!
BO (WHOOSH)
BUN (SWING)
GYUN (SWERVE)

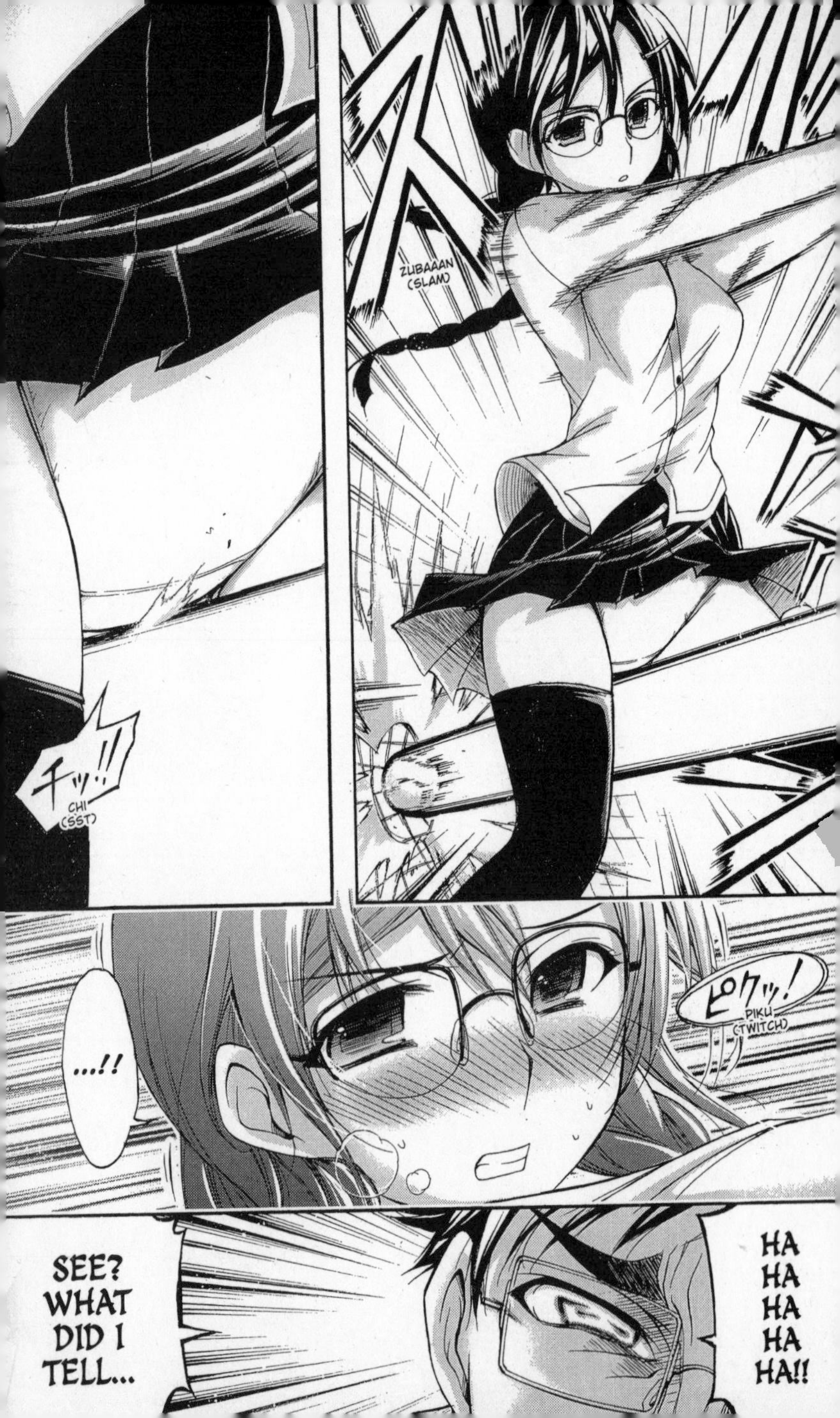
ZUBAAAN (SLAM)
チッ!!
CHI (SST)
ピクッ!
PIKU (TWITCH)
...!!
HA HA HA HA HA!!
SEE? WHAT DID I TELL...

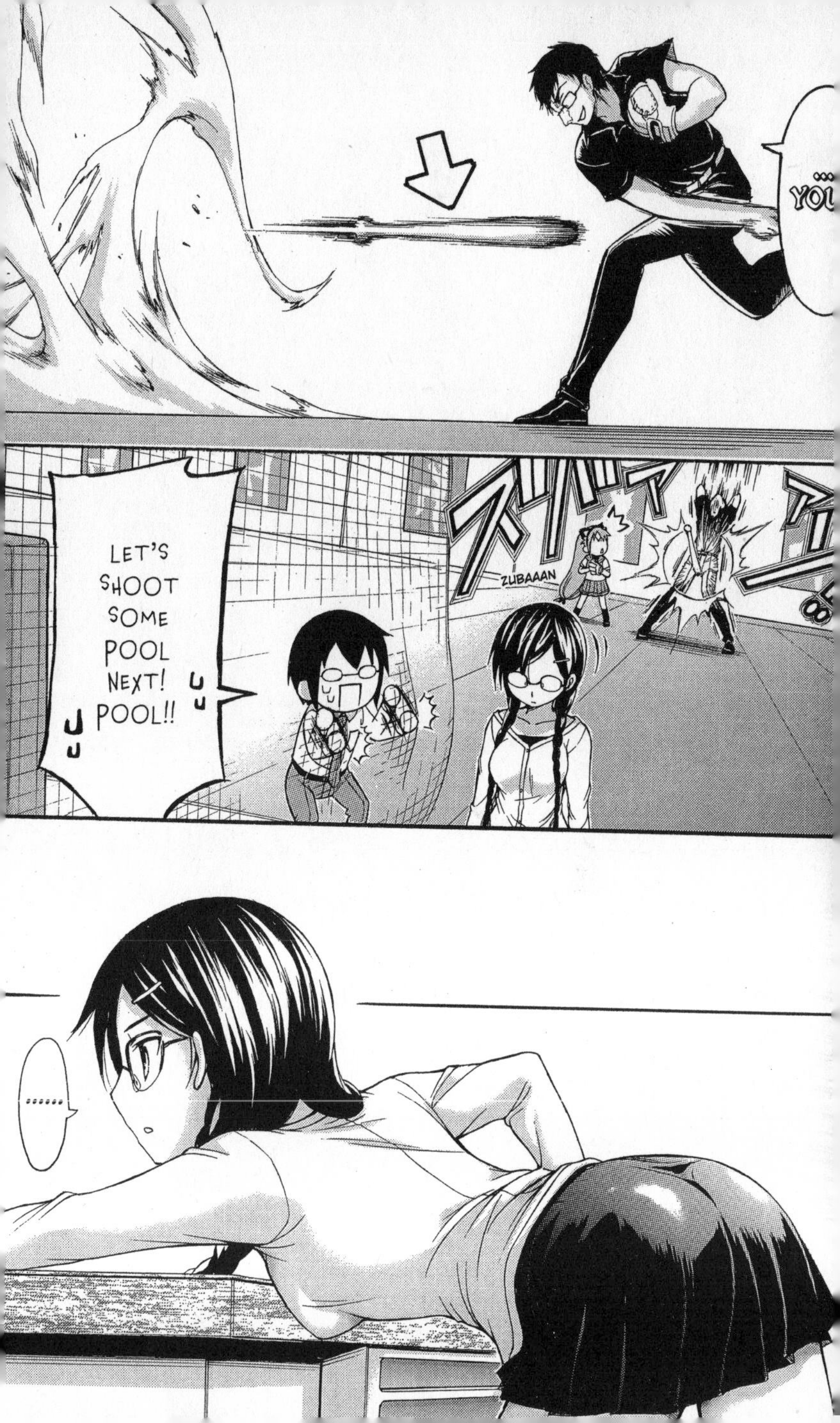
...YOU
LET'S SHOOT SOME POOL NEXT! POOL!!
ZUBAAAN
......

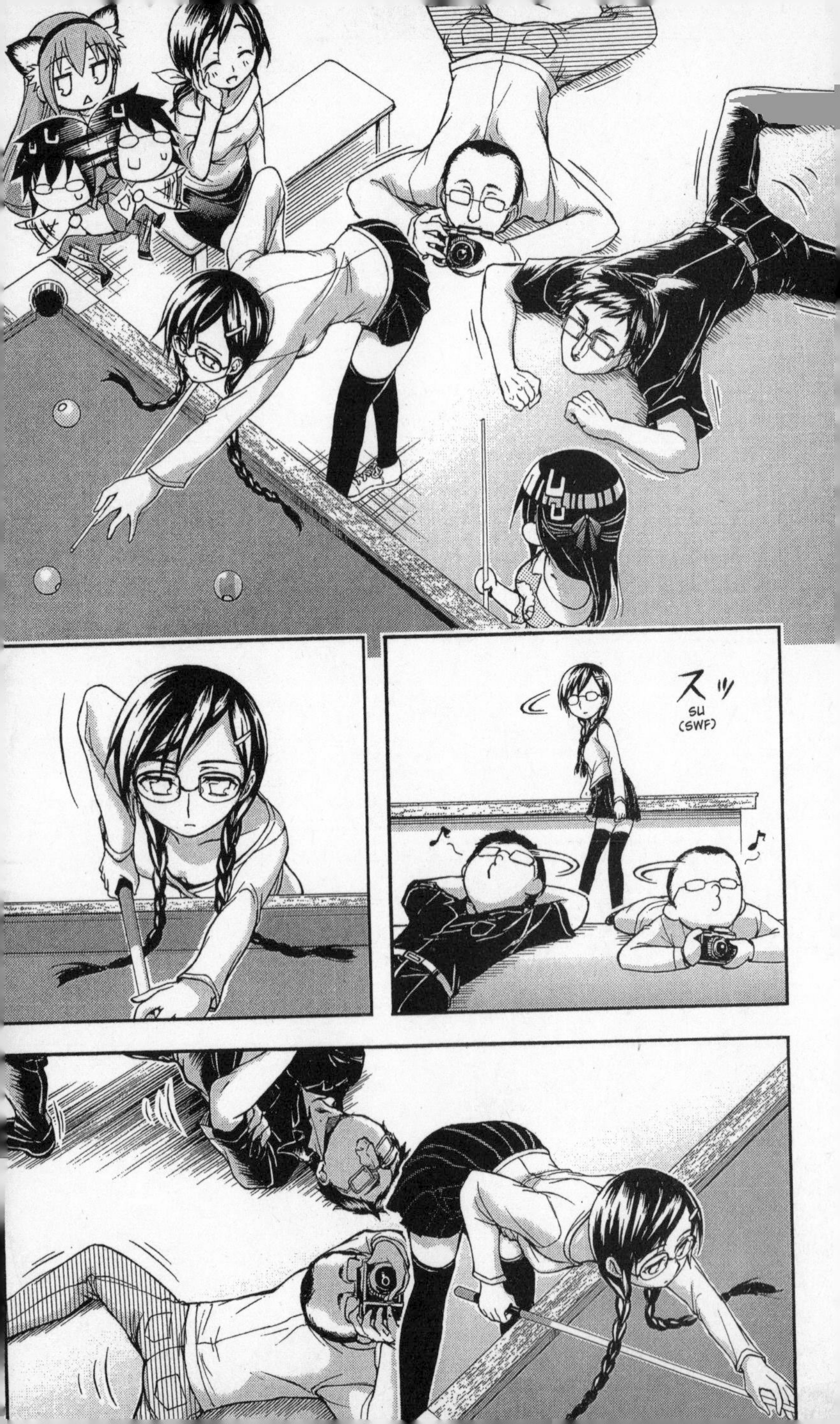
スッ
SU
(SWF)

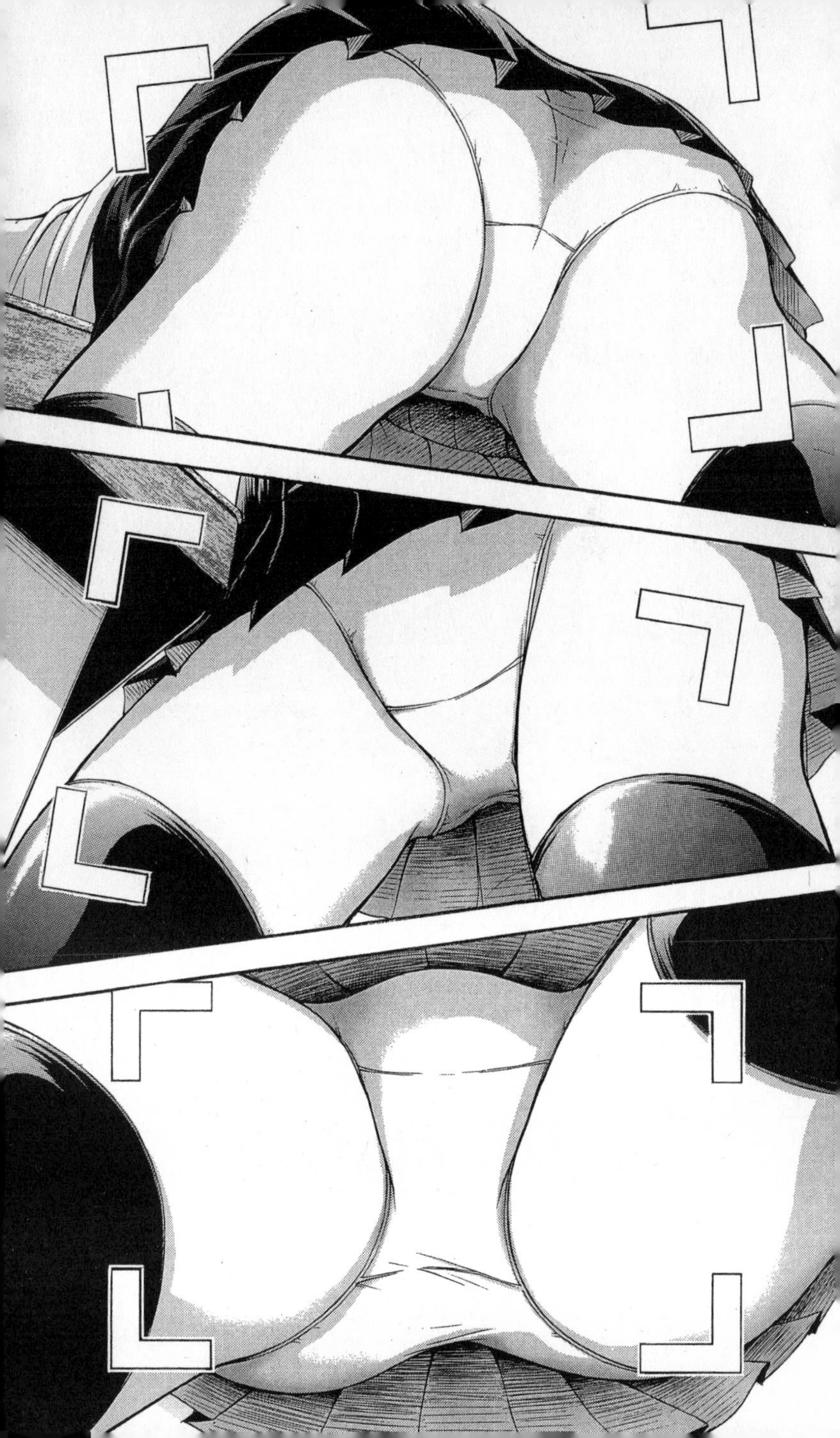

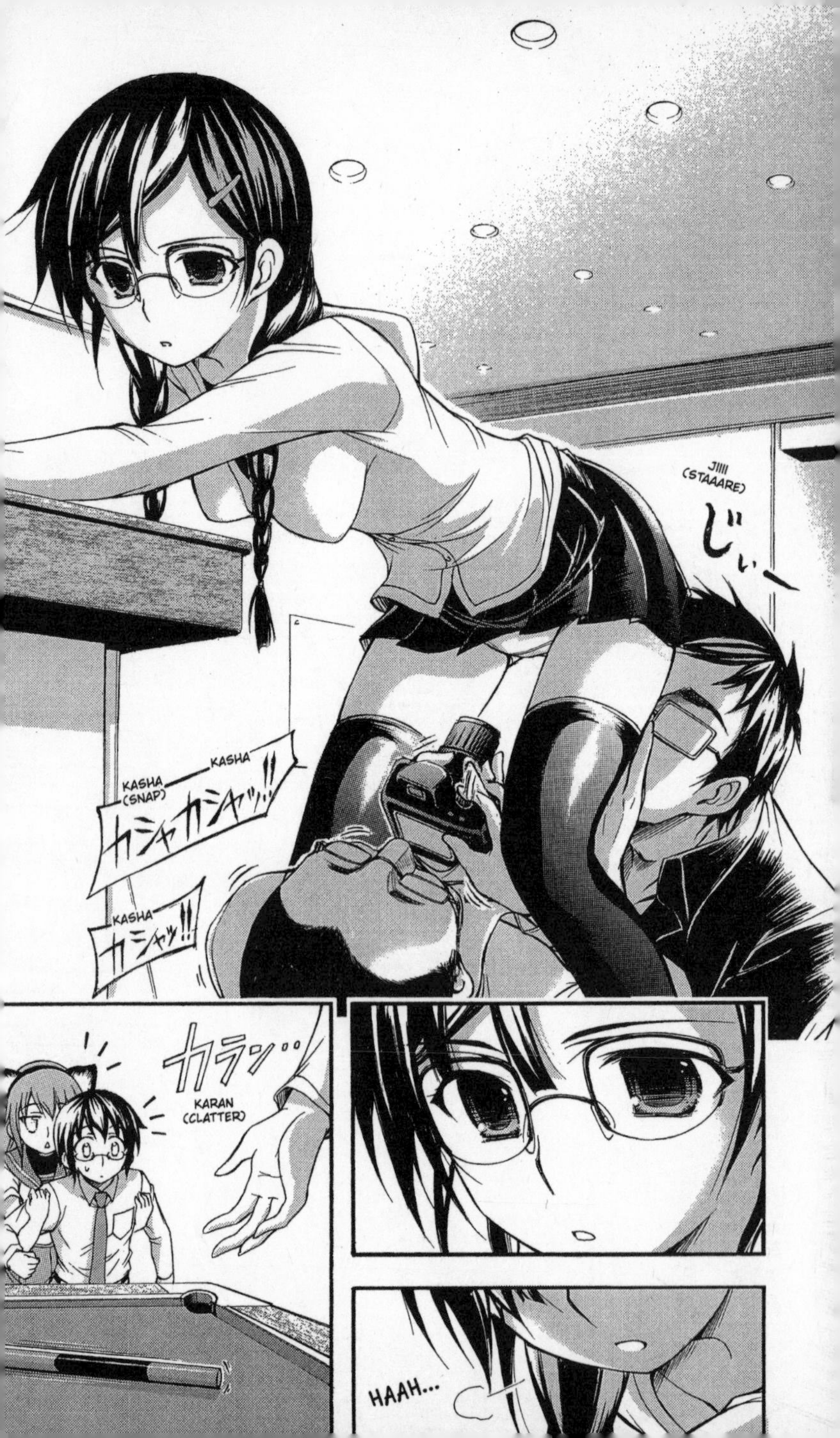
JIIII (STAAARE)
じぃー
KASHA (SNAP)
KASHA
カシャカシャッ!!
KASHA
カシャッ!!
HAAH...
カラン‥
KARAN (CLATTER)

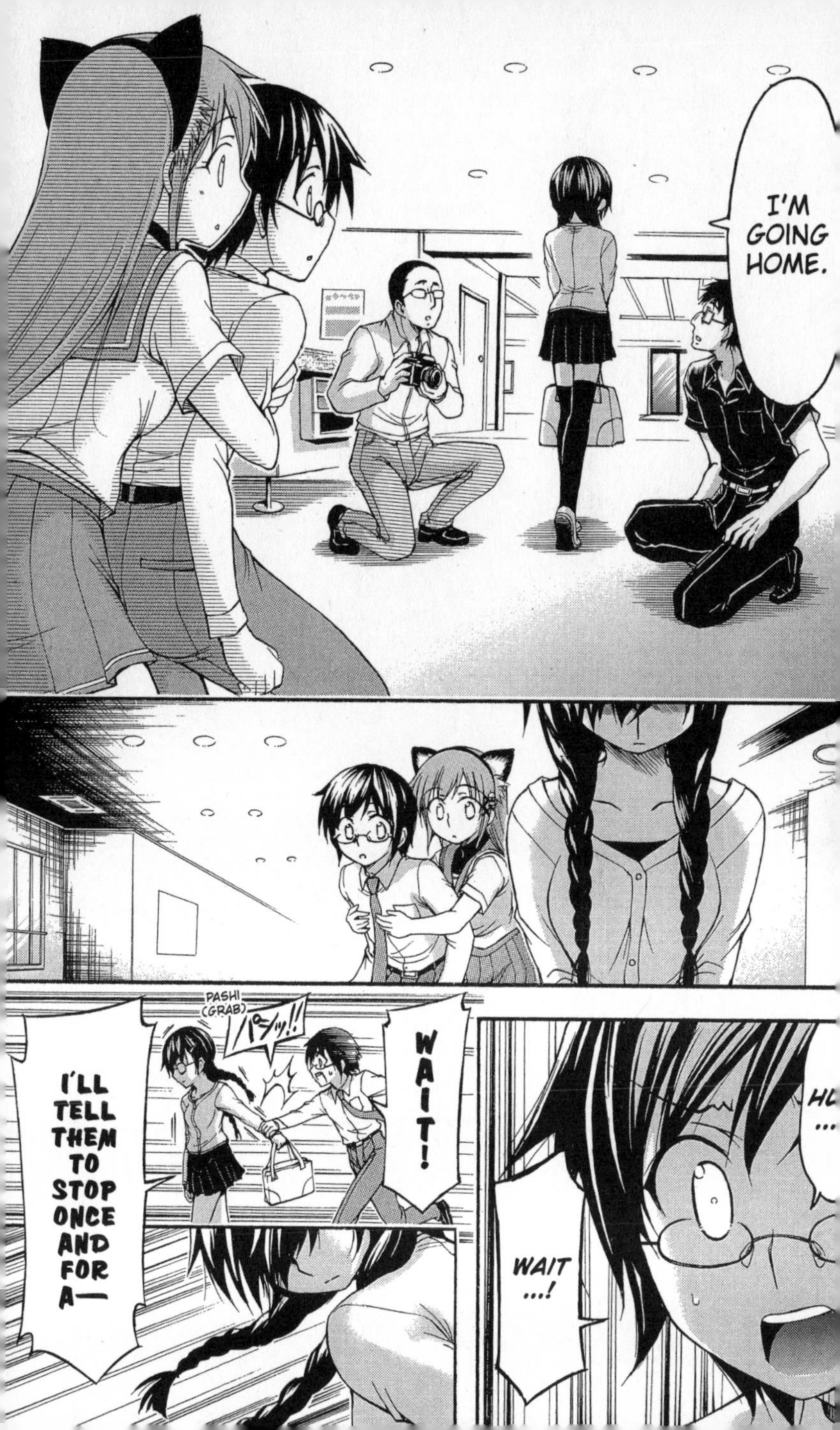
I'M GOING HOME.
HU ...
WAIT ...!
WAIT!
PASHI (GRAB)
パシッ!!
I'LL TELL THEM TO STOP ONCE AND FOR A—

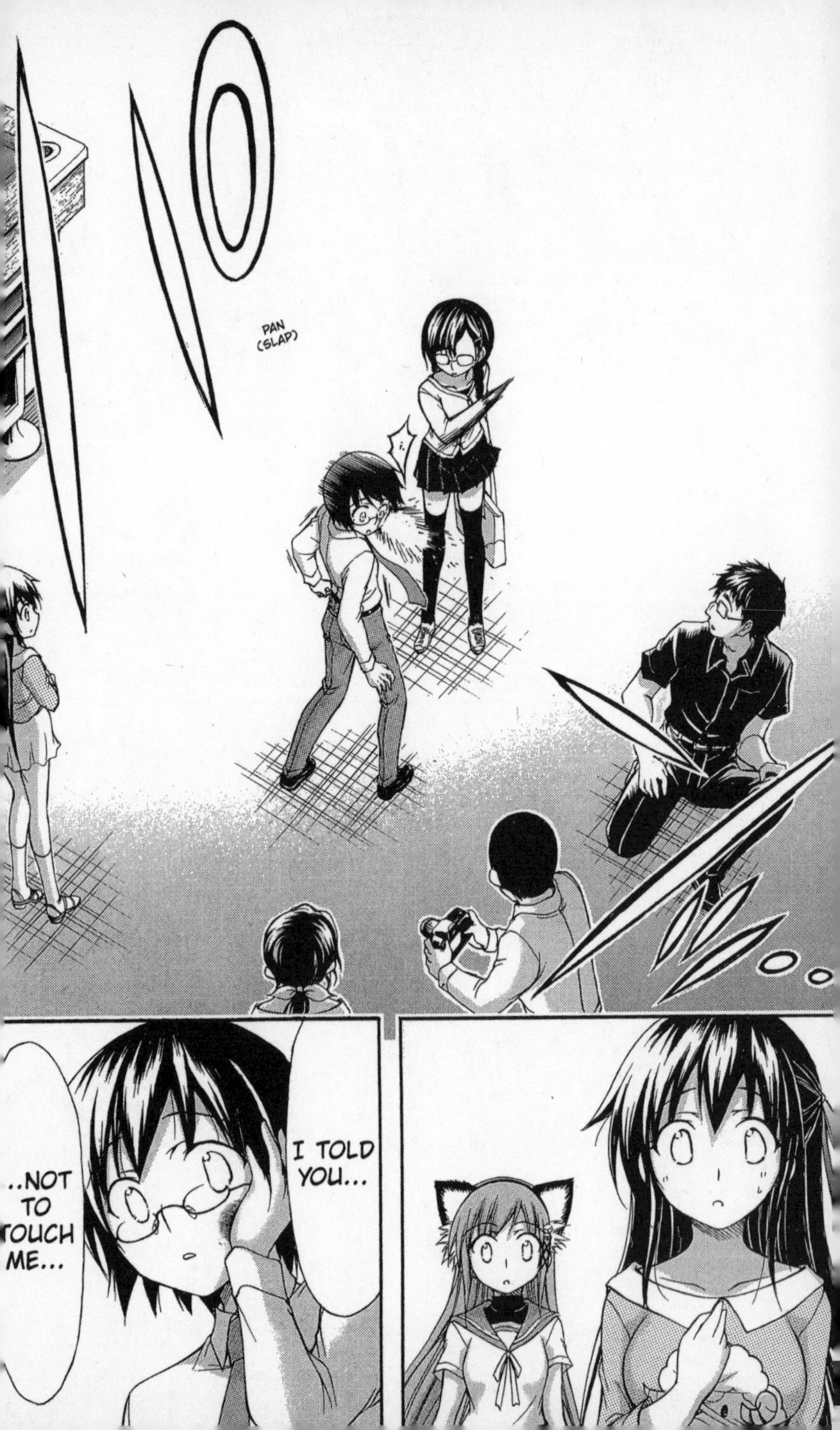
PAN (SLAP)
I TOLD YOU...
...NOT TO TOUCH ME...

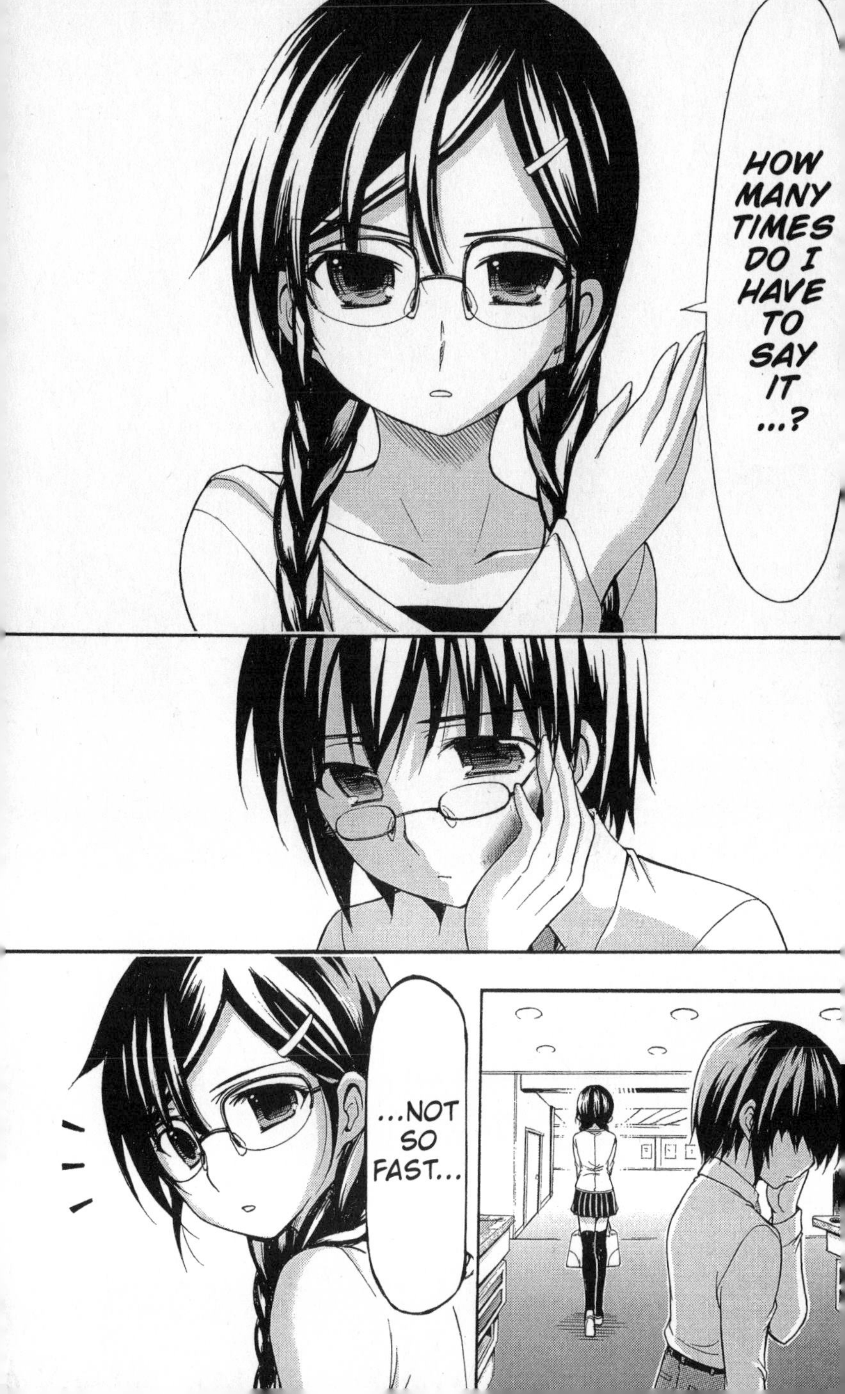
HOW MANY TIMES DO I HAVE TO SAY IT ...?
...NOT SO FAST...

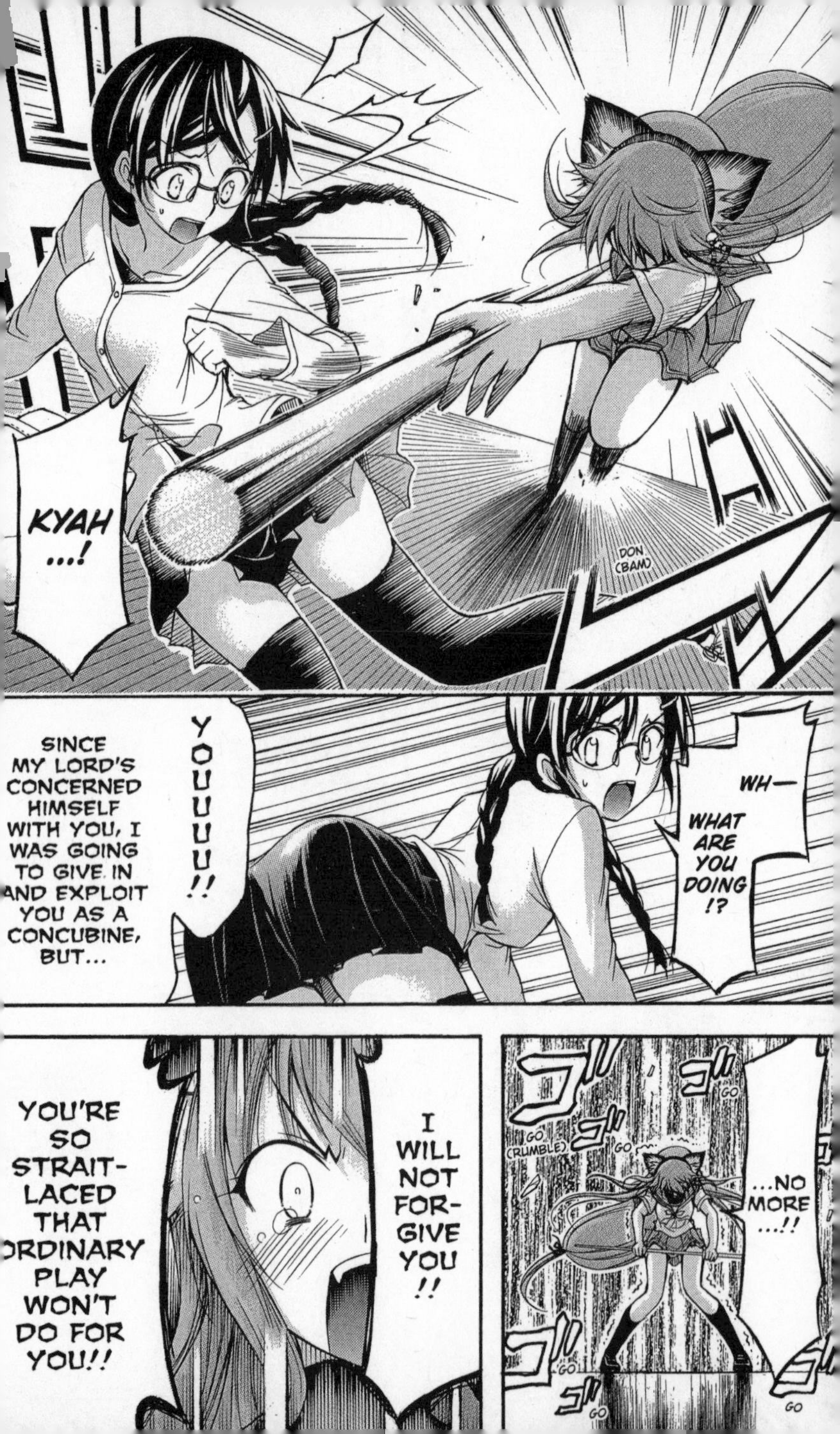
KYAH ...!
DON (BAM)
WH— WHAT ARE YOU DOING !?
YOUUUUU!!
SINCE MY LORD'S CONCERNED HIMSELF WITH YOU, I WAS GOING TO GIVE IN AND EXPLOIT YOU AS A CONCUBINE, BUT...
GO
GO (RUMBLE)
GO
...NO MORE ...!!
GO
GO
GO
I WILL NOT FOR-GIVE YOU !!
YOU'RE SO STRAIT-LACED THAT ORDINARY PLAY WON'T DO FOR YOU!!

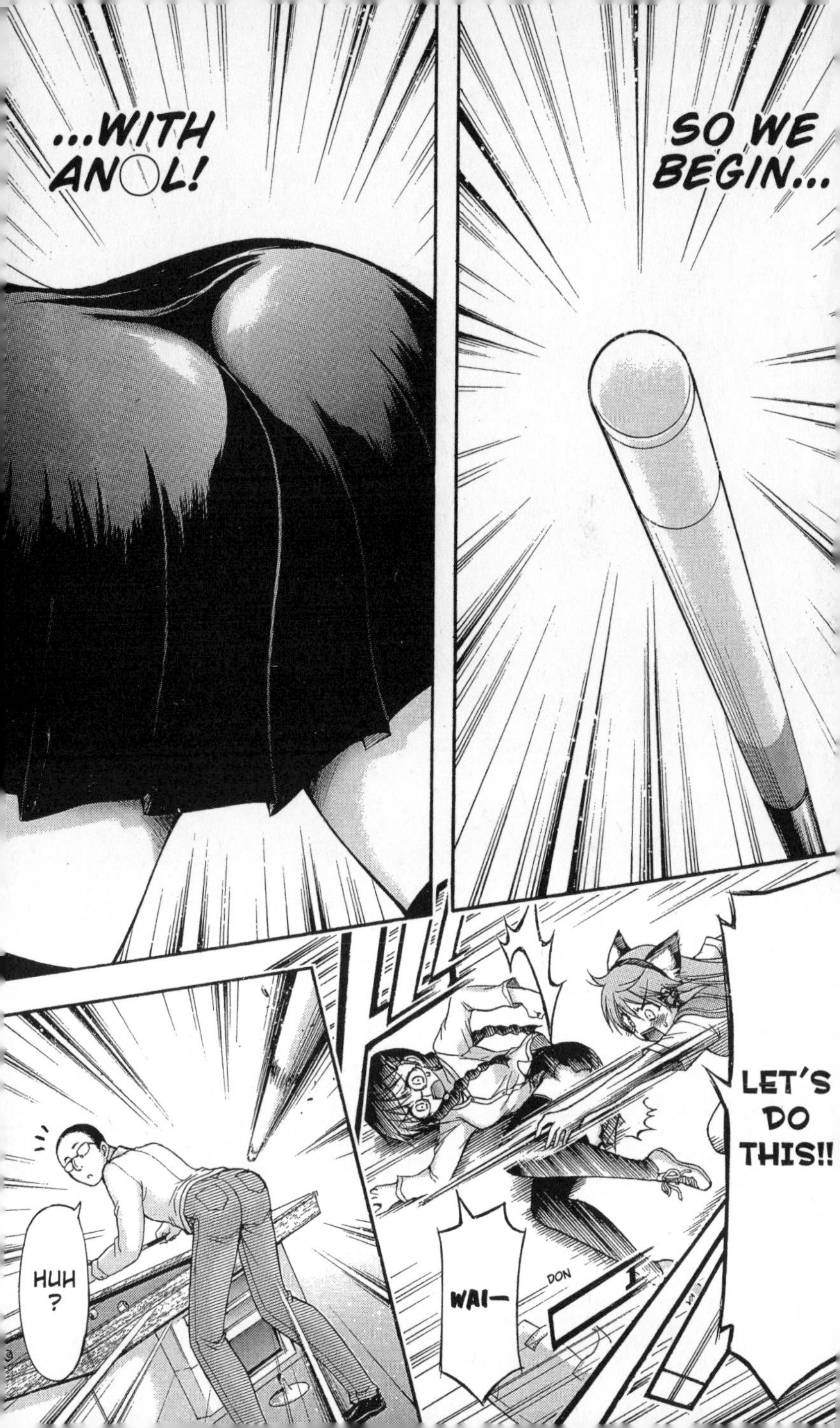
SO WE BEGIN...
...WITH AN◯L!
LET'S DO THIS!!
WAI—
DON
HUH?

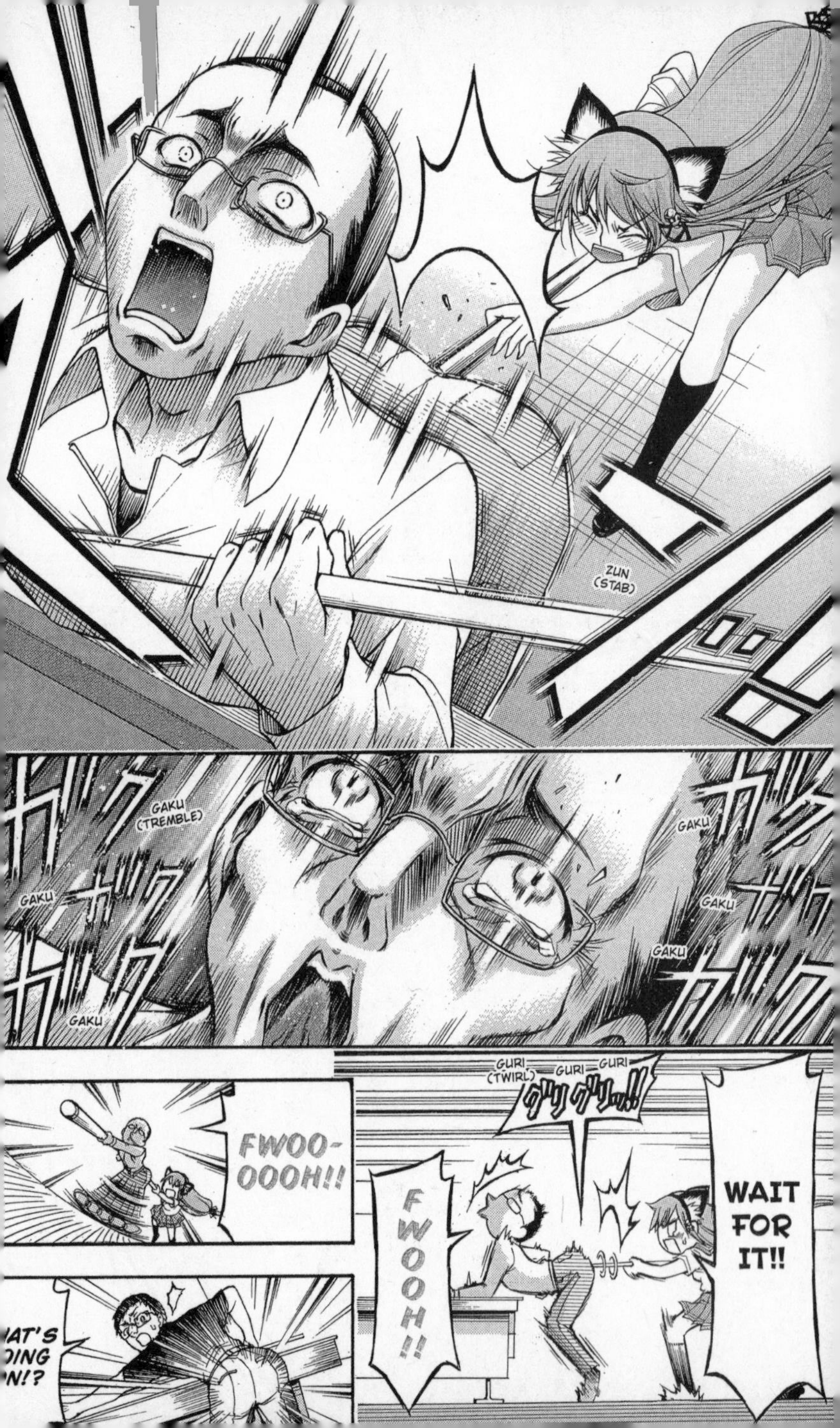
ZUN (STAB)
GAKU
GAKU
GAKU
GAKU (TREMBLE)
GAKU
GAKU
WAIT FOR IT!!
GURI (TWIRL) GURI GURI
グリグリッ!!
FWOOOOH!!
FWOO-OOOH!!
AT'S OING N!?

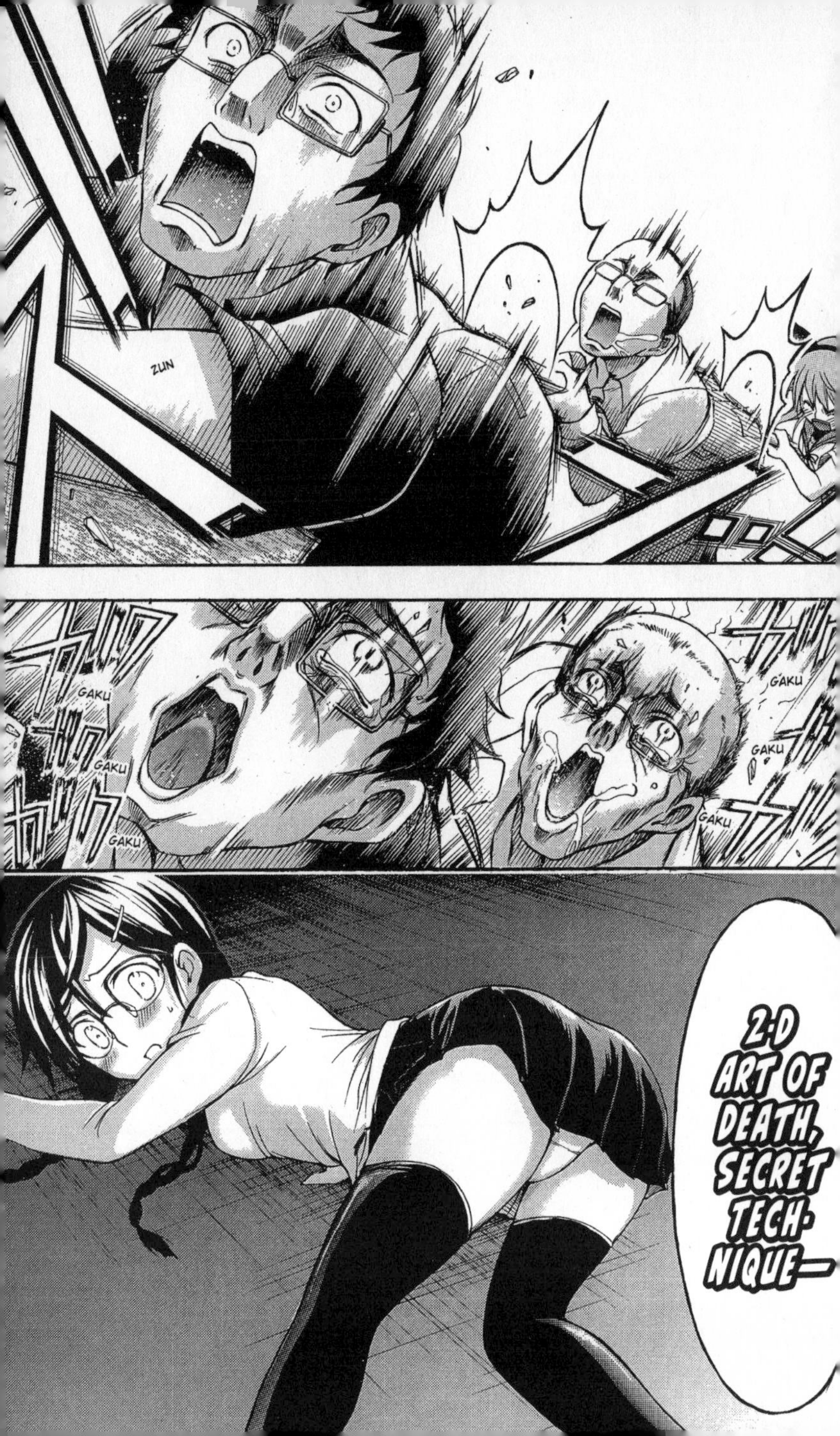
ZUN
GAKU
GAKU
GAKU
GAKU
GAKU
GAKU
GAKU
2-D ART OF DEATH, SECRET TECH-NIQUE—

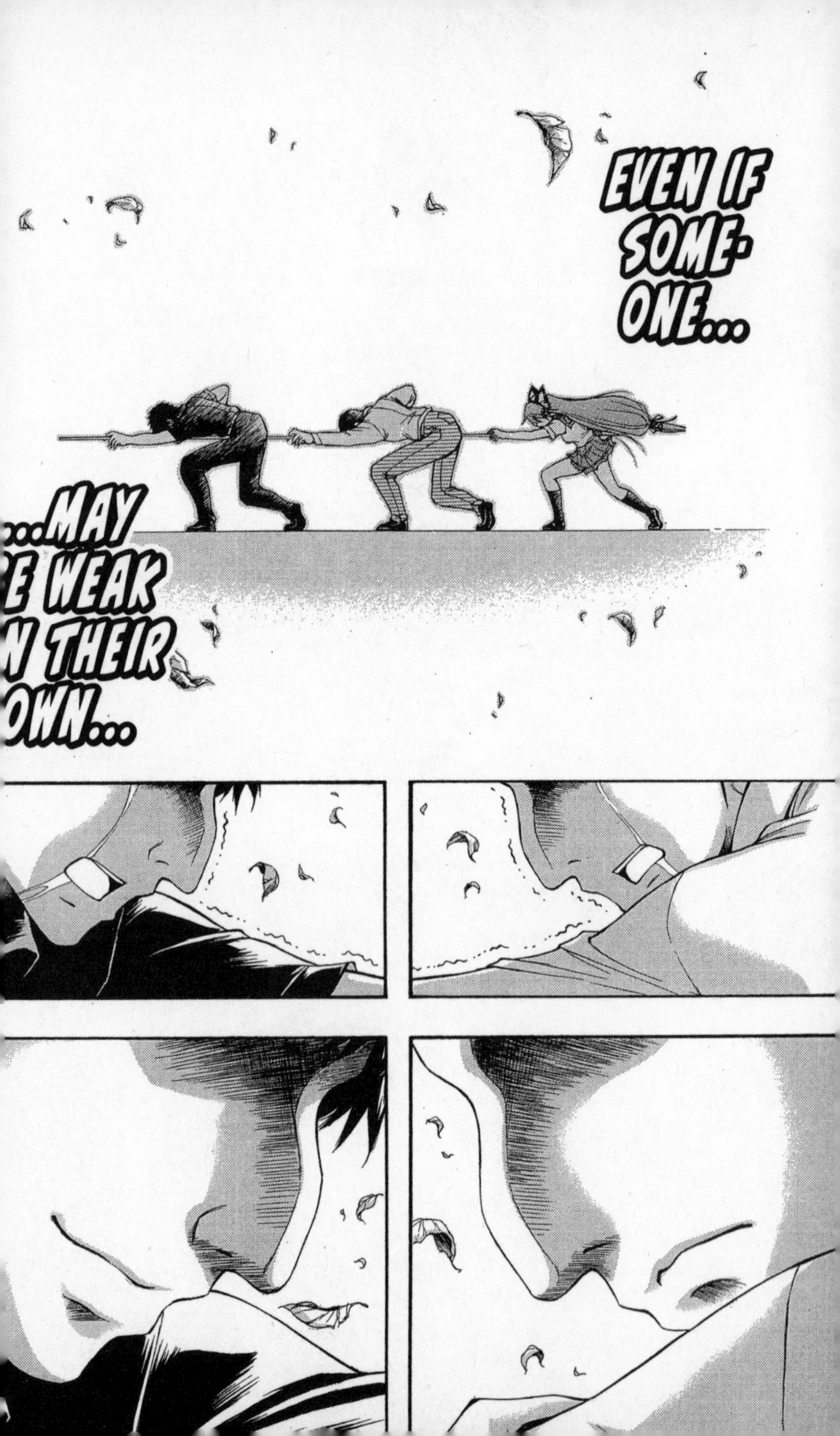
EVEN IF SOME-ONE...
...MAY E WEAK N THEIR OWN...

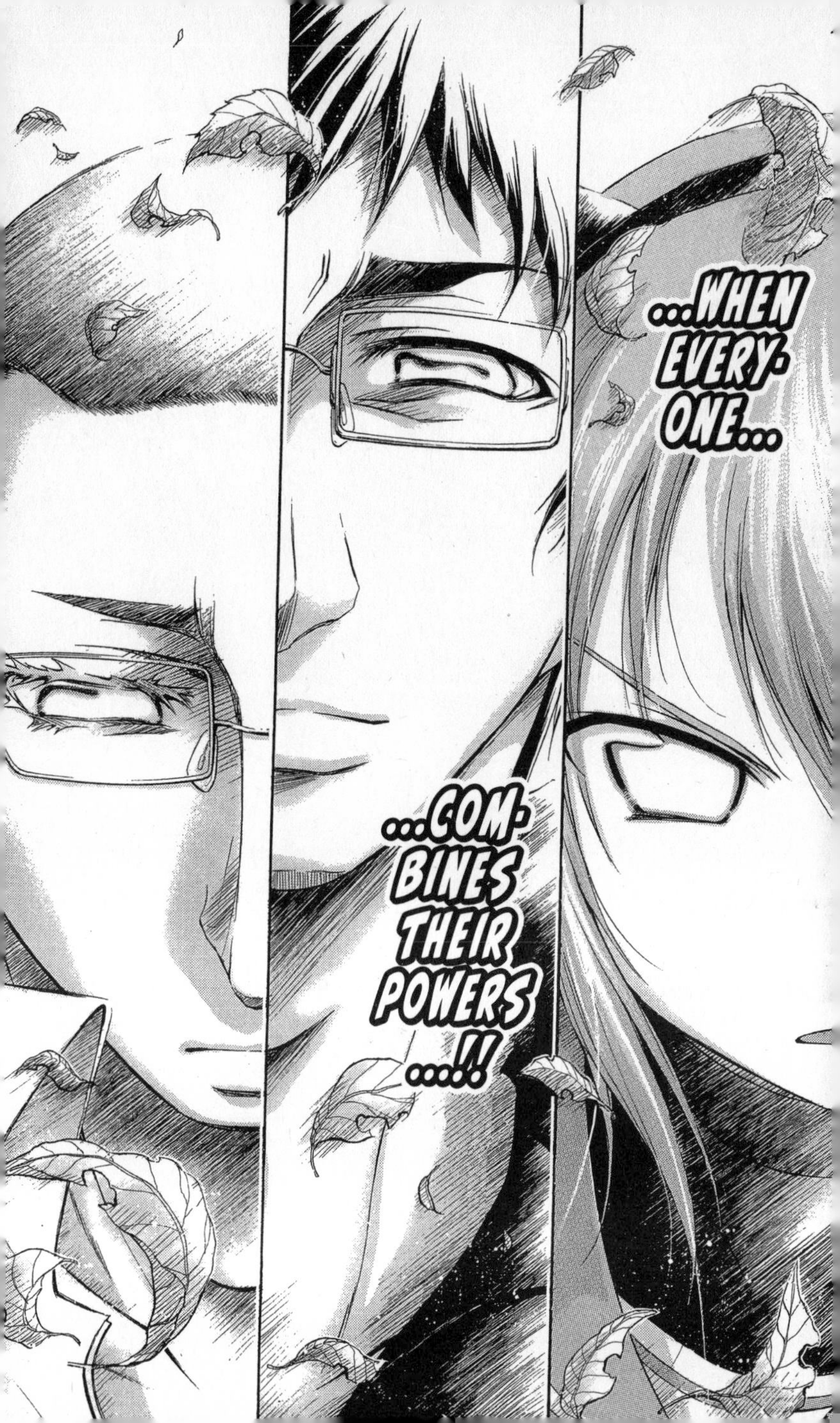
...WHEN EVERY-ONE...
...COM-BINES THEIR POWERS ...!!

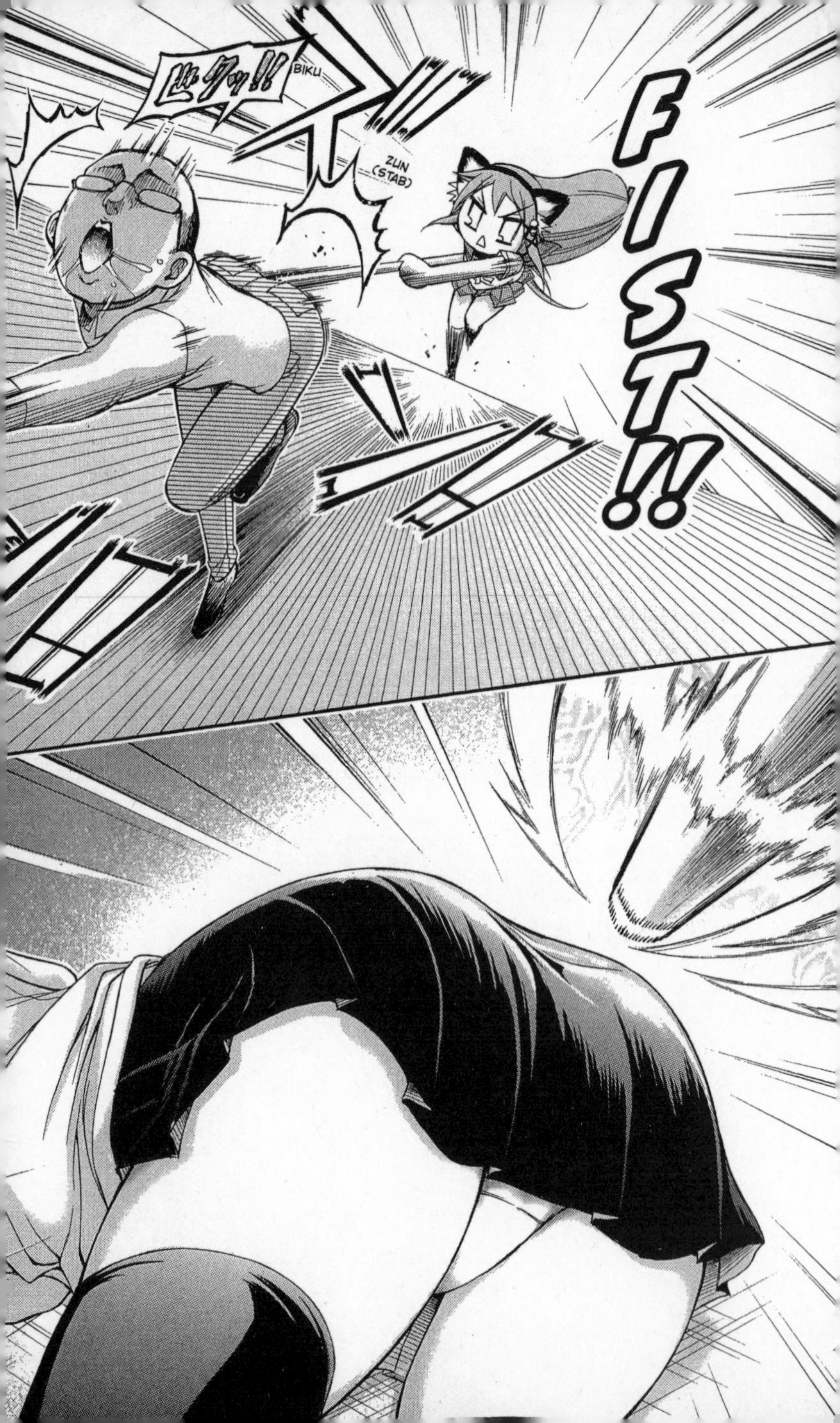
FIST!!
ZUN (STAB)
ビクッ!!
BIKU

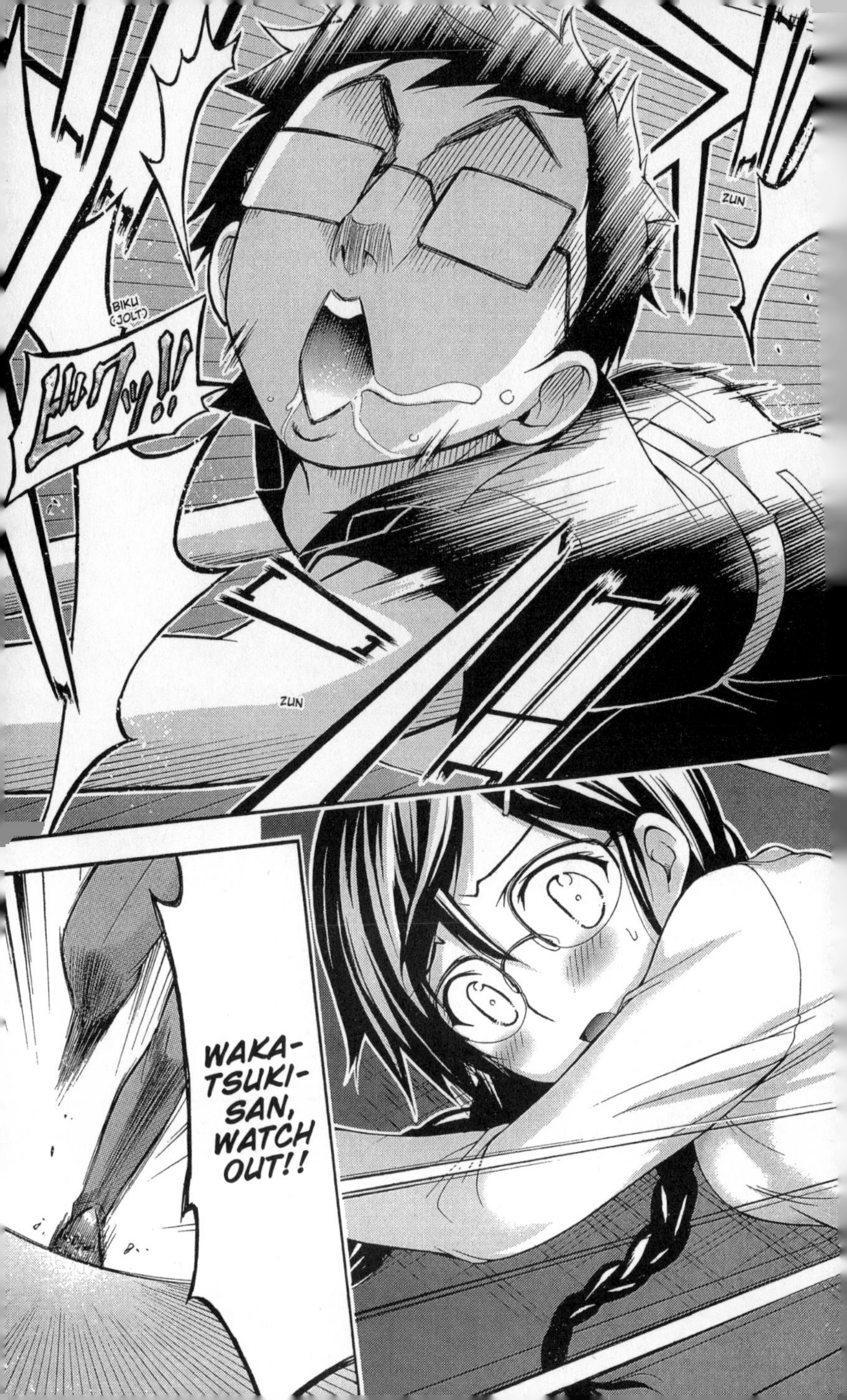
ZUN
BIKU
(JOLT)
ビクッ!!
ZUN
WAKA-TSUKI-SAN, WATCH OUT!!

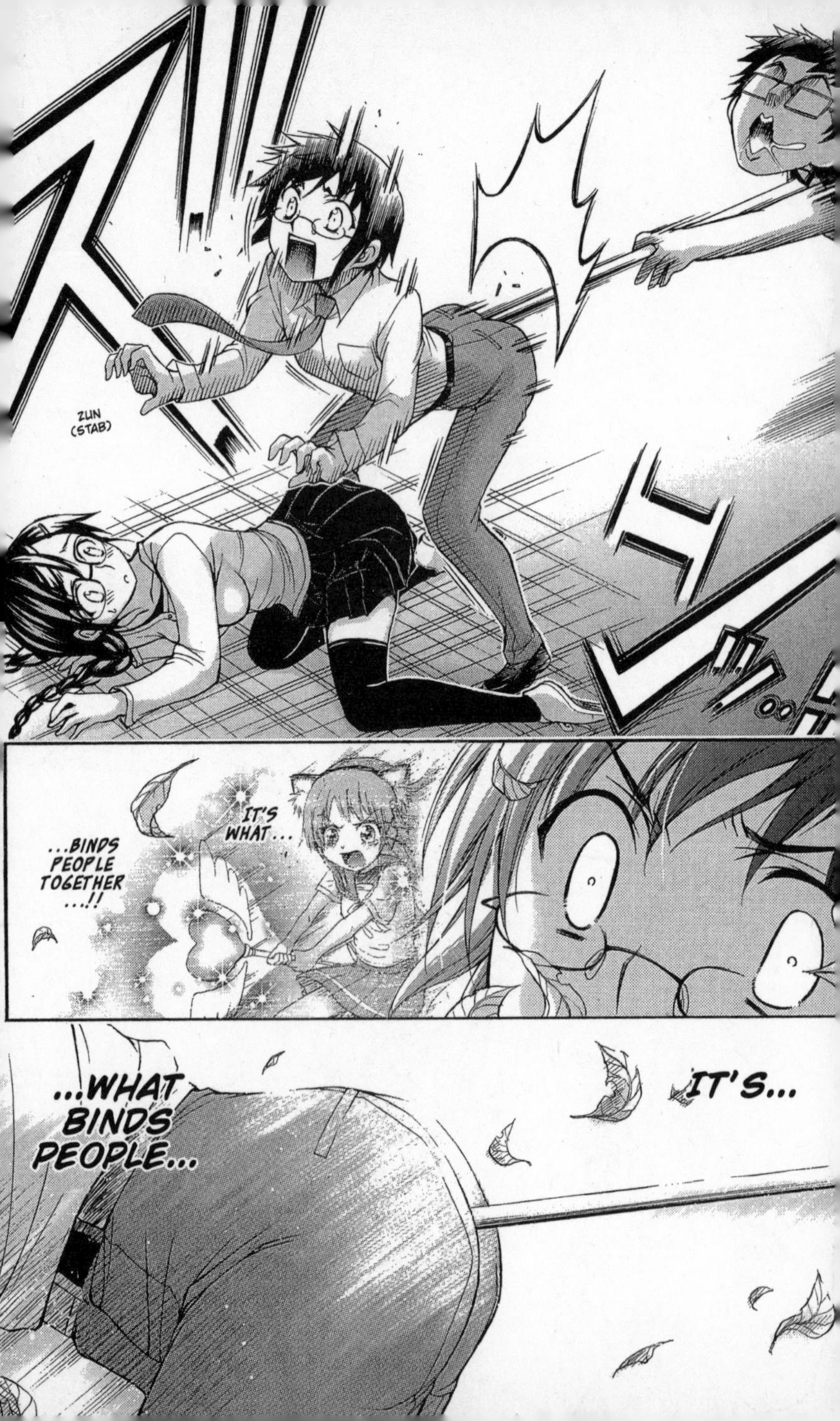
ZUN
(STAB)
IT'S WHAT...
...BINDS PEOPLE TOGETHER ...!!
IT'S...
...WHAT BINDS PEOPLE...

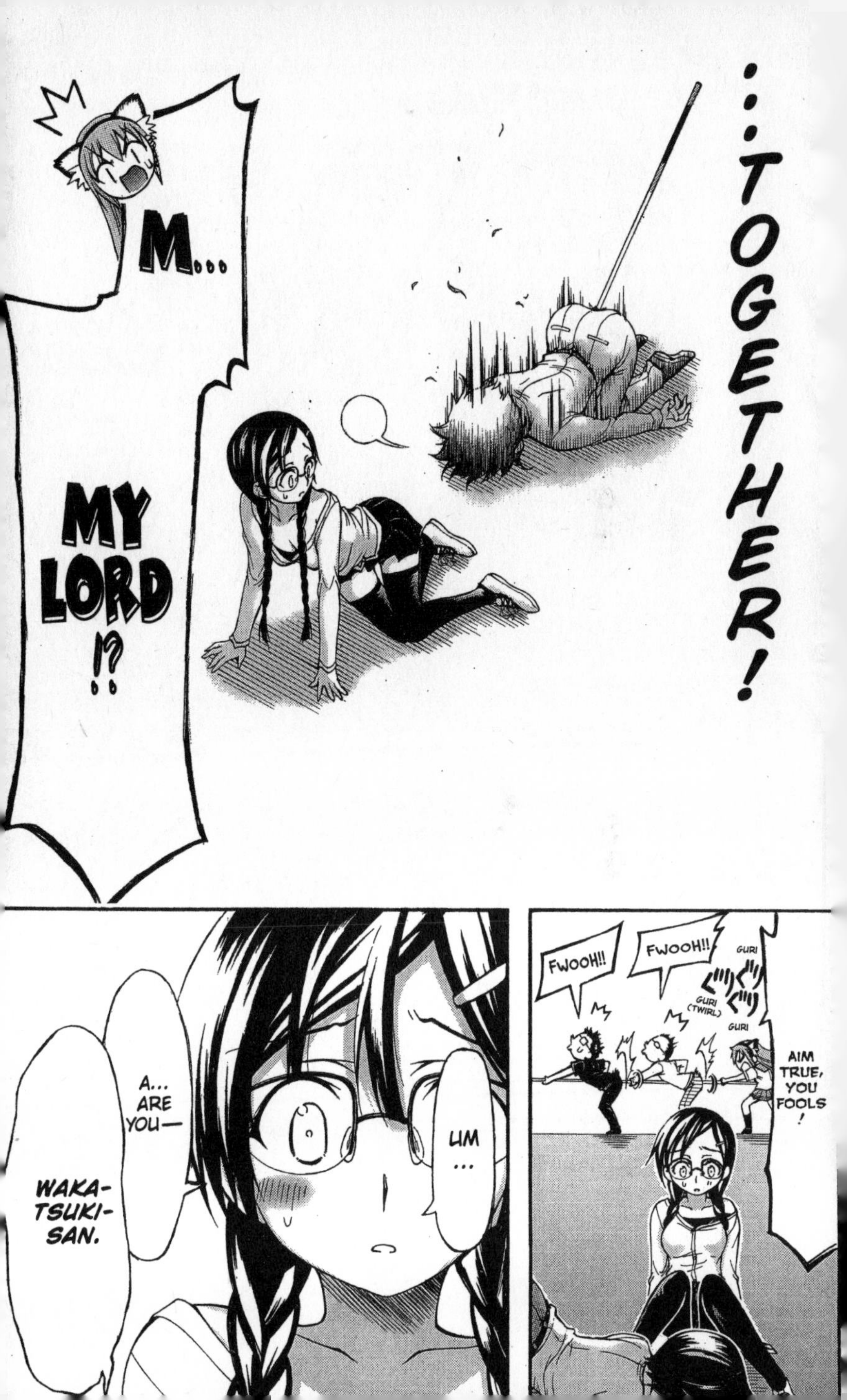
...TOGETHER!
M... MY LORD!?
GURI
FWOOH!!
GURI (TWIRL)
GURI
FWOOH!!
AIM TRUE, YOU FOOLS!
UM...
A... ARE YOU—
WAKA-TSUKI-SAN.

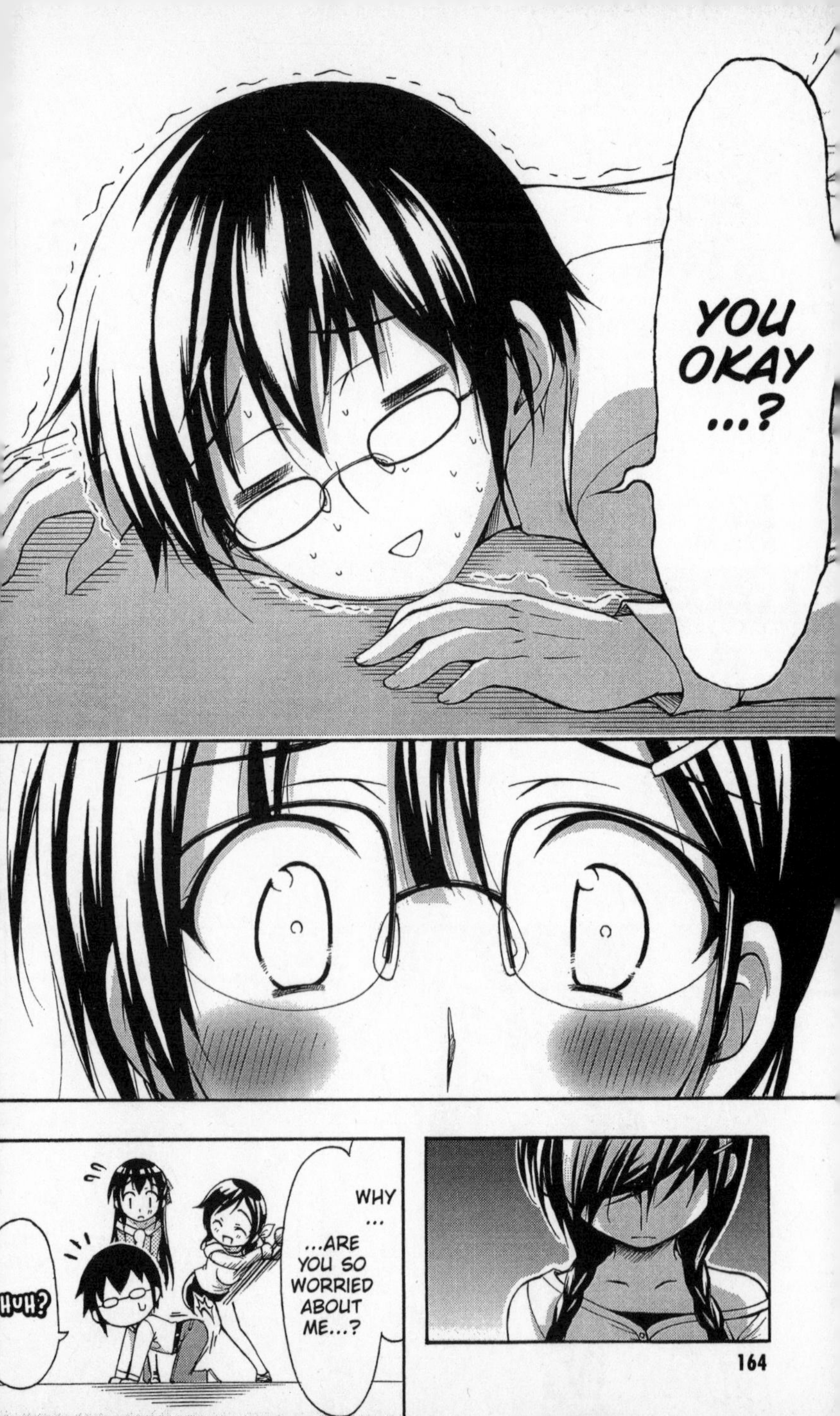
YOU OKAY ...?
WHY ... ...ARE YOU SO WORRIED ABOUT ME...?
HUH?

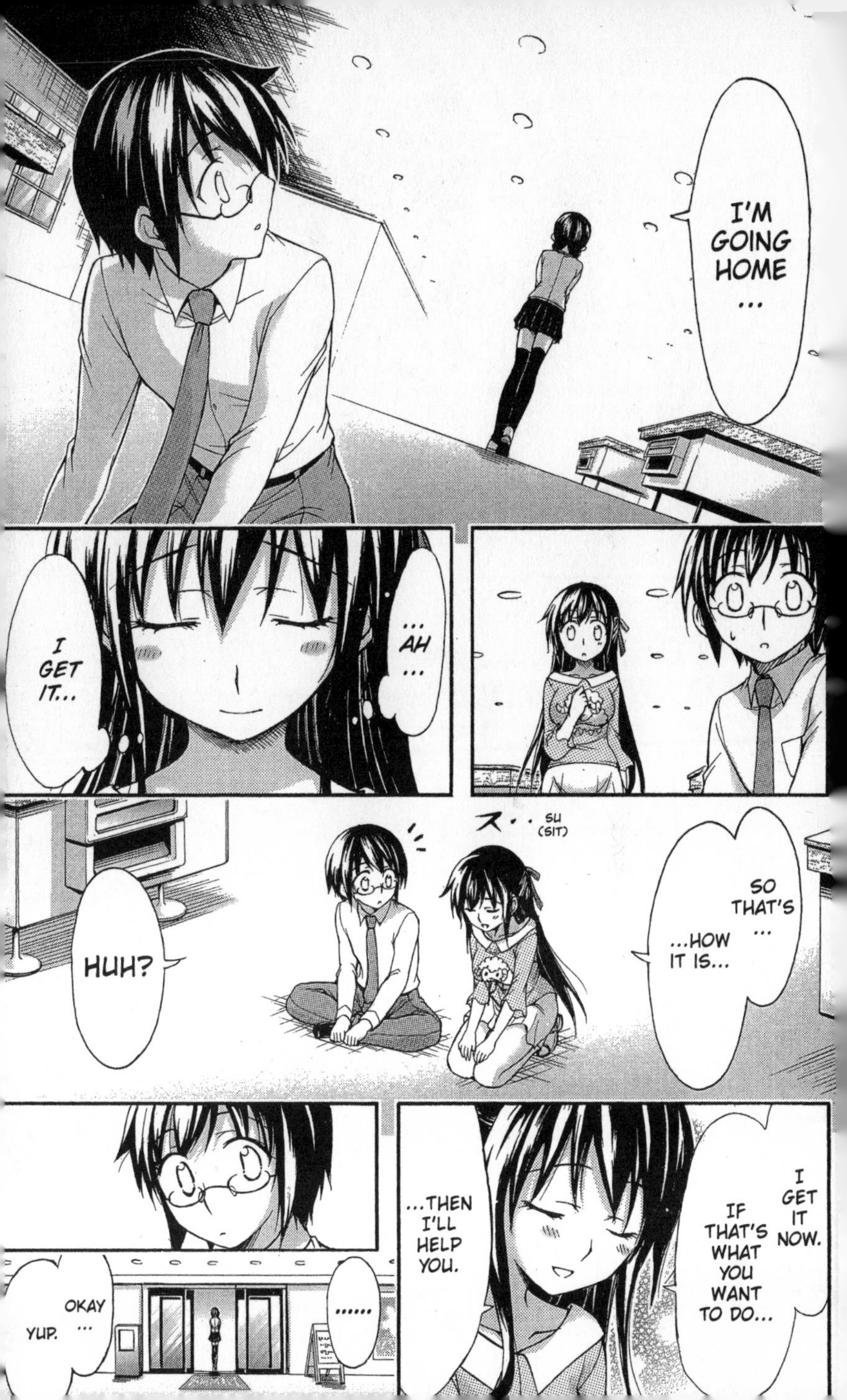
I'M GOING HOME ...
... AH ...
I GET IT...
SO THAT'S ... ...HOW IT IS...
ス・・ SU (SIT)
HUH?
I GET IT NOW.
IF THAT'S WHAT YOU WANT TO DO...
...THEN I'LL HELP YOU.
......
OKAY ...
YUP.

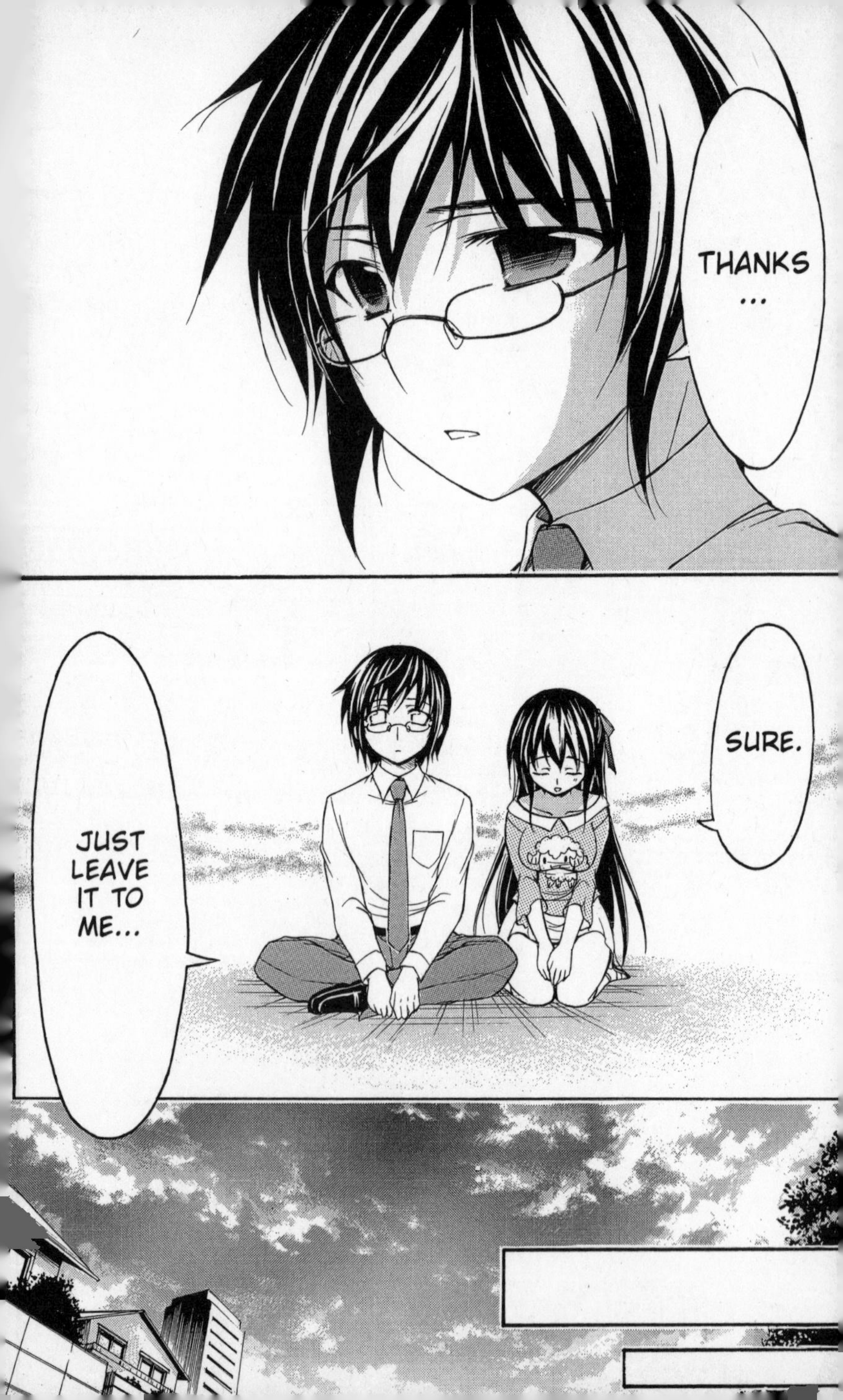
THANKS ...
SURE.
JUST LEAVE IT TO ME...

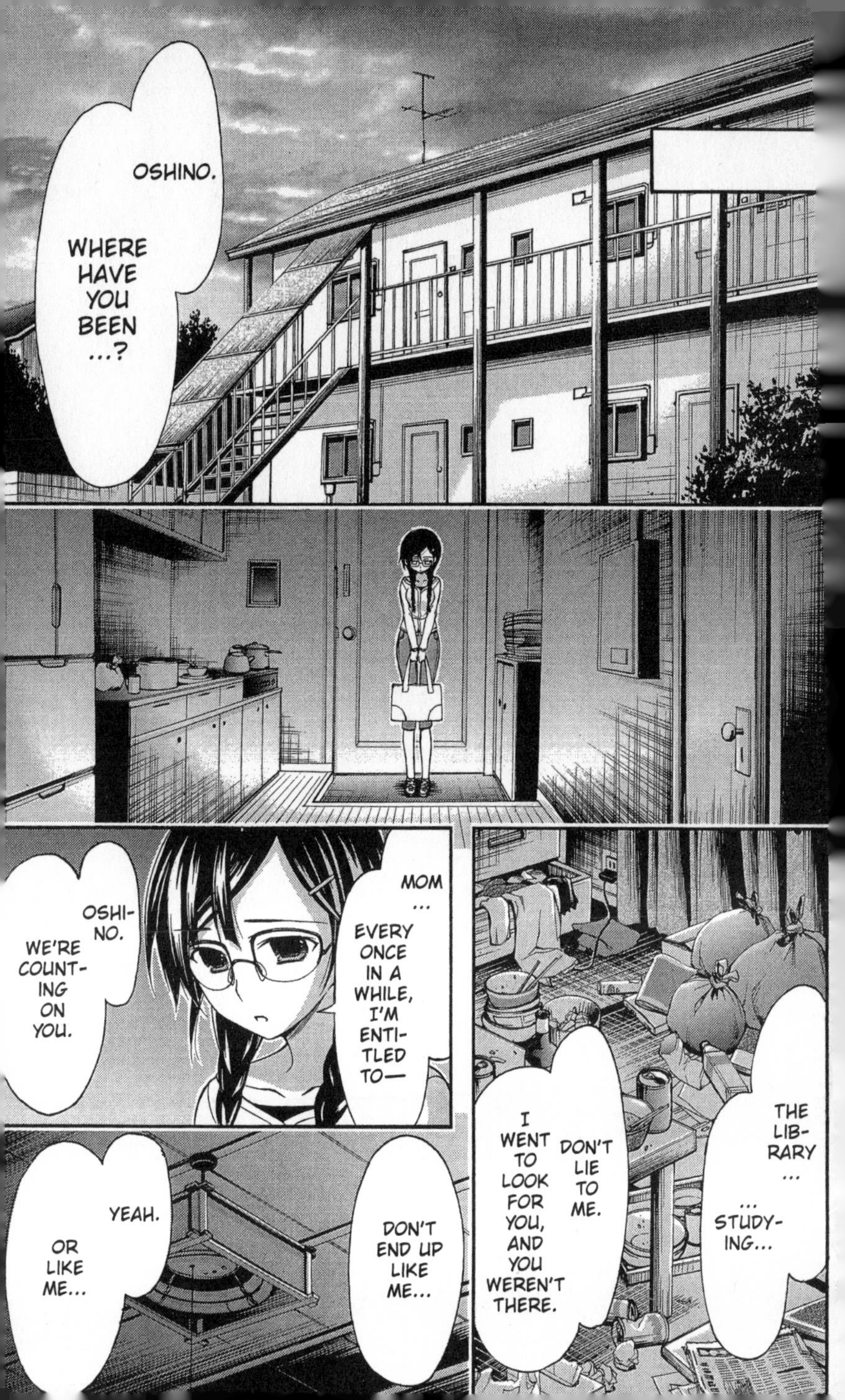
OSHINO.
WHERE HAVE YOU BEEN ...?
THE LIBRARY ... ... STUDYING...
DON'T LIE TO ME.
I WENT TO LOOK FOR YOU, AND YOU WEREN'T THERE.
MOM ... EVERY ONCE IN A WHILE, I'M ENTITLED TO—
OSHINO. WE'RE COUNTING ON YOU.
DON'T END UP LIKE ME...
YEAH.
OR LIKE ME...

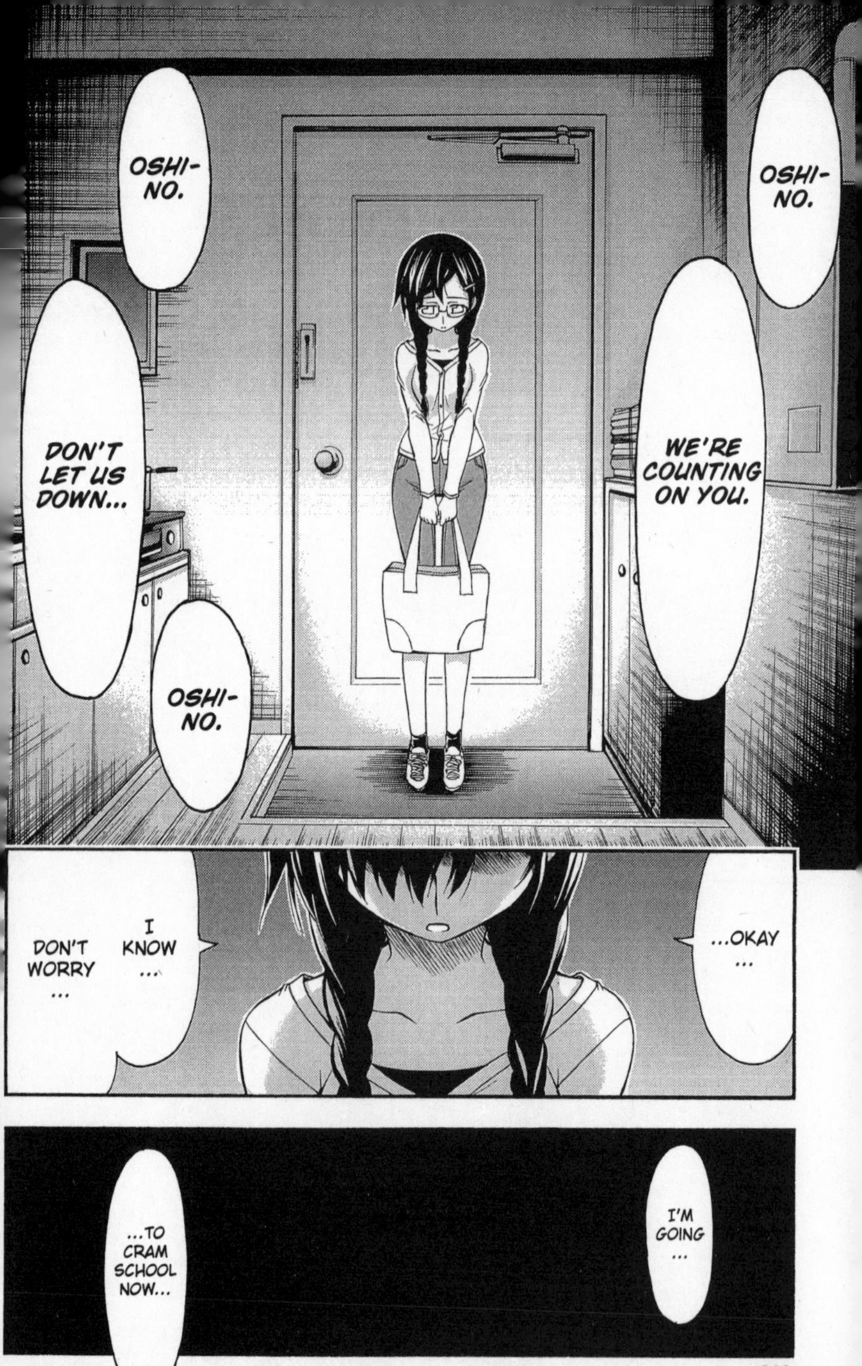
OSHI-NO.
WE'RE COUNTING ON YOU.
OSHI-NO.
DON'T LET US DOWN...
OSHI-NO.
...OKAY...
I KNOW...
DON'T WORRY...
I'M GOING...
...TO CRAM SCHOOL NOW...

17TH OFFENSE • THE END

GOU-DERE
SORA NAGIHARA

SORA NAGIHARA NOTES

PAGE 2
A Childhood Friend's Lost Property is a parody of the English title of Suu Minazuki's other manga series, *Heaven's Lost Property* (*Sora no otoshimono*).

PAGE 2
My Childhood Friend Can't Be This Awesome!! is a parody of the light novel/anime/manga series *Oreimo* by Tsukasa Fushimi. The full Japanese title of this series translates to "My Little Sister Can't Be This Cute."

PAGE 23
A **komusou** is a Zen beggar monk of the Fuke sect, known for wearing a basketlike straw hood and playing a *shakuhachi*, a kind of Japanese flute.

PAGE 86
Piroriiiin is the sound of their cell phones taking photos. Japan was first to have photo-taking cell phones, and to protect people from having their pictures taken unannounced, they added this loud melodic sound to play when a shot is snapped.

READ ON FOR
A PREVIEW OF

GOU-DERE
SORA NAGIHARA

VOLUME 4!!

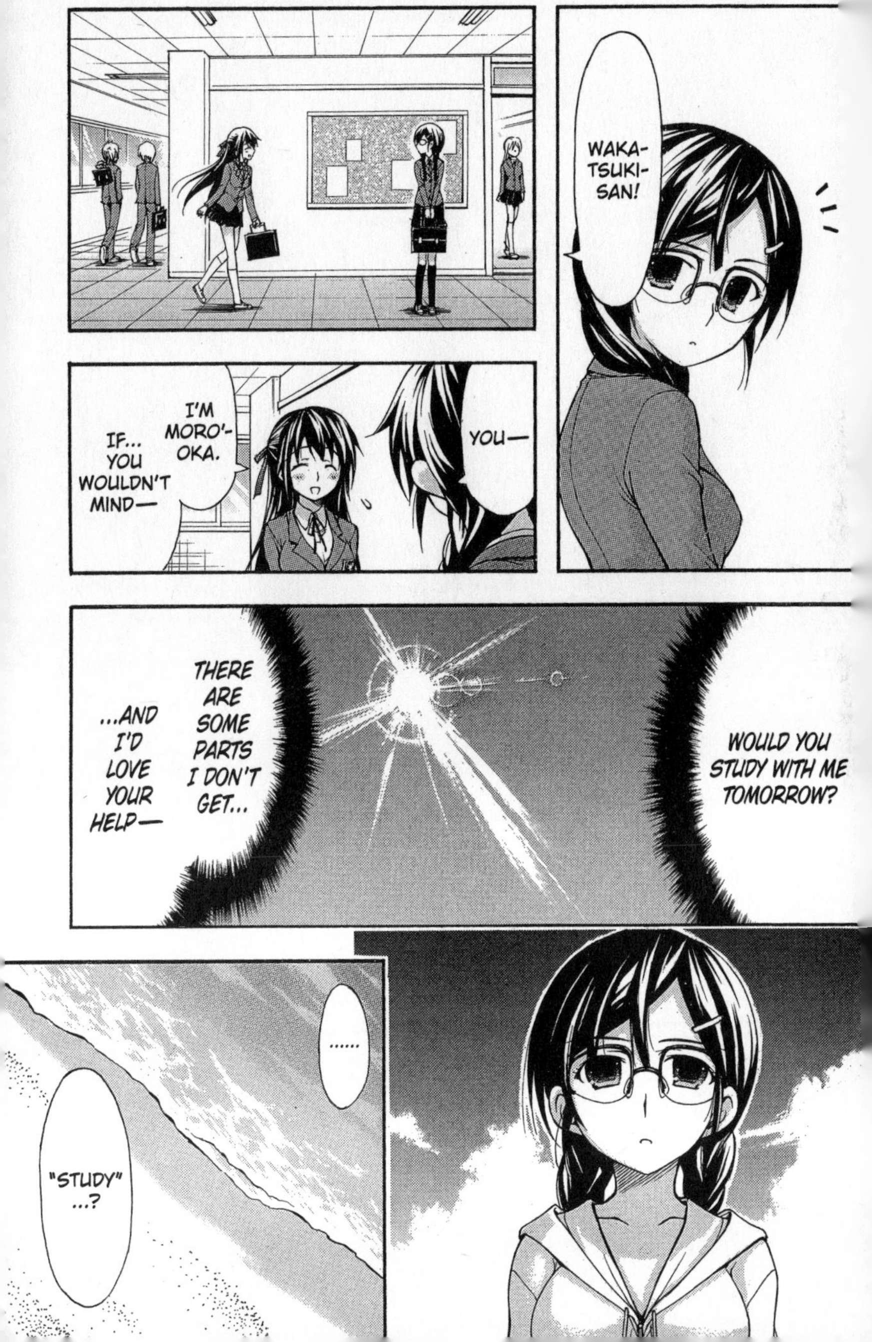
WAKA-TSUKI-SAN!
YOU—
I'M MORO'-OKA.
IF... YOU WOULDN'T MIND—
WOULD YOU STUDY WITH ME TOMORROW?
THERE ARE SOME PARTS I DON'T GET...
...AND I'D LOVE YOUR HELP—
......
"STUDY" ...?

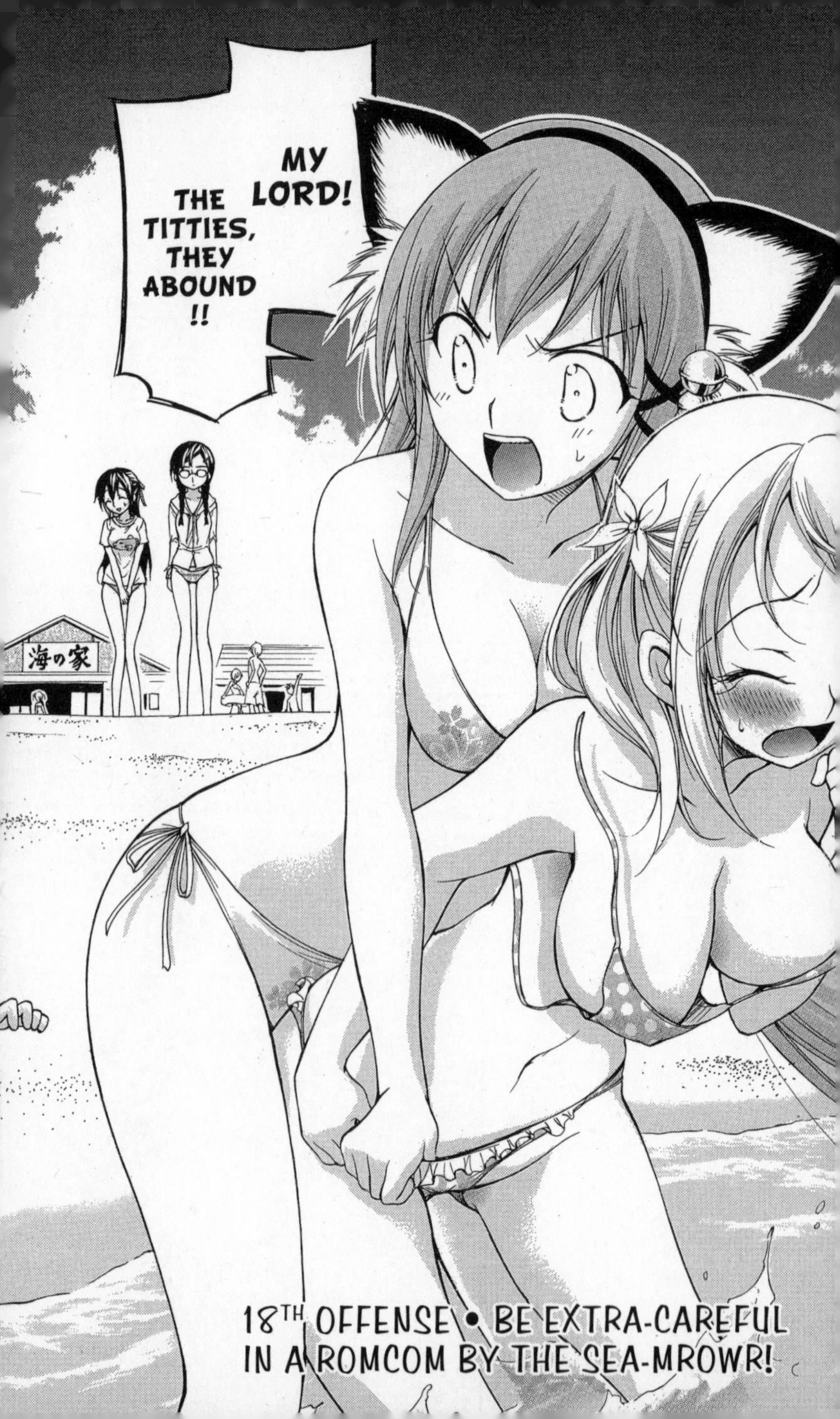
MY LORD! THE TITTIES, THEY ABOUND !!
海の家
18TH OFFENSE • BE EXTRA-CAREFUL IN A ROMCOM BY THE SEA-MROWR!

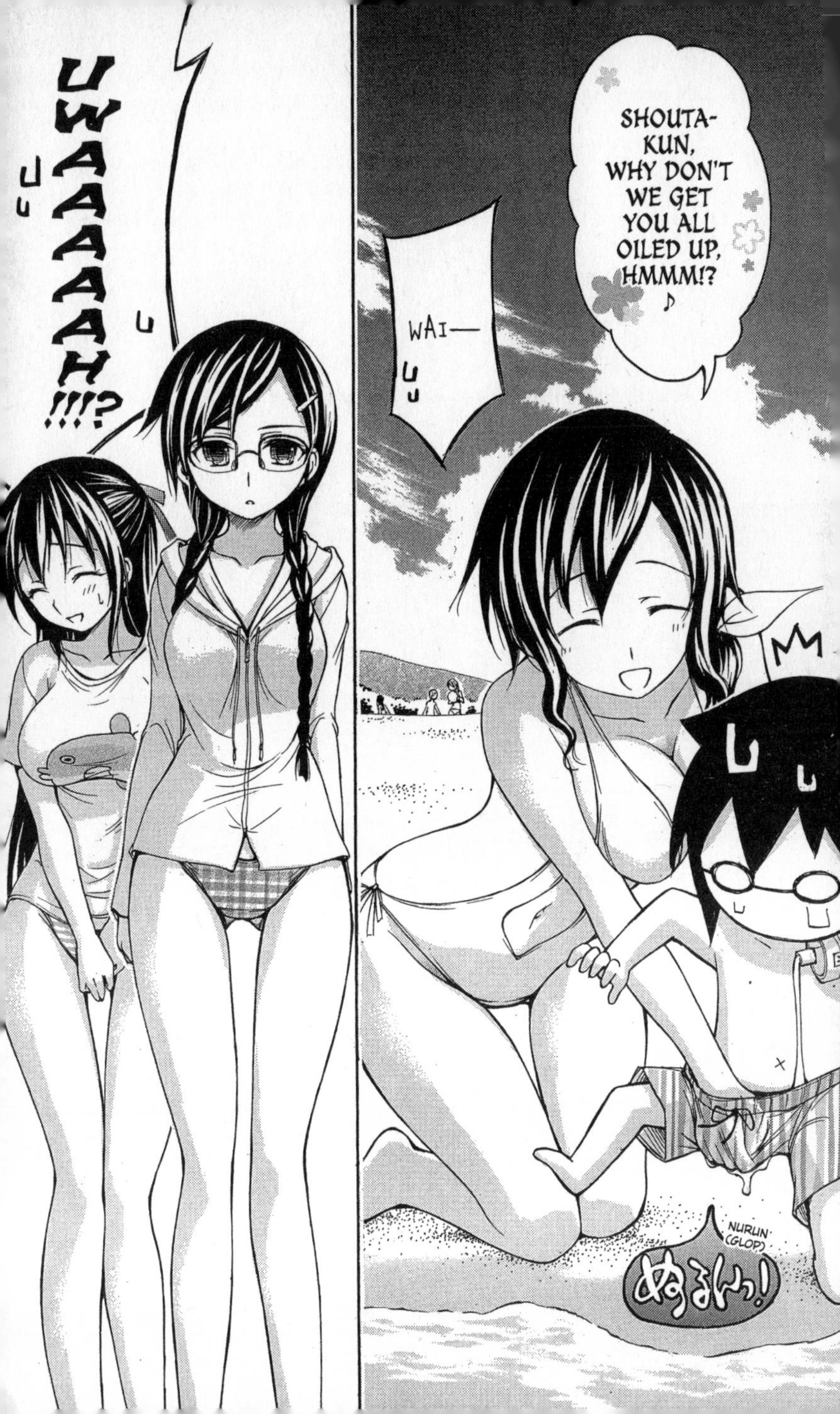
SHOUTA-KUN, WHY DON'T WE GET YOU ALL OILED UP, HMMM!? ♪
WAI—
NURUN (GLOP)
ぬるんっ!
UWAAAAAH!!!?

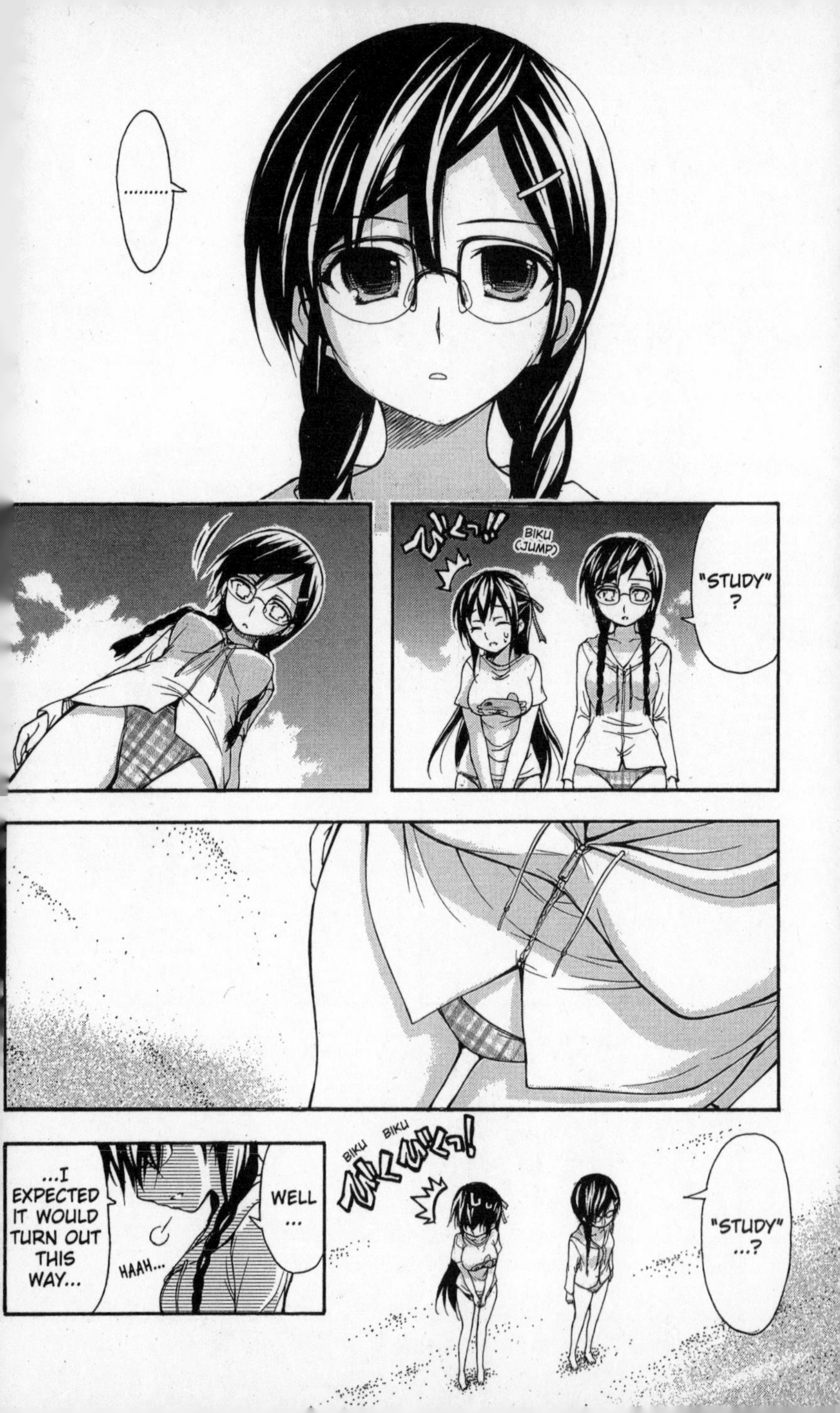
....
BIKU (JUMP)
"STUDY" ?
"STUDY" ...?
BIKU BIKU
WELL ...
HAAH...
...I EXPECTED IT WOULD TURN OUT THIS WAY...

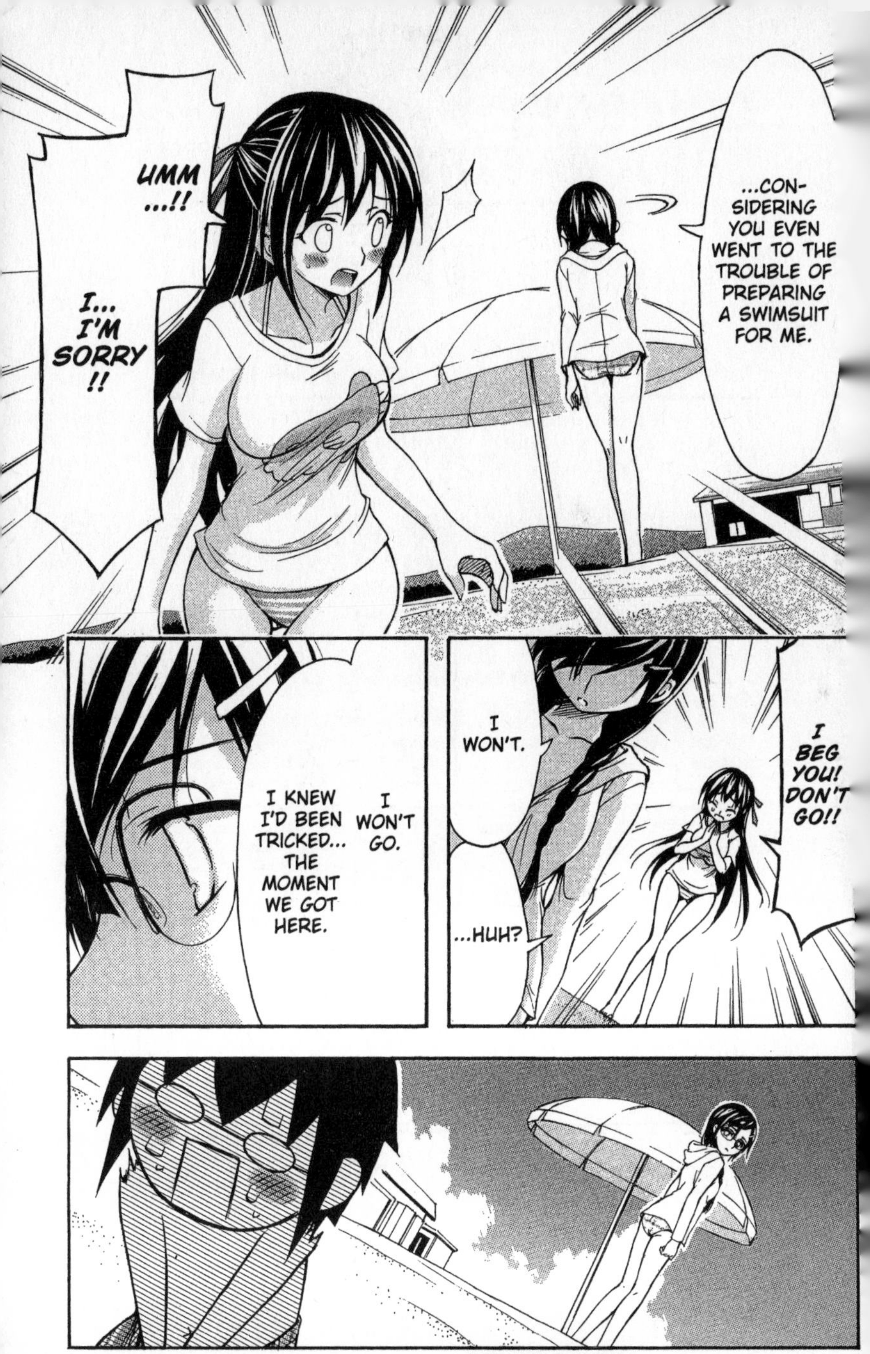
...CON-SIDERING YOU EVEN WENT TO THE TROUBLE OF PREPARING A SWIMSUIT FOR ME.
UMM ...!!
I... I'M SORRY !!
I BEG YOU! DON'T GO!!
I WON'T.
...HUH?
I WON'T GO.
I KNEW I'D BEEN TRICKED... THE MOMENT WE GOT HERE.

>>TO BE CONTINUED IN VOLUME FOUR!!

GOU-DERE
SORA NAGIHARA ❸

SUU MINAZUKI

Translation: Christine Dashiell • Lettering: James Dashiell

This book is a work of fiction. Names, characters, places, and incidents are the product of the author's imagination or are used fictitiously. Any resemblance to actual events, locales, or persons, living or dead, is coincidental.

Gou-Dere Bishojo Nagihara Sora by Suu Minazuki
© Suu Minazuki 2013
All rights reserved.
First published in Japan in 2013 by HAKUSENSHA, INC., Tokyo. English language translation rights in U.S.A., Canada and U.K. arranged with HAKUSENSHA, INC., Tokyo through Tuttle-Mori Agency Inc., Tokyo.

Translation © 2015 Hachette Book Group, Inc.

Yen Press
Hachette Book Group
1290 Avenue of the Americas
New York, NY 10104

www.HachetteBookGroup.com
www.YenPress.com

Yen Press is an imprint of Hachette Book Group, Inc. The Yen Press name and logo are trademarks of Hachette Book Group, Inc.

The publisher is not responsible for websites (or their content) that are not owned by the publisher.

First Yen Press Edition: May 2015

ISBN: 978-0-316-29880-3

10 9 8 7 6 5 4 3

BVG

Printed in the United States of America